# Lecture Notes in Artificial Intelligence 8335

Subseries of Lecture Notes in Computer Science

T0212612

Lecture Notes in Artificial Intelligence 8435

Subseries of Lecture Notes in Computer Science

LNAI Series Editors

Randy Goebel
University of Alberta, Edmonton, Canada
Yuzuru Tanaka
Hokkaido University, Sapporo, Japan
Wolfgang Wahlster
DFKI and Saarland University, Saarbrücken, Germany

LNAI Founding Series Editor

Joerg Siekmann
DFKI and Saarland University, Saarbrücken, Germany

Qingfeng Chen   Baoshan Chen   Chengqi Zhang

# Intelligent Strategies for Pathway Mining

## Model and Pattern Identification

 Springer

Authors

Qingfeng Chen
Guangxi University, State Key Laboratory for Conservation and Utilization
of Subtropical Agro-Bioresources, School of Computer, Electronic and Information
100# Daxue Road, Nanning, Guangxi 530004, China
E-mail: qingfeng@gxu.edu.cn
*and* University of Technology Sydney
Centre for Quantum Computation and Intelligent Systems
P.O. Box 123, Broadway, NSW 2007, Australia
E-mail: qingfeng.chen@uts.edu.au

Baoshan Chen
Guangxi University, State Key Laboratory for Conservation and Utilization
of Subtropical Agro-Bioresources
100# Daxue Road, Nanning, Guangxi 530004, China
E-mail: chenyaoj@gxu.edu.cn

Chengqi Zhang
University of Technology Sydney
Centre for Quantum Computation and Intelligent Systems
P.O. Box 123, Broadway, NSW 2007, Australia
E-mail: chengqi.zhang@uts.edu.au

ISSN 0302-9743                                    e-ISSN 1611-3349
ISBN 978-3-319-04171-1                            e-ISBN 978-3-319-04172-8
DOI 10.1007/978-3-319-04172-8
Springer Cham Heidelberg New York Dordrecht London

Library of Congress Control Number: 2013956129

CR Subject Classification (1998): I.2, H.3, H.4, J.3, H.2.8, F.1

LNCS Sublibrary: SL 7 – Artificial Intelligence

*Typesetting:* Camera-ready by author, data conversion by Scientific Publishing Services, Chennai, India

Printed on acid-free paper

Springer is part of Springer Science+Business Media (www.springer.com)

*To my wife, Dongqin Jiang,*
*and my lovely boy, Zishen Chen.*
*I dedicate this book to my family*
*for their constant support*
*and all the wonderful things they do.*

*Qingfeng Chen*

# Preface

Bioinformatics is the application of mathematics and computer science to the field of molecular biology. It has played central roles in developing databases, algorithms, computational techniques and the theory needed to extract and manage interesting knowledge from biology data over the past two decades. The major research areas include sequence alignment, gene finding, genome assembly, drug design, drug discovery, protein structure alignment, protein structure prediction, gene expression and protein–protein interactions, genome-wide association studies, and the modeling of evolution. In particular, owing to the application of high-throughput techniques and the development of systems biology, the analysis and management of a tremendous amount of data has become a big challenge, such as metagenome analysis. Recently, with the completion of the genome of a number of species, the value of these sequence data has attracted increasing attention. For example, the exploration of genes aids in molecular medicine and results in improving the diagnosis of diseases, while knowledge of other animal and plant genomes should enhance agriculture. Functional genomics has become a critical step in this biological revolution, not simply the function annotation for the discovered genes but the organization and interaction of genetic pathways that work together to form the physiology of an organism.

The development of these efficient strategies is motivated by predicting the function of a gene and even modeling signaling pathways in which it may act. At the molecular level, functional information can be acquired through the analysis of DNA and RNA expression arrays, and has been widely discussed among researchers in this field. These attempts to contribute to the investigation of novel and efficient ideas and techniques are made available through some important conferences and journals, such as the *Proceedings of the National Academy of Sciences of the United States of America* (PNAS), *International Conference of the IEEE Engineering in Medicine and Biology Society* (EMBC), *IEEE Computer Society Bioinformatics* (CSB), *ACM International Conference on Research in Computational Molecular Biology* (RECOMB), *Annual International Conference on Intelligent Systems for Molecular Biology* (ISMB), *European Conference on Computational Biology* (ECCB), *ACM Conference on Management of Data* (SIGMOD), *ACM International*

*Conference on Very Large Data Bases* (VLDB), *IEEE International Conference on Bioinformatics and Biomedicine* (BIBM), *IEEE International Conference on Data Engineering* (ICDE), and *PLoS Computational Biology, Bioinformatics, BMC Bioinformatics, IEEE/ACM Transactions on Computational Biology and Bioinformatics*. As a result, the exploration of signaling pathways has played an important role in functional genomics and systems biology, such as understanding of environmental signals, regulatory mechanisms (activation or inhibition), and the corresponding expression of target genes involved in signal transduction. A complicated signaling pathway can include a cascade of signals within the cell, which leads to a change in the cell, either in the gene expression or in the activity of enzymes. The analysis of signaling pathways including modeling and featured pattern mining is the primary issue in the post-genomic era.

Many studies recently started to explore the regulatory pathway of kinases from the aspect of the genome. Although the regulation must be positive or negative, the difficulty is to identify the specific nucleotide sequences involved in the regulation and to classify them into different groups. A gene may be present in more than one kinase pathway and a kinase pathway may be related to more than one gene. There are still insufficient methods to handle kinase pathway data by combining the gene expression, structural information, and potential structure–function relationships. Traditional computational linguistics has been applied in computational biology toward abstracted, hierarchical views of biological sequences, whereas they show limitations in modeling complicated secondary structures. The generated set of all the ideal strings using grammar is inappropriate for data analysis. This calls for the use of sophisticated and effective computational and modeling techniques for the systematic collection and interpretation of kinase pathway data. Association rule mining has recently emerged as a popular summarization and pattern-extraction algorithm to identify correlations between items in transactional databases. Several attempts have been made to mine biological databases using association rule mining. The most critical issue to be solved by researchers is the development of efficient algorithms for the collection, storage, modeling, and analysis of diverse and complex pathway data.

As a result, this book takes these interesting and challenging issues into account and aims to develop innovative approaches for the sequential and cumulative actions of genetically distinct but functionally related objects. The present volume was motivated by the demand for a comprehensive understanding of the roles and features of a collection of signal pathways, including activities of functional factors, gene expression, and activators and inhibitors, and aims to serve as an overall course-aid and self-study material for researchers and students in bioinformatics and applications in signaling pathway data collection, analysis, and interpretation. These require a systematic way of combining technologies, signaling pathways, and genomic data. In fact the volume can be useful to anyone else who is interested in interdisciplinary research with respect to data mining, artificial intelligence, signaling pathways, and bioinformatics.

The book is organized into 13 chapters that range over the relevant approaches and tools in data integration, modeling, analysis, and knowledge discovery for signaling pathways. Bearing in mind that the book is also addressed to students, the contributors present the main results and techniques in an easily accessed and understood way together with many references and examples.

Chapter 1 presents an introduction to signaling pathways, including motivations, background knowledge, and relevant data mining techniques for pathway data analysis. Chapter 2 presents a variety of data sources and data analysis techniques with respect to signaling pathways, including data integration and relevant data mining applications. Chapter 3 describes a framework to measure the inconsistency between heterogenous biological databases. A GO-based (genome ontology) strategy is proposed to associate different data sources. Chapter 4 presents the identification of the positive regulation of kinase pathways in terms of association rule mining. The results derived from this project could be used when predicting essential relationships and may enable a comprehensive understanding of kinase pathway interactions. Chapter 5 deals with graphical model-based methods to identify regulatory networks of protein kinases. A framework using negative association rule mining is introduced in Chapter 6 to discover the featured inhibitory regulation patterns and the relationships between the involved regulation factors. It is necessary not only to detect the objects that exhibit a positive regulatory role in a kinase pathway but also to discover those objects that inhibit the regulation. Chapter 7 presents methods to model ncRNA secondary structure data in terms of stems, loops, and marked labels, and illustrates how to find matched structure patterns for a given query. Chapter 8 shows an interval-based distance metric for computing the distance between conserved RNA secondary structures. Chapter 9 describes a framework to explore structural and functional patterns of RNA pseudoknot structures according to a probability matrix. Chapter 10 presents methods to model miRNA data and identify miRNA interactions of cross-species and within-species type. Chapter 11 presents an approach to measure the importance of an miRNA site and the adjacent base by using information redundancy and develops a novel measure to identify strongly correlated infrequent item sets. The discovered association rules not only present important structural features in miRNAs, but also promote a comprehensive understanding of regulatory roles of miRNAs. Chapter 12 deals with bioinformatics techniques for protein kinase data management and analysis, kinase pathways and drug targets, and describes their potential application in the pharmaceutical industry. Chapter 13 offers a summary of the chapters and gives a brief discussion of some emerging issues.

It is difficult for us to include all the related investigations in this book, owing to the increasingly varied biology data and complicated regulatory networks. We believe that this book is sufficiently comprehensive to provide a useful and handy guide for both beginners and experienced researchers in the fields of computer science and biology.

November 2013

*Qingfeng Chen*
*Baoshan Chen*
*Chengqi Zhang*

# Acknowledgments

This book is the outcome of the authors' work in computer science and biology and includes a review of recent articles and books. Many people have directly or indirectly helped us in our efforts. Their ideas or comments may have appeared insignificant at the time, but they have had a significant causal effect. Special thanks must first go to our families, who may have been neglected in the past few years during our concentrated effort. We would like to express our sincere thanks to all our mentors and colleagues who provided us with constructive comments and support during our drafting of this book. They include Professor Phoebe Chen from La Trobe University and Professor Shichao Zhang and Longbing Cao from the University of Technology Sydney, Professor Qiang Yang from the Hong Kong University of Science and Technology, Professor Limsoon Wong from the National University of Singapore, Professor F.H.D. van Batenburg from Leiden University, Professor Wen-Hsiung Li from the University of Chicago, Professor Taoshen Li from Guangxi University, Dr. Scott Mann from La Trobe University, Professor. Ming Chen from Zhejiang University, Dr. Gang Li from Deakin University, Mr. Xiaobin Zhang from IBM, and Dr. Liang Zhao from Baylor College of Medicine.

We also wish to especially thank Alfred Hofmann, Editor at Springer, for his enthusiasm, patience, and great efforts to make this book available, as well as his staff for their conscientious work. We are very grateful to all of the reviewers for their useful and valuable feedback. We would also like to thank our students, Qingzhen Song, Xiaoyan Hu, Wei Lan, Keli Li, Chaowang Lan, and Huizhe Pang, who contributed to the data collection, system implementation, and experimentation.

Most especially, Qingfeng Chen would like to thank his family and friends, words alone cannot express what I owe them for their encouragement–their patient love allowed me to complete this book. Without their persistent support throughout this project, this dissertation could not have been written. A special thanks to Professor Shuo Bai and Professor Ju Wang for guiding me throughout my initial academic program. I would also like to warmly acknowledge Ms. Li Liu and Professor Bingbing Zhou for their help and care during my PhD study in Australia. In addition, a special thanks to Professor Changan Yuan, Professor Jinyan Li, Professor Haiqiong

Luo, Dr. Jinyu Hou, Ms. Jia Guo, Mr. Zhiqiang Wang, and all my colleagues for their consideration and motivation.

This work was partially supported by the National Natural Science Foundation of China project 61363025, and key project of the Natural Science Foundation of Guangxi 053006 and 019029.

# Contents

# Chapter 1
# Introduction

Pathway analysis is an important subfield of bioinformatics, including pathway algorithms, ontology, visualizations, databases. A pathway comprises one or more processes, each of which begins with input signals, uses various combinations of other input signals, such as cofactors, activators and inhibitors, and ends with output that exhibits functions. To discover the complex regulatory pathways and the potential characterized patterns of their components, a number of bioinformatics techniques and tools have been developed for varied purposes. They are proved to be useful in dealing with pathway data, and have been widely applied in exploring metabolism, genetic and environmental information processing, cellular processes, organismal systems, human diseases and drug development. One of the most critical issues to be solved by researchers is the development of efficient algorithms for collection, storage, modeling and deep analysis of diverse and complex pathway data. The knowledge gained can lead to comprehensive understanding of the molecular interaction and reaction networks in genomics, transcriptomics, proteomics, and metabolomics.

For both beginners and experienced researchers, this monograph will provide information with respect to concepts, data sources, modeling, algorithms and tools that are related to pathway data analysis. A comprehensive description to the critical issues and core techniques will be presented. This chapter aims to describe what is regulatory pathways, including fundamental components, how they can be used for functional genomics and biomedicine engineering, and the state of arts of relevant works and efforts. We will also describe the limitations of current approaches and techniques and the motivations and needs to develop new methods in combination of mathematics, computer science and biology for handling emerging challenging issues in signaling pathways. In particularly, this monograph will focus on protein kinases and non-coding RNA(ncRNA) and their featured regulatory patterns and functional roles, which are directly or indirectly related to pathways.

## 1.1   What Is Signaling Pathway?

There has been an explosion of knowledge with respect to signal transduction pathways, impacting virtually all areas of biology and medicine. For example, in energy metabolism, $5'$-AMP-activated protein kinase (AMPK) has been proved to be a potent regulator of skeletal muscle metabolism and gene expression [78]. The regulatory mechanisms are actually controlled by a collection of kinase genes. Further, there are increasing evidences that the activation or inhibition of AMPK plays a crucial role in regulation of metabolism in the development of many diseases, such as heart disease and type 2 diabetes. In addition, over the last decade, the understanding of plant signaling pathways due to the use of genetic tools in Arabidopsis has assisted in the identification of hormonal, developmental and environmental signal transduction pathways and cross-talk between them. As a result, the deep study of regulatory features of pathways has emerged as an important, efficient and safe way in biology and medicine.

Signal transduction is the process, by which an extracellular signaling molecule activates a membrane receptor protein, which in turn alters intracellular molecules eliciting a physiological response [73]. Environmental stimuli at the cellular level is able to impact on signal transduction processes. These essential signals in their environment lead to a series of responses from Cells, which are often chemicals in the extracellular fluid (ECF) from distant locations in a multicellular organism, nearby cells, or even secreted by themselves. The chemicals may also react to signaling molecules on the surface of adjacent cells, which may trigger (http://users.rcn.com/jkimball.ma.ultranet/BiologyPages/C/CellSignaling.html):

- an immediate alteration in the metabolism of the cell or in the electrical charge across the plasma membrane;
- an alteration in the gene expression, including transcription within the nucleus. This class of responses often needs more time due to its complexity.

There are a variety of signal pathways responsible for different regulatory purposes. For example, neuroscience signaling is related to diseases, including dopamine signaling in Parkinson's disease and neurofibrillary tangle formation in Alzheimer's disease; AMPK signaling and insulin receptor signaling for Glucose metabolism; mTOR signaling for translation control; protein acetylation and histone methylation signaling for chromatin regulation/acetylation; and plants use ethylene pathways, to modulate various developmental programs and coordinate responses to a multitude of external stress factors [168]. As defined by Wikipedia, a signal pathway consists of the following components to receive signal from various stimuli, transduce the signal in cell and generate a physiological response:

- **Signaling molecules.** A signaling molecule is a chemical that participates information transmission between cells. Biological processes are controlled by complex systems of functionally interacting signaling molecules. They communicate with specific receptors in another cell, and trigger a response in that cell by activating a collection of enzyme controlled reactions which give rise to alterations inside the cell. Hence, systems biology approaches in combination with the understanding of each molecule are ideal to discover signaling networks/pathways involved in the biologically important processes.

- **Environmental stimuli.** In single-celled organisms, the variety of signal transduction processes influence its reaction to its environment. In contrast, in multicellular organisms, many signal transmission processes are required for coordinating individual cells to support the organism as a whole. Examples include photons hitting cells in the retina of the eye, and light intensity, day length, gravity, and temperature to regulate the growth of plants. In general, the complexity of these processes tend to increase with the complexity of the organism.

- **Receptors.** A receptor is a protein molecule most often found on the surface of a cell, which includes cell surface receptors and nuclear receptors. The former are embedded in the plasma membrane, and the latter are embedded in the cytoplasm or nucleus of a cell. Further, they are attached by one or more specific kinds of signaling molecules, such as ligand, peptide, or other small molecule, such as hormone, a pharmaceutical drug.

- **Second messengers.** Second messengers are molecules inside cells that acts to transmit signals from receptors to target molecules in the cytoplasm and/or nucleus. For example, in cAMP messenger system, epinephrine alone would not convert glycogen to glucose, and has to trigger a second messenger, cyclic AMP, for the liver to complete the conversion.

- **Cellular response.** Gene activations and metabolism alterations are primary examples of cellular responses to extracellular stimulation that require signal transduction. The former leads to further cellular effects, since the products of responding genes include instigators of activation and transcription factors can directly or indirectly activate even more genes. As a result, an initial stimulus can give rise to the expression of numerous genes, leading to physiological events.

There are varied classifications for signal pathway. In KEGG pathway database (http://www.genome.jp/kegg/), it divides the pathways into seven classes in terms of molecular interactions, reactions, and relations, including metabolism, genetic information processing, environmental information processing, cellular process, organism systems, human diseases and drug development. It is noted that these pathways are not independent but often interact with each other. However, it is not our target to intentionally discover the interacted molecules in pathways and study their features from the aspect of biochemistry.

From the above observation, signal transduction pathways play a central role in biological processes that a large number of gene or metabolism regulation are attributed to their deregulation. The arisen regulation impacts on different functional aspects of organisms and may lead to diseases, such as mechanism of stress/infection resistance of plant, and diseases arisen from defects in pathways. For example, Figure 1.1 presents an example for AMPK roles in regulating energy metabolism. This monograph will focus on the topic of signaling pathway that may be related to gene expression and metabolism, especially relevant bioinformatics application for discovery of featured patterns of involved regulatory factors, such as miRNA and protein kinases. We will examine their central roles and interesting featured regulation patterns for prediction of regulatory network, investigate some of the major pathways by which the arrival of a chemical signal at a cell switches on a new pattern of gene expression and metabolism regulation, and study the properties of pathway component, such as sequence and structure.

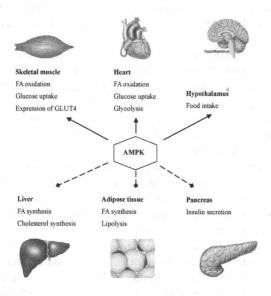

**Fig. 1.1** Roles of AMPK in regulating energy balance metabolism. Solid arrows represent positive effects, and dash lines with diamonds indicate negative effects.

In recent years, a variety of signaling pathways have been reported to play central roles in controlling the gene expression and cellular proliferation. Many disease processes, such as diabetes and heart disease arise from defects in these pathways, highlighting the importance of this process in biology and medicine. It is observed that the signaling pathways may be varied and complex since they show discrepancy between different organisms, at different growth stages, and even in different organs or tissues. Further, the above pathways including their components are not independent and actually correlate with each other by constructing a complicated regulatory network. There have been an explosive growth of genome and proteome data due to the development of high throughput techniques. These valuable and tremendous data not only provide useful resources to understand pathways and are a big challenge to us. In order to be useful to the research community, this information must be synthesized and integrated into understandable paradigms of cellular communication. This demands application of multi-discipline by combining biology scientists and outside experts to provide succinct and current overviews of selected signaling pathways.

## 1.2  Motivations of Bioinformatics for Signaling Pathways

Signaling pathways are divided into two main groups depending on how they are activated. Most of them are activated by external stimuli and function to transfer information from the sensor on cell surface to internal downstream effector systems that are responsible for controlling different cellular processes. In contrast, some of the pathways respond to information generated from within the cell, usually in the form of metabolic messengers. Without exception, protein-protein interactions and second messengers are two primary ways to convey information. Cells usually depend on a collection of such signal pathways, and cross-talk between them is an important feature. As described at http://www.cellsignalingbiology.org/csb/, there has been an explosion in the characterization of signaling components and pathways. The next major challenge is to understand how cells use this large signaling toolkit to assemble the specific signaling pathways they require to communicate with each other. This monograph focuses on introducing current bioinformatics methods and tools for investigating property and role of major components of intracellular signaling pathways operating in cells to regulate their cellular activity.

Defects in signaling pathways may give rise to a large amount of diseases. Most of the serious diseases in humans, such as heart disease, diabetes, hypertension and many forms of mental illness, seem to arise from subtle phenotypic modifications of signaling pathways. Such phenotypic remodeling changes the behaviour of cells and subvert their normal functions, leading to disease.

The regulatory signals usually function in complex networks, composing of a large number of activators or inhibitors. Further, multiple specific inhibitors of all conserved signal pathways have been identified as modulators in organ or tissue development, regulators in metabolism, and cause of diseases. All these findings support the hypothesis that the biological diversity of species may have originated from tinkering with the conserved signal pathways, organized into complex networks, during evolution.

To meet these requirements, we must develop innovative approaches aimed at the sequential and cumulative actions of genetically distinct, but functionally related objects. However, there is a lack of intelligent technology strategies to tackle the high-dimensional pathway data. We have developed effective methods for data integration of biological databases, identification of association rule between stimuli and subunits of kinase and modeling-based structure-function relationship of RNA. It is essential that these aspects are understood and integrated into new algorithms and tools used in kinase pathway data collection, analysis and management. These require a systematic way of combining technologies, signaling kinase pathways and genomic data. The current and potential demands for bioinformatics for pathway analysis may be motivated by several sakes listed below:

- **Genes interaction.** Since the chromosome theory of inheritance was formally proposed by Walter Sutton and Theofore Boveri in 1903, there have been an exploration of efforts to study the genetics and explain the physical reality of Mendel's principles of inheritance. Initially, scientists recognize genes are segments of the DNA that code for specific proteins that are responsible for the expression of the phenotype, such as the human blood type and flower color. Although one gene may generate only one protein in theory, the effect of those proteins are often interact with each other. A lot of novel phenotypes have been proved to often result from the interactions of more than one gene[216]. The interfered expression between one gene with another can result in epistasis. Further, phenotypes are often affected by environmental stimuli, such as water and temperature. In other words, environment determines the phenotype patterns of gene expression. This includes the investigations of gene-gene or gene-environment interaction in complex diseases.

- **Pathway modeling and simulation.** A big challenge in the post-genomic era is how to represent the cell and the organism in virtue of computer. This will assist in computational prediction of higher-level complexity of cellular processes and organism behaviors from genomic information. A number of pathways can be obtained by publicly accessed site/databases like KEGG, BioCYC, BioPACS. They use varied formats to represent pathways or convert databases to a common format, such as proprietary XML. It is important to construct a pathway model to specify processes and reactions according to their input and output entities. This enables the simulation of the pathway once initial conditions of the various entities and processes are specified.

- **Management of biological data.** There have been increasingly growth of proprietary data with information from public sources. This requires us to give researchers a cost-effective, and easy to use system for effective integration[51], intelligent management, and effective utilization of biological data. The data from multi-sources are usually needed to organized, normalized and standardized, making it amenable to precise and complex querying and network construction. A powerful search and visualization interfaces can help researchers integrate data with public and third party datasets and provide context within the literature for interpretation; document literature-derived and internal analyzed data on proteins, complexes, genes, interactions, and compounds in own database; and build and visualize molecular interaction networks dynamically with information in database.

- **Visualization of gene expression.** To assist in the development of a library of pathways that will include all known genes in the primary model organisms, it is important to have a computer application designed to visualize gene expression data on maps representing biological pathways and group of genes[107, 268]. Further, this demands for multidisciplinary collaboration since the pathways regarding gene expression are complex and include various tasks, such as format exchange for biological pathways data and pathway conversion.

- **Pathway and sequence analysis.** It is important to provide a comprehensive reference data set for genes, transcripts and proteins. Thus, it is necessary for us to model relationships between proteins, genes, complexes, cells, tissues, drugs and diseases. Annotation assists us in collecting all available information about any sequence. The creation and interpretation of pathways are viewed as the starting point for the target validation process. Genome visualization provides single or multiple genes in context with information from many different sources mapped to a genome sequence, and RNA structure[50] and protein structure provide an overview of secondary and tertiary structures related to a given target sequence.

- **Protein-protein interaction(PPI).** One of the most important objectives in functional genomic is to investigate and construct protein-protein interaction networks[21, 278]. Interactions between proteins are important for the majority of biological functions. Actually, protein-protein interactions are regarded as the core in the entire interactomics system of any living cell. Functional analysis, such as structure-function relationships and microarrays, has been prevalent and played an important role in biology study. It is crucial to understand the patterns with respect to protein-protein and protein-DNA interactions, transcriptional factors, signaling, metabolism, small molecules and cellular processes.

Signal regulatory networks assist in deeper understanding of organism living activities. The application of advanced experimental approaches in the signal transduction field generate abundant mechanisms of signaling pathways. This demands for bioinformatics analysis methods for signal networks, including public database resources, methods of constructing the network structures, including structural Motif finding and automated pathways generation, modeling and simulation of signaling networks, as well as the relevant components in this area[296, 302]. For example, bioinformatics has been applied to describe the miRNAs target genes function and identify the mRNA interaction networks that are responsible for various cellular processes. This provides a useful approach to observe the function of microRNA in physiological and pathological conditions. However, bioinformatics analysis to predict the target genes and miRNAs gene networks is still underdeveloped owing to the increasing data and potential complicated correlations in biology system.

In recent years, the investigation of signal transduction has been developed from small-scale experiments to large-scale network analysis, and dynamic simulation of networks is closer to the real system, such as synthetical biology. With the study of signal pathways going deeper and becoming more complex, their bioinformatics analysis would become more important. In more details, it is critical to achieve the specific goals below:

- Collect and standardize regulatory pathway data, and provide online data upload, download, and communication between different databases.
- Identify positive and negative regulation of kinase pathways. It is necessary to not only detect the objects that exhibit a positive regulatory role in a kinase pathway but also to discover those objects that inhibit the regulation.
- Structure modeling of genes potentially involved in the activation of kinase pathways, clustering of conserved structures and discovery of potential structure-function relationships for inferring regulatory networks. The results derived from this monograph could be used when predicting essential relationships and enable a comprehensive understanding of kinase pathway interaction.

This monograph is motivated by the desire to develop a comprehensive understanding of the roles and features of a collection of biological regulatory pathways, including activities of functional factors, gene expression, protein-protein interaction, and activators and inhibitors. As a result, this gives rise to the need for bioinformatics including mathematics, computer science, information theory and biology for collection, normalization, modeling, management, analysis, visualization and interpretation of increasing, complex and valuable biology data.

This book will include the work with respect to computer science, biomedicine engineering, and biology. We have already applied relevant methods and algorithms to handle critical problems in biological systems. For example, integration of biological information [49], identification of kinase pathways and structure-function correlations in RNA molecules by data mining [47, 48], and association rule mining in analyzing RNA secondary structures. These studies demonstrate the importance of bioinformatics to tackle the emerging issues in exploring signaling pathways. In particular, we present algorithms for mining top-ranked characteristic correlations from the data; discretization methods for quantitative attribute partition of pathway data; algorithms for identifying both activated and inhibitory patterns; and modeling gene structure and measuring structure similarity using specified distance vectors.

## 1.3  Background

A variety of genomic and proteomic databases are now publicly accessible via the Internet. With the explosion of recorded information, researchers have for the first time found it necessary to develop intelligent strategies for the collection, storage, modeling, analysis and interpretation of diverse biological data. Data mining is an advanced tool and has been widely used for automatic analysis, classification and summarization of data, and automatic prediction and characterization of its trend [126, 339]. However, traditional methods have showed their limitations in dealing with complicated biological data owing to the complexity of biological systems and inherent genetic relationships. In particular, kinase pathways comprise processes controlled by the combination of input signals such as activators and inhibitors. There might be a certain group of kinase pathways that are regulated by a subset of activators and inhibitors, or several kinase pathways can work together to perform an important function. The formalization of this research challenge in signaling kinase pathway data analysis has generated a new impetus in datasets to be analysed and efficient mining techniques to fit that research. An example is the association between pathways, kinome, inhibitors, diseases and targets shown in Figure 1.2 which highlights the importance of bioinformatics.

Many studies recently started to explore the regulatory kinase pathways from the aspect of the genome [1, 22]. Although the regulation must be positive or negative, the difficulty is to identify the specific nucleotide sequences involved in the regulation and classify them into different groups. A gene may present in more than one kinase pathway and a kinase pathway may be related to more than one gene. There are still insufficient methods to handle kinase pathway data by combining the gene expression, structural information and potential structure-function

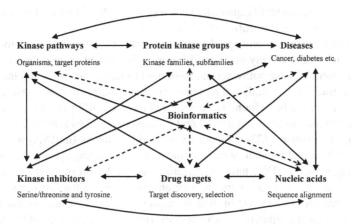

**Fig. 1.2** Typical roles of bioinformatics for kinase pathway components

relationships. Traditional computational linguistics have been applied in computational biology toward abstracted, hierarchical views of biological sequences [279], whereas they show limitations in modeling complicated secondary structures [254]. The generated set of all the ideal strings using grammar is inappropriate for data analysis. These call for the use of sophisticated and effective computational and modeling techniques for systematic collection and interpretation of kinase pathway data. Association rule mining has recently emerged as a popular summarization and pattern extraction algorithm to identify correlations between items in transactional databases [4, 47, 318]. Several attempts have been made to mine biological databases using association rule mining [154, 332].

Several issues are challenging: First, it has been found that a tremendous number of rules can be discovered from the high-dimensional data set [66, 318]. This makes it difficult to filter out the most significant rules. The high dimensionality along with the huge number of rules results in extremely deep mining processes. Second, this method requires a user to specify a minimum support threshold and a confidence threshold for the generation of all the itemsets. However, without specific knowledge, it is difficult for users to set the support threshold and confidence threshold. Therefore, it would be better to identify top-N interesting itemsets, instead of specifying a fixed threshold value for all itemsets of all sizes like [87, 126, 318]. In particular, discrete values about interval of numbers have an important role in data mining and knowledge discovery since they are concise, easier to use and interpret than continuous values [237]. Many studies show rules with discrete values which are normally shorter and more understandable, and this discretization can lead to improved predictive accuracy. Many applications using data mining have been reported in analyzing various biological data sets [47, 49, 51]. Most of them [4, 126] however show limitations in handling the data with multi-valued variables including categorical multi-valued valuables (such as color red, blue, green) and quantitative multi-valued variables (such as weight [40, 50], [50, 75]). A model is proposed in [339] to identify quantitative association rules, in which the domain of multi-valued variables is partitioned into intervals.

For regulating critical biological processes such as cell growth, movement and death, living organisms rely on a family of enzymes called protein kinases [237]. Thus, the protein kinase pathways are important to understand how organisms respond to extracellular stimuli and regulate various cellular activities. Further, many protein kinases have been found to be activated by RNA. RNA regulation has been increasingly recognized as a potential and perhaps overlooked aspect of the genetics of higher organisms [224], especially non-coding RNAs (ncRNA) which play various catalytic and regulatory roles in the genetic operating system. Unlike protein coding genes, ncRNA has insufficient comparable information or outstanding signal. Nevertheless, a comprehensive understanding of the functions of RNA molecules requires knowledge of their structures. Thus, it is critical to analyze the kinase pathways in conjunction with structure-function relationships in RNA.

The authors have developed efficient association rule mining algorithms for mining the most significant interesting patterns for AMPK regulation on skeletal muscle [47] and a framework to discover the structural and functional features in RNA pseudoknots [48]. A method is proposed to measure the inconsistency in biological databases using ontologies (a formal representation of a set of concepts within a knowledge domain) for further mining applications [51]. Also, we developed a novel, unsupervised correlation preserving algorithms for continuous attribute discretization, which transfers a continuous attribute into a discrete one with minimum loss of information. It has been applied to analyse RNA secondary structure data and identify interesting structure-function relationships of RNA. It is essential that they are understood and are incorporated into the analysis of different kinase pathway data.

To sum up, the signaling pathway data is a big challenge to existing computational analysis. Thus, it is critical to develop effective algorithms and tools that are appropriate to deal with the complex pathway data and extract interesting patterns in biology.

## 1.4 Data Mining for Pathway Analysis

Data mining is usually defined as collection, search, analysis of a large amounts of data to discover relationships, patterns, or any significant statistical correlations. With the advent of computer and high throughput techniques, it is easier than ever to generate and obtain tremendous data that can then be systematically analyzed to help identify interesting patterns, by which to find right solutions for difficult problems. In addition to its application in finance to explore strong consumer patterns and relationships, data mining is able to uncover trends, statistical correlations, relationships and patterns that can help your research become more efficient, effective and streamlined. There have been a wide application in diverse fields, such as weather forecast, earthquake, educational institutions to find significant correlations that can enhance our society. For example, The supermarket can now figure out which brands sell the most, what time of the day, week, month or year is the most busiest, what products do consumers frequently buy together with certain items.

In recent years, data mining has been widely used for biology data analysis in post genomic era. It is observed that data mining needs sufficient data samples. This is to ensure the correctness and soundness of identified patterns from the statistical aspect. However, data quality is also critical in data mining as well as data quantity. Without high quality data, it is possible to result in obtaining redundant patterns or missing interesting knowledge. As a result, it is critical to perform data cleaning, data normalization and data standardization before going to practical data analysis. Especially, the biological data are varied and are usually derived from heterogenous biological databases, which are developed, published and maintained by different universities, institutions, labs, organizations, or countries. The inconsistencies in name, languages and used dictionary etc. between databases prevent us from extracting interesting biological knowledge. Further, biological data include both sequence data and structure data, which are different from traditional market basket data. This requires us to develop modeling methods to incorporate both sequence and structure data together for deep data mining application.

There are a number of data mining algorithms and methods for addressing signal pathway data analysis. Sometimes, we may have several options to deal with an issue. It may be hard to say which one is the best in comparison with others. Although we can perform experiments to compare their accuracy, correctness and efficiency, there may be no much difference in the experimental results. A reasonable way is to select the most significant *top-k* patterns, reserve and highlight the potential interesting patterns with low support in current data set.

### 1.4.1 Association Rule Mining

Association rule mining was first introduced in [4] and is one of the most important and well researched techniques of data mining. It aims to extract interesting correlations, frequent patterns, associations or casual structures among sets of items in the transaction databases or other data sources. Association rules have been widely used in various areas such as market and risk management, stock market prediction etc. A brief introduction of various association mining techniques and algorithms will be provided in this section.

Association rule mining aims to identify association rules that satisfy the predefined minimum support and confidence from a given database. This includes two primary processes. One is to find itemsets whose occurrences is equal to or greater than a predefined support threshold in the database. Those itemsets are called frequent itemsets. The other is to generate association rules from those frequent itemsets with the constraints of minimum confidence.

Suppose $I = \{I_1, I_2, \cdots, I_n\}$ is a set of $n$ distinct attributes, $T$ is a transaction that contains a set of items such that $T \subseteq I$, $D$ is a database with different records $T$s.

An association rule is an implication of the form $X \Rightarrow Y$, where $X, Y \subset I$ are called itemsets consisting of a collection of items, and $X \cap Y = \emptyset$, $X$ and $Y$ are called antecedent and consequent, respectively.

Support *supp* and confidence *conf* are two important measures for association rules. Since users are interested in only those frequently occurred items in the databases, it is important to have appropriate thresholds of support and confidence to prune those rules that are not so interesting or useful. The two thresholds are called *minimum support* and *minimum confidence*, respectively. Given a rule $X \Rightarrow Y$, we have

- Supports of itemset $X$ and $Y$, namely $supp(X) = |X(t)|/|D|$ and $supp(Y) = |Y(t)|/|D|$ are defined as the proportion of records in the data set which contain $X$ and $Y$, respectively. $X(t) = \{t \in D \mid t \text{ contains } X\}$ and $Y(t) = \{t \in D \mid t \text{ contains } Y\}$.
- Support of the association rule $X \Rightarrow Y$ is defined as the percentage/fraction of records that contain $X \cup Y$ to the total number of records in the database, namely $supp(X \Rightarrow Y) = supp(X \cup Y)$. Support is a measure of frequency of the association rules.
- Confidence of the rule $X \Rightarrow Y$ is defined as $conf(X \Rightarrow Y) = \frac{supp(X \cup Y)}{supp(X)}$ of records that contain $X \cup Y$ to the total number of records that contain $X$. Confidence is a measure of strength of the association rules.

Association rules need to satisfy a specified minimum support and a user-specified minimum confidence at the same time. Association rule identification usually consists of two separated steps:

- First, *minimum support* is applied to identify all frequent itemsets in a database.
- Second, based on the generated frequent itemsets, the *minimum confidence* constraint is further applied to generate rules.

There have been a number of measures proposed to evaluate the interestingness for rules as well as confidence. Some popular measures are:

- **Any-confidence.** An association is deemed interesting if any rule that can be produced from that association has a confidence greater than or equal to minimum any-confidence value. Suppose $t$ and $D$ represent a record and a database, respectively. Any-confidence of an itemset $X$ can be represented as

$$any - confidence(X) = \frac{supp(X)}{min(supp(x), x \in X)} \qquad (1.1)$$

- **All confidence.** An association is deemed interesting if all rule that can be produced from that association has a confidence greater than or equal to minimum all-confidence value. $max(supp(x), x \in X))$ is the support of the item with the highest support in $X$. All-confidence presents that all rules which can be generated from itemset $X$ have at least a confidence of *all-confidence(X)*. All-confidence has the downward-closed closure property.

$$all - confidence(X) = \frac{supp(X)}{max(supp(x), x \in X)} \tag{1.2}$$

- **Collective strength.** Collective strength gives 0 for perfectly negative correlated items, infinity for perfectly positive correlated items, and 1 if the items co-occur as expected under independence. As for items with medium to low probabilities, the observations of the expected values of the violation rate is dominated by the proportion of records which do not contain any of the items in $X$. For those itemsets, collective strength produces values close to one, even if the itemset appears several times more often than expected together.

$$C(X) = (1 - v(X))/(1 - E[v(X)]) * E[v(X)]/v(X) \tag{1.3}$$

where $v(X)$ presents the violation rate and $E$ is the expected value for independent items. The violation rate is defined as the fraction of transactions which contain some of the items in an itemset but not all.

- **Conviction.** Conviction is used as an alternative to confidence which was found to not capture direction of associations adequately. Conviction compares the probability that $X$ appears without $Y$ if they were dependent with the actual frequency of the appearance of $X$ without $Y$. From the observation, it is similar to *lift* described below, whereas, in contrast to *lift*, it is a directed measure since it also uses the information of the absence of the consequent.

$$conviction(X \Rightarrow Y) = \frac{(1 - supp(Y))}{(1 - conf(X \Rightarrow Y))} = \frac{P(X)P(\neg Y)}{P(X \cup \neg Y)} \tag{1.4}$$

- **Leverage.** Leverage measures the difference of $X$ and $Y$ appearing together in the data set and what would be expected if $X$ and $Y$ were statistically dependent. The rational in a sales setting is to find out how many units (items $X$ and $Y$ together) are sold than expected from the independent sells. Using *minimum leverage* thresholds, one first can use an algorithm to find all itemsets satisfy *minimum support* and then filter the found item sets using the leverage constraint. This property leverage also suffers from the rare item problem.

$$leverage(X \Rightarrow Y) = P(X \cup Y) - (P(X)P(Y)) \tag{1.5}$$

- **Lift.** Lift measures how many times more often $X$ and $Y$ occur together than expected if they were statistically independent. Lift is not down-ward closed and does not suffer from the rare item problem. Also lift is susceptible to noise in small databases. Rare itemsets with low counts (low probability) which perchance occur a few times (or only once) together can produce enormous lift values. The lift of a rule is defined as

$$lift(X \Rightarrow Y) = \frac{supp(X \cup Y)}{supp(X)supp(Y)} \tag{1.6}$$

There are many similar measures such as *cross support ratio, chi-square statistic, cosine/IS measure, gini index, hyper-lift, hyper-confidence, improvement, phi* (correlation), *odds ratio*. Some of these measures are presented and compared by Tan et al [303]. Looking for techniques that can model what the user has known (and using this models as interestingness measures) is currently an active research trend under the name of *Subjective Interestingness*.

There are a number of algorithms developed for association rule mining. Some well known algorithms are *Apriori*, *Eclat* and *FP-Growth*, but they only do half the job, since they are algorithms for mining frequent itemsets. Another step needs to be done to generate rules from frequent itemsets found in a database. It is not our primary goal to describe and discuss details of algorithms in this monograph. We will just list several typical and representative algorithms in association rule mining and focus on the identification of frequent itemsets.

- *Apriori algorithm*. Apriori is the well-known algorithm to discover association rules. A breadth-first search strategy is applied to calculate the support of itemsets and a candidate generation function is used to exploit the downward closure property of support.
- *Eclat algorithm* [334]. Eclat is a depth-first search algorithm using set intersection. The basic idea for the eclat algorithm is to use the set intersections to compute the support of a candidate itemset avoiding the generation of subsets that does not exist in the prefix tree.
- *FP-growth algorithm*. FP-growth (frequent pattern growth) [126] uses an extended prefix-tree (FP-tree) structure to store the database in a compressed form. A divide-and-conquer approach is applied to decompose both the mining tasks and the databases. It uses a pattern fragment growth method to avoid the costly process of candidate generation and testing like Apriori.

The above algorithms are for mining frequent itemsets. According to the derived frequent itemsets from databases, another process needs to be conducted for generating rules

- GUHA procedure is a general method for exploratory data analysis that has theoretical foundations in observational calculi. The ASSOC procedure [4] is a GUHA method that uses fast bitstrings operations for generating association rules. The obtained association rules by this method are more general than those output by Apriori, for example *"items"* can be connected both with conjunction and disjunctions and the relation between antecedent and consequent of the rule is not restricted to setting *minimum support* and *confidence*. An arbitrary combination of supported interest measures can be used.
- One-attribute rule [33]. The one-attribute rule, or OneR, is an algorithm for finding association rules. The idea of the OneR algorithm is to find one attribute to use to classify a novel data point that makes fewest prediction errors. For example, to forecast weather you are not sure, the following rule might be used: *If Windy Then Rainy*, as opposed to a rule with multiple attributes in the condition: *If Windy And Thunder And Cloudy Then Rainy*.
- OPUS search. OPUS is an efficient algorithm for rule discovery that, in contrast to most alternatives, does not require either monotone or anti-monotone constraints such as minimum support. It is initially used to find rules for a fixed

consequent, and it has subsequently been extended to find rules with any item as a consequent.

- Zero-attribute rule. The zero-attribute rule, or ZeroR, does not involve any attribute in the condition part, and always returns the most frequent class in the training set. This algorithm is frequently used to measure the classification success of other algorithms.

There are many other types of association mining. The following algorithms are more or less extended or adapted from the above algorithms. For example, *contrast set learning* is a form of associative learning. Contrast set learners use rules that differ meaningfully in their distribution across subsets; *weighted class learning* is another form of associative learning in which weight may be assigned to classes to give focus to a particular issue of concern for the consumer of the data mining results; *K-optimal pattern discovery* provides an alternative to the standard approach to association rule learning that requires that each pattern appears frequently in the data; *mining frequent sequences* use support to find sequences in temporal data; *generalized association rules* use hierarchical taxonomy (concept hierarchy); *quantitative association rules* use categorical and quantitative data; *interval data association rules* e.g. partition the discrete values of attribute into interval; *sequential aromatization rules* focus on sequential and temporal data e.g. first buy computer, then CD Roms, then a web camera.

## 1.4.2 Bayesian Network

A Bayesian network, belief network or directed acyclic graphical model is a probabilistic graphical model that represents a set of random variables and their conditional dependencies via a directed acyclic graph (DAG)[127]. An example of a Bayesian network could be the probabilistic relationships between disease and gene expression. Given gene expression, the network can be applied to predict the probabilities of the presence of various diseases.

Formally, Bayesian networks are directed acyclic graphs whose nodes represent random variables in the Bayesian sense: they may be observable quantities, latent variables, unknown parameters or hypotheses. Edges represent conditional dependencies; nodes which are not connected represent variables which are conditionally independent of each other. Each node is associated with a probability function that takes as input a particular set of values for the node's parent variables and gives the probability of the variable represented by the node.

Many efficient algorithms are available and perform inference and learning in Bayesian networks. Bayesian networks that model sequences of variables (e.g. speech signals or protein sequences) are called dynamic Bayesian networks. Generalizations of Bayesian networks that can represent and solve decision problems under uncertainty are called influence diagrams.

Several equivalent definitions can be applied for Bayesian network. Suppose $G = (V, E)$ be a directed acyclic graph (or DAG), and suppose $X = (X_v)_{v \in V}$ be a set of random variables indexed by $V$. $X$ is viewed as a Bayesian network with respect to $G$ if its joint probability density function (with respect to a product measure) can be written as a product of the individual density functions, conditional on their parent variables.

$$p(x) = \prod_{v \in V} p(x_v | x_{pa(v)})$$  (1.7)

where $pa(v)$ is the set of parents of $v$ pointing directly to $v$ via a single edge.

For any set of random variables, the probability of any member of a joint distribution can be calculated from conditional probabilities using the chain rule. Suppose the variables from any of their non-descendents are conditionally independent, given the values of their parent variables.

$$p(X_1 = x_1, \cdots, X_n = x_n) = \prod_{i=1}^{n} p(X_i = x_i | X_j = x_j, \forall X_j \in X_{pa(i)})$$  (1.8)

$X$ is a Bayesian network with respect to $G$ if it satisfies the *local Markov property*. Namely, each variable is conditionally independent of its non-descendents given its parent variables. Similar to the first definition, this can be expressed as

$$p(X_i = x_i | X_j = x_j, \forall X_j \notin X_{de(i)}) = p(X_i = x_i | X_j = x_j, \forall X_j \in X_{pa(i)})$$  (1.9)

where $de(i)$ is the set of descendants of $i$.

To develop a Bayesian network, we often first develop a DAG, where $X$ is supposed to satisfy the local Markov property with respect to $G$. We then ascertain the conditional probability distributions of each variable given its parents in $G$. In many cases, if we define the joint distribution of $X$ to be the product of these conditional distributions, then $X$ is a Bayesian network regarding $G$.

- Markov blanket. The Markov blanket of a node is its set of neighboring nodes: its parents, its children, and any other parents of its children. $X$ is a Bayesian network with respect to $G$ if every node is conditionally independent of all other nodes in the network, given its Markov blanket.
- $d$-separation. It can be defined in more general $d$-separation of two nodes, where $d$ stands for dependence. Let $P$ be a a path from node $u$ to $v$. Then $P$ is said to be $d$-separated by a set of nodes $Z$ if and only if (at least) one of the following holds:

  1. $P$ contains a chain, $i \to m \to j$, such that the middle node $m$ is in $Z$,
  2. $P$ contains a chain, $i \leftarrow m \leftarrow j$, such that the middle node $m$ is in $Z$,
  3. $P$ contains a fork, $i \leftarrow m \to j$, such that the middle node $m$ is in $Z$, or
  4. $P$ contains an inverted fork, $i \to m \leftarrow j$, such that the middle node $m$ is not in $Z$ and no descendant of $m$ is in $Z$.

Thus $u$ and $v$ are said to be $d$-separated by $Z$ if all trails between them are $d$-separated. If $u$ and $v$ are not $d$-separated, they are called $d$-connected. $X$ is a

Bayesian network with respect to $G$ if, for any two nodes $u$, $v$, which are conditionally independent given $Z$. $Z$ is a set which $d$-separates $u$ and $v$. The Markov blanket is the minimal set of nodes which $d$-separates node $v$ from all other nodes.

- Causal networks. Although Bayesian networks are often used to represent causal relationships, this need not be the case: a directed edge from $u$ to $v$ does not require that $X_v$ is causally dependent on $X_u$. For example, in Bayesian networks $a \rightarrow b \rightarrow c$ and $a \leftarrow b \leftarrow c$ impose exactly the same conditional independence requirements.

A causal network is a Bayesian network with an explicit requirement that the relationships are causal. The additional semantics of the causal networks specify that if a node $X$ is actively caused to be in a given state $x$, then the probability density function changes to one of the network obtained by cutting the links from $X$'s parents to $X$, and setting $X$ to the caused value $x$. Using these semantics, one can predict the impact of external interventions from data obtained prior to intervention.

### 1.4.3  Neural Network

Traditionally, neural network was used to refer to a circuit of biological neurons that are connected or functionally relevant in the peripheral nervous system or the central nervous system. In addition, the term neural network also refers to artificial neural networks, which consist of artificial neurons or nodes. In the computing environment, the term Neural Network (NN) is usually used as synonym for artificial neural network. Artificial Neural Networks (ANNs) are of primary research interest at present, involving researchers of many different disciplines. Subjects contributing to this research include biology, computing, electronics, mathematics, medicine, physics, and psychology. The basic idea of this approach is to use the knowledge of the nervous system and the human brain to design intelligent artificial systems.

Biologists and psychologists are trying to model and understand the brain and parts of the nervous system and searching for interpretations for human behavior and the limitations in brain. In contrast, computer scientists and electronic engineers are looking for efficient ways to solve problems for which conventional computers are currently used. Biological and psychological models and ideas are often the resource of inspiration for these scientists.

Artificial neural networks consist of interconnecting artificial neurons. They may either be applied to obtain an understanding of biological neural networks, or for addressing artificial intelligence problems without necessarily generating a model of a real biological system. ANN algorithms attempt to abstract this complexity of NN and focus on what may hypothetically matter most from an information processing point of view. Good performance can then be used as one source of evidence towards supporting the hypothesis that the abstraction really captured something important from the point of view of information processing in the brain. Another motivation is to reduce the amount of computation to simulate artificial neural networks.

Artificial intelligence and cognitive modeling as well as neural networks are also information processing approaches inspired by the way biological neural systems process data. Artificial intelligence and cognitive modeling try to simulate some properties of biological neural networks. While similar in their techniques, the former is based on statistical estimations, classification optimization and control theory, and has the aim of solving particular tasks such as speech recognition, image analysis. In contrast, the cognitive modeling aims to build mathematical models of biological neural systems.

### 1.4.4   Clustering

Clustering is the unsupervised classification of patterns (observations, data items, or feature vectors) into groups (clusters). Cluster analysis is the organization of a collection of patterns (usually represented as a vector of measurements, or a point in a multidimensional space) into clusters based on similarity[160]. Intuitively, patterns within a valid cluster are more similar to each other than they are to a pattern belonging to a different cluster. The clustering problem has been addressed in many contexts and by researchers in many disciplines.

There is difference between clustering (unsupervised classification) and discriminant analysis (supervised classification). In supervised classification, a collection of labeled (preclassified) patterns are provided and the problem is to label a newly encountered, yet unlabeled, pattern[161]. Typically, the given labeled (training) patterns are applied to learn the descriptions of classes which in turn are used to label a new pattern. In the case of clustering, it aims to group a given set of unlabeled patterns into interesting clusters. In a sense, labels are related to clusters also, whereas these category labels are data driven. In other words, they are derived solely from the data. In general, a pattern clustering activity includes the following steps:

- *Pattern representation* (optionally including feature extraction and/or selection) refers to the number of classes, the number of available patterns, and the number, type, and scale of the features available to the clustering algorithm[161]. Feature selection is viewed as the process of discovering the most effective subset of the original features to use in clustering.
- A *pattern proximity* measure appropriate to the data domain. Pattern proximity is usually measured by a distance function defined on pairs of patterns. A variety of distance measures are in use in the various communities [8, 160]. A simple distance measure like *Euclidean* distance can often be used to reflect dissimilarity between two patterns, whereas other similarity measures, such as *Hausdorff* distance can be used to characterize the conceptual similarity between patterns.
- *Clustering or grouping*. The grouping step can be performed in a number ways. The output clustering can be hard or fuzzy (where each pattern has a variable degree of membership in each of the output clusters). Hierarchical clustering algorithms generate a nested series of partitions based on a criterion for merging

or dividing clusters in terms of similarity. Partitional clustering algorithms identify the partition that optimizes (usually locally) a clustering criterion. Additional techniques for the grouping operation include probabilistic and graph-theoretic clustering methods.

- *Data abstraction* (if needed) is able to extract a simple and compact representation of a data set. In general, simplicity is either from the perspective of automatic analysis (so that a machine can perform further processing efficiently) or it is human-oriented (so that the representation obtained is easy to understand and intuitively appealing). In the clustering context, a compact description of each cluster is a typical data abstraction, usually based on cluster prototypes or representative patterns such as the centroid[161].
- *Assessment of output.* A clustering procedure output can be evaluated from several aspects. One is actually to assess the data domain rather than the clustering algorithm itself. Data which do not contain clusters should not be processed by a clustering algorithm. More information can refer to [84]. *Cluster validity analysis*, by contrast, often uses a specific criterion of optimality. Validity assessments are objective and are performed to determine whether the output is meaningful. A clustering structure is valid if it cannot reasonably have occurred by chance or as an artifact of a clustering algorithm. When statistical approaches is applied for clustering, validation is achieved by carefully applying statistical methods and testing hypotheses. There are three types of validation studies. An external assessment of validity compares the recovered structure to a priori structure. An internal validity assessment attempts to determine if the structure is intrinsically appropriate for the data. A relative test compares two structures and measures their relative merit.

*Pattern representation* can often yield a simple and easily understood clustering. A poor pattern representation may result in a complex clustering whose true structure is difficult or impossible to discern. A careful study of the available features and any available transformations (even simple ones) can give rise to significantly improved clustering results. Patterns are represented conventionally as multi-dimensional vectors. Each dimension can be viewed as a single feature, which is either quantitative or qualitative. For example, if weight and color are the two features used, then [20, black] is the representation of a black object with 20 units of weight. The features can be subdivided into the following types:

- *Quantitative features* can be measured on a ratio scale (with a meaningful reference value, such as temperature), or on nominal or ordinal scales, such as (1) continuous values (e.g., *weight*); (2) discrete values (e.g., the number of computers); (3) interval values (e.g., the duration of an event).
- *Qualitative features* consist of (1) nominal or unordered (e.g., *color*); (2) ordinal (e.g., military rank or qualitative evaluations of temperature (*cool* or *hot*) or sound intensity (*quiet* or *loud*)).

It is often useful to sort out only the most descriptive and discriminatory features in the input set. Those features are exclusively applied in subsequent analysis.

Feature selection techniques enable discovery of a subset of the given features for subsequent use. In contrast, feature extraction techniques generate new features from the original set. In either case, they focus on improving classification performance and/or computational efficiency. Although feature selection is a well-explored topic in statistical pattern recognition, this process is of necessity, in a clustering context without class labels for patterns. Further, it might involve a trial-and-error process where various subsets of features are selected, the resulting patterns clustered, and the output evaluated using a validity index.

*Similarity measure.* Since similarity is fundamental to the definition of a cluster, a measure of the similarity between two patterns derived from the same feature space is critical to most clustering procedures. Owing to the variety of feature types and scales, the distance measure must be selected carefully. It is most common to compute the dissimilarity between two patterns using a distance measure defined on the feature space. The most popular metrics include

- *Euclidean distance* for continuous features. Suppose $X_i = (X_{i1}, \cdots, X_{im})$ and $X_j = (X_{j1}, \cdots, X_{jm})$ represent two variables. Their distance can be presented as

$$d(X_i, X_j) = \sqrt[2]{\sum_{k=1}^{m} (X_{ik} - X_{jk})^2} \qquad (1.10)$$

where *Euclidean distance* is a special case of the Minkowski distance in case of $q = 2$ in the formula below.

$$d(X_i, X_j) = \sqrt[q]{\sum_{k=1}^{m} (X_{ik} - X_{jk})^q} \qquad (1.11)$$

*Euclidean distance* shows good performance when a data set has compact or isolated clusters. The limitation to direct use of the Minkowski metrics is the tendency of the largest-scaled feature to dominate the others. Thus, it is necessary to include normalization of the continuous features (to a common range or variance) or other weighting schemes.

- *Mahalanobis distance* relies on correlations between variables by which different patterns can be identified and analyzed. Unlike *Euclidean distance*, it does not consider the correlations of the data set and is a multivariate effect size. Suppose $X = (X_1, \cdots, X_m)\}^T$ is a multivariate vector from a group of values with mean $u = (u_1, \cdots, u_m)\}^T$ and covariance matrix $S$

$$d(X) = \sqrt{(X - u)^T S^{-1} (X - u)} \qquad (1.12)$$

This distance assigns different weights to different features based on their variances and pairwise linear correlations. Here, it is implicitly assumed that class conditional densities are unimodal and characterized by multidimensional spread, i.e., that the densities are multivariate Gaussian. Recently, the *Hausdorff distance* is applied in a point set matching context.

- *Cosine* is used to measure the variance between two vectors $X_1 = (X_{11}, \cdots, X_{1n})$ and $X_2 = ((X_{21}, \cdots, X_{2n}))$.

$$\cos(\theta) = \frac{\sum_{k=1}^{n} X_{1k} X_{2k}}{\sqrt{\sum_{k=1}^{n} X_{1k}^2} \sqrt{\sum_{k=1}^{n} X_{2k}^2}} \tag{1.13}$$

- *Jaccard similarity coefficient*
  Suppose $X$ and $Y$ are two sample sets. *Jaccard coefficient* aims to measure similarity between $X$ and $Y$.

$$J(X,Y) = \frac{|X \cap Y|}{|X \cup Y|} \tag{1.14}$$

*Jaccard distance* is to measures dissimilarity between the sample sets $X$ and $Y$, is complementary to the Jaccard coefficient.

$$J_\delta(X,Y) = 1 - J(X,Y) = \frac{|X \cup Y| - |X \cap Y|}{|X \cup Y|} \tag{1.15}$$

Suppose $p$, $q$, $r$, $s$, $t = p + q + r + s$ represent number of variables that positive for both objects, number of variables that positive for the $X$ objects and negative for the $Y$ object, number of variables that negative for the $X$ object, and positive for the $Y$ object, number of variables that negative for both objects, and total number of variables, respectively. By removing $s$ from simple matching coefficient, Jaccard's coefficient can be presented as

$$s_{XY} = \frac{p}{p+q+r} \tag{1.16}$$

According to Formula 1.16, in the similar way, Jaccard's distance can be represented as

$$d_{XY} = 1 - s_{XY} = \frac{q+r}{p+q+r} \tag{1.17}$$

- *Correlation coefficient* developed by Karl Pearson is a measure of the correlation (linear dependence) between two variables $X$ and $Y$.

$$p_{XY} = \frac{Cov(X,Y)}{\delta_X \delta_Y} = \frac{E((X - u_X)(Y - u_Y))}{\delta_X \delta_Y} \tag{1.18}$$

where $Cov$ and $\delta$ represent covariance and standard deviation, respectively. As a result, the correlation distance is defined as

$$d_{XY} = 1 - p_{XY} \tag{1.19}$$

Substituting estimates of the covariances and variances based on a sample give the sample correlation coefficient, commonly denoted $r$ :

$$r = \frac{\sum_{i=1}^{n}(X_i - \overline{X})(Y_i - \overline{Y})}{\sqrt{\sum_{i=1}^{n}(X_i - \overline{X})^2}\sqrt{\sum_{i=1}^{n}(Y_i - \overline{Y})^2}} \tag{1.20}$$

where $\overline{X}$ and $\overline{Y}$ represent the sample mean of $X$ and $Y$, respectively.

A difficulty is how to calculate the distances between patterns with some or all features being noncontinuous since the different types of features are not comparable and (as an extreme example) the notion of proximity is effectively binary- valued for nominal-scaled features. A number of other metrics have been reported by Diday and Simon and by Ichino and Yaguchi for computing the similarity between patterns represented using quantitative as well as qualitative features. Further, patterns can also be represented by string or tree structures. Several measures of similarity between strings are described in [15]. A good summary of similarity measures between trees is given in [340].

The above describes the primary distance metrics for similarity measures. Most existing distance functions are extended or adapted from these metrics. Further, unlike distance metrics, , there are a number of methods to evaluate the correlation between objects, such as entropy, mutual information, rough set. They actually take into account the degree of dependence between two objects from the aspect of contained information. They will be described in the following sections.

### 1.4.5   Information Theory

Information theory was initially proposed by Claude E. Shannon to discover fundamental limits on signal processing operations such as compressing data and on reliably storing and communicating data. It can be viewed as a branch of applied mathematics and electrical engineering involving the quantification of information. Information theory has been widely applied in a variety of applications, including statistical inference, natural language processing, cryptography, communication networks as in neurobiology, the evolution and function of molecular codes, model selection in ecology, thermal physics, quantum computing, and other forms of data analysis.

Information theory is based on probability theory and statistics. Entropy is one of the most important key measures of quantities of information. It is usually expressed by the average number of bits needed for storage or communication. Entropy assists in quantifying the uncertainty involved in predicting the value of a random variable. Further, mutual information aims to measure the amount of information in common between two random variables. The former quantity indicates how easily message data can be compressed while the latter can be used to find the communication rate across a channel.

**Entropy.** The entropy, $H$, of a discrete random variable $X$ is a measure of the amount of uncertainty associated with the value of $X$. The choice of logarithmic base in the following formulae determines the unit of information entropy that is used. The most common unit of information is the *bit*, based on the binary logarithm.

Other units include the *nat*, which is based on the natural logarithm, and the *hartley*, which is based on the common logarithm. Suppose $X$ is the set of all messages $\{x_1, \cdots, x_n\}$ that $X$ could be, and $p(x)$ is the probability of $X$ given some $x \in X$, then the entropy of $X$ is defined as

$$H(X) = E_X[I(x)] = -\sum_{x \in X} p(x) \log p(x) \tag{1.21}$$

where $I(x)$ represents the self-information, namely the entropy contribution of an individual message and $E_X$ represents the expected value. An important property of entropy is that it is maximized when all the messages in the message space are equiprobable. In other words, we have $p(x) = 1 / n$ and $H(X) = \log n$. A special case of information entropy for a random variable with two outcomes is the binary entropy function, usually taken to the logarithmic base 2, namely $H(X) = -p \log_2 p - (1 - p)\log_2(1 - p)$.

**Joint Entropy.** The joint entropy of two discrete random variables $X$ and $Y$ is merely the entropy of their pairing: $(X, Y)$. This implies that if $X$ and $Y$ are independent, then their joint entropy is the sum of their individual entropies.

$$H(X, Y) = -\sum_{x \in X} \sum_{y \in Y} p(x, y) \log_2[p(x, y)] \tag{1.22}$$

where $x$ and $y$ are particular values of $X$ and $Y$, respectively, $p(x, y)$ is the probability of these values occurring together, and $p(x, y)\log_2[p(x, y)]$ is defined to be 0 if $p(x, y) = 0$. For more general form including a collection of variables, it can be defined as

$$H(X_1, \cdots, X_n) = -\sum_{X_1} \cdots \sum_{X_n} p(x_1, \cdots, x_n) \log_2[p(x_1, \cdots, x_n)] \tag{1.23}$$

**Conditional Entropy.** The conditional entropy or conditional uncertainty of $X$ given random variable $Y$ is the average conditional entropy over $Y$. This allows us to quantify dependence.

$$H(X|Y) = -\sum_{y \in Y} p(y) \sum_{x \in X} p(x|y) \log p(x|y) = -\sum_{x,y} p(x, y) \log \frac{p(x, y)}{p(y)} \tag{1.24}$$

Some properties of joint entropy and conditional entropy are:

- *Chain Rule*, namely $H(X, Y) = H(X|Y) + H(Y) = H(Y|X) + H(X)$
- *Conditional Entropy Maximum*, namely $H(X|Y) \leq H(X)$.
- *Addition Rule*, namely $H(X, Y) \leq H(X) + H(Y)$.
- *Independence*. If $X$ and $Y$ are independent, we have $H(X, Y) = H(X) + H(Y)$.

**Mutual Information.** It measures the amount of information that can be obtained about one random variable by observing another. The mutual information between random variables $X$ and $Y$ is defined as

$$I(X;Y) = \sum_{x,y} p(x,y) log \frac{p(x,y)}{p(x)p(y)} \tag{1.25}$$

Mutual information has two basic properties.

- $I(X;Y) = H(X) - H(X|Y)$
- $I(X;Y) = H(X) + H(Y) - H(X, Y) = I(Y;X)$

### 1.4.6 Sequence and Structure Modeling

**Linguistic Methods.** Noam Chomsky developed a formal representation of the rules or syntax of language, called generative grammar, that could provide finite-indeed, concise-characterizations of such infinite languages. The Chomsky hierarchy of language classes has proven especially durable as a means of stratifying formal languages according to their expressive power and resulting computational and mathematical complexity. Generative grammars were also soon integrated into the framework of the theory of computation, and in addition now form the basis for efforts of computational linguists to automate the processing and understanding of human language[151].

DNA is a richly-expressive language for specifying the structures and processes of life, also with the potential for a seemingly infinite variety. There is an increasing trend throughout the field of computational biology toward abstracted, hierarchical views of biological sequences, which is prevalent in the spirit of computational linguistics. In the 1980s, several workers began to follow various threads of Chomsky's legacy in applying linguistic methods to molecular biology. The utility of grammars is able to capture not only informational but also structural aspects of macromolecules.

*Chomsky hierarchy and formal language theory.* A grammar is a rule-based approach to specifying a language, consisting of a set of rewriting rules that take forms such as $A \rightarrow xB$. Here, upper-case letters denote temporary or nonterminal symbols, which do not occur in the alphabet, whereas lower-case letters are terminal symbols that do. The example rule specifies that any occurrence of the nonterminal $A$ may be replaced by an $x$ followed by a $B$.

Suppose $S$ is a starting nonterminal. A derivation from a grammar consists of a series of rewriting steps that end when the last nonterminal is eliminated. For example, the simple grammar with an alphabet $x$ and $y$, which contains the rules $S \rightarrow xS$ and $S \rightarrow y$. This grammar generates all strings beginning with any number of $x$' and ending in a single $y$. It produces derivations such as $S \Rightarrow xS \Rightarrow xxS \Rightarrow xxxS \Rightarrow xxxy$, where each double arrow signifies the application of a single-arrow rule. In this case there are three applications of the first rule followed by a single application of the second to produce a terminal string, one of the infinite number of such strings in this language. An equivalent means of generating such languages is a finite-state automaton (FSA), which is a notional machine used to reason about computation, built out of states which are interconnected by transitions (arrows) that emit symbols from the alphabet as they are traversed.

Context-free grammars allow any arrangement of terminals and nonterminals on the right-hand sides of rules and have greater expressive power, such as $S \rightarrow xS$, $S \rightarrow 0A$. They can generate not only all regular languages, but also non-regular languages such as strings of $x$'s followed by the same number of $y$'s (for example, $xxxxyyyy$). Such languages cannot be specified by a regular grammar or FSA because these devices have no mechanism for 'remembering' how many $x$'s were generated when the time comes to derive the $y$'s.

Even context-free grammars are inadequate for some languages, for instance strings of consecutive $x$'s, $y$'s and $z$'s in equal number (for example, $xxxyyyzzz$). This entails dependencies that necessarily cross one another, called cross-serial dependencies, and to capture these with a grammar requires context-sensitive rules that have additional symbols on their left-hand side. Such a grammar will be called context-sensitive if the left-hand side of each rule is not longer than its right-hand side, such as $S \rightarrow xSAB$, $S \rightarrow 0A$, $0S \rightarrow 0A$.

It is observed that the requirement that each rule's right-hand side is at least as long as its left-hand side guarantees that strings produced by successive derivations never grow longer than the final terminal string, and thus exceed the memory available to the automaton. If there is no constraint on the number of symbols on the left hand sides of rules, the grammar is called unrestricted.

*Structural Linguistics of Nucleic Acids.* Linguistics have been widely applied to encompass various phenomena observed in nucleic acids that are literally structural, namely depending on the physical nature of DNA and RNA. This demonstrates the utility of grammars in capturing not only informational but also structural aspects of macromolecules.

There are varied relationships in linguistics, called dependencies, including nested dependency and cross dependency. For example, a folded RNA secondary structure entails pairing between nucleotide bases and contains the most basic stem-loop secondary structure, which establishes nested dependency. This can be described by context-free base-pairing grammar.

$$S \rightarrow aSu, S \rightarrow gSc, S \rightarrow cSg, S \rightarrow uSa, S \rightarrow \varepsilon$$

where $a$, $g$, $c$, $u$ represent nucleotides of *Adenine, Guanine, Cytosine, Uracil*, respectively. The symbol $\varepsilon$ in the fifth rule describes that an $S$ is removed.

Based on these rules, hairpin sequences of secondary structure can be derived, such as

$$S \rightarrow aSu \Rightarrow S \rightarrow agScu \Rightarrow S \rightarrow aguSacu \Rightarrow \cdots \Rightarrow S \rightarrow agucSgacu$$

In a realistic stem-loop, the derivation would terminate in an unpaired loop of at least several bases and might also contain, for example, non-Watson-Crick base pairs and 'bulges'. But such features are easily added to the grammar without affecting the fundamental result that any language consisting of RNA sequences that fold into these basic structures requires context-free expression. Figure 1.3 presents a simple stem structure, which creates the nested dependencies of the stem. In contrast, Figure 1.4 describes a structure containing stems and unpaired loops together. There are diverse types of secondary structures apart from stem-loop structure, whereas they can be easily captured by simply adding to the grammar corresponding rules. For example, the arbitrarily branched folded structures in Figure 1.5 requires an additional rule $S \rightarrow SS$.

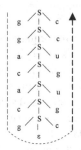

**Fig. 1.3** A structure of Stem

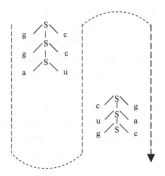

**Fig. 1.4** A structure of stem-loop

It is observed that there is no base-pairing cross dependency with respect to the stem and branch tree like structure in the first two subfigures. Although the base-pairing dependencies in Figure 1.5 are more complex than Figure 1.3, it is still non-crossing. As a result, the resulting grammar is formally ambiguous, and more than one kind of tree can be derived. Such ambiguity allows users to embody the ensemble of potential secondary structures, and use more specific grammars to specify particular forms, such as transfer RNA cloverleafs.

A stochastic context-free grammar (SCFG) extends the standard context-free formalism by adding probabilities to each production:

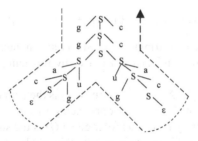

**Fig. 1.5** A structure of branch

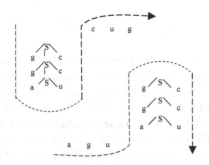

**Fig. 1.6** A structure of attenuator

$$X \to \lambda \; [p]$$

where the rule probability $p$ is usually written as $P(X \to \lambda)$. This notation to some extent hides the fact that $p$ is a conditional probability, of production $X \to \lambda$ being chosen,

A stochastic grammar assigns a probability to each string which it derives and hence defines a probability distribution on the set of strings. Stochastic (probabilistic) automata are the probabilistic counterpart of finite automata that are known as hidden Markov models (HMMs). Stochastic context-free grammars (SCFGs) is a superclass and goes one step beyond hidden Markov models in the Chomsky hierarchy.

A stochastic context-free grammar (SCFG) $G$ consists of a set of nonterminal symbols $X$, and a string $x$ over the alphabet $\Sigma$ of $G$. The three basic problems to deal with SCFGs, which are the same as in HMMs, can be solved efficiently. The first two problems, calculating the probability of a given string $w$ assigned by a SCFG $G$ and finding the most likely derivation tree of $w$ by $G$, can be solved using dynamic programming methods analogous to the Cocke-Younger-Kasami or early parsing methods.

- The probability of a (partial) derivation $v_1 \Rightarrow v_2 \Rightarrow \cdots v_n$ is inductively defined by

1. $P(v_1) = 1$
2. $P(v_1 \Rightarrow v_2 \Rightarrow \cdots v_n) = P(X \rightarrow \lambda)P(v_1 \Rightarrow v_2 \Rightarrow \cdots v_n)$

where $v_1$, $v_2$, $\cdots$ $v_n$ are strings of terminals and nonterminals, $X \rightarrow \lambda$ is a production of $G$, and $v_2$ is derived from $v_1$ by replacing one occurrence of $X$ with $\lambda$.

- The string probability $P(X \Rightarrow x)$ (of $x$ given $X$) is the sum of the probabilities of all left-most derivations $X \Rightarrow \cdots \Rightarrow x$ producing $x$ from $X$.
- The sentence probability $P(S \Rightarrow x)$ (of $x$ given $G$) is the string probability given the start symbol $S$ of $G$. In other words, this is also the probability $P(x|G)$ assigned to $x$ by the grammar $G$.
- The prefix probability $P(S \Rightarrow_L x)$ is the sum of probabilities of all sentence strings having $x$ as a prefix

$$P(S \Rightarrow_L x) = \sum_{y \in \Sigma^*} P(S \Rightarrow xy)$$

From the above observation, the grammar complexity is increasing from regular languages, context-free languages, context-sensitive languages to recursively-enumerable languages. Accordingly, their recognition is changed from linear, polynomial, exponential to undecidable. Further, a significant finding is that there exist phenomena in RNA that in fact raise the language even beyond context-free. The most obvious of these are so-called non-orthodox secondary structures such as pseudoknots, which are pairs of stem-loop elements in which part of one stem resides within the loop of the other like Figure 1.4. This configuration induces cross-serial dependencies in the resulting base pairings, requiring context-sensitive expression. Using formalisms called tree-adjoining grammars and their variants, which are considered to be mildly context-sensitive and relatively tractable, it is possible to encompass a wide range of RNA secondary structures. Moreover, new types of grammars have been invented to deal with such biological examples.

There has been less activity in modeling proteins with linguistic methods, perhaps because they are viewed as having a richer basic repertoire of interactions and conformations than nucleic acids, and perhaps also more of a sense of emergent properties. Nevertheless, linguistic methods have been more or less applied to certain abstracted depictions of protein structure, such as domain schematics, which describes the highly variable arrangements of 'mobile' domains or topology 'cartoons', which annotates dependencies between secondary structural elements.

Specific aspects of protein structure have been modeled explicitly with grammars. Secondary structural elements, and in particular the hydrogen bonding between strands in a b-sheet, may be displayed in antiparallel form, creating nested dependencies by analogy with stem-loop structures in RNA, or in parallel form, which creates cross-serial dependencies. However, translocation of segments of a string due to insertion or deletion may result in cross-serial dependencies where none existed before, and thus the block movements typical of genomic rearrangements may lead to pressure in the Chomsky hierarchy that is inherent in evolution. Nevertheless, within proteins there is evidence that at the level of domains there is again a relative insufficiency of non-context-free forms. As a result, it is interesting that the special case of head-to-tail rearrangements actually preserve context-free status from a mathematical perspective.

The results summarized above all relate to structural aspects of macromolecules. Nevertheless, genes do convey information, and furthermore this information is organized in a hierarchical structure whose features are ordered, constrained and related in a manner analogous to the syntactic structure of sentences in a natural language.

**Index-Based Modeling.** RSEARCH [188], and PHMMTS [267] use variants of stochastic context-free grammars as descriptors, whereas ERPIN [106] uses sequential and structural profiles. Although descriptor-based tools available today is fast compared to other methods, they have a running time that is, in the best case, linear in the size of the target sequence database. This makes their application challenging while it copes with large sequence databases. A solution with sublinear running time would require index data structures. However, widely used index structures like suffix trees or arrays or the FM-index have bad performance on typical RNA sequence-structure patterns, because they cannot utilize the RNA structure information. Meyer etc. present a fast descriptor-based method and software for RNA sequence-structure pattern matching. This method is composed of initially building an affix array, i.e. an index data structure of the target database. Affix arrays cope well with structural pattern constraints by allowing for an efficient matching order of the bases constituting the pattern. Structurally symmetric patterns like stem-loops can be matched inside out, such that first the loop region is matched and, in subsequent extensions, pairing positions on the boundaries are matched consecutively.

Suppose $S$ is a sequence over an alphabet $\mathscr{A}$ and $|S|$ denotes the length of $S$. $S_i$, $0 \leq i < n$ denotes the character of $S$ at position $i$. Let $\varepsilon$ denote the empty sequence. The set of all possible sequences over $\mathscr{A}$ including the empty sequence is denoted by $\mathscr{A}^\star$. Given a sequence $S = S_0 S_1 \cdots S_{n-1}$ and $0 \leq i \leq j < n$. The reverse sequence of $S$ is denoted by $S^{-1} = S_{n-1} S_{n-2} \cdots S_0$. Given $S = uv$, $u$ and $v \in \mathscr{A}^\star$. $u$ is a prefix of $S$, and $v$ is a suffix of $S$. The $k$th suffix of $S$ starts at position $k$, while the $k$th prefix of $S$ ends at $k$. The $k$th reverse prefix of $S$ is the $k$th suffix of $S$.

For $0 \leq k < n$, we use the following notation for substring of $S$.

- $(i : S: j)$ denotes the substring $S_i S_{i+1} \cdots S_j$ of $S$.
- $(k : S)$ denotes the $k$th suffix of $S$
- $(S: j)$ denotes the $j$th prefix of $S$

Let $\mathscr{A}$ denote the RNA alphabet $\{A, C, G, U\}$. Its characters code for the nucleotides adenine (A), cytosine (C), guanine (G), and uracil (U). In the following, a sequence $S$ is fixed over the RNA alphabet $\mathscr{A}$. The RNA secondary structure is formed by Watson-Crick pairing of complementary bases and also by the slightly weaker wobble pairs. Two bases $(c, d) \in \mathscr{A} \times \mathscr{A}$ can form a complementary base pair if and only if $(c, d) \in \{(A, U), (U, A), (C, G), (G, C), (G, U), (U, G)\}$.

A non-crossing RNA structure $R$ of length $m$ is a set of base pairs $(S_i, S_j)$, $0 \leq i < j < m$, stating that the base at position $i$ pairs with the base at position $j$, such that for all $(i, j), (i', j') \in R$: $i < i' < j' < j$ or $i' < i < j < j'$ or $i < j < i' < j'$ or $i' < j' < i < j$. An important structural motif occurring in many RNA molecules is the stem-loop structure. $R$ is called a stem-loop RNA structure if and only if for all $(i,j), (i',j') \in R$: $i < i' < j' < j$ or $i' < i < j < j'$.

Affix array is a widely used method for index data structure. This index structure can be used for efficient unidirectional as well as bidirectional searches and is more space efficient than the affix tree. Until now, affix arrays have received little attention in bioinformatics. This has been to some extent owing to the lack of an open and robust implementation.

Suppose $S^F = S$, $S^R = S^{-1}$, and $S^X$ represents the statements that apply to $S^F$ and $S^R$. $\$ \notin \mathscr{A}$ is the reserved *terminator symbol* to present the end of a sequence. In other words, $\$$ is lexicographically larger than all the characters in $\mathscr{A}$. The affix array data structure of a sequence $S$ consists of six tables,

- $suf_F$ means suffix arrays of $S^F$;
- $suf_R$ means suffix arrays of $S^R$;
- $lcp_F$ means longest common prefix arrays of $S^F$;
- $lcp_R$ means longest common prefix arrays of $S^R$
- $aflk_F$ means affix link arrays of $S^F$;
- $aflk_R$ means affix link arrays of $S^R$.

where $suf_X$ is an array of integers in the range 0 to $n$ specifying the lexicographic order of the $n + 1$ suffixes of the string $S^X\$$. That is, $S^X_{suf_X[0]}, S^X_{suf_X[1]}, \cdots S^X_{suf_X[n]}$ is the sequence of suffixes of $S^X\$$ in ascending lexicographic order. Figure 1.7 presents a atomic suffix tree for AGAGG. For example, $suf[1]$ and $suf[2]$ represent strings GAGG and AGG, respectively.

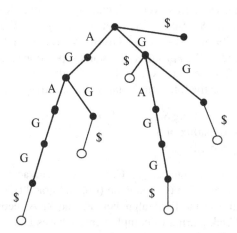

**Fig. 1.7** Atomic suffix tree for string AGAGG. The end symbol $\$$ is appended to indicate the end-position of suffixes. Explicit branching nodes are marked by boxes.

**Definition 1.1.** $lcp_X$ (longest common prefix) is a table in the range 0 to $n$.

$$lcp_X[i] = \begin{cases} 0 & , \quad if \; i = 0 \; or \; i = n \\ max\{j | (0 : suf_{i-1} : j) = (0 : suf_i : j)\} + 1 & , \quad otherwise \end{cases}$$

where $n$ is the length of the string, and $lcp_X[i]$ is the length of the longest common prefix between $S^X_{suf_X[i-1]}$ and $S^X_{suf_X[i]}$ for $1 \le i \le n$. In other words, it is the length of the longest common prefix of $suf_i$ and $suf_{i-1}$.

The underlying concepts of this data structure is described by using intervals in the suffix array $suf_X$. Two important concepts of affix arrays are *suffix-intervals* and *lcp-intervals*. An interval $[i, j]$ representing the set of suffixes $S^X_{suf_X[i]}, \cdots, S^X_{suf_X[j]}$, 1 $\le i, j \le n$, of width $j - i + 1$, is a *suffix-interval* in $suf_X$ with depth (prefix length) $\ell$ $\in \{0, \cdots, n\}$, or $\ell$-*suffix-interval*, denoted $\ell$ -$[i, j]$, if and only if the following three conditions hold:

- $lcp_X[i] < \ell$;
- $lcp_X[j + 1] < \ell$; and
- $lcp_X[k] \ge \ell$ for $\forall k \in \{i + 1, \cdots, j\}$.
- $lcp_X[k] = \ell$ for at least one $k \in \{i + 1, \cdots, j\}$.

Table 1.1 shows the suffix array for the string in Figure 1.7. $suff_F[I] = j$ means $suf_j$ starts at the string position $j$, such as $suff_F[2] = 1$, $suff_F[1] = 2$. According to Definition 1.1, $lcp[i]$ presents the length of the longest common prefix of $suf_i$ and $suf_{i-1}$. As a result, we have $lcp[1] = 2$, which is the length of the longest common prefix of AGAGG\$ ($suf_0$) and AGG\$ ($suf_1$), namely $|AG| = 2$.

**Table 1.1** Suffix array for string $S$ = AGAGG

| $I$ | $suff_F[I]$ | $lcp_F[I]$ | $S^F_{suff_F[i]}$ |
|---|---|---|---|
| 0 | 0 | 0 | AGAGG\$ |
| 1 | 2 | 2 | AGG\$ |
| 2 | 1 | 0 | GAGG\$ |
| 3 | 3 | 1 | GG\$ |
| 4 | 4 | 1 | G\$ |
| 5 | 5 | 0 | \$ |

**Shape-Based Modeling.** Structures of individual RNA family members, which naturally have different lengthes and sequence compositions, may exhibit structural variation in detail, but overall, they have a common shape in a more abstract sense. According to a given collection of structure data, we can compute these abstract shapes for all families, namely a shape index. If a query sequence belongs to a certain family, it must be able to fold into the family shape with reasonable free energy. As a result, it is efficient to first (and quickly) compute its feasible shape(s), and use the shape index to access only the families where a match is possible owing to a common shape with the query, rather than matching the query against all families in the data base.

Abstract shapes of RNA were introduced in [110], in which the functional RNA classes usually refer to abstraction instead of concrete structures. There are a variety of RNA structures. A tRNA has a cloverleaf structure, a microRNA precursor is a lengthy hairpin, oxyS RNA has three adjacent hairpins. It is observed that the most important structural characteristic is the specific arrangement of RNA helices, governed by the two principles of adjacency and embedding. The cloverleaf, for example, is a helix which embeds three helices adjacent to each other.

In most case, a less abstraction is expected. Thus, a shape abstraction is a mapping from concrete RNA structures to abstract shapes. Concrete structures are modeled as trees, as frequently used in linguistics and conventional indexing. This is natural, as trees incorporate the two principles of adjacency and embedding. Although abstract shapes are viewed as trees either, they contain less detail.

**Definition 1.2.** Suppose $S$ and $P$ represent the tree-like domain of structures, and a tree-like domain of shapes, respectively. A shape abstraction is a mapping $\pi$ from $S$ to $P$ that preserves adjacency and embedding.

Suppose $x$ and $y$ are two structures, and $s$ is sequence.

- If $\pi(x) = \pi(y)$, $x$ and $y$ have the same shape.
- If $\pi(x_{s_1}) = \pi(x_{s_2})$, two sequences $s_1$ and $s_2$ have the same shape.

A given RNA sequence $s$ consists of concrete shape and abstract shape in terms of the above definition. The former presents the set of all legal structures according to the rules of base pairing. The latter presents the set of mapping from concrete shapes. A sequence $s$ is said to be a $p$-shaped structure, if $\pi(x) = p$. In [110], a representative structure $\hat{p}$ is defined as the element that has minimal free energy among all structures in the shape class $p$. There are different structural components in RNA, which are *single stranded regions*, *hairpin loops*, *stacking regions*, *bulges* on the 5' or on the 3' side, *internal loops*, *multiloops*, and *adjacent structure*. These structural components are represented by SS, HL, SR, BL and BR, IL, ML and AD, respectively.

A collection of equations are defined for the abstraction mapping $\pi$. Suppose $l$ and $l'$ describe loop sequences, $a$ for a list of adjacent components and $x$ for arbitrary structures. The shapes mainly consist of open and closed structures and branching and adjacency, which are represented by OP, CL and FK (fork), respectively.

$$\pi(SS(l)) = OP \tag{1.26}$$

$$\pi(HL(a_1, l, a_2)) = CL \tag{1.27}$$

$$\pi(SR(a_1, x, a_2)) = \pi(x) \tag{1.28}$$

$$\pi(BL(a_1, l, x, a_2)) = \pi(x) \tag{1.29}$$

$$\pi(BR(a_1,x,l,a_2)) = \pi(x) \qquad (1.30)$$

$$\pi(IL(a_1,l,x,l',a_2)) = \pi(x) \qquad (1.31)$$

$$\pi(ML(a_1,c,a_2)) = FK(\pi(c)) \qquad (1.32)$$

$$\pi(AD(SS(l),c)) = \pi(c) \qquad (1.33)$$

$$\pi(AD(x,c)) = AD(\pi(x),\pi(c)) for\ x \neq SS(l) \qquad (1.34)$$

Figure 1.8 presents two structures with different shapes. Their sequences can be seen in Figure 1.9 and Figure 1.10, respectively. In[110], the above two shapes are represented in a simple manner using square bracket, like [ [] [] ] and [], respectively.

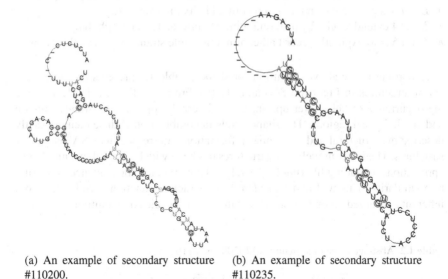

(a) An example of secondary structure #110200.

(b) An example of secondary structure #110235.

**Fig. 1.8** Examples of different structures

ACCUCUCCCCUGUUUUCUCUAGGGACAGCGUUCCCCACUCAUCCUUCUCUCUAUUACAGCUGCCCCUGAUGAUUAAAUAUCAGUACCAAGCAGCUUUGUAGUAUAUUCUCCUAGGAGACU

...(((((..............((((......))))...............(((((((((((((..(((((......)))))).......)))))..))))))).........))))..

**Fig. 1.9** Sequence and equivalent notation as dot-bracket string of structure #110200

AUCAGAAAUGUAAGGCAUUGGUGAUGUUUGCAUUUACCCUCCUGUAAGCAACACUUUAACGUCUUACAUU

......(((((((((((...((((.(((((((((..........))))))))).)))).....)))))))))))

**Fig. 1.10** Sequence and equivalent notation as dot-bracket string of structure #110235

In [162], they improve the notations by using square brackets to denote helices (or helix parts) and underscores for unpaired regions. Further, the shape is separated into different shape levels for describing their precise meaning. Usually, it consists of five abstract levels.

- *Level* 1 abstracts from all helix interruptions (bulge and internal loops), and ignores single stranded regions.
- *Level* 2 accounts for helix interruptions by internal loops (but not by bulges).
- *Level* 3 is alternative and aim to record all helix interruptions.
- *Level* 4 extend level 3 by differentiating in between left and right bulges.
- *Level* 5 is to explicitly record all continuous single stranded or helical regions.

According to the above definition for shapes, Table 1.2 presents the shape levels of structures in Figures 1.8(a) and 1.8(b). From the Table, it is clear to see the occurrence of helix interruption, bulge, internal loops, single stranded region and single helical regions. The shape levels in combination with sequence exactly describe the structural and sequential information with respect to RNA secondary structures. The index modeling of structures has been widely applied in a number of applications, including filtering for search and computation for sequence and structure similarity. This will assist in identifying structure-function correlations from inherent conserved secondary structures in relevant species of evolution.

**Table 1.2** Abstract shape of structures #110200 and #110235

| #110200 | shape | #110235 | shape |
|---------|-------|---------|-------|
| level 1 | [ [] [] ] | level 1 | [] |
| level 2 | [ [] [[]] ] | level 2 | [ [] ] |
| level 3 | null | level 3 | [ [ [] ] ] |
| level 4 | [ [] [_[]_] ] | level 4 | [ [_ [] _] ] |
| level 5 | _[ _[_] _[_[_]_]_ ]_ | level 5 | _[_ [_ [_] _]_ ]_ |

## 1.5 Significance and Methods

### 1.5.1 Significance and Innovation

Around 50 years ago, Martin Rodbell and his colleagues found that signals are transferred in entire organisms following a varied and significant kinase pathway. This was confirmed by the Nobel Prize winner Alfred G. Gilman and Martin Rodbell who have studied this particular aspect of the communication problem (1994). Morgane et al said that data mining is a powerful approach for the dissection of signaling kinase pathways in Oncogene (Nature publication) [233]. The priority goal of this monograph will be smart information use.

The significance of this book is that (a) it enhances the analysis and management of signaling kinase pathway data, and (b) leads to improvement in understanding of regulatory networks by combining gene expression and structure information. This book will bring together the expertise of researchers from mathematics, statistics and computational biology to deal with this important problem. The investigators will generate a publicly accessed kinase pathway data resource using ontologies, and are responsible for the data sharing between collaborators. The algorithms and tools introduced in this book will also enable continuous data analysis of regulation in other organisms such as dog and mouse, which will add to our understanding of the kinase pathways.

- The algorithms and tools developed in this book will enhance the application of data mining, including discretization and classification in handling high-dimensional biological data, and improve the predictive accuracy and mining efficiency.
- The approach for discovering top-ranked patterns of regulation assists us in efficiently sorting out the most significant kinase pathway knowledge.
- The identification of both positive and negative regulatory kinase pathways avoids missing those patterns that are usually hidden but valuable to us.
- The framework for modeling secondary structures ensures the accuracy and correctness of data mining.

Therefore, this research program is essential to develop a better understanding of regulatory kinase pathways and will assist in both biotechnology and computer science sectors.

The innovation in this book is the application of powerful data mining technology for kinase pathway data analysis by combining kinase pathways, gene expression and structural information of genes. A small set of patterns rather than a large number of rule groups will be returned as answers, which can be easily interpreted by the biologists. The other innovations in this book are highlighted below.

The computational techniques developed in this monograph are an innovative advance in systems biology and for the first time we will be able to deal with high-dimensional signaling kinase pathway data and identify the most significant patterns from the data. Specifically we will be able to:

- Accurately identify different relationships in kinase pathway data in terms of specified association groups.
- Determine a threshold in terms of the amount of results, rather than fix a threshold for all itemsets of all sizes.
- Develop unsupervised correlation preserving algorithms for the discretization of the continuous attributes in multivariate data sets. This uses both categorical and continuous attributes and the underlying correlation structure in the data set to generate the discrete intervals.
- Model the conserved secondary structures of RNA using distance vectors and search the matched structures for query using an innovative distance function for intervals.

Also, the developed techniques are innovative in biomedical studies:

- The discovered patterns of regulation will confirm previous experimental results, and those suggesting new hypotheses will warrant further investigation.
- Not only do we identify the helpful regulations that are good to health but also the harmful regulations that cause disease. The latter are often hidden and infrequent but extremely important for preventing disease.
- The targeting protein kinase [237] and relevant genes are considered in the treatment of diseases such as cancer and diabetes. The components of the discovered regulatory kinase pathways are potentially useful therapeutic targets.
- The combination of kinase pathways and genes together can help researchers identify the root cause of diseases, not just the symptoms.

The recent increasing interest in functional and genetic studies demands innovative approaches for understanding the mechanisms of signaling kinase pathways. The authors have analyzed varied types of data sets [47, 51] that are relevant to this book. The normalization, standardization techniques and established databases can be adopted or extended to for signaling pathway data analysis. For example, the AMPK data and conserved secondary structure data have been collected by authors [47]. The data are actually extracted from published literatures and recognized database such as PseudoBase. Further, the database, methods and significant results have been published in [48, 49, 51]. Thus, we are especially interested to analyse the kinase pathway-based human genome/proteome. We also plan to analyse data from a few closely related model organisms (e.g., mouse) to develop techniques which can be applied to regulatory kinase pathways of human.

## 1.5.2  Framework Design and Methods

This book will focus on the signaling pathways and will consist of five main parts:

**Preprocessing of Experimental Data.** The data process is illustrated by using the published experimental data of AMPK regulation, in which AMPK is activated or inhibited by endurance training in skeletal muscle or by acute or chronic stresses

**Table 1.3** Activity and expression of $\alpha_{1a}$ and $\alpha_{1e}$ of AMPK in skeletal muscle

| $\alpha_{1a}$ | $\alpha_{1e}$ | Training | Glycogen | Diabetes | N | I | D |
|---|---|---|---|---|---|---|---|
| 2 | 5 | 50 | 60 | 70 | 80 | 92 | 101 |
| 1 | 5 | 51 | 60 | 70 | 80 | 90 | 103 |
| 1 | 6 | 51 | 60 | 70 | 80 | 91 | 100 |
| 1 | 6 | 51 | 60 | 70 | 80 | 91 | 101 |

in heart. Some raw data can be accessed by [46], in which each row of the data set corresponds to an experiment and each column corresponds to the items under the attribute.

Table 1.3 presents a random example of the activity and expression of AMPK in skeletal muscle, in which N, I and D represent *nicotinic acid, intensity* and *duration*, respectively. Each column corresponds to an experiment. The subscript a and e means *activity*, and *protein expression*, respectively. The raw data are transferred into integers. For example, 1 and 5 represent *no change* in corresponding items; 100, 101 and 103 represent the duration under 20 minutes, between 20 and 60 minutes and above 90 minutes, respectively; 90, 91 and 92 represent the *maximal oxygen uptake* (VO(2)max) under 50%, VO(2)max between 65% and 75%, and VO(2)max between 80% and 100%, respectively. In reality, the continuous attributes need to be partitioned into discrete values using intervals, which can lead to improved predictive accuracy. Thus, we need to extend or adapt appropriate discretization method for the above continuous features, such as C 4.5 [256].

The integration of biological databases is usually confronted with semantic issues. Ontologies such as GO [112], consisting of an agreed upon vocabulary of concepts (terms) and specification of the relationships among these concepts, are an ideal option to handle the semantic heterogeneity of databases and promote the reliable and reusable biological knowledge. Our recently developed method [51] can be applied to solve this problem.

**Mining Regulation Data with Item Constraints.** According to the support-confidence framework [339], a rule $A \Rightarrow B$ is of interest if $supp(A \cup B) \geq minsupp$ and $conf\ (A \Rightarrow B) \geq minconf$. In this book, the conventional association rule mining is extended for analysing kinase regulation data. FP-tree algorithm [117, 126] based on support-confidence framework [4] constructs a frequent pattern tree that has an extended prefix-tree structure and stores quantitative information about frequent patterns. It can generate a complete set of frequent patterns. FP-tree algorithm is applied to generate all frequent itemsets and find association rules that make sense biologically.

To extract frequent itemsets, users usually need to specify a fixed minimum support but this method has been criticized due to its difficulty [208, 318, 339]. As described above, it is quite subtle to set a minimum support [318] and a minimum confidence support [66]: a too small threshold may result in the output of many redundant patterns, whereas a too big one may generate no answer or miss interesting knowledge. In addition, the probability of occurrence of a larger size itemset is inherently much smaller than that of a smaller size itemset [208]. A more flexible option is to allow users to specify different thresholds in accordance with different itemsets. Consequently, the top-$N$ interesting itemsets using item constraints [66] and the *top-k* covering rule group [48] are returned as answers.

To generate constraint specification, we group the items from the same attribute into a bin [318]. Although each bin corresponds to only one attribute, each attribute can contain several state measurements. Thus, each bin can have more than one item. Table 1.4 presents an example of bins, by which to explore correlations between itemsets from specified bin sets, such as $\{\alpha_{1a}, \alpha_{2a}\}$ from $\{B_1, B_2\}$.

**Table 1.4** An example of bins and corresponding attributes

| Bin | $\alpha_{1a}$ | $\alpha_{1e}$ | $\alpha_{2a}$ | $\alpha_{2e}$ | Training | Diabetes |
|-----|------|------|------|------|----------|----------|
| $B_1$ | yes | yes | no | no | no | no |
| $B_2$ | no | no | yes | yes | no | no |
| $B_3$ | no | no | no | no | yes | yes |

The obtained itemsets, due to the item constraints, need to be sorted in light of their supports in descending order, by which we can generate the *top-$N_i$* interesting itemsets for each corresponding bin constraint $IC_i$. Therefore, the mining will focus on finding out association rules on the basis of these *top-N* interesting itemsets. To obtain the top-$k$ covering rule groups, we define a rule as a set of items, or specifically a set of conjunctive stimuli level intervals (*antecedent*) with a single class label (*consequent*) (activator or inhibitor). The general form of a rule is: $stimulus_1[a_1, b_1]$, $\cdots$, $stimulus_n[a_n, b_n] \rightarrow class$, where $stimulus_i$ represents the name of the stimulus and $[a_i, b_i]$ represents its expression interval. A rule group $r_1$ is more significant than $r_2$ if $(r_1.conf > r_2.conf) \vee (r_1.sup > r_2.sup \wedge r_1.conf = r_2.conf)$, where *conf* and *sup* mean confidence and support, respectively. Given the data set and a user specified **minsup**, the *top-k* covering rule groups for each $r_i$ is the set of rule groups $\{R_{r_ij}\}$, where $R_{r_ij}.sup > minsup$.

There are many algorithms for association rule mining, whereas only limited works handle the problem of *top-N* patterns. To discuss alternative approaches and the comparative advantage of different approaches, Chen and Chen [47, 48] have presented comprehensive discussion of miner, local causal discovery and probability partition matrix and showed comparative advantage of our approach in terms of data set, applicability, *top-k* rule group, correctness (*frequent patterns*) and efficiency (*CPU time*).

**Modeling RNA Secondary Structures.** To understand the functional roles of kinase-related RNA, we need to characterize RNA secondary structures by modeling for further mining application. A given RNA secondary structure includes not only sequence information but structure information. This book presents a novel approach to model the predicted RNA secondary structures and a filtering schema to identify matched models for the queried secondary structures in an efficient way. Given a nucleotide sequence s with length $|s| = n$. We define a $(k, l)$ stack as a pair of indices $(i, j)$ if $(j - i) \leq 1$, $s[i \cdots i + k -1]$, and $s[j \cdots j + k -1]$ can form an energetically favorable base-pair stack. Although the $(k, l)$ stack of nucleotide string can be used to express predicted secondary structures, two genetic mutations (*insertion* or *deletion*) that may decrease the effective value of $k$, and the variability of $l$ that may increase the effective value of $l$. Thus, more complicated models are needed to develop. For example, stack $S_1$ may be nested within stack $S_2$ (*nested stack*), stack $S_1$ may be parallel to stack $S_2$ (*parallel stack*) and stack $S_1$ is said to be a multiloop stack if it contains a parallel stack $S_2$ and each of the stack is nested in a $(k, l)$ stack. Figure 1.11 presents an example of multiloop stack, in which $s_2$ and $s_3$ are parallel and are nested in $s_1$.

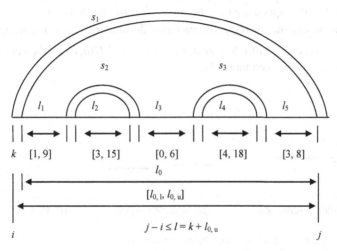

**Fig. 1.11** A $(k, 3)$ multiloop stack with a distance vector $= \{[1, 9], [3, 16], [0, 6], [4, 18], [3, 8]\}$

The above nested, parallel and multiloop stacks can be observed in all the families of ncRNA. There are particular conserved structural features in every ncRNA family that give rise to correct folding. Thus, it is feasible to use the nested and multiloop stacks to model the conserved secondary structures. Usually, each stack comprises a pair of substrings corresponding to a fixed length. However, the distance between stacks is varied due to the various loop (*bulge, interior loops, multiloop*) regions. Thus, it is necessary to use distance constraints to specify a variety of $(k, l)$ stacks. A model that satisfies the distance constraint can be written as $(k, \overrightarrow{l}, h)$. Suppose $l_0, \cdots, l_{2n-1}$ represent a set of distance ranges, in which $l_0$ is the range between the first and the last substrings, and $l_j, j > 0$ is the range in the substrings ordered from left to right. We have $\overrightarrow{l} = \{l_0, \cdots, l_{2n-1}\}$ (distance vector). Let $l_{i,l}$ and $l_{i,u}$ be the lower limit and upper limit of the interval $l_i$, respectively.

Given several groups of range intervals and a query, we need to decide which group the query belongs to. Two key points to solve this problem are

- The definition of a distance function for two intervals
- The definition of the distance between a query of intervals and a group of range intervals.

We define two important attributes for each interval, center and radius. Given two intervals $a = [a_1, a_2]$ and $b = [b_1, b_2]$, they have three possible relationships as described in Figure 1.12. Suppose $d(a, b)$ denotes the distance from interval $a$ to $b$; $H(a, b)$ denotes the Hausdorff distance from interval $a$ to $b$; $O(a, b)$ denotes the overlapped area between interval $a$ and $b$; and $2r_a$ denotes the area of an interval $a$. Then, the ratio between the overlapped area and the area of $a$ is defined as $\frac{O(a,b)}{2r_a}$, which represents the similarity intensity from $a$ to $b$. Since we want to combine the overlapped area method with the Hausdorff distance, and the intuition tells us that the bigger the overlapped area is, the lower $d(a, b)$ should be. Then we use $(1 - \frac{O(a,b)}{2r_a+1})$ to represent the overlapped-area-based dissimilarity intensity, which multiplies $H(a, b)$ to generate $d(a, b) = H(a, b) * (1 - \frac{O(a,b)}{2r_a+1})$ $H(a, b)$ can be varied due to different relations between intervals.

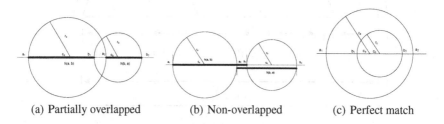

| (a) Partially overlapped | (b) Non-overlapped | (c) Perfect match |
|---|---|---|

**Fig. 1.12** An example of relationships between intervals

**Identification of RNA-Mediated Kinase Pathways.** Using the structure data after modeling, we can further explore the kinase pathways with respect to the RNA structures. A RNA pseudoknot consists of non-nested double-stranded stems connected by single-stranded loops. There is an expanding rate of studies into RNA pseudoknotted structures as well as increasing allocation of function. To capture the features of RNA pseudoknots, we present a novel framework using quantitative association rule mining to analyse the pseudoknot data. The derived rules are classified into specified association groups regarding structure, function and category of RNA pseudoknots.

The previous techniques can only identify rules among simple variables, such as *tea* → *sugar* or *state* → *united*. They have limitations in discovering rules among multi-valued variables from large databases and representing them. For example, *stem* and *loop* are categorical multi-value variables.

Usually, we may obtain a number of rules in traditional association rule mining. However, it is uneasy to sort those rules that are ranked higher than the others. Further, an inappropriate threshold might lead to missing interesting rules or generating redundant rules. Thus, this book extends and adapts traditional methods by representing a rule as the form of $X \rightarrow Y$ in conjunction with a probability matrix $M_{Y|X}$ in terms of Bayesian rules. This captures the relationship that the presence of $X$ results in the occurrence of $Y$. $M_{Y|X}$ is defined as

$$M_{Y|X} = \triangleq P(Y = y | X = x) = \begin{pmatrix} p(y_1|x_1) \ p(y_2|x_1) \ \cdots \ p(y_n|x_1) \\ p(y_1|x_2) \ p(y_2|x_2) \ \cdots \ p(y_n|x_2) \\ \cdots \\ p(y_1|x_m) \ p(y_2|x_m) \ \cdots \ p(y_n|x_m) \end{pmatrix}$$

Suppose $M_{Y|X}$ corresponding to an association $AS$ consists of a set of rows $\{r_1, \cdots, r_n\}$. Let $A = \{A_1, \cdots, A_m\}$ be the complete set of antecedent items of $AS$, and $C = \{C_1, \cdots, C_k\}$ be the complete set of consequent items of $AS$, then each of the row $r$ includes an antecedent item from $A$ and a set of consequent items from $C$. Suppose $PS$ (Point-paris Support Set) is the set of point-pairs whose conditional probabilities are unequal to zero. A rule group is defined as $G_x = \{x \rightarrow C_j \mid (x, C_j) \in PS(x)\}$ be a rule group with an antecedent item $x$ and consequent support set $C$. It is observed that the rules from different rule groups might have different supports and confidences. Further, there might be different numbers of valid rules derived from different groups. The *top-k* covering rule groups are thus applied to encapsulate the most significant association of the dataset while enabling users to control the number of rules in a convenient manner. Using *top-k*, we distinguish our method from other association rule works as this technique is significant and lacking in research by others in the field, hence the need of our proposed contributions.

With respect to statistical significance, we are able to assign statistical significance to select top-ranked patterns (ranked according to measures such as gain ratio, chi-square etc.) using statistical and machine learning methods to discover frequent patterns and to alleviate the computational problems of high-dimensional data. However, such methods have two main problems. Firstly, it is difficult to determine how many top-ranked patterns to be used for classification model. Secondly, low-ranked patterns are often contained in significant rules that are sometimes necessary for perfect classification accuracy. Our proposed methods not only rely on the feature selection to reduce the number of dimensions for computational efficiency; we also try to mine all rules that satisfy *minimum support* or *minimum confidence* thresholds. Finally we sort and prune these discovered rules to get the classification rules.

**Interpretation.** We try to find out potential relationships between the protein kinase's isoform expression and activity, between subunits and between activation and inhibition. They are usually hidden in derived experimental data and are difficult to identify by traditional statistics. From the results in this study, we will select similar association rules to describe kinase's regulation in different tissue or organs, such as $\{\alpha_{1e}|\} \rightarrow \{\alpha_{2e}|\}$ and $\{\alpha_{1e}|, \alpha_{2e} \downarrow\} \rightarrow \{\beta_{1e} \downarrow, \beta_{2e}|\}$ in skeletal muscle. We will compare the items in each rule by using their frequencies occurring in relevant experiments. In other words, the items in identified rules occur much more frequently than those from other rules under the same indexes. These can be secondary evidence to support the fact that our chosen rules are more important than the other ones. In addition, we also focus on those rules have slightly low *minimum confidence* or *minimum support* threshold than the specified cut-off threshold, by which we can predict some latent associations that are selected for biologists to test in future experiments. In particular, we will compare the rule with partially identical conditions.

The extracted rules of RNA pseudoknots not only present that in the most of simple pseudoknots their stems and loops favor different numbers of nucleotides and different base compositions, but also indicate that potential associations may exist between category and pseudoknot structure, and between function and pseudoknot structure. Further, several significant ratios regarding stems and loops are reported. For example, in most of the cases, the number of nucleotides of pseudoknot of mRNA (messenger RNA that is transcribed from a DNA template, and carries coding information to the sites of protein synthesis: the ribosomes) may peak at 6 base pairs. In the similar manner, the remaining rules can be interpreted. The rules in fact unveil the structural features of RNA pseudoknots and potential structure-function relationship. Specific comparisons will be conducted between stems, between loops, between different classes and between different functions, respectively. Moreover, this book provides a novel facility to predict some potential correlations by combining several association rules together, which can be left for biologists to examine in the future experiments. By doing so, it is able to generate new biological knowledge. The book has significant innovation in its methodology as it is the only monograph to add innovation in rule mining and result pruning to discover association rules. This three-stage process negates the undesirable qualities of other techniques in this research area, namely the use of feature selection to reduce dimensionality.

Recently, many evidences have indicated that the sequence similarity with the query string is insufficient to get the candidate regions. A number of cases show complete conservation of the structure, but low sequence similarity. It is impractical for a tool using sequence similarity to be effective in identifying RNA homologs. Therefore, the structure similarity is viewed as the basis of modeling RNA secondary structures. The sequence similarity will be used as a secondary evidence to evaluate homologs. We do not discuss the conservation of secondary structure in comparison with sequence similarity in this book. The secondary structure of RNA is usually presented as a tree like shape and may consist of various stems and loops (bulge, interior loops, multi-loops) regions. Each stem in this tree contains energetically favorable stacked base-pairs. In addition to the most energetically favorable Watson-Crick base-pairing (A $\leftrightarrow$ U, C $\leftrightarrow$ G), the other pairings such as the wobble base-pair (G $\leftrightarrow$ U) are possible as well. Each stem comprises a pair of substrings. These pairs are nonintersecting. Although intersected stacks, or pseudoknots, they can be ignored since we focus on modeling the predicted RNA secondary structures. Our proposed methodology compares well with other techniques in the field whereby past solutions have focused on weighted correlations of protein networks [21] and Bayesian techniques [266].

**New Methodologies.** This book will deliver many new methodologies in the fields of data mining and high dimensional data pathway analysis.

- Methodologies to remove inconsistencies from biological databases and integrate sources to support greater knowledge mining from experimental data
- Algorithmic development for mining regulation data with item constraints
- Development of new methodologies for modeling RNA secondary structures.
- The development of association rule techniques for the identification of RNA mediated kinases pathways

**Benefits and Prospects** A number of protein kinase, such as AMPK are now recognised as a major regulator of metabolism and gene transcription in response to varied stimuli such as exercise and nutritional stress. They have been viewed as the new hot drug target of the Pharmaceutical Industry with applications in obesity, diabetes, cardiovascular disease. Additional benefits, including knowledge, expertise and technology in this work, are listed below:

- The knowledge in studying the protein kinase's regulation from the subunit activity and stimuli has the potential to enhance the identification of pathways for potential pharmacologic targets and the prediction of useful activations to affect the treatment of relevant diseases.
- The developed association rule mining tools can be applied to other protein kinases regulation and assist biologists in examining or predicting experimental results in an intelligent way. A full understanding of the kinases regulation networks including their correlations enable a more accurate prediction of metabolic kinase pathways.
- The studies of protein kinase's regulations in different tissues enable the comparison between the regulations in different destinations. We will have a better understanding of syndromes in terms of their potential interaction.

# Chapter 2
# Data Resources and Applications

There has been a rapid growth of biology data in the past few years. Their deep studies are important in post genome era and are essential for modern human life, such as importance as drug and fuel resources, disease diagnosis and treatment and as fundamental knowledge for recombinant technology. Considering these applications, database infrastructure for model systems of species deserves much more attention. Study of biological signal transduction, the interconnection between these pathways and systems biology on the whole has in general lagged behind the functional genomic. In this chapter, we review a variety of pathway databases and the resources that are currently available. We highlight trends and challenges in the ongoing efforts to integrate pathway databases and the applications of data analysis in terms of database integration. We also discuss how progress in bioinformatics can serve as an example for the improvement of the pathway database landscape and thereby allow quantitative modeling of biosystems. We propose several feasible and successful database applications as a possible model for collaboration and to ease future integration efforts of signal transduction.

## 2.1 The Importance of Pathways

A biological pathway is a programmed sequence of molecular events in a cell. This chain of events executes a particular cellular function or brings about a specific biological effect. Knowledge of an organism's pathways is essential to understand a biological system at different levels, from simple metabolism to complex regulatory reactions. Many pathways are complex and hierarchical and are themselves interconnected to form, to participate in, or to regulate a network of events. Over the last couple of decades, there has been an exponential increase in the information on these pathways, their components and their functions. This stems from the biotechnological advancements in genomics and proteomics and high throughput technologies like microarray and next generation sequencing (NGS). For the purpose of this review, pathway databases are broadly classified into four types: metabolic pathways, gene regulatory networks, protein-protein interaction networks, and signaling pathways.

**Signaling pathways** are used by cell to regulate their activity. This module focusses on the ON mechanisms responsible for transmitting information into the cell. There has been an explosion in the characterization of signaling components and pathways. The next major challenge is to understand how cells exploit this large signaling toolkit to assemble the specific signaling pathways they require to communicate with each other. The emerging information on cell signaling pathways is integrated and presented within the context of specific cell types and processes. It is thus critical to understand the mechanisms that different pathways are combined and adapted to control a diverse array of cellular processes in widely different spatial and temporal domains[301].

Many of the same signaling systems that control development come into play again to regulate a wide range of specific processes in adult cells, such as contraction, secretion, metabolism, proliferation, information processing in neurons and sensory perception. These examples illustrate how cell signaling pathways are adapted and co-ordinated to regulate many different cellular processes. This intimate relationship between cell signaling and biology is providing valuable insights into the underlying genetic and phenotypic defects responsible for many of the major human diseases.

For numerous species, this has increased our knowledge about normal pathways as well as rogue/aberrant pathways that lead to a variety of diseases. Examples include pathways that lead to cancer or pathways that lead to aberrant leaf development in plants. Production of large amounts of data necessitates the creation of pathway databases and repositories, where information about the pathways along with their molecular components and reactions is stored. These data sets often become data-sources in their own right, and are shared with the public, explaining in part the large number of databases[39, 61] that exist today.

At http://www.biochemj.org/csb/, a large number of intracellular signaling pathways are reported to be responsible for transmitting information within the cell. They fall into two main categories.

- The majority responds to external stimuli arriving at the cell surface, usually in the form of a chemical signal (neurotransmitter, hormone or growth factor). For example, *Cyclic AMP signaling pathway* functions includes control of metabolism, gene transcription and ion channel activity, and regulation of the activity of other signaling pathways. *Voltage-operated channels* (*VOCs*) are found predominantly in excitable cells such as muscle cells (skeletal, cardiac and smooth muscle cells), neurons, and neuroendocrine and endocrine cells. *Mitogen-activated protein kinase* (*MAPK*) *signaling pathway* function to control many cellular processes and particularly those related to gene transcription, metabolism, motility, cell proliferation, apoptosis, synaptic plasticity and long-term memory.
- The other categories are the pathways that are activated by signals generated from within the cell. There are a number of metabolic messengers that act from within the cell to initiate a variety of signaling pathways. For example, *Endoplasmic*

*reticulum* *(ER)* *stress* *signaling* transmit information to the nucleus about the state of protein processing within the lumen of the ER. *AMP signaling pathway* is activated by an increase in the AMP/ATP ratio, which leads to the activation of AMP-activated protein kinase (AMPK).

From the observation, the signaling pathways are ubiquitous in biology system. The above mentioned functions of signaling pathways for information transmission is just the tip of the iceberg, but overall this demonstrates their importance in various molecular activities, such as metabolism, genetic information processing, environmental information processing, cellular processes, and biomedicine, such as human disease and drug development. As a result, a deep study of signaling pathways is interesting and critical for us to understand their modulatory roles in molecular interactions, reactions, and relations.

**Metabolic Pathways.** Metabolism is organized by metabolic pathways, which enable cells to keep living, growing and dividing. There are two subcategories of metabolic processes, namely anabolism and catabolism. The former is metabolic reactions that result in the synthesis of larger/ more complex molecules. The latter is metabolic reactions in the cell that degrade a substrate into smaller/simpler products..

In [20], the key features of metabolic signaling pathways to modulate age-related disease risk and longevity is presented. The aging process is characterized metabolically by insulin resistance, changes in body composition, and physiological declines in growth hormone (GH), insulin-like growth factor-1 (IGF-1), and sex steroids. Novel approaches and unexpected discoveries have revealed an important paradox regarding the role of IIS (insulin/IGF-1 signaling) signaling in aging.

In human, a number of important metabolic pathway interact in a complex way for regulation of glycolysis, oxidative phosphorylation, gluconeogenesis. Plants use complex metabolic pathways to fend off pathogens, to coordinate reproduction with changes in day length, to accommodate environmental changes, and to select developmental pathways most suited to a given place and time. For these and other physiological processes, metabolism integrates inputs from both genome and environment. The process often involves the production and use of unusual chemicals that function for the plant as signals or defenses. Some of these chemicals are exploited by humans as pharmaceuticals, insecticides, spices, and nutritional supplements[139].

**Protein-Protein Interaction Networks.** Cells are stuffed with the proteins they produce that carry on the life processes. Technological advances in proteomics have resulted in unprecedented quantities of protein-protein interaction (PPI) data. Protein-protein interaction is also a critical component of a subject that is perhaps the core of molecular genetics research: transcription regulation. Genetic transcription is the process by which the cell "decodes" information stored in DNA and copies it into RNA. Selecting which information will be decoded, and when, is the most fundamental and important decision that any cell makes. This has stimulated research into the properties of the PPI network, with a view to understanding the biological properties of the systems that underlie them. The topology of the network potentially has a wide range of biological implications. For example, it has been suggested that the structure of the PPI network is related to whether or not a given protein is essential. Analysis of network structure has been used to propose evolutionary mechanisms of how cellular complexity arose and has also led to controversy as to whether network modularity is dynamically organized. Topological analysis of large scale protein-protein interaction networks (PINs) is thus important for understanding the organizational and functional principles of individual proteins.

The challenges we face conducting genetic analyses are derived from the complexity of the genotype- and phenotype-mapping relationship that results from phenomena such as epistasis (gene-gene interactions) and plastic reaction norms (gene-environment interactions).

**Gene Regulatory Networks.** Gene regulatory networks explicitly represent the causality of developmental processes. They explain exactly how genomic sequence encodes the regulation of expression of the sets of genes that progressively generate developmental patterns and execute the construction of multiple states of differentiation. Based on gene regulatory network, the regulatory genome can be transformed as a logic processing system. In other words, every regulatory module contained in the genome receives multiple disparate inputs and processes them in ways that can be mathematically represented as combinations of logic functions (e.g., and functions, switch functions, or functions). The reasons why genes are expressed when and where they are in the spatial domains of the developing organism are revealed in causality network architecture. For example, a review[248] discloses that heart development is controlled by an evolutionarily conserved network of transcription factors that connect signaling pathways with genes for muscle growth, patterning, and contractility. During evolution, this ancestral gene network was expanded through gene duplication and co-option of additional networks. Mutations in components of the cardiac gene network cause congenital heart disease, the most common human birth defect.

## 2.2   The Pathway-Related Database Landscape

There are a variety of classification strategies for pathways in different databases, organizations or institutes. It is not easy to present all of them in this book. Thus, several representative and widely used public databases with respect to pathways are selected to present below. In particular, we focus on describing those databases regarding protein kinase pathway and RNA-based pathways.

### 2.2.1   Kinase Pathway

**Pathguide**(http://www.pathguide.org/), an online pathway resource meta-database, provides an overview of more than 300 biological pathway resources that have been developed to date. These include pathway databases, tools for data analysis, visualization and data extrapolation and other (peripheral) databases that can be linked with pathway databases to provide additional information. Some databases are specific to a particular organism, e.g. AraCyc deals with the metabolic pathways of Arabidopsis thaliana. Some pathway databases are specific to a certain disorder or disease, e.g. the Human Cancer Protein Interaction Network (HCPIN); other contain information about a certain system in an organism, e.g. InnateDB, a repository for pathways involved in the innate immune system of humans and mice.

**KEGG**(Kyoto Encyclopedia of Genes and Genomes) is established and developed by Kanehisa Laboratories since 1995. It is a database resource for understanding high-level functions and utilities of the biological system, such as the cell, the organism and the ecosystem, from molecular-level information, especially large-scale molecular datasets generated by genome sequencing and other high-throughput experimental technologies). It consists of sixteen main databases, which are broadly categorized into systems information, genomic information and chemical information. More details can be seen at http://www.genome.jp/kegg/.

There have been considerable efforts undertaken to manually create a knowledge base for such systemic functions by capturing and organizing experimental knowledge in the computable forms of molecular networks called KEGG pathway maps, BRITE functional hierarchies and KEGG modules. Continuous efforts have also been made to develop and improve the cross-species annotation procedure for linking genomes to the molecular networks through the KEGG Orthology (KO) system. Thus, KEGG has been widely applied as a reference knowledge base for integration and interpretation of large-scale datasets generated by genome sequencing and other high-throughput experimental technologies. In addition to support basic research, KEGG targets towards more practical applications integrating human diseases, drugs and other health-related substances as perturbations of the KEGG molecular networks.

**KinBase** at http://kinase.com/ holds information on over 3,000 protein kinase genes found in the genomes of human, mouse, fly, worm, yeast and many other sequenced genomes. The database can be searched by a variety of different gene names and accessions, or according to the sequence based classification. In addition, the users can search the database by class: group, family or subfamily. Especially, KinBase can also be searched by NCBI Blast, including

- blastp: compares an amino acid query sequence against a protein sequence database;
- blastn: compares a nucleotide query sequence against a nucleotide sequence database;
- blastx: compares a nucleotide query sequence translated in all reading frames against a protein sequence database;
- tblastn: compares a protein query sequence against a nucleotide sequence database dynamically translated in all reading frames;
- tblastx: compares the six-frame translations of a nucleotide query sequence against the six-frame translations of a nucleotide sequence database.

The databases used for BLAST search consist of peptide sequence databases, DNA sequence databases, and Human kinome cDNAs. The last contains predicted cDNA sequences of the 518 human protein kinases and 106 human protein kinase pseudogenes.

In addition to the database search and Blast services, this database also provides logos tool. It uses sequence logos to show patterns of sequence conservation within each kinase class. Every kinase group, family, and subfamily is aligned to generate a HMM. From this, the provided custom software is able to build a logo view.

**Kinase Pathway Database** at http://kinasedb.ontology.ims.u-tokyo.ac.jp/ is an integrated database concerning completed sequenced major eukaryotes, which contains the classification of protein kinases and their functional conservation and orthologous tables among species, protein-protein interaction data, domain information, structural information, and automatic pathway graph image interface. The protein-protein interactions are extracted by natural language processing (NLP) from abstracts using basic word pattern and protein name dictionary GENA. In this system, pathways are easily compared among species using protein interactions data more than 47,000 and orthologous tables.

Kinase families are classified by eukaryotic protein kinase, protein kinase-like kinase, un-classified protein kinase, and diacylglycerol kinase. It provides search services for different purposes, including

- Pathway Search
- Protein/Gene/Compound Interaction Data Search
- Protein Data Search (including GO based functions)
- Orthologue Data Search
- Phylogenetic Tree Search
- Protein Structure Search
- Domain Search
- Protein Family Search

**KSD** (Kinase Sequence Database) at http://sequoia.ucsf.edu/ksd/ is a collection of protein kinase sequences grouped into families by homology of their catalytic domains. The aligned sequences are available in MS Excel format, as well as in HTML. After a recent update, the database features a total of 287 families, which contain 7128 protein kinases from 948 organisms. Excel spreadsheets are available in two versions: for PC's and Macs. The users can find the kinase of interest by its name (e.g., c-Src) or by its GenBank or SwissProt accession number. Sequences can also be found by description and organism. The database provides tools for alignments by GI accession number or sequence name and supplies statistics service of different purposes, including Conservation profile, search for residue patterns, residue distribution statistics, kinase signature profile, and differential profile display.

**Kinweb** at http://www.itb.cnr.it/kinweb/ is a collection of protein kinases encoded in the human genome. This site provides:

- a comprehensive analysis of functional domains of each gene product;
- a prediction of secondary and tertiary structure motifs by using machine learning based programs;
- a collection of conserved sequence elements identified by comparative analysis of human kinase genes and their murine counterparts, useful to the identification of additional coding sequences, such as alternatively spliced exons, or other regulatory elements.

For each kinase, GenBank RefSeq and the SwissProt entry name are available along with information about kinase classification (Hanks and Hunter classification). A graphic browser is used to view kinase genes at various levels of magnification.

**Protein Kinase Resource** at http://pkr.genomics.purdue.edu/pkr/Welcome is designed for providing cross-links with other online resources. In addition, it introduced several new technologies to integrate information search, retrieval and visualization, including varied search tools, such as structure search, BLAST search, motif search, and alignment. In particularly, this site collects a completed list of primary available kinase resources in this field.

## 2.2.2  Plant Pathway Databases

Plant pathway databases are fewer in number and much less diverse in comparison with human pathway databases[301]. Despite increasing awareness about the importance of plants as new energy and food crops, but it appears that the resources and efforts devoted to uncovering and understanding plant pathways is insufficient. A comparison of the number of genomes sequenced to date for mammals and higher plants shows that plants receive less attention from the sequencing community. Many biologically, medically and economically important plants may have much difference in their physiology. This urges us to not only have more genomes and proteomes information to be studies, but also uncover complete pathways of plants.

Metabolic pathway databases like MetaCyc (http://www.metacyc.org) contain experimentally verified metabolic pathways and enzyme information for more than 2000 pathways from more than 2391 organisms and can be used to provide a reference data set for computationally predicting the metabolic pathways of organisms from their sequenced genomes, supporting metabolic engineering, and help compare biochemical networks. A dedicated portal for plant metabolic pathway databases is SolCyc (http://solcyc.solgenomics.net/). SolCyc is a Pathway Tools-based pathway genome database (PGDB) currently containing small molecule metabolism data for one plant belonging to family rubiaceae (coffee), and five plants belonging to family solanaceae (tomato, potato, tobacco, pepper and petunia).

Gramene database (http://www.gramene.org, a database for grasses) contains the known and predicted biochemical pathways of rice (RiceCyc) and sorghum (SorghumCyc). Plant Metabolic Network (PMN) (http://www.plantcyc.org/) is a collaborative project to build a broad network of plant metabolic pathway databases. PlantCyc is the central feature of PMN and serves as a multi-species reference database containing manually curated or reviewed information of catalytic enzymes and genes about shared 800 metabolic pathways present in more than 300 plant species. Further, PMN also contains ten single species/taxon based databases. Additionally, PMN has a small number of pathways that are known to be present in other organisms and are predicted to exist in plants.

Gene regulatory networks consist of transcription factors and the genes that they regulate. A regulatory network is composed of a series of events where regulation of one gene results in the control of another, such as protein-DNA interactions, sRNA/miRNA and sRNA/miRNA target gene interaction. An example of a regulatory network database is the Arabidopsis Gene Regulatory Information Server (AGRIS) (http://arabidopsis.med.ohio-state.edu/) which contains information on the transcription factors and cis-regulatory elements that are regulated by them in A. thaliana. AGRIS also contains a Regulatory Networks Interaction Module (ReIN), that allows creation, visualization and identification of regulatory networks in A. thaliana. Unlike data from sequence annotations, TRANSFAC (http://www.gene-regulation.com/pub/databases.html) is a gene regulatory network database that contains data on transcription factors, their experimentally proven binding sites and the genes they regulate in 300 species. It is one of the few proprietary plant database resources in PathGuide. Gene co-expression network databases for plants are under development. Such databases contain information on co-expression of genes with respect to a number of experimental conditions. These can be used for discovering genes involved in a certain function, identifying cis-regulatory elements, and constructing regulatory networks.

PPI (Protein-protein interactions) take place when two or more proteins bind together. Interactions between proteins are critical to carry out the majority of biological functions, such as signal transduction. The A.thaliana protein interactome database (AtPID)(http://www.megabionet.org/atpid/webfile/) is one such database. It contains protein interaction pairs found through manual text mining or in silico predictions using various bioinformatics methods, along with protein pairs that have been confirmed. STRING (http://string-db.org/) is a database of known and predicted protein interactions, including 5214234 proteins from 1133 organisms. The interactions include direct (physical) and indirect (functional) associations. It is now recognized that the experiments required to generate protein interaction data often give false positives as well as false negatives and hence it is important to use this type of data with caution. To discern whether a certain result is reliable, one needs to know the type of experiment and the conditions used, as well as details about the results. The IntAct database (http://www.ebi.ac.uk/intact/), which contains protein-protein interaction information on several organisms, provides such high level details.

Signaling pathways consist of a collection of molecular networks in the signal transduction. These are involved in transmission of information from one part of the cell to another or from one cell to another. Extracellular stimuli can also give rise to the activation or inhibition of a pathway and thus a change in the cellular environment. Signaling pathways often involve protein-protein interactions at different levels like protein modification (e.g. protein phosphorylation), protein translocation and protein complex formation or dissociation. Several signaling pathway databases, for example SPIKE(http://www.cs.tau.ac.il/~spike/), developed for non-plant eukaryotes. SignaLink ( http://signalink.org/) is a cross-species pathway database regarding human, D. melanogaster and Caenorhabditis elegans. However, there are few plant signaling pathway databases in comparison to their non-plant counterparts.

Most plant pathway databases contain information on the networks in their own right, e.g. metabolic or regulatory networks in A. thaliana or soybean. However, the specialized pathway databases for plant immunity, plant growth or for controlling the size of plant organs have been underdeveloped. Metabolic pathways are the earliest discovered and best studied pathways. Metabolic pathways are represented by a series of enzymatic reactions that take place at the level of small molecules. These have been elaborated and characterized for many organisms. According to the signaling pathways and their properties that these affect in plants, it can be concluded that these pathways are cross connected instead of independent with each other. As a result, it is critical to understand these pathways and to integrate this information with other databases in order to obtain a more complete and comprehensive picture to help scientists modulate certain plant properties without affecting other mechanisms and pathways.

### 2.2.3 RNA-Based Resources

There have been an increasing growth of RNA data in the past decade due to application of new experimental techniques and sequencing tools. However, there is insufficient work to identify and explore RNA-mediated pathways. To construct complete RNA pathways, it is important to know primary RNA databases including sequence and structure as well as pathway resources.

RNApathwaysDB, available online at http://iimcb.genesilico.pl/rnapathwaysdb, is an online resource about maturation and decay pathways involving RNA as the substrate. The current release presents information about reactions and enzymes that take part in the maturation and degradation of tRNA, rRNA and mRNA, and describes pathways in three model organisms: Escherichia coli, Saccharomyces cerevisiae and Homo sapiens. RNApathwaysDB can be queried with keywords, and sequences of protein enzymes involved in RNA processing can be searched with BLAST. Options for data presentation include pathway graphs and tables with enzymes and literature data. Structures of macromolecular complexes involving RNA and proteins that act on it are presented as 'potato models' using DrawBioPath-a new javascript tool[230].

MODOMICS at http://modomics.genesilico.pl/ is a complementary resource with RNApathwaysDB. While MODOMICS presents RNA modification pathways on the level of nucleosides, RNApathwaysDB deals with RNA metabolism with respect to whole RNA molecules. MODOMICS is the first comprehensive database resource for systems biology of RNA modification. It integrates information about the chemical structure of modified nucleosides, their localization in RNA 15 sequences, pathways of their biosynthesis and enzymes that carry out the respective reactions. MODOMICS also provides literature information, and links to other databases, including the available protein sequence and structure data. MODOMICS can be queried by the type of nucleoside (e.g. A, G, C, U, I, m1A, nm5s2U, etc.), type of RNA, position of a particular nucleoside, type of reaction (e.g. methylation, thiolation, deamination, etc.) and 30 name or sequence of an enzyme of interest. Options for data presentation include graphs of pathways involving the query nucleoside, multiple sequence alignments of RNA sequences and tabular forms with enzyme and literature data.

The web site http://www.science.co.il/biomedical/RNA-Databases.asp includes a list of major RNA databases. Since it is impractical to describe all of them in this monograph, several typical databases are presented herein. fRNAdb available at http://www.ncrna.org/frnadb/ is a database for comprehensive non-coding RNA sequences. It has two main bioinformatics tools, CentroidHomfold and CentroidFold. The former predicts an RNA secondary structure of an input (target) sequence by employing automatically collected homologous sequences of the target. Currently, the input sequence should be less than or equal to 500 bases. The latter predicts an RNA secondary structure from an RNA sequence. FASTA and one-sequence-in-a-line format are accepted for predicting a secondary structure per sequence. It also predicts a consensus secondary structure when a multiple alignment (CLUSTALW format) is given. Currently, the input sequence should be less than or equal to 2000 bases.

MiRBase at http://www.mirbase.org/ is a database of published miRNA sequences and annotation. Each entry in the miRBase represents a predicted hairpin portion of a miRNA transcript (termed mir in the database), with information on the location and sequence of the mature miRNA sequence (termed miR). Both hairpin and mature sequences are available for searching and browsing, and entries can also be retrieved by name, keyword, references and annotation. All sequence and annotation data are also available for download. Current release 19 contains 21264 entries representing hairpin precursor miRNAs, expressing 25141 mature miRNA products, in 193 species.

The noncoding RNA (ncRNA) database aims to provide information on the sequences and functions of transcripts which do not code for proteins, but perform regulatory roles in the cell. Current database includes over 30,000 individual sequences from 99 species of Bacteria, Archaea and Eukaryota. The primary source of sequence information, annotation information and genome mapping information were from the GenBank, FANTOM3 database and the UCSC Genome Browser site. The sequences and annotations of small cytoplasmic RNAs were derived from the Rfam database. The database can be retrieved by searching organism name, RNA symbol or GenBank accession number, BLAST sequence, and downloading data.

The Rfam database at http://rfam.sanger.ac.uk/ contains a collection of RNA families, each represented by multiple sequence alignments, consensus secondary structures and covariance models (CMs). The families in Rfam break are divided into three broad functional classes: non-coding RNA genes, structured cis-regulatory elements and self-splicing RNAs. Many evidences show that these functional RNAs often have a conserved secondary structure which may be better preserved than the RNA sequence. CMs can simultaneously model RNA sequence and the structure in an elegant and accurate form. FSDB (frameshift database) at http://wilab.inha.ac.kr/fsdb/ is a comprehensive compilation of experimentally known or computationally predicted data about programmed ribosomal frameshifting. The database provides the graphical view of the frameshift cassettes and the genes utilizing frameshifting for their expression. It also allows the user to find frameshift sites himself/herself from the genome sequences using a program called FSFinder.

## 2.3 Bioinformatics Application of Pathway Databases

### 2.3.1 Pathway Database Integration

The integration of pathway databases bring about many potential advantages for the biologist and computer scientist alike. There have been numerous applications to follow the integrated databases and yield a number of interesting or even unthinkable results. In order to better understand the potential of integration, a few case studies from other fields are presented.

A study [301] integrated three metabolic pathways-fatty acid synthesis genes from Arabidopsis Lipid Gene Database (http://lipids.plantbiology.msu.edu/) and starch metabolism genes from http://www.starchmetnet.org/. The integration uncovers that each of these pathways is structured as a co-expressed module in a hierarchical form. The transcripts from each module co-accumulate over a wide range of environmental and genetic perturbations and developmental stages. In another case study [213], A. thaliana pathways from protein interaction databases were combined with co-expression data by virtue of the Ondex system (http://www.ondex.org/). This method enabled the discovery of co-expression of the interacting protein partners and the levels of expression.

An interesting example of using database integration to obtain enhanced information about a system is AraGEM [77]. AraGEM is an attempt at building genome scale reconstruction of the primary metabolic network in A. thaliana. It used A. thaliana metabolic genome information from KEGG as a core enriched with information on the cellular compartmentalization of metabolic pathways from literature and databases. A total of 75 essential primary metabolism reactions were identified for which genetic information was unknown. AraGEM exemplifies how genome-scale models can be first built and then used to explore highly complex and compartmentalized eukaryotic networks and to construct and examine testable, non-trivial hypotheses.

A thorough literature search on pathways and newly discovered mechanisms can enable design of new applications through database integration. In plants, for example, hormonal and defense signaling pathways have been found to cross-talk through identical components [118]. An integration of these two types of information can point towards new targets to counteract the microbial components that decrease plant resistance and lead to disease.

Two approaches exist to perform database integration: through the use of tools and through already integrated databases [240]. Pathway database integration tools along with integrated pathway databases play a very important role in easing data integration for biologists. These tools can also be used for various other purposes like data visualization, pathway prediction, pathway gap-fillers and biological network analysis. Applications of pathway databases and tools help further knowledge of the pathways and on the inner workings of living systems.

CORNET(http://cornet.psb.ugent.be/) aims to provide functional context to genes and conversely, to provide an ability to predict functions of genes that have unknown functions. It is a tool that could also, in the future, use the information on A.thaliana to extrapolate networks in other plant species.

The 'MetNet' platform(http://metnet.vrac.iastate.edu/MetNet_overview.htm) contains both metabolic and regulatory networks of A.thaliana, soybean and grapevine. It aims to integrate metabolic data from AraCyc and regulatory data from AGRIS, with additional manually collected signal transduction pathways (in A.thaliana). The pathway information is combined with other resources, such as GO-classifications. Protein information is obtained from PPDB(http://ppdb.tc.cornell.edu/), AMPDB, AtNoPDB, AraPerox, and BRENDA(www.brenda-enzymes.org/). These also provide the subcellular localization information for the entities. Metabolite data from PubChem, KEGG, NCI are also included in the database.

### 2.3.2   Pathway Visualization

Visualization of pathway data not only provides an intuitive way to understand the data, but also assists in analyzing and building valid hypotheses in terms of these data. To address these requirements, many pathway/network visualization tools have been constructed for different purposes of functionalities. The level of visualization that these tools offer range from simple two-dimensional pathway maps like those provided by KEGG, to three-dimensional and hierarchical visualizations like those provided by MetNetGE [164]. In particular, interactive visualization allows users to analyze, edit and modify the pathways according to their own experimental data, such as GenMAPP(http://www.genmapp.org/). In [107], it has thoroughly reviewed available pathway visualization tools and they have been broadly separated into two partly overlapping categories-tools focused on automated methods for interpreting and exploring large biological networks and tools regarding assembly and curation of pathways. Many of these tools integrate with public databases, enabling the users to analyze and visualize their own data. Another comprehensive overview of visualization tools was presented by [301, 302]. A critical evaluation of the requirements for biological visualization tools and the need for further pathway analysis can be seen from [274].

iPath (interactive Pathways Explorer) at http://pathways.embl.de/ (iPath) is a web-based tool for the visualization, analysis and customization of the various pathways maps. Current version provides three different global overview maps, including metabolic pathways constructed by 146 KEGG pathways, and an overview of the complete metabolism in biological systems, 22 KEGG regulatory pathways, and 58 KEGG pathways involved in biosynthesis of secondary metabolites. In addition to the KEGG based overview maps, iPath is used for visualization of various species specific, manually created pathway maps. MetaboAnalyst at http://www.metaboanalyst.ca/ is an integrated web-based platform for comprehensive analysis of quantitative metabolomic data. One of the most recent enhancements has been the incorporation of metabolite set enrichment analysis (MSEA) and metabolic pathway analysis into MetaboAnalyst to assist in the high-level functional interpretation of quantitative metabolomic data.

### 2.3.3 Pathway Interaction

Protein interaction networks model the interaction of proteins in an organism. More precisely, they represent proteins as nodes and their mutual interactions as edges. Each edge can be labeled by a so-called interaction reliability [278], which can be interpreted as the probability that the respective proteins interact with each other in one or more signaling pathways, where a signaling pathway is a cascade of successive protein interactions that the cell uses to react to various external and internal stimuli.

A recent tool focuses on the detection of linear pathways. The basic idea is that a 'good' candidate path is a path that maximizes the product of its edge probabilities. They can serve as a seed structure for experimental investigation of more complex mechanisms [156]. A number of algorithms have been designed to automate the discovery of linear pathways in protein interaction networks [278, 296]. Although this approach indeed yields biologically meaningful results, there are two problems that have remained so far:

- Detecting paths that maximize the product of edge probabilities is an NP-hard problem.
- There is a lack of effective evaluation of pathway candidates derived by this approach.

The analysis of large-scale and high-dimensional phenotyping screens is moving to the center stage of computational systems biology as more and better experimental equipments and systems get established in model organisms. Nested effects models (NEM) are a class of models introduced to analyze the effects of gene perturbation screens visible in high-dimensional phenotypes like microarrays or cell morphology. NEMs achieve two goals:

- reveal clusters of genes with highly similar phenotypic profiles;
- order (clusters of) genes according to subset relationships between phenotypes.

These subset relationships show which genes contribute to global processes in the cell and which genes are only responsible for sub-processes. The NEM structure helps to understand signal flow and internal organization in a cell. NEMs offer complementary information to traditional graphical models including correlation graphs, Bayesian networks and Gaussian graphical models [218]. Thus, they are relevant for theoretical researchers developing methods in systems biology. In addition, a wide range of applications shows the broad impact of NEMs on both molecular biology and medicine: NEMs were successfully applied to data on immune response in Drosophila melanogaster, to the transcription factor network in Saccharomyces cerevisiae.

PathBuilder at http://www.zope.org/ annotates biological information pertaining to signaling pathways and, with minimal additional effort, to create web-based pathway resources. PathBuilder enables annotation of molecular events including protein-protein interactions, enzyme-substrate relationships and protein translocation events via manual or automatic methods. The data is stored in a MySQL database, processed in an application layer implemented in Python programming language and published to the web using DTML, a Zope HTML templating language.

Experimental research to elucidate biological pathways in detail has generated large amounts of data that are spreaded across the published literature. Due to the complexity of pathway data, it is necessary to have biologists and computer scientists to work together to manually collect and curate biological information. A major issue that needs to be addressed is to store, retrieve and visualize the collected data in a simple form and accessible format with provision for integration with other pathway resources. Though software like cPath is available for storing, visualizing and analyzing biological pathways [174], there is currently no publicly available open-source software that allows biologists to rapidly deploy a web-based pathway resource. The importance of pathways is underscored by the fact that there are an increasing growth of biological pathway related resources.

## 2.4  Discussion and Conclusion

Although a number of pathway resources have been developed, it is observed that these databases and resources are no longer accessible. such as aMAZE, Sentra and EMP in Pathguide. Some databases may may change location, whereas most resources is due to lack of long term financial support for maintenance, curation and development. Several of these databases contained high quality data and current absence is a significant loss to the scientific community at large and can thus hinder the development of the field.

The genome scale metabolic networks now being reconstructed from annotation of genome sequences demand new network-based definitions of pathways to facilitate analysis of their capabilities and functions, such as metabolic versatility and robustness, and optimal growth rates. This demand has led to the development of a new mathematically based analysis of complex, metabolic networks that enumerates all their unique pathways that take into account all requirements for cofactors and byproducts. Applications include the design of engineered biological systems, the generation of testable hypotheses regarding network structure and function, and the elucidation of properties that can not be described by simple descriptions of individual components (such as product yield, network robustness, correlated reactions and predictions of minimal media). Recently, these properties have also been studied in genome-scale networks. Thus, network-based pathways are emerging as an important paradigm for analysis of biological systems.

Pathway databases play an important role in advancing our knowledge of the biological functions and mechanisms. Increased understanding of living systems as a whole can, in turn, aid successful application design in biomedicine. Plants are important as veritable food, drug and fuel sources, as well as bioremediation and biotechnological tools. These provide a strong incentive to create better, more integrated and easily accessible pathway databases. Such efforts would lead to discovery and elucidation of the yet unknown components involved in various valuable pathways and their potential function. This would also result in the creation of testable models that can further enrich the knowledge on biology systems. This could gives rise to the design of more specialized intervention technologies along with potential commercial applications: innovation as a result of integration.

# Chapter 3
# Detecting Inconsistency in Biological Molecular Databases Using Ontologies

The rapid growth of life science databases demands the fusion of knowledge from heterogeneous databases to answer complex biological questions. The discrepancies in nomenclature, various schemas and incompatible formats of biological databases, however, result in a significant lack of interoperability among databases. Therefore, data preparation is a key prerequisite for biological database mining. Integrating diverse biological molecular databases is an essential action to cope with the heterogeneity of biological databases and guarantee efficient data mining. However, the inconsistency in biological databases is a key issue for data integration. This chapter proposes a framework to detect the inconsistency in biological databases using ontologies. A numeric estimate is provided to measure the inconsistency and identify those biological databases that are appropriate for further mining applications. This aids in enhancing the quality of databases and guaranteeing accurate and efficient mining of biological databases.

## 3.1 Introduction

Recent development in laboratory technology has resulted in the explosive growth of biological data. Initially, biological data was published and collected using HTML (Hypertext Markup Language) format. However, it cannot describe complex structured documents. This has a negative impact on the presentation of biological information and the integration of biological databases. In addition, the varied organizations, storages and publications of biological data lead to different information types. For example, the representative database NCBI (National Center for Biotechnology Information) [239] adopts mostly the binary ASN.1 format, whereas flat-files are used in EMBL(European Molecular Biology Laboratory) [93], GenBank [23] and DDBJ(DNA DataBank of Japan) [232].

Biological databases (nucleotide sequences and proteins) have been widely used by biologists for data analysis and querying. For example, signaling pathways is crucial in functional genomics since it provides clue to systematically connect genes or gene products to cellular functions. Databases have accumulated masses of data concerning pathways that include signaling pathways, metabolic pathways, molecular interactions as well as molecular complexes. Due to the growth in the number of databases and their contents, it is necessary to answer a complex biological question by consulting more than a single database. However, the heterogeneity among independently designed and maintained biological databases has greatly impeded accessibility to these databases [297]. Therefore, data preparation is a key prerequisite to biological database mining. Integrating diverse biological molecular databases is an essential action to cope with the heterogeneity of biological databases and to also guarantee efficient data mining.

The data are collected either from literatures or from large scale high throughput experiments. Further, most data collected in databases are descriptions of sequence and structure, or signaling phenomena at molecular level. It is necessary to proceed with systematical construction of functional information on the data for reconstruction of cellular phenomena. However, the data collected so far have been represented in different dictionaries or models. For example, two different models called *binary relation* and *state transition* used for signal pathways. Binary relation model regards a pathway as a series of molecular interactions, such as interactions between an enzyme and a substrate, a receptor and a ligand, and a transcription factor and DNA. The state transition model regards a pathway as a series of state changes of molecules, such as a change of chemical modification states, localization states, and compositions of a molecular complex. Each model represents a different aspect of pathways, namely starting a reaction and effect of a reaction on a molecular. It remains to be elucidated how the two aspects contribute to entire nature of pathways. Such an integrated model will provide us with a unique representation of pathways that enables us to do cross-species comparative analysis to find biological essence conserved among species. However the problem to integrate them into a general model is not yet solved. The disagreement between the present two data models arises from their simplifying conceptualizations of biochemical phenomena observed in pathways. Both of them lack fundamental concept structures that systematize more abstract characteristics common to the two models.

The integration of biological databases is usually confronted with technical and semantical problems. The technical problems can be overcome as most biological molecular databases are implemented on relational database management systems (RDBMS) that provide standard interfaces like JDBC and ODBC for data and metadata exchange [191, 251]. The remaining problems involve semantic issues as described in [178, 320]. The inconsistency that arises from semantic issues, such as attribute conflicts, thus challenges current methods to integrate biological databases.

When we want to integrate heterogenous biological databases, they are situations in which we expect some degree of inconsistency in the obtained data. Suppose $D_i$ represent a biological database. The databases may contain some data that is semantically inconsistent, such as an English species name *mouse* and a systematic species name *Mus Musculus* in $D_1$ and $D_2$, respectively. The mining on highly inconsistent biological databases is inefficient and may result in uninteresting and even inaccurate results. Inconsistency must be dealt with before mining biological databases.

It is critical to achieve efficient and accurate mining of biological databases using integration to enhance the quality of biological databases for users or data providers. In addition, the advancements of technologies that allow access to discovery of novel pathway information have leaded to the creation of many more pathway databases that target different organisms, processes and mechanisms. Information aggregated from different pathway databases is often more useful than information from individual databases. Integration of information from various pathway databases can be used to reveal novel information about a system. This urges us to find an intuitive way to measure the inconsistency and to identify the databases that are acceptable for further mining applications.

There have been considerable efforts to address the inconsistency issues in knowledge bases. Hunter presented a method to measure inconsistency in knowledge bases and analyzed inconsistent knowledge by considering the conflicts arising in the minimal quasi-classical (QC) models for that knowledge [153]. Hunter also proposed a framework for characterizing inconsistency that can be used in processes for conflict resolution [152]. Lin presented a knowledge merging operator based on Dalal distance that is capable of measuring the inconsistency between a given world and the knowledge bases in an intuitive way [206]. Although Hunter and Lin have shown an ability to deal with the inconsistency in knowledge bases, their models are inappropriate when addressing the semantic heterogeneity of biological databases due to the databases' inherent complexity and diverse terminologies.

To measure inconsistency in biological databases, we often need to access semantically conflicting data. Although each biological database uses its own terminology to share languages for communication, the biological knowledge from a database is not 'machine understandable' and prevents us from accurately measuring the inconsistency in databases. Ontologies such as GO [13, 112], consisting of an agreed upon vocabulary of concepts (terms) and specification of the relationships among these concepts, are an ideal option to handle the semantic heterogeneity of databases using precise description of the data's semantics and promote the reliable and reusable biological knowledge.

Nevertheless, biological database integration by ontologies is not as good as we might expect due to (1) ontologies with independent terminologies and structures are often incompatible, which causes difficulties in knowledge acquisition from biological databases; (2) heterogeneity, such as synonyms results in a significant lack of interoperability between biological databases; (3) biological databases with high inconsistency are subject to inefficient integration, and may lead to uninteresting knowledge. Although considerable efforts have been devoted to create OBO (Open Biomedical Ontologies), its ability to handle inconsistency is still far from perfect due to diverse heterogenous biological databases. It is desirable that the practical mining is only operated on consistent biological databases.

In this chapter, we present a framework to measure the inconsistency in biological molecular databases by using ontologies. This not only helps us to determine those biological databases that are appropriate for further mining applications, but also ensures efficient mining of biological databases. The presented experiments demonstrate that our framework is useful and promising in detecting inconsistency in biological molecular databases and enhancing the quality of databases for data mining.

The reminder of this chapter is organized as follows. Section 3.2 presents related work. In Section 3.3, the basic concepts and preliminaries are defined. The framework to measure inconsistency in biological databases is shown in Section 3.4. In Section 3.5, experiments are presented. Section 3.6 briefly discusses our methodology and future directions. Section 3.7 concludes this chapter.

## 3.2 Related Work

In the past decades, over several hundred biological molecular databases such as GenBank and NCBI have been publicly available on the Internet. Not only do they provide a convenient and efficient way to access biological data but also pose a big challenge to extract interesting knowledge from these databases [153]. The heterogeneity of biological databases greatly impedes knowledge sharing and further database integration. How to derive high quality and reliable data from diverse biological databases has been a key issue in data mining. To achieve this goal, we should put extra emphasis on the stage of data preparation [343, 344].

Pathway database analysis can be used to discover patterns in the pathways that are related to a disease and assist in the identification of new drug targets [301]. Another application is targeted drug discovery by screening the complete pathway as compared to a single pathway component. Pathway analysis can also be used to find molecular switches that lead to disease and to efficiently turn them off to silence them without affecting the rest of the system. For example, a riboswitch is able to rebuild components of a pathways to regulate expression of multiple genes.

An individual pathway database includes a variety of information. This diversity has been a big challenge to scientists who want to access and utilize this information. Information is scattered across various databases that are different not only in the type of data they contain, but also the format in which they exist. Further, the pathways are often interconnected in an actual living cell. This gives rise to an imperative demand for integration of pathway databases in order to explore a biological regulatory mechanism in its entirety. Given a particular biological mechanism, researchers should be able to easily access all the data they need, without having to go through the difficult process of collecting and cleaning data from various databases that are based on different platforms. One of the biggest challenges to the integration of databases is their diversity and inconsistency. The major issue is syntactic differences between the existing databases, including the varied forms of data file formats and retrieval methods, and semantic differences in the terminologies and data models.

There have been several pathway database resources listed in Pathguide. However, they have insufficient machine-readability and are vastly inconsistent. This prevents us from processing and automatic data retrieval and mining. Thus, the above challenging issues require increased efforts to establish standards for domain-specific analytical data models, such as pathway ontology standards. Systems Biology Markup Language (SBML) is a representative standard using XML for storing and communicating of computational models of biological networks, including metabolic networks, cell signalling pathways and regulatory networks. BioPAX is another standard language developed for detailed pathway depiction and for permitting data exchange. Other data exchange formats exist that are peripherally associated with network-data and can certainly serve as input for other software packages that determine such networks. The Chemical Markup Language (CML) can be used to describe small molecules and ligands that participate in networks, whereas the Protein Markup Language (ProML), along with its predecessor PDB, can be used to characterize larger binding-partners. The Microarray Gene Expression Markup Language (MAGE-ML) can be used as input to determine gene co-expression networks under various conditions.

There are many options of formats for end-users in current pathway databases. Although all standards are now being used by at least some pathway databases, the proliferation of different data formats lead to new problems. Providers have to determine which formats to support and this may cause a laborious and resource-intensive effort. As a result, end-users need to convert the data formats in most cases. In particular, fewer plant genomes have been sequenced compared to other life forms and plant pathways are more dispersed. Therefore, it is critical to incorporate and support already existing standard formats for better integration of information and knowledge extraction from plant pathway databases.

Database integration, which mainly includes data warehousing methods and federated database methods, has been an important action to cope with heterogeneities of multiple databases. Data warehousing methods, like SRS [94] and DBGET/LinkDB [102], directly provide integrated access by using indexed flat-files. Federated database methods, such as DiscoveryLink [123], integrate multiple autonomous database systems into a single federated database by using a meta-database management system (DBMS). Although the above approaches are effective in the integration of heterogeneous databases, the semantic issues as described in [178] have been greatly ignored.

A number of efforts have been devoted to achieve automated, intelligent and reliable integration of biological databases. One option is to combine all possible application programs into web service, and use them to make connections to other services. Oinn proposed a tool for the composition and enactment of bioinformatics workflows [246]. Another way is to use ontology technology which specifies a set of concepts (conceptualization) with precise semantics. SEMEDA (Semantic meta database) [191] supports querying databases via a powerful interface and which enables users to query databases without requiring any details about the data sources. The interoperation of information requires a consistent and shared understanding of the meaning of that information, however the metadata, such as flat-files in biological databases, is often implicit. The terminologies provide common vocabularies of a domain but cannot ensure that everyone has a consistent understanding amongst each other. Therefore, a comprehensive reusable reference ontology of biological concepts is a prerequisite for the integration of biological databases.

There have been several ontologies that were used as repositories of potentially reusable biological knowledge. RiboWeb [55] aims at facilitating the construction of three-dimensional models of ribosomal components such as bonded molecules, biological macromolecules and regions of molecules. EcoCyc ontology [176] covers *E.coli* gene regulation, metabolism and signal transduction. RiboWeb and EcoCyc both use frames as the type of knowledge representation. Gene ontology (GO) [112] project intends to produce a controlled vocabulary for all organisms, even as knowledge of gene and protein roles in cells is accumulating and changing. TAMBIS ontology [17] enables biologists to ask questions about multiple external databases using a query interface. It uses DLS (description logics) as a knowledge representation language instead of frames. They include an individual vocabulary of terms and specification.

Recently, a number of ontology-based applications have also been developed [191, 297]. Philippi [251] proposed a method for the ontology-based semantic integration of life science databases using XML technology. Karp [177] presented an ontology for biological function according to molecular interactions. Yeh [330] proposed methods for knowledge acquisition, consistency checking and concurrency control for Gene Ontology. In addition, XML has also become commonly used as a means for data exchange in different areas due to the fact that XML can facilitate the carrying out of sophisticated retrievals and provide information about their structure. DNA data bank of Japan (DDBJ) [232] itemizes the pieces of information in an entry (genome sequence) by XML, and proposes the DDBJ-XML format for presenting the contents of an entry. Fujibuchi [102] proposed a general architecture for ontology driven data integration based on XML technology and described a prototypical implementation of this architecture based on a native XML database and an expert system shell.

The previous studies have been useful in prompting the interoperability of life science databases. However, the method to measure the inconsistency in biological databases is underdeveloped. Without a qualification of inconsistency, it is difficult to identify databases that are appropriate for further mining applications.

## 3.3   Semantics Description

### 3.3.1   Symbols and Formal Semantics

Suppose $\mathscr{L}$ denotes a set of proposition formulae formed in the usual way from a set of atom symbols $\mathscr{A}$. We use variables $c \in \mathscr{A}$ for concepts such as *Gene* and *Protein*; $\phi$, $X$ and $Y$ for formulas; and $\alpha$, $\gamma$, $\beta \in \mathscr{A}$ for database attributes. Let $\equiv$ be logical equivalence, let $\varpi$ be the weight of biological databases in a taxonomy and let $CV_E$ and $CV_S$ be *controlled vocabulary English species name* and *controlled vocabulary systematic species name*, respectively. A model of a formula $\phi$ is a possible set of atoms where $\phi$ is true in the usual sense.

Database *metadata* usually presents database schema information, data about the **DBMS** and relevant data such as mark-up in flat-files that are required to access a data source. The schema of databases consists of datatypes (*domains*) and tables (*relations*). Tables consist of attributes (*fields*) and corresponding datatypes, and may contain data within the limits of these domains.

*Controlled vocabularies* are a set of named concepts that may have an identifier. The concepts or their identifiers are often used as database entries.

**Definition 3.1.** Suppose $t$, *def*, *id* and *sn* denote term, definition, identifier and synonyms, respectively. Let $C$ be the set of concepts of databases.

$$Controlled\ Vocabulary\ CV := \{c \mid c = (t, def, id, sn) \in C\}$$

For example, in *Gene Ontology*, each concept (*biological process*) includes a term (*recommended name*), an identifier (*id: GO: number*), definition (*explanation and references*) and synonyms (*other names*). Apart from concepts, an ontology also includes relationships, including 'is-a' (*Specification relationships*) and 'part-of' (*Partitive relationships*). Thus, concepts can correlate with each other, such as '*Enzyme* is a *Protein*' and '*Membrane* is part of *Cells*'. Although 'part-of' relationship can be defined, only the transitive 'is-a' hierarchy is required for querying databases. Ontology can be viewed as a tree, where the nodes and directed edges denote concepts and relationships, respectively.

**Definition 3.2.** Let $O$ be an ontology, and $r$ be relationships that link concepts. An ontology can be defined as a set of tuples.

$$Ontology\ O := \{(c_1, c_2, r) \mid c_1, c_2 \in CV, \text{ and } r : c_1 \rightarrow c_2\}$$

where $c_1 \rightarrow c_2$ denotes the relation $r$ from $c_1$ to $c_2$, such as '$c_1$ *is-a* $c_2$'.

*Example 3.1.* In Figure 3.1, *Vertebrate*, *Animal*, *Plant* and *Organism* are connected by 'is-a' relationship. (*Animal, Organism, Animal* $\rightarrow$ *Organism*), (*Plant, Organism, Plant* $\rightarrow$ *Organism*), (*Vertebrate, Animal, Vertebrate* $\rightarrow$ *Animal*) and (*Invertebrate, Animal, Invertebrate* $\rightarrow$ *Animal*) represent the ontology.

To measure inconsistency in biological databases, the databases have to be semantically defined by ontologies. One of the key processes is to link the attributes of databases to a specified ontology. Then, users can execute queries to obtain data from them. To search in attributes of heterogenous databases, a number of complex query operations need to be implemented. If the attributes cannot be found in a current database, it is often the case that the queried attributes have to be mapped to corresponding concepts of ontology, to enable the search for semantically equivalent attributes in the other databases. Occasionally, additional operations are needed, such as translation and cross-reference.

The above facts can be stated in the form of expressions called *sentences*. We define an *atomic sentence* by the following $n$-ary relation operator $\pi$. Let $a_i$, $1 \leq i \leq n$, be atom symbol.

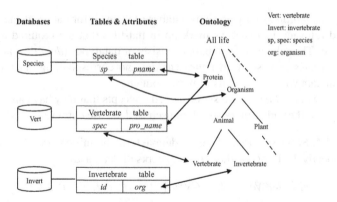

**Fig. 3.1** Biological database attributes are linked to ontology concepts. Attributes *pname* and *pro_name* from databases *Species* and *Vert* have different attribute names, but they can be connected by a common concept *protein* of the ontology.

$$\pi (a_1, a_2, \ldots, a_n)$$

where the atom symbols can be ontologies, controlled vocabularies such as $CV_E$, database attributes such as *pname* and *pro_name*, concepts such as *animal* and *organism*.

There are entailment relationships between the above operations. Let $Att_1$ and $Att_2$ be attributes of database $DB_1$ and $DB_2$, respectively.

**Mapping**

$$maps(Att_1, c) \wedge maps(Att_2, c) \rightarrow Att_1 \equiv Att_2 \qquad (3.1)$$

states that if $Att_1$ and $Att_2$ can be mapped to a common concept $c$ of ontology $O$, $Att_1$ and $Att_2$ are viewed as having the same semantic definition regarding $c$, such as *pname* and *pro_name* in Figure 3.1.

**Translation**

$$translates((CV_1, CV_2), < Att_1, Att_2 >, c) \rightarrow Att_1 \equiv Att_2 \qquad (3.2)$$

states that if $Att_1$ and $Att_2$ can be translated into a common concept $c$ by synonymous concepts, $Att_1$ and $Att_2$ are regarded as having the same semantic definition in relation to $c$, such as, in Figure 3.2, *mouse* in the attribute '*systematic_spec_name*' and *Mus Musculus* in the attribute '*english _spec_name*' by $CV_E$ and $CV_S$.

**Cross-reference**

$$cross\text{-}reference(CV, Att_1, Att_2, c) \rightarrow Att_1 \equiv Att_2 \qquad (3.3)$$

states that if $Att_1$ and $Att_2$ can be linked to a common concept $c$ by *cross-reference*, they are semantically equivalent by $c$, such as, in Figure 3.2, *pn* in *DB2* and *DB3* by the concept *protein_ID*.

**Taxonomy**

$$\forall c_1, c_2, c_3 \in O, is\text{-}a(c_1, c_2) \wedge is\text{-}a(c_2, c_3) \rightarrow is\text{-}a(c_1, c_3) \tag{3.4}$$

states that if $c_1$ '$is\text{-}a$' $c_2$, and $c_2$ '$is\text{-}a$' $c_3$, we can deduce $c_1$ '$is\text{-}a$' $c_3$. It actually indicates the '$is\text{-}a$' relationship holds transitivity.

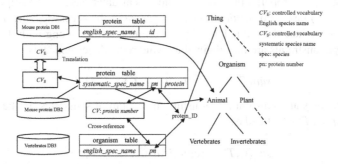

**Fig. 3.2** Translation by mapping synonymous concepts of controlled vocabularies is used to link databases with synonyms. Database attributes corresponding to the same concept and sharing the same controlled vocabulary can be viewed as cross-references of attributes.

The above axioms describe the possible processes in response to user's queries about database attributes. Ontology plays a central role in mapping the attributes to common concepts or translating attributes between different controlled vocabularies. The query can be classified into two categories according to entered attributes.

- if a queried attribute is found in databases, it will be mapped to a concept of ontology, by which to connect to other database attributes;
- if no existing database attribute is matched, a corresponding concept of ontology is selected. Its *sub-concepts* and *super-concepts* will be searched for the attribute. The details can be seen below.

In the first category, users usually search in the attribute *Att* in conjunction with a specified term *T*. *T* is actually a complementary description that locates the relevant databases. For example, in Figure 3.1, if a user wants to search in attribute *pname* for *mouse*, the term *mouse* will be combined with *pname* to locate databases *Species* and *Vert*. As to the latter, the queries first attempt to find the concept of ontology that is related to the queried attributes. The *sub-concepts* and *sup-concepts* will be searched for the specified *term*. They are defined as:

$$sub(C) = \{c | \forall c, is\text{-}a(c, C)\} \tag{3.5}$$

$$sup(C) = \{c | \forall c, is\text{-}a(C, c)\} \tag{3.6}$$

where the ontology $O$ can be regarded as a tree, $sub(C)$ consists of all child nodes of the parent node $C$ and $sup(C)$ includes all parent nodes of the child node $C$.

However, some unwanted concepts can be returned, which will result in unnecessary queries and results. For example, for the query *animal : mouse*, we can get $sub(Animal) = \{Vertebrate, Invertebrate\}$. It is obvious that *mice* is exactly in the *Vertebrate*, rather than *Invertebrate*, concept by the taxonomic tree in [153]. Thus, the database attributes should be semantically defined as specifically as possible to facilitate the interoperability between biological databases. For example, (*vertebrate, mouse*) instead of (*Animal, mouse*) can avoid the access to '*invertebrate*'. Also, we can reduce the redundancy by including a term $T$ along with the query. The concept constraints are thus defined to avoid redundancy concepts.

$$sub(C,T) = \{c | \forall c, is\text{-}a(c,C), c \sqsupseteq T\} \tag{3.7}$$

where $\sqsupseteq$ denotes an inclusion relationship on account of semantics. In the similar manner, $sup(C, T)$ is defined as

$$sup(C,T) = \{c | \forall c, is\text{-}a(C,c), c \sqsupseteq T\} \tag{3.8}$$

*Example 3.2.* Suppose the queried database attribute is '*Animal: parrot*'. In Figure 3.1, we have $sub(Animal, parrot) = \{Vertebrate\}$, $sup(Animal, parrot) = \{Organism\}$.

It is observed that $Vertebrate \in sub(Animal, parrot)$ is irrelevant to the term *parrot*. Therefore, ontologies should also be defined as specifically as possible. For example, if a *Mammals* concept is included to be a subconcept of *Vertebrate*, the search for the unwanted concepts such as *Fish* and *Reptiles* can be avoided. The obtained concept $c \in sub(C, T) \cup sup(C, T)$ can then be mapped to the desired attributes of other databases.

**Definition 3.3.** Let $ATT_{DB} = \{a_1, a_2, ..., a_n\}$ be the set of attributes of biological database DB. $ATT_R$ and $ATT_C$ denote the set of attributes from reference database and compared databases, respectively.

The reference database is the database that includes the queried attribute or the attribute that can be mapped to the concepts in $sub(C, T) \cup sup(C, T)$. It aids in deciding whether the attributes in compared databases are consistent with the queried attribute.

*Example 3.3.* In Figure 3.1, $ATT_{Species} = \{sp, pname\}$, $ATT_{Vert} = \{pro\_name, spec\}$ and $ATT_{Invert} = \{id, org\}$. Given a query *pname*, then $ATT_R = \{sp, pname\}$ and $ATT_C = \{pro\_name, spec, id, org\}$.

**Definition 3.4.** Let $\models$ be a support relationship. For a set of database attributes $ATT_{DB}$, $ATT_{DB} \models$ is defined as follows.

(1) if the queried database attribute $\alpha$ is found in current databases, we have

$$\begin{cases} ATT_R \models \alpha & \text{iff "} ATT_R \text{ contains } \alpha \text{"} \\ ATT_C \models \neg\alpha & \text{iff "} ATT_C \text{ contains } \beta \text{"} \end{cases}$$

Here $\beta$ is a database attribute of compared databases, which is semantically equivalent to $\alpha$ by a medium concept of ontology.

(2) if the queried database attribute $\alpha$ is not in the databases but can be mapped to a concept of ontology, we have

$$\begin{cases} ATT_R \models \alpha_1 & \text{iff "} ATT_R \text{ contains } \alpha_1 \text{"} \\ ATT_C \models \neg\alpha_1 & \text{iff "} ATT_C \text{ contains } \alpha_2 \text{"} \end{cases}$$

where $\alpha_1$ represents the mapped attribute in reference database by $c \in sub(C, T) \cup sup(C, T)$, and $\alpha_2$ is the corresponding database attribute to $c$ in compared databases.

In reality, $(\alpha, \beta)$ and $(\alpha_1, \alpha_2)$ are called synonyms because they use different names to mean the same thing.

## 3.4 Detecting Inconsistency of Biological Databases

### 3.4.1 Minimal Models of Queried Biological Database Attributes

This section defines an operator by the models of database attributes to measure the inconsistency in biological databases.

**Definition 3.5.** Suppose $ATT \in \wp(\mathscr{L})$, $X \in \wp(\mathscr{A})$, where $\wp$ is the power set function. Let $ATT_{DB}$ be attributes from $DB \in \{R, C\}$. Let $X \models ATT$ denote that $X \models \alpha$ holds for every $\alpha$ in $ATT$.

$$model(ATT) = \{X \in \wp(\mathscr{A}) \mid X \models ATT\}$$

where $ATT$ denotes a set of database attributes. The model of $ATT$ actually represents a set of atoms that support $ATT$.

For each atom $\alpha \in ATT_R$ or $ATT_C$, $X \models \alpha$ means that $X$ contains $\alpha$. On the contrary, $X \models \neg\alpha$ means that a semantically equivalent attribute of $\alpha$ supported by $X$ exists, which can be linked to $\alpha$ via ontology. In particular, if no equivalent attribute is found in $ATT_{DB}$, we also have $X \models \neg\alpha$. The set of database attributes $ATT$ is the union of $ATT_R$ and $ATT_C$. Thus, we have

$$ATT = ATT_R \sqcup ATT_C$$

where $\sqcup$ denotes a multiset union operator but the repeated items are reserved. For example, let $ATT_R = \{\alpha\}$ and $ATT_C = \{\alpha, \beta\}$. Hence $ATT_R \sqcup ATT_C = \{\alpha, \alpha, \beta\}$. If $ATT_R \sqcup ATT_C = \emptyset$, it represents that the biological databases do not support the queried attribute. In other words, the accessible databases are irrelevant to the queried database attribute.

*Example 3.4.* (Continue Example 3.3) $ATT = ATT_R \sqcup ATT_C = \{sp, pname, pro\_name,$ $spec, id, org\}$. Thus, $\{sp, pname\} \models ATT_R$, $\{pro\_name, spec, id, org\} \models ATT_C$ and $\{sp, pname, pro\_name, spec, id, org\} \models ATT$ denote a model of $ATT_R$, $ATT_C$ and $ATT$, respectively.

The models of queried attributes might include not only database attributes but also the pathways of ontology, such as $maps(pname, Protein) \wedge cross\text{-}reference(pname, pro\_name, Protein) \rightarrow pro\_name$ with $ATT_R$, and $maps(pro\_name, Protein) \wedge cross\text{-}reference(pname, pro\_name, Protein) \rightarrow pname$ with $ATT_C$. However, the pathways and medium concepts, such as *Protein*, have no influence in measuring inconsistency. Thus, they should be ignored in the model.

To measure inconsistency in biological databases, we use minimal models *Mmod*.

**Definition 3.6.** Let $ATT \in \wp(\mathscr{L})$. The set of minimal model for $ATT$ is defined as

$$Mmod(ATT) = \{X \in model(ATT) \mid \text{if } Y \subset X, \text{then } Y \notin model(ATT)\}$$

*Example 3.5.* (Continue Example 3.2) Let $ATT_1 = \{spec\}$ and $ATT_2 = \{sp\}$ be the set of attributes with respect to *sub(Animal, parrot)* and *sup(Animal, parrot)*, respectively. Thus, $ATT_C = ATT_1 \cup ATT_2$ and $ATT_R = \{Animal\}$. Let $ATT = ATT_C \cup ATT_R$. Then, we have $Mmod(ATT) = \{\{Animal, spec, sp\}\}$.

## 3.4.2  Detecting Inconsistency of Minimal Models

We now consider a measure of inconsistency called compatibility of biological databases. The *consistentset* of a minimal model $Y$ includes the database attributes that have identical names with the reference attributes. The *conflictset* of $Y$ consists of (1) the database attributes that are semantically equivalent to the queried attribute; and (2) the *null* attribute that denotes no attribute is semantically equivalent to the reference attribute.

**Definition 3.7.** Let $Y \in \wp(\mathscr{A})$ be a minimal model of the queried attribute. Let $\alpha$ be a selected reference attribute from reference database $R$. The consistentset and conflictset are defined as

$$Consistentset(\alpha) = \{\beta \mid \beta \in Y, \beta \equiv \alpha\} \qquad (3.9)$$

$$Conflictset(\alpha) = \{\beta \mid \beta \in Y, \beta \equiv \neg\alpha \text{ or } \beta \equiv null\} \qquad (3.10)$$

If $Consistentset(\alpha) = \emptyset$, $Y$ is totally inconsistent with $\alpha$, and vice versa; if $Conflictset(\alpha) = \emptyset$, $Y$ is totally consistent with $\alpha$, and vice versa. For simplicity, we use $\neg\alpha$ to represent both *null* attributes and *semantically equivalent* attributes of $\alpha$.

By *consistentset* and *conflictset*, the compatibility function from $\mathscr{A}$ into $[0, 1]$, is defined below when $\alpha$ is not empty, and $Compatibility(\emptyset) = 0$.

$$Compatibility(\alpha) = \frac{|Consistentset(\alpha)|}{|Consistentset(\alpha)| + |Conflictset(\alpha)|} \times 100\% \quad (3.11)$$

where $|Consistentset(\alpha)|$ and $|Conflictset(\alpha)|$ denote the cardinality of *Consistentset*$(\alpha)$ and *Conflictset*$(\alpha)$, respectively. If $Compatibility(\alpha) = 0$, the minimal model $Y$ has no conflict upon $\alpha$ and vice versa; if $Compatibility(\alpha) = 1$, there is no negative attribute $\neg\alpha$ in $Y$.

*Example 3.6.* (Continue Example 4.2) Due to $Mmod(ATT) = \{\{spec, sp, Animal\}\}$. Let $\alpha = $ 'Animal'. Thus, we have $spec = \neg\alpha$ and $sp = \neg\alpha$. Thus, we have *Conflictset*$(Animal) = \{spec, sp\}$ and *Consistentset*$(Animal) = \{Animal\}$, and thus *Compatibility*$(Animal) = 1/3 = 33\%$.

The above definition ideally assumes that the databases have an equal degree of importance. In reality, they are assigned different weights. It is reasonable that the databases with high authority, such as NCBI, GenBank and EMBL should have higher weight than other databases. This paper assumes that each biological database is associated with a *weight* which represents the relative degree of importance of the databases. If $\varpi_{DB_i} > \varpi_{DB_j}$, $i \neq j$, it indicates $DB_i$ is more important than $DB_j$, and more of its opinion will be reflected in measuring the inconsistency in databases.

**Definition 3.8.** Let $\varpi_R$ and $\varpi_{C_1}, \ldots, \varpi_{C_k}$ be the weight of the reference database and compared databases respectively. The weighted compatibility of the set of database $\{R, C_1, \ldots, C_k\}$ regarding database attribute $\alpha$ is defined as follows, and $Compatibility(\emptyset, \varpi) = 0$.

$$Compatibility(\alpha, \varpi) =$$

$$= \frac{\sum_{i \in \{R, C_1, \ldots, C_k\}} |Consistentset_i(\alpha)| * \varpi_i}{\sum_{i \in \{R, C_1, \ldots, C_k\}} (|Consistentset_i(\alpha)| + |Conflictset_i(\alpha)|) * \varpi_i} \quad (3.12)$$

The number of occurrence of $\alpha$ and $\neg\alpha$ in databases are equal in case of *Consistentset*$(\alpha) = $ *Conflictset*$(\alpha)$. In this scenario, the databases are definitely inconsistent with respect to $\alpha$. Hence, it seems reasonable to define a number that is greater than $0.5$ as the threshold of *minimal compatibility*, namely $mincomp > 0.5$. Increasing the *mincomp* will lead to higher expectation of the consistency in biological databases. The beliefs in the compatibility are defined as

$$\begin{cases} consistent & \text{if } Compatibility(\alpha, \varpi) \geq mincomp \\ inconsistent & \text{if } Compatibility(\alpha, \varpi) < mincomp \end{cases}$$

The compatibility function provides an intuitive way to measure the inconsistency in biological databases. If the databases are highly inconsistent, they may contain too many incompatible terminologies or most of current databases do not contain the queried database attributes at all. From the results, we are able to identify those databases that are appropriate for further mining applications and enhance the quality of biological databases.

### 3.4.3   Algorithm Design

The presented algorithm identifies database attributes that are semantically equivalent to the queried attribute.

**begin**

*Input: D: biological database; att: T: queried database attribute with constraint T;*

(1) **let** *Consistentset* $\leftarrow \emptyset$; *Conflictset* $\leftarrow \emptyset$; $DB \leftarrow; \emptyset$; $ATT_R \leftarrow \emptyset$;
   $ATT_C \leftarrow \emptyset$;

(2) **forall** $d \in D$ **do**
       **if** $d$ satisfies $T$ **then** $DB \leftarrow DB \cup d$;
   **end**

(3) **if** $\exists DB_i \in DB$ contains $att$ **then** {
       (3.1) $ATT_R \leftarrow ATT_R \cup ATT_{DB_i}$;
       (3.2) $ATT_C \leftarrow ATT_{DB} - ATT_R$;
       (3.3) *Consistentset* $\leftarrow$ *Consistentset* $\cup att$;
       (3.4) **forall** $att_c \in ATT_C$ **do**
           **if** $att_c$ is identical with $att$ **then**
               *Consistentset* $\leftarrow$ *Consistentset* $\cup att_c$;
           **else**
               **if** $att_c$ is synonymous with $att$ via ontology **then**
                   *Conflictset* $\leftarrow$ *Conflictset* $\cup att_c$;
       **end**
   }

(4) **else** {
       **if** $\exists$ concept $c$ in ontology that can be mapped to $att$ **then**
           the set of relevant concepts $con \leftarrow sub \cup sup$;
       (4.1) $ATT_{con} \leftarrow$ a set of database attributes that can be
           mapped to concepts of $con$;
       (4.2) Find out *Consistentset* and *Conflictset* with respect
           to specified $att' \in ATT_{con}$;
   }

**end**

In step 1, an empty set is assigned to the variable of *Consistentset, Conflictset, DB, ATT_R* and *ATT_C*, respectively. In the following processes, some new elements can be added if the condition is satisfied. We aim to obtain *Consistentset* and *Conflictset* by virtue of *DB, ATT_R* and *ATT_C*. Thus, we have to first find out *DB, ATT_R* and *ATT_C*.

Step 2 represents a cycle operation to decide whether a database satisfies the constraint *T*. If the database does not satisfy *T*, it will be ignored before constructing *ATT_R* and *ATT_C*. For example, the database irrelevant to the *mammal* will not be considered in the query regarding *Mus musculus*.

In Step 3, if a database $DB_i$ contains the queried attribute *att*, then we can add its attributes $ATT_{DB_i}$ to the attribute of reference database $ATT_R$ (Step 3.1). The remaining attributes of database *DB* are then stored into the $ATT_C$ (Step 3.2). Step 3.3 includes the *att* in *Consistentset* since $DB_i$ contains it. According to the obtained $ATT_C$, step 3.4 checks whether $att_c$ is identical with *att*. If so, it is saved to *Consistentset*, otherwise, it is saved to *Conflictset*.

However, if a database $DB_i$ does not contain the queried attribute *att*, we will go to Step 4. This attempts to find out the medium concept in the ontology that can be mapped to *att* in terms of *sub-concepts* and *super-concepts*. The attribute that can be mapped to the concept of *con* will be stored into $ATT_{con}$ (4.1). The obtained $ATT_{con}$ is then used to generate *Consistentset* and *Conflictset* (Step 4.2). As a result, we can measure the inconsistency in databases.

## 3.5 Experiments

To demonstrate the potential of the principles of semantic inconsistency measures as described above, a prototype system was developed. It focuses on illustrating the measure of inconsistency, whereas the well-established features in other systems, like integration of bioinformatic analysis tools/applications and knowledge acquisition [191], are not considered.

**Dataset.** We evaluate our approach on real-world gene association data of mouse from GOA (GO Annotation@EBI) [7] which is responsible for the integration and release of GO [109] annotations to the multi-species proteomes. Using GOA, a query can be linked to various database sources, e.g, mouse genome information in MGI (Mouse genome informatics), DoTs (Database of transcribed sequences, 43164 human and 78054 mouse DoTS Transcripts (DTs)), UniGene (1313562 UniGene entries), NIA Mouse Gene Index (28219 protein-coding genes (81629 transcripts) 10334 additional gene candidates) and Entrez Gene (2585453 genes). There are 70861 records in the training dataset and of which a gene product can have one or more molecular functions. The gene product may be used in one or more biological processes and may be associated with one or more cellular components. The details of the file format is described in the Annotation Guide [109].

Three sets of records GO0005201, G00007160 and GO0005578 are selected to form the dataset. GO0005201 is the extracellular matrix structural constituent data

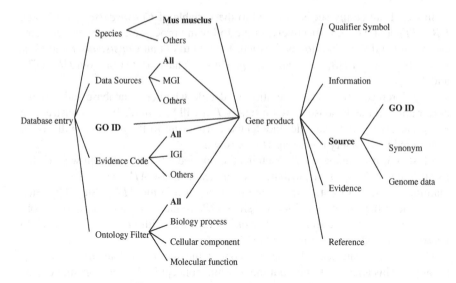

**Fig. 3.3** Relations between concepts and database entries

of molecular function, containing 20 records retrieved from AmiGO using keyword
"0005201". G00007160 is the cell-matrix adhesion data of biological process, containing 42 records retrieved from AmiGo using keyword "0007160". GO0005578
is the extracellular matrix (sensu Metazoa) data of cellular component, containing 132 records retrieved from AmiGo using keyword "0005578". All three GO
terms were retrieved only for *Mus Musculus*. After removing duplicated records
in "GO0005578", there are 123 unique gene products. Figure 3.3 illustrates the
relations between concepts and database entries. Each database entry consists of
species, data sources, GO ID, evidence code and ontology filter. The entries are
highlighted on the left of gene product in bold. Of course, a background translation
between English species name (mouse) and systematic species name (Mus musculus) is needed at the beginning. On the right of gene product, it shows how to link
to other database sources and obtain the genome data.

**Implementation.** For simplicity, we assume all databases are assigned equal weight
*1* in this study. Three queries are executed below by varying the *GO ID* from

**Table 3.1** Query results of gene product

| GO ID | Qualifier Symbol | Source | Evidence | Reference |
|---|---|---|---|---|
| 0005201 | Col4a3 | MGI | RCA | PMID:12466851 |
| 0007160 | 4733401I12Rik | MGI | RCA | PMID:12466851 |
| 0005578 | Adamts10 | MGI | RCA | PMID:12466851 |

0005201, 0007160 to 0005578, which represents *extracellular matrix structural constituent, cell-matrix adhesion* and *extracellular matrix(sensu Metazoa)*, respectively.

1. *'0005201 : Mus musculus'* – search in the term *'0005201'* for *'Mus musculus'*,
2. *'0007160 : Mus musculus'* – search in the term *'0007160'* for *'Musculus'*, and
3. *'0005578 : Mus musculus'* – search in the term *'0005578'* for *'Mus musculus'*.

Three datasets of gene product are obtained. Table 3.1 shows three records in which **PMID** and **RCA** denote 'PubMed ID' and 'inferred from Reviewed Computational Analysis', respectively. For brevity, the *information* attribute is not included in the table. The *source* attribute can be used to link to other biological databases. Table 3.2 shows that the first record in Table 3.1 can be connected to the database DoTs, TIGR, NIA Mouse Gene Index and Entrez Gene via database MGI.

**Table 3.2** Conversion of synonym of gene product without GO

| Source | Synonym | GO ID | Conversion without GO |
|---|---|---|---|
| MGI | Col4a3 | 0005201 | 1 |
| DoTs | DT.55281263 | 0005201 | −1 |
| DoTs | DT.91365816 | null | −1 |
| TIGR | TC1422845 | null | −1 |
| TIGR | TC1556182 | null | −1 |
| NIA Mouse Gene Index | Col4a3 | 0005201 | 1 |
| Entrez Gene | Col4a3 | 0005201 | 1 |

**Results and Interpretation.** Although most of the databases include the uniform GO ID, they use either the same name of the gene product or a semantically equivalent name. Table 3.2 presents the synonym of gene product in different databases, in which *null* denotes no GO ID or no predicted GO function was provided in the databases. It is observed that inconsistency exists within the terminology of gene product between database sources, such as *Col4a3* in databases MGI, NIA Mouse Gene Index and Entrez Gene, and *TC1422845* and *TC1556182* in database TIGR. Obviously, it is impractical for a normal user to know that they actually mean the same thing, and that the user could be expected to extract interesting knowledge from such raw data.

In the same manner, each query described above can bring out an association file of gene product, which contains the synonyms in different linked database sources. The details of association files can be reached by http://bioinformatics.gxu.edu.cn/bio/data/LNAI8335/8335-5.zip.

To measure the inconsistency, we convert the *synonym of gene product* to integers. The positive integers and negative integers represent coherent name, and synonym or null value, respectively. For example, the last column in Table 3.2, illustrates the converted synonyms of gene product without GO. In the same way, we can perform the conversion for other records. To distinguish different records, the integer is varied by increasing 1 each time until the end of the association file. As a result, the intervals of retrieved records using 0005201, 0007160 and 0005578 will be [−20, 20], [−42, 42] and [−123, 123], respectively. The numbers 20, 42 and 123 represent the result sizes and denote the above three ranges, respectively.

In the association files, the name of gene product of MGI is selected as the reference attribute. A comparison between "without GO" and "with GO" was conducted. In the case of "without GO", if the name of the gene product in other databases is inconsistent with MGI, the conversion will be assigned a positive integer, otherwise a negative integer. In the case of "with GO", the conversion will be assigned a negative integer only if the name of gene product in the database is inconsistent with MGI and the database includes no GO ID. Table 3.3 presents the first four records of Table 3.2 using the GO conversion. Using the converted data, we are able to generate the *conflictset* and *consistentset*, by which to evaluate the inconsistency in biological databases.

**Table 3.3** Conversion of synonym of gene product with GO

| Source | Synonym | GO ID | Conversion with GO |
|--------|---------|-------|--------------------|
| MGI | Col4a3 | 0005201 | 1 |
| DoTs | DT.55281263 | 0005201 | 1 |
| DoTs | DT.91365816 | null | −1 |
| TIGR | TC1422845 | null | −1 |

The statistics of synonym gene products in biological databases with consistent name is compared to those with inconsistent name. Figure 3.4, Figure 3.5 and Figure 3.6 present the comparison between "without GO" and "with GO" with respect to GO:0005201, GO:0007160 and GO:0005578, respectively.

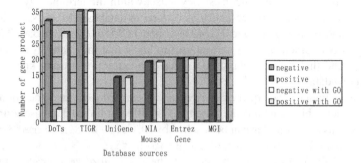

**Fig. 3.4** The statistics of synonym of gene products regarding GO: 0005201 in biological databases

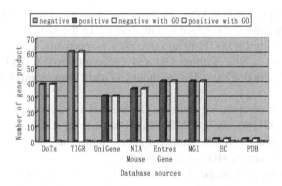

**Fig. 3.5** The statistics of synonym of gene products regarding GO: 0007160 in biological databases

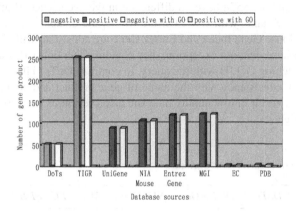

**Fig. 3.6** The statistics of synonym of gene products regarding GO: 0005578 in biological databases

In Figure 3.4, the sources UniGene, NIA mouse gene index, Entrez gene and MGI have high consistency with the name of the gene product. However, the sources DoTs and TIGR have high inconsistency with the name of the gene product. In particular, some gene products in DoTs include the same GO ID as the query, therefore the query can directly link to this database using ontology. That is why we can see many positives if GO is applied. Using Equations (9), (10) and (11), we have *Compatibility*(0005201) = 52% without GO and *Compatibility*(0005201) = 72% with GO. This implies that we are able to decrease the inconsistency in biological databases using ontology.

In Figure 3.5 and Figure 3.6, UniGene, NIA mouse gene index, Entrez gene and MGI still show their high coherence with the name of the gene product. In comparison with Figure 3.4 and Figure 3.5, Figure 3.6 includes more negative numbers of gene product from TIGR. This indicates that TIGR is the primary source that causes the inconsistency. In addition, two new sources, EC and PDB, are included. It is not surprising that very few gene products are found from these sources since they are not very relevant to our queries. In the same way, we can compute the compatibility for 0007160 and 0005578, respectively. Thus, we have *Compatibility*(0007160) = 59% without GO and *Compatibility*(0007160) = 59% with GO; *Compatibility*(0005578) = 58% without GO and *Compatibility*(0005578) = 58% with GO.

It is observed that the compatibility without GO is equal to the compatibility with GO in both queries, 0007160 and 0005578. This is because no matching GO ID is available in database sources and the names of gene products are inconsistent with the reference database, such as MGI used in this study.

Table 3.4 presents the percentage of occurrence of positive attributes and negative attributes in database sources with respect to the queries, in which "+" and "−" denote positive and negative, respectively. In particular, $0005201_G^+$, $0007160_G^+$ and $0005578_G^+$ denote the percentage of occurrence of attributes with GO. Except for 0005201, 0007160 and 0005578 have no difference in the occurrence of attributes between "without GO" and "with GO". On the whole, the database sources Uni-Gene, MGI, NIA Mouse Gene Index and Entrez Gene are consistent with the name of gene product because, without exception, they contain either consistent name of gene product or matching GO ID with the query. In contrast, DoTs, TIGR, EC and PDB show very low consistency with the name of gene product and contain even no GO ID. This may result in low quality data and also prevent us from extracting interesting knowledge.

**Table 3.4** Percentage of occurrence of attributes

| Query | DoTs | TIGR | UniGene | NIA | Entrez | MGI | EC | PDB |
|---|---|---|---|---|---|---|---|---|
| $0005201^+$ | 0 | 0 | 10% | 13.6% | 14.3% | 14.3% | 0 | 0 |
| $0005201^-$ | 22.9% | 25% | 0 | 0 | 0 | 0 | 0 | 0 |
| $0005201_G^+$ | 20% | 0 | 10% | 13.6% | 14.3% | 14.3% | 0 | 0 |
| $0005201_G^-$ | 2.9% | 25% | 0 | 0 | 0 | 0 | 0 | 0 |
| $0007160^+$ | 0 | 0 | 12.4% | 14.5% | 16.5% | 16.5% | 0 | 0 |
| $0007160^-$ | 15.7% | 24.5% | 0 | 0 | 0 | 0 | 0.8% | 0.8% |
| $0005578^+$ | 0 | 0 | 12% | 14.2% | 15.8% | 16.2% | 0 | 0 |
| $0005578^-$ | 7% | 33.6% | 0 | 0 | 0 | 0 | 0.4% | 0.7% |

As a consequence, our approach is not only able to measure the inconsistency in biological databases, but also report to the users the sources that cause the inconsistency. This benefit improves the interoperability between databases, and enhances the data quality for data mining.

## 3.6 Discussion

To achieve efficient and reliable data mining, one of the most important steps is to obtain high quality data that is complete, consistent and clean. In addition, we have to collect data from multiple database sources. Thus, data integration has been a key issue in data mining. There have been many efforts in developing tools for collecting data from biological databases. However, the inconsistent terminology, duplicated records, and even conflicting identifier in different databases can remarkably influence the interoperability between database sources. The obtained raw data is definitely unready for further mining applications and may lead to inefficient mining, missing of interesting patterns and even incorrect knowledge. To confront these significant challenges, this chapter provides an intuitive way to measure the inconsistency in biological databases using ontology by identifying the sources that are appropriate for further mining applications.

The initial dataset of GO:0005578 contains duplicate records that have the same name of gene product and PMID. This may arise from (1) the same gene product may be submitted by the biologist to more than one database; (2) the gene product is submitted repeatedly to the same database; or (3) fragment and partial entries of the gene product may be saved in different database records. Although the duplicate records are removed from the dataset, it warns us that they may give rise to incorrect evaluation of inconsistency. On the other hand, most of the predicted GO ID in DoTs is *unreviewed* or *none*. In that case, we ignore the records in DoTs.

Although the inconsistency in biological databases can be evidence for further data analysis, the database entries should be input as specifically as possible. For example, the query 0005201:Mus musculus will return more interesting gene products in comparison with 0005201 only. Occasionally, a query is too simple to search but the inconsistency in databases might be low. Our approach depends on the quality of databases. As described above, we can see some duplicate records in the association files and many unreviewed GO ID in the database DoTs. In addition, the accuracy of ontology is also critical to accurately evaluate the inconsistency in biological databases. For example, if there is no translation between English species name and systematic species name, the query 0005201:Mus musculus might return nothing. Thus, the database attributes should be semantically defined to be as specific as possible. In other words, no database attributes are semantically defined as general top-level concepts such as 'thing'. Nevertheless, these should not impact the capability of our approach to detect inconsistency in biological databases.

Another issue that might influence the efficiency and accuracy of further mining applications is the extra or unpredictable consumption of time and computation due to the use of ontology. It is clear that an unperfect and complex ontology might result in low efficient mining and even inaccurate results. Regardless of the difficulties, it may be an optimal way to unify the terminology by formalizing the collected data from biological databases before commencing mining, or establish a complete mapping relation between them using ontology.

In this study, we measure the inconsistency in biological databases using a numeric estimate and compare their different effects on inconsistency. Based on the comparison, we not only discovered the databases that are appropriate for further data mining but also the databases that need to be further improved.

Although we present a framework to measure the inconsistency between biological databases, until now, we do not directly talk much about the applications and tools of pathway database integration because it is complex and still a new research field in bioinformatics. Despite this, the methods and tools for biological database integration proposed in this monograph can be applied to pathway data analysis since the diversity in data format and terminology is the common issue in database integration. The aforementioned methods and tools can be adapted or extended for further mining of pathway databases.

A thorough literature search on pathways and newly discovered mechanisms can enable design of new applications through database integration. For example, hormonal and defense signaling pathways in plant have been found to cross-talk through identical components. An integration of these two types of information can aid in finding new targets to counteract the microbial components that decrease plant resistance and lead to disease.

There are two main approaches to perform database integration: through the use of tools and through already integrated databases (that hopefully get rebuilt periodically to stay current). These tools can also be used for various other purposes such as data visualization, pathway prediction, pathway gap-fillers and biological network analysis. Applications of pathway databases and tools help learn further knowledge of the pathways and on the inner workings of living systems. For example, Eu.Gene Analyzer [39] is an easy-to-use, stand-alone application that allows rapid and powerful microarray data analysis in the context of biological pathways. It uses two different statistical methods to evaluate which pathways are most affected by differences in gene expression observed in a functional genomic experiment. Human Pathway Database (HPD) [61] was proposed for integrating heterogeneous human pathway data that are either curated at the NCI Pathway Interaction Database (PID), Reactome, BioCarta, KEGG or indexed from the Protein Lounge Web sites.

## 3.7 Conclusion

Data preparation is a key prerequisite for mining life science databases. However, the heterogeneity caused by varied data formats and data schemas of biological databases results in a significant lack of interoperability among databases and prevents users from extracting interesting patterns from multiple sources. Ontology-based approaches have been successfully used to exploit biological knowledge by reducing the semantic heterogeneity and thus promoting the flexible and reliable interoperability between biological databases. This chapter proposes an ontology-based framework to detect the inconsistency in biological databases, to allow users to identify the sources that are appropriate for further mining application, and data providers can enhance the quality of databases.

Pathway databases play an important role in advancing our knowledge of the biological functions and mechanisms. Increased understanding of living systems as a whole can, in turn, aid successful application design in silico, in vitro and in vivo. This provides a strong incentive to create better, more integrated and easily accessible pathway databases. Such efforts would lead to discovery and elucidation of the yet unknown components involved in various pathways and their function. This would also result in the creation of testable models that can further enrich the knowledge on biological systems. This then could lead to the design of more specialized intervention technologies along with potential commercial applications: innovation as a result of integration.

Unlike the general data integration, our approach provides an intuitive compatibility function to measure the inconsistency. It enables us to not only discover the sources with duplicate or inconsistent records but also to minimize data loss due to discrepant terminology. The mining can be implemented either on the sources with high consistency or on the sources after enhancement. Thus, it has good potential for guaranteeing accurate and efficient mining of biological databases. The conducted experiments demonstrate that our approach is useful and promising.

# Chapter 4
# Exploration of Positive Frequent Patterns for AMP-Activated Protein Kinase Regulation

AMP-activated protein kinase (AMPK) has emerged as a significant signaling intermediary that regulates metabolisms in response to energy demand and supply. An investigation into the degree of activation and deactivation of AMPK subunits under exercise can provide valuable data for understanding AMPK. In particular, the effect of AMPK on muscle cellular energy status makes this protein a promising pharmacological target for disease treatment. As more AMPK regulation data are accumulated, data mining techniques can play an important role in identifying frequent patterns in the data. Association rule mining, which is commonly used in market basket analysis, can be applied to AMPK regulation.

This chapter proposes a framework that can identify the potential correlation, either between the state of isoforms of $\alpha$, $\beta$ and $\gamma$ subunits of AMPK, or between stimulus factors and the state of isoforms. Our approach is to apply item constraints in the closed interpretation to the itemset generation so that a threshold is specified in terms of the amount of results, rather than a fixed threshold value for all itemsets of all sizes. The derived rules from experiments are roughly analyzed. It is found that most of the extracted association rules have biological meaning and some of them were previously unknown. They indicate direction for further research.

Our findings indicate that AMPK has a great impact on most metabolic actions that are related to energy demand and supply. Those actions are adjusted via its subunit isoforms under specific physical training. Thus, there are strong co-relationships between AMPK subunit isoforms and exercises. Furthermore, the subunit isoforms are correlated with each other in some cases. The methods developed here could be used when predicting these essential relationships and enable an understanding of the functions and metabolic pathways regarding AMPK.

## 4.1 Introduction

AMP-activated protein kinase (AMPK) has emerged as a significant signaling intermediary that regulates metabolisms in response to energy demand and supply.

An investigation into the degree of activation and deactivation of AMPK subunits under exercise can provide valuable data for understanding AMPK. In particular, the effect of AMPK on muscle cellular energy status makes this protein a promising pharmacological target for disease treatment. As more AMPK regulation data are accumulated, data mining techniques can play an important role in identifying frequent patterns in the data. Association rule mining, which is commonly used in market basket analysis, can be applied to AMPK regulation.

In recent years, there has been a tremendous growth in biological data and the emergence of new, efficient experimental techniques. A variety of genomic and proteomic databases are now publicly accessible over the Internet. However, it is widely recognized that the mere gathering of discrete data is insufficient for us to discover the potential correlations amongst them. The biological interpretation and analysis of these data are crucial. Such biological data not only provides us with a good opportunity for understanding living organisms, but also poses new challenges. This has led us to the development of a new method to analyze the data.

Protein kinases regulation data can be a good foundation for understanding their structure, function, and expression. One goal, in terms of analyzing protein kinase regulation data, is to determine how an external stimulus might affect the catalytic subunit and regulatory subunit of protein kinases. Figure 4.1 presents Protein kinase $X$ uses $IRS_i$, a regulatory subunit (a second protein molecule) to control the activity of a catalytic subunit $ICS_j$. Each subunit consists of several gene encoding isoforms. Another goal is to determine what isoforms are expressed or unchanged in expression as a result of certain conditions. AMP-activated protein kinase (AMPK) has recently emerged as a potential key signaling pathway, in the regulation of exercise-induced changes in glucose and lipid metabolism in skeletal muscle [37, 237]. This enzyme is activated as a result of the alterations in cellular energy levels [181]. The activation of AMPK also exerts long-term effects at the level of both gene expression and protein synthesis, such as positive effects on glucose uptake of heart, food intake of hypothalamus, and negative effects on insulin secretion of pancreas and cholesterol synthesis of liver [130]. Hence, the investigation into the degree of activation and deactivation of subunit isoforms of AMPK will contribute to a greater understanding of AMPK and disease treatment [235].

Unfortunately, the traditional computational methods have been mainly used in sequence alignment [6], gene prediction [87], and microarray analysis. However, the efforts to develop robust methods to analyze AMPK regulation data lag behind the rate of data accumulation. Most of the current analysis rests on isolated discussion of single experimental results. Also, there has been a lack of systematical collection and interpretation of diverse AMPK regulation data. Besides, the existing approaches that seek to analyze biological data cannot cope with the AMPK regulation data that contains status messages of subunit isoforms and stimulus factors. This calls for the use of sophisticated computational techniques.

Recently, data mining techniques have emerged as a means of identifying patterns and trends from large quantities of data. Among them, association rule mining is a popular summarization and pattern extraction algorithm to identify correlations between items in transactional databases [339]. Several attempts have been made

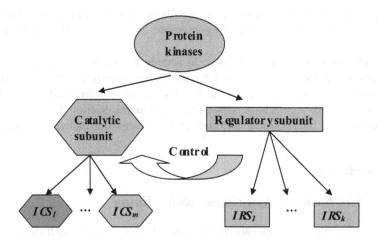

**Fig. 4.1** Catalytic subunit and Regulatory subunit of Protein kinases, in which *ICS* and *IRS* represent the isoform of catalytic subunit and regulatory subunit respectively

to mine biological databases using association rule mining [82, 298]. Earlier investigations mainly focus on discovering an association between the gene expression, genetic pathways and protein-protein interaction. However, not much work has been found to address AMPK regulation data. Hence, it is necessary to identify implicit, but potentially useful, frequent patterns from the AMPK regulation data.

An association rule is an implication of the form $X \Rightarrow Y$, where $X$ and $Y$ are itemsets. For example, as for AMPK regulation, $Y$ and $X$ can represent the subunit isoforms of AMPK that is highly expressed or unchanged in expression, and stimulus factors that describe the certain conditions such as the intensity and duration, respectively. A rule might be {moderate intensity} $\Rightarrow \{\alpha_{1a}|, \alpha_{2a} \uparrow\}$ where $\alpha_{1a}$ and $\alpha_{2a}$ represent the activity of $\alpha$ subunits of AMPK. It shows that $\alpha_{1a}$ usually has no change in expression, and $\alpha_{2a}$ is highly expressed in most experiments where the exercise intensity is moderate. Typically, this method requires a user to specify a minimum support threshold for the generation of all itemsets. However, without specific knowledge, it is difficult for users to set the support threshold. Therefore, it would be better to identify top-N interesting itemsets, instead of specifying a fixed threshold value for all itemsets of all sizes like [59].

This chapter presents a framework by which to analyze the AMPK regulation data derived from the published experimental results. FPtree (Frequent Pattern Tree) algorithm [126] is used to extract frequent itemsets efficiently, and item constraints in the closed interpretation are proposed to specify general constraints on itemset generation. A number of rules of interest are discovered from mining AMPK data. A cursory analysis of some of the like reveals numerous potential associations between the states of subunit isoforms of AMPK, or between the stimulus factor and the state of isoforms, many of which make sense biologically. Those suggesting new hypotheses may warrant further investigation. If a data set from existing experiments has missing values for some subunit isoforms that are intentionally untested in corresponding experiments, these items are filtered out ahead of mining. Furthermore, the items that are not tested by adequate experiments will be reserved in databases for future use.

This chapter is organized as follows. In Section 4.2, the basic concepts used in this chapter, are discussed. Section 4.3 presents the procedure to find association rules from AMPK regulation data. Section 4.4 explains implementation of the algorithm to discover association rules using experiments. Section 4.5 refers to our methodology and future directions. Finally, this chapter is concluded in Section 4.6.

## 4.2 Methods

### 4.2.1 The Basics of Association Rule Mining

An association rule is an implication of the form, $A \Rightarrow B$, where $A$ and $B$ are itemsets, and $A \cap B = \emptyset$. The following criteria can be used to evaluate the association rule:

1. *support* for a rule $A \Rightarrow B$ is the percentage of transactions in $D$ that contain $A \cup B$, and is defined as $supp(A \cup B)$; and
2. *confidence* for a rule $A \Rightarrow B$ is defined as $conf(A \Rightarrow B) = supp(A \cup B)/supp(A)$.

According to the support-confidence framework [4], a rule $supp(A \Rightarrow B)$ is of interest if $supp(A \cup B) \geq minsupp$ and $conf(supp(A \Rightarrow B)) \geq minconf$. In this chapter, the conventional association rule mining is extended for analyzing AMPK regulation data. Suppose $E = \{E_1, \cdots, E_n\}$ is a set of experiments. Each experiment consists of an *eid* (experiment identifier) and two itemsets, $E_i = (eid, S_i, ST_i)$; $ST_i \Rightarrow S_i$ is treated as an initial rule. Let $I = \{x \mid x \in S_i \cup ST_i, 1 \leq i \leq n\}$ be a set of items, and $A \subseteq I$ and $B \subseteq I$ be itemsets. A rule $supp(A \Rightarrow B)$ has support, $s$, in the set of experiments if $s\%$ of experiments contains $A$ and $B$. The rule has confidence, $c$, if $c\%$ of experiments containing $A$, also contain $A$ and $B$.

### 4.2.2 Definition of Problem

For regulating critical biological processes such as memory, hormone responses, and cell growth, living organisms rely on a family of enzymes called *protein kinases*. In particular, AMPK is activated in skeletal muscle in response to exercise, phosphorylating target proteins along diverse metabolic pathways, such as glucose uptake and fatty-acid oxidation. The response to environmental demands is accomplished by signal transduction by which an extracellular signal interacts with receptors at the cell surface, activating factors in signaling pathways and ultimately sustaining muscle performance by activating skeletal muscle remodeling genes. Furthermore, recent findings point to the AMPK pathway as a potential target for therapeutic strategies to restore metabolic balance to patients, such as type 2 diabetic and obesity patients. Thus, AMPK pathway is a particularly challenging problem in bioinformatics.

Recent studies [37, 235] have shown that AMP-activated protein kinase (AMPK) plays an important role in the regulation of exercise-induced changes, which occur in glucose and lipid metabolism in skeletal muscle, and gene expression and protein synthesis. AMPK contains *catalytic subunit isoforms* $\alpha_1$ and $\alpha_2$ and *regulatory subunit isoforms* $\beta_1$, $\beta_2$, $\gamma_1$, $\gamma_2$ and $\gamma_3$, and the regulation controlled by subunits is shown in Figure 4.2. The subunit isoforms congregate together to perform the functions of AMPK. Therefore, interpretation and analysis of AMPK regulation data and identification of potential associations from the data, may lead to a better understanding of its structure, function and expression. However, only limited studies have been conducted to analyze this valuable data, and the majority of these studies have focused on isolated experiments. In this chapter, a framework is proposed to discover association rules from a collection of AMPK regulation data.

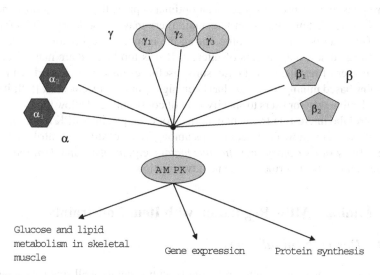

**Fig. 4.2** Subunit isoforms of AMPK and its functions

Given a set of experimental results, $E$, each result is described by a set of items. The items can be classified into two categories:

1. *Stimulus item (ST)* represents a parameter that is used to measure stimuli. For example, intensity, load and duration are generally used to measure the exercise stimuli. +++, ++, + and - indicate that the stimulus is *intense*, *high*, *moderate* and *low*, respectively.
2. *State item (S)* represents isoforms of $\alpha$, $\beta$ and $\gamma$ subunits of AMPK. ↑, |, ↓ are used to indicate *highly expressed*, *expressed* and *no change* in expression, respectively.

Items collected from different experiments contain a great deal of hidden information that may be meaningful. For example, in an observed experiment based on the training of moderate intensity treadmill, $\beta_2$ and $\gamma_2$ isoforms of AMPK are found to be highly expressed in terms of activation in white quadriceps [86]. The initial rule for this experiment can be written as $A = \{moderate\ intensity\ treadmill\} \Rightarrow B = \{\beta_{2a} \uparrow, \gamma_{2a} \uparrow\}$. It is hypothetically derived from an experiment. Nevertheless, in practice, the association rules have to be mined from an experimental data set.

The best known strategy to mining frequent itemsets is Apriori [4], which lives on the essential assumption that all itemsets have a uniform minimum support. However, in reality, the minimum support is not uniform. For example, rules containing *coffee* and *milk* or *coffee* and *sugar* usually have higher support than rules containing *coffee* and *tea*. The occurrence of a large itemset is inherently smaller than that of a small itemset in accordance with probability [318]. On the other hand, it is still troublesome for users to specify an optimal support threshold for all itemsets of all sizes. If the threshold is set too small, there may be too many results for the users. This may be time consuming during the computational phase and result in extra efforts to sort out answers of interest. If it is too large, there may be only a small number of results. In that case, some useful results can be missed. Thus, the constraint-based mining technique has been highlighted in recent work [59]; it provides a flexible way for users to specify a set of constraints and allow them to search and control the interesting frequent patterns. For example, in AMPK regulation, we may only want to know the relationships among items of different attributes, such as the activity of $\alpha_1$ *isoform* and *stimulus factors*, e.g. *intensity* and *duration*. Their explanation will be described in the next two sections.

## 4.3   Mining AMPK Regulation with Item Constraints

### 4.3.1   Deriving Initial Items

In general, mining of association rules starts with generating all frequent itemsets. The mined data set can be derived from different experimental results. The experimental conditions have to be considered in order to find out correct association rules. To discover frequent itemsets, initial items from experimental data, including experimental conditions such as moderate intensity and treadmill training, are to be derived. Also, the item derived from AMPK regulation data includes not only its status measurement but also item name such as $\alpha_{1a} \mid$ and $\beta_{2a} \uparrow$.

In AMPK regulation data, *activity*, *protein expression* and *phosphorylation* are used as testing indexes for $\alpha$, whereas only protein expression is used for $\beta$ and $\gamma$. The following steps can be used to generate initial items from experimental data:

- Generate initial rules $ST \Rightarrow S$ from experimental data where $S$ and $ST$ represent *state itemset* and *stimulus itemset*, respectively and
- Derive a set of initial items $I = S \cup ST$.

It is illustrated in the form of $\{x_1, x_2, \cdots, x_n\}$ where $x_i \in I$. Let the experimental universe be $EID = \{E_1, E_2, E_3, E_4\}$. Table 4.1 represents an example of initial items derived from different experiments. Each row in Table 4.1 corresponds to one experiment for AMPK regulation. There are four initial rules, $\{\phi^+, \varphi^-\} \Rightarrow \{\alpha_{1a} \downarrow, \alpha_{1p} \uparrow\}$, $\{\phi^+, \varphi^-\} \Rightarrow \{\alpha_{1a} \downarrow, \alpha_{1e}|, \alpha_{1p}|, \beta_{1e}|, \beta_{2e}|\}$, $\{\phi^+, \varphi^+\} \Rightarrow \{\alpha_{1a} \downarrow, \alpha_{1e}|, \beta_{1e}|\}$, and $\{\phi^{++}, \varphi^+\} \Rightarrow \{\alpha_{1a}|, \alpha_{1e} \downarrow, \alpha_{1p}|, \beta_{1e}|, \beta_{2e}|\}$ where subscripts $a, p$ and $e$ represent *activity*, *phosphorylation* and *protein expression*, respectively. Hence we can say $\forall A \subseteq \{\alpha_{1a} \downarrow, \alpha_{1a}|, \alpha_{1e}|, \alpha_{1e} \downarrow, \alpha_{1p} \uparrow, \alpha_{1p}|, \beta_{1e}|, \beta_{2e}|, \phi^+, \phi^{++}, \varphi^-, \varphi^+\}$ is an itemset as usual, and $\forall y \in \{\alpha_{1a} \downarrow, \alpha_{1a}|, \alpha_{1e}|, \alpha_{1e} \downarrow, \alpha_{1p} \uparrow, \alpha_{1p}|, \beta_{1e}|, \beta_{2e}|, \phi^+, \phi^{++}, \varphi^-, \varphi^+\}$ can be viewed as an initial item.

**Table 4.1** An example of experiment database

| EID | Items | | | | | $\phi$ | $\varphi$ |
|-----|-------|---|---|---|---|--------|-----------|
| | $\alpha_1$ | | | $\beta$ | | | |
| $E_1$ | $\alpha_{1a} \downarrow$ | $-$ | $\alpha_{1p} \uparrow$ | $-$ | $-$ | $\phi^+$ | $\varphi^-$ |
| $E_2$ | $\alpha_{1a} \downarrow$ | $\alpha_{1e}|$ | $\alpha_{1p}|$ | $\beta_{1e}|$ | $\beta_{2e}|$ | $\phi^+$ | $\varphi^-$ |
| $E_3$ | $\alpha_{1a} \downarrow$ | $\alpha_{1e}|$ | $-$ | $\beta_{1e}|$ | $-$ | $\phi^+$ | $\varphi^+$ |
| $E_4$ | $\alpha_{1a}|$ | $\alpha_{1e} \downarrow$ | $\alpha_{1p}|$ | $\beta_{1e}|$ | $\beta_{2e}|$ | $\phi^{++}$ | $\varphi^+$ |

In order to determine association rules, the frequent itemsets need to be sorted out from the obtained initial items.

## 4.3.2 Specifying Item Constraints

*FP-tree* algorithm [126] constructs a frequent pattern tree that has an extended prefix-tree structure and stores quantitative information about frequent patterns. It can generate a complete set of frequent patterns. The typical data format for using this algorithm is shown in Table 4.1. We notice that not every item does occur in all experiments in this Table. Our method marks these items with *filtering symbols* so as to filter out the itemsets that contain such items during the itemset generation. Actually, if an itemset is not tested in most of the experiments, it will not be considered when finding association rules for the time being, instead it will be reserved for future use.

Suppose *support*$(X, E)$ denotes the support of $X$ in experiment $E$ and $f(X, E)$ represents the occurrence of itemset $X$ in $E$, it can be defined as:

$$support(X,E) = |f(X,E)|/|E| \tag{4.1}$$

where $f(X, E) = \{E_i \in E \mid E_i \text{ contains } X\}$. For example, *suppotr*$(\alpha_{1e}|, E)$ in Table 4.1 is equal 2/4 or 50%.

$X$ is a high occurrence itemset if *support*$(X, E) \geq$ *minoccur* (*minimum occurrence*). To avoid missing valuable initial itemsets, we assume *minoccur* = $2/|E|$, which is the lower bound of minimum support corresponding to the support requirement of at least 2 experiments. Otherwise, it is called a *low occurrence itemset*. Consequently, a collection of *initial interesting itemsets* can be obtained in light of the initialized *filtering symbols* and given *minimum occurrence*.

To extract frequent itemsets, users usually need to specify a fixed minimum support but this method has been criticized due to its difficulty [59, 126, 318]. As described above, it is quite subtle to set a minimum support: a too small threshold may result in the output of many redundant patterns, whereas a too big one may generate no answer or miss interesting knowledge. In addition, the probability of occurrence of a larger size itemset is inherently much smaller than that of a smaller size itemset [59]. A more flexible option is to allow users to specify different thresholds in accordance with different itemsets [59]. Consequently, the *top-N* interesting itemsets are returned as answers.

Suppose a ***k-itemset*** denotes a set of items containing $k$ items. We have the following two definitions.

**Definition 4.1.** *Top-N interesting k*-itemsets. Suppose a ***k-itemset*** is sorted in descending order by their supports. Let $s$ be the support of the *Nth k-itemset* in the sorted list. The ***top-N interesting k*-itemsets** represent the set of *k-itemsets* whose supports are equal to or larger than $s$.

From the observation, it is possible that there are multiple itemsets that have the same support $s$. The ***top-N interesting k*-itemsets** may contain more than $N$ itemsets. In this extreme case, it will be reported to the user, rather than returning all of them [59].

**Definition 4.2.** *Top-N* interesting itemsets is the union of the ***top-N* interesting *k*-itemsets** where $1 \leq k \leq k_{max}$ and $k_{max}$ is the upper bound of the size of itemsets we would like to find. An itemset is of interest if, and only if, it is in the ***top-N* interesting itemsets**.

*Example 4.1.* In Table 4.1, we specify $k_{max} = 7$ because the maximal tested items in every experiment are 7. The **interesting 1-itemsets** is $\{\alpha_{1a} \downarrow, \alpha_{1e}|, \alpha_{1p}|, \beta_{1e}|, \beta_{2e}|, \phi^+, \varphi^-, \varphi^+\}$ after filtering $\alpha_{1a}|, \alpha_{1e} \downarrow, \alpha_{1p} \uparrow$ and $\phi^{++}$ by formula 4.2. As a result, ***top-1* interesting 1-itemsets** $= \{\alpha_{1a} \downarrow\}$ and ***top-2* interesting 1-itemsets** $= \{\alpha_{1a} \downarrow, \beta_{1e}|, \phi^+\}$.

From the observation, it is clearly impractical to enumerate all ***top-N* interesting itemsets**. Although several ***top-N*** mining algorithms [59, 66, 126, 318] already exist, they focus, without exception, on finding all ***top-N* itemsets**. However, this may be time-consuming and can lead to many useless or uninteresting itemsets. For example, itemsets from {*training, glycogen, diabetes, nicotinic acid, intensity, duration*} rather than their subsets are of interest because a part of the testing indexes cannot correctly describe an experiment. Our method is to partition a set of items, $I$, into several bins, where each bin $B_j$ contains a subset of items in $I$. We use item constraint in a similar way to the enumeration-based specification defined in [318] so that the items in a bin are not distinguished in terms of the specification.

For example, $B_1 = \{\beta_{1e}, \beta_{2e}\}$ and $B_2 = \{\alpha_{1a}, \alpha_{1e}\}$ represent that the user is interested in protein expression of $\beta$, rather than $\alpha$ and $\gamma$, and only *activity* and *protein expression* of $\alpha$, rather than *phosphorylation*. The constraint can be expressed in the following brief formula:

$$IC_i(B_{i1}, \cdots, B_{im}) = N_i \qquad (4.2)$$

where $B_{ij} \cap B_{ik} = \emptyset$, $1 \leq j, k \leq m, j \neq k$. $N_i$ is the number of itemsets satisfying $IC_i$ in terms of a derived support described in Section 4.6. It explicitly defines what particular items we focus on and which should be presented in the identification of frequent patterns.

The concept of *closed interpretation* in [318] is adopted as well. An itemset $X \in I$ satisfies a constraint $IC_i$ in the closed interpretation if $X$ contains exactly one item from each $B_{ij}$ in $IC_i$, and these items are completely different. Suppose $IC_j$ is an item constraint, and $|IC_j| = k$. As for close interpretation, a collection of *k-itemsets* can be generated. These itemsets are sorted in light of their support in descending order. Let the $N_j$th greatest support be $\theta$. Consequently, all *k-itemsets*, with support not less than $\theta$, are interesting due to the constraint. We call them **top-$N_j$** interesting itemsets of $IC_j$ in the closed interpretation. Usually, users can specify several item constraints. In this scenario, we want to find **top-$N_j$** interesting itemsets for each **top-$N_i$** in the closed interpretation.

Suppose, for example, we partition the items in Table 4.1 into seven bins: $B_1 = \{\alpha_{1a} \downarrow, \alpha_{1a}|\}$, $B_2 = \{\alpha_{1e}|, \alpha_{1e} \downarrow\}$, $B_3 = \{\alpha_{1p} \uparrow, \alpha_{1p}|\}$, $B_4 = \{\beta_{1e}|\}$, $B_5 = \{\beta_{2e}|\}$, $B_6 = \{\phi^+, \phi^{++}\}$, $B_7 = \{\varphi^-, \varphi^+\}$. Let $IC_1(B_1, B_2, B_3) = 2$, $IC_2(B_4, B_5) = 3$ and $IC_3(B_6, B_7) = 2$. Consider itemset $X_1 = \{\alpha_{1a} \downarrow, \alpha_{1e}|\}$, $X_2 = \{\beta_{1e}|, \beta_{2e}|\}$ and $X_3 = \{\phi^+, \varphi^-\}$, they correspond to bin patterns $(B_1, B_2, B_3)$, $(B_4, B_5)$ and $(B_6, B_7)$, respectively. Therefore, we say that $X_1$ satisfies $IC_1$ in the closed interpretation; $X_2$ satisfies $IC_2$ in the closed interpretation; and $X_3$ satisfies $IC_3$ in the closed interpretation.

Until now, we have not referred closely to how the filtering symbols are specified. The untested items in experiments need to be pruned before going on to set up item constraints. Our approach converts the initial items of experiments into the format of non-negative integer. Consequently, each bin can contain several non-negative integers but any two bins must be disjoint. Table 4.2 is a conversion of Table 4.1, in which 8, 12, 29 and 30 correspond to the untested items regarding $\alpha_{1e}$, $\alpha_{1p}$, $\beta_{1e}$ and $\beta_{2e}$, respectively. Therefore, the bins defined in the last paragraph can be converted into $B_1 = \{1, 2\}$, $B_2 = \{5, 6\}$, $B_3 = \{10, 11\}$, $B_4 = \{26\}$, $B_5 = \{29\}$, $B_6 = \{91, 92\}$, and $B_7 = \{100, 101\}$. These filtering symbols are reserved in the data set and will be skipped when finding patterns from the initial interesting itemsets.

*Example 4.2.* In Table 4.2, the non-negative integers 8, 12, 27 and 30 represent the specified filtering symbols. They correspond to the untested items with respect to $\alpha_{1e}$, $\alpha_{1p}$, $\beta_{1e}$ and $\beta_{2e}$, respectively.

**Table 4.2** A converted experiment dataset

| EID | Items | | | | | | |
|-----|-------|----|----|----|----|----|-----|
| | $\alpha_1$ | | | $\beta$ | | $\phi$ | $\varphi$ |
| $E_1$ | 1 | 8 | 11 | 27 | 30 | 91 | 100 |
| $E_2$ | 1 | 6 | 10 | 26 | 29 | 91 | 100 |
| $E_3$ | 1 | 6 | 12 | 26 | 30 | 91 | 101 |
| $E_4$ | 2 | 5 | 10 | 26 | 29 | 92 | 101 |

### 4.3.3 Discovering Association Rules

The obtained *top-$N_i$* **interesting itemsets** for item constraints in the closed interpretation can then be used to construct association rules. There are two approaches to identify association rules, depending on which antecedents or consequents of rules the item constraint *IC* are defined. Let $X$ and $X'$ be top interesting itemsets from *IC* and *IC'*, respectively, and $X' \subset X$.

1. if $supp(X)/supp(X') \geq minconf$, $X' \to X - X'$ is a rule of interest.
2. if $supp(X)/supp(X - X') \geq minconf$, $X - X' \to X'$ is a rule of interest.

In addition, those rules that do not make sense biologically are pruned while mining AMPK regulation data. Hence, the valid rules should conform to the rules as given below:

- *Rule*1: $A \Rightarrow B$, $A \subseteq S$ and $B \subseteq S$ and
- *Rule*2: $A \Rightarrow B$, $A \subseteq ST$ and $B \subseteq S$.

If the antecedent or consequent of a rule contains either both state items and stimulus items, or only stimulus items, it will be pruned. Obviously, the relation between only stimulus items such as *intensity* and *time* is not meaningful in biology at all. Besides, state items actually rely on stimulus items; therefore, they should not be included in the antecedent and consequent of a rule simultaneously. These kinds of rules are uninteresting and need to be pruned, and the search space can be reduced.

## 4.4 Results

### 4.4.1 Pre-processing of Experimental Data

FP-tree algorithm is applied to generate all frequent itemsets and find association rules that make sense biologically. We experimented on the published experimental data of AMPK regulation, in which AMPK is activated by endurance training in human skeletal muscle. The data is collected through searching the NCBI database and surely ranges over all the openly available data. Originally, the data contained

17 attributes, 46 items and 45 experiments. After conversion into the format of non-negative integer, there are 57 items owing to the insert of filtering items. In addition, initial items from experiments are divided into state items and stimulus items. Each item corresponds to an attribute/value pair.

AMPK consists of state items: *catalytic subunit* ($\alpha$) and *regulatory subunit* ($\beta$, $\gamma$). The isoforms ($\alpha_1$, $\alpha_2$) of $\alpha$ are measured by *activity*, *phosphorylation* and *protein expression* but the isoforms of $\beta$ and $\gamma$ ($\beta_1$, $\beta_2$, $\gamma_1$, $\gamma_2$, $\gamma_3$) are measured only by *protein expression*. As a result, there are 11 state items including all isoforms of AMPK, $\alpha_{1a}$, $\alpha_{1e}$, $\alpha_{1p}$, $\alpha_{2a}$, $\alpha_{2e}$, $\alpha_{2p}$, $\beta_{1e}$, $\beta_{2e}$, $\gamma_{1e}$, $\gamma_{2e}$ and $\gamma_{3e}$. Six stimulus indexes, including *training*, *glycogen*, *diabetes*, *nicotinic acid*, *intensity* and *duration*, are considered.

Table 4.3 is a random example of the activity and expression of AMPK in skeletal muscle, in which $N$, $I$ and $D$ represent *nicotinic acid*, *intensity* and *duration*, respectively. Each column corresponds to an experiment. The subscripts $a$ and $e$ mean *activity*, and *protein expression*, respectively. 1 and 5 represent *no change* in corresponding items; 2 and 6 represent *expressed*; 50 and 51 represent *trained* and *untrained*, respectively; 60 represents *normal glycogen*; 70 represents *normal nicotinic acid*; 100, 101 and 103 represent the duration under 20 minutes, between 20 and 60 minutes and above 90 minutes, respectively; 90, 91 and 92 represent the *maximal oxygen uptake* (VO(2)max) under 50%, VO(2)max between 65% and 75%, and VO(2)max between 80% and 100%, respectively.

**Table 4.3** Activity and expression of $\alpha_{1a}$ and $\alpha_{1e}$ of AMPK in skeletal muscle

| $\alpha_{1a}$ | $\alpha_{1e}$ | Training | Glycogen | Diabetes | N | I | D |
|---|---|---|---|---|---|---|---|
| 2 | 5 | 50 | 60 | 70 | 80 | 92 | 101 |
| 1 | 5 | 51 | 60 | 70 | 80 | 90 | 103 |
| 1 | 6 | 51 | 60 | 70 | 80 | 91 | 100 |
| 1 | 6 | 51 | 60 | 70 | 80 | 91 | 101 |

To generate constraint specification, we group the items from the same attribute into a bin, yielding 17 bins for the 17 attributes. Although each bin corresponds to only one attribute, each attribute can contain several state measurements. Thus, each bin can have more than one item. We organise these items into seventeen disjoint non-negative integer intervals so that each bin $B_i$ contains the items matching integers in the $i$th interval. Table 4.4 shows the specified intervals, and the details can be found at http://bioinformatics.gxu.edu.cn/bio/data/LNAI8335/8335-4.zip. We specify item constraint $IC_i$ in the closed interpretation. Suppose $BV_i$ represents a bin variable.

$$IC_i(BV_1, \cdots, BV_k) = N_i, 0 \leq k \leq k_{max} \tag{4.3}$$

where $k_{max}$ is the upper bound of the size of itemsets that users want to find. We specify $N_i$ as the number of itemsets that satisfies constraint $IC_i$ with supports $\geq$ $\theta_i(BV_1, \cdots, BV_k)$, where

**Table 4.4** The bins and corresponding interval

| $B_i$ | Attribute | Interval | $B_i$ | Attribute | Interval |
|-------|-----------|----------|-------|-----------|----------|
| $B_1$ | $\alpha_{1a}$ | [1, 4] | $B_{10}$ | $\gamma_{2e}$ | [34, 37] |
| $B_2$ | $\alpha_{1e}$ | [5, 8] | $B_{11}$ | $\gamma_{3e}$ | [38, 40] |
| $B_3$ | $\alpha_{1a}$ | [9, 12] | $B_{12}$ | training | [50, 51] |
| $B_4$ | $\alpha_{1a}$ | [13, 16] | $B_{13}$ | glycogen | [60, 62] |
| $B_5$ | $\alpha_{1e}$ | [17, 20] | $B_{14}$ | diabetes | [70, 71] |
| $B_6$ | $\alpha_{2p}$ | [21, 24] | $B_{15}$ | nicotinic acid | [80, 81] |
| $B_7$ | $\alpha_{1e}$ | [25, 27] | $B_{16}$ | intensity | [90, 93] |
| $B_8$ | $\alpha_{2e}$ | [28, 30] | $B_{17}$ | duration | [100, 103] |
| $B_9$ | $\gamma_{1e}$ | [31, 33] | | | |

$$\theta_i(BV_1, \cdots, BV_k) = \begin{cases} 0.044 & if \ \lambda^{k-1} \times S(BV_1) \times \cdots \times S(BV_k) \leq 0.044 \\ 1 & if \ \lambda^{k-1} \times S(BV_1) \times \cdots \times S(BV_k) > 1 \\ \lambda^{k-1} \times S(BV_1) \times \cdots \times S(BV_k) & otherwise \end{cases}$$

(4.4)

where $S(BV_i)$ is the smallest support of the items in the bin $BV_i$. $\lambda$ is an integer larger than 1 used to slow down the decrease of $S(BV_1) * \cdots * S(BV_k)$ in case of large $k$ [318].

### 4.4.2 Rule Generation

Unlike traditional methods, our approach starts with pruning items of low occurrence, rather than generating *frequent itemsets* directly. *FP-tree* algorithm is implemented on the obtained initial items to generate initial interesting itemsets. The process is repeated until all initial interesting itemsets are extracted. The procedure of finding association rules consists of four phases:

1. Generate *initial interesting itemsets* from *initial items*.
2. Sort out the itemsets containing no filtering symbols.
3. Set up bin $B_j$ and item constraint $IC_i$.
4. Identify association rules using $IC_i$.

The value of $N_i$ is determined by formulas 4.3 and 4.4. We assign $\lambda$ with 5 like [59]. $k_{max} = 9$ is set using the principle of rule generation in Section 4.3 because the itemsets containing more than 9 items are not interesting according to the specified maximum item constraints $IC(B_9, B_{10}, B_{11}, B_{12}, B_{13}, B_{14}, B_{15}, B_{16}, B_{17})$. There are 47 item constraints specified in a file for the itemsets in the closed interpretation such as $IC(B_{12}, B_{13}, B_{14}, B_{15}, B_{16}, B_{17})$ and $IC(B_1, B_4)$. The constraints are classified into two categories:

1. Contain all items of stimulus factors at least; and
2. Contain only items of AMPK subunits.

They enumerate the items in a bin in the closed interpretation, on the basis that the user is interested in only the items with respect to specification, rather than all possible combinations of items.

Based on Definition 4.2, the obtained itemsets, due to item constraints, need to be sorted in light of their supports in descending order, by which we can generate the *top-$N_i$* interesting itemsets for each corresponding bin $IC_i$. Therefore, the mining will focus on finding out association rules on the basis of these top-N interesting itemsets. Table 4.5 shows the results of *initial interesting itemsets, itemsets without filtering symbols, sorted itemsets in bins in the closed interpretation* and *top-N interesting itemsets in bins*. From the observation, the search space is greatly reduced as a result of the use of filtering symbols and item constraints.

**Table 4.5** The result of itemset generation

| itemset | Number |
| --- | --- |
| Initial interesting itemset | 964519 |
| Itemset without filtering symbols | 14985 |
| Sorted itemset in bins | 97 |
| Top-N interesting itemset in bins | 97 |

The *top-N* interesting itemsets are then used to identify frequent patterns based on the defined criteria in Section 4.3.3, by which some uninteresting rules are pruned. We vary the minimum confidence starting from 0.4 to 1 by increasing 0.1 each time. Figure 4.3 shows the result of frequent patterns. We observe that there is no sharp drop in rule output when setting the minimum confidence from 0.7 to 1 in comparison with 0.6. Therefore, we select the results by 0.7 in contrast to the results by 0.6 in the following analysis. There are 74 and 51 association rules by minimum confidence 0.6 and 0.7, respectively. From these rules, we can find many potential correlations between itemsets. The rules by 0.7 are classified into the form of Rule1 (40 rules) and the form of Rule2 (11 rules) in terms of the definition in section 4.3.3. Nevertheless, the rules need to be pruned because some of them can overlap with each other. Suppose $R_i: A_i \rightarrow B_i$ and $R_j: A_j \rightarrow B_j$ are two rules. The pruning complies with the principles below:

- *Delete $R_j$, if $A_i = A_j$ and $B_i \supseteq B_j$*
- *Replace $R_i$ and $R_j$ with $A_i \vee A_j \rightarrow B_i$, if $B_i = B_j$, $A_i \not\subset A_j$ and $A_j \not\subset A_i$*

Finally, we obtain 32 rules after pruning. For example, $29 \Rightarrow 32$ are removed due to $29 \Rightarrow 6, 32$; $14 \Rightarrow 1$ and $13 \Rightarrow 1$. are replaced by $14 \vee 13 \rightarrow 1$ where 1, 6, 13, 14, 29 and 32 denote $\alpha 1a \downarrow$, $\alpha 1e|$, $\alpha 2a \downarrow$, $\alpha 2a|$, $beta2e|$ and $gamma2e|$, respectively. For convenience, we reconvert the integers into readable symbols in Section 4.2. Table 4.6 shows some selected association rules mined from the AMPK regulation data set, in which $t$, $I$, $T$, $ng$, $lg$, $hg$, $nc$, $ut$ and $nd$ represent *time, intensity, trained, normal glycogen, low glycogen, high glycogen, untrained* and *normal diabetes*, respectively.

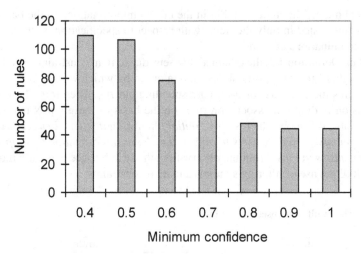

**Fig. 4.3** The frequent patterns for AMPK regulation data

**Table 4.6** Selected association rules from AMPK regulation data set

| Association rule |
|---|
| 1  $\{t^+, ng, I^+, nc, ut, nd\} \vee \{t^+, hg, I^+, nc, nd, T\} \vee \{t^{++}, nc, I^+, ut, ng, nd\} \rightarrow \{\alpha_{1a}\downarrow\}$ |
| 2  $\{t^+, ng, I^+, lg, nc, nd, T\} \rightarrow \{\alpha_{1a}\downarrow, \alpha_{2a}\vert\}$ |
| 3  $\{t^+, ng, I^{++}, ng, nc, nd, T\} \rightarrow \{\alpha_{2a}\vert\}$ |
| 4  $\{t, ng, I^{++}, ut, nc, nd\} \rightarrow \{\alpha_{2a}\uparrow\}$ |
| 5  $\{t^+, ng, I^{++}, ng, nc, nd\} \rightarrow \{\alpha_{2p}\vert, \alpha_{1p}\vert\}$ |
| 6  $\{\alpha_{1a}\uparrow\} \rightarrow \{\alpha_{2a}\uparrow\}$ |
| 7  $\{\alpha_{1e}\vert\} \rightarrow \{\alpha_{2e}\vert\}$ |
| 8  $\{\alpha_{1p}\uparrow\} \rightarrow \{\alpha_{1a}\downarrow, \alpha_{2a}\uparrow, \alpha_{2p}\uparrow\}$ |
| 9  $\{\beta_{1e}\vert, \beta_{2e}\vert\} \vee \{\gamma_{1e}\vert, \gamma_{2e}\uparrow, \gamma_{3e}\vert\} \rightarrow \{\alpha_{2a}\uparrow, \alpha_{1a}\downarrow\}$ |
| 10  $\{\gamma_{1e}\vert, \gamma_{3e}\vert\} \rightarrow \{\gamma_{2e}\uparrow, \beta_{1e}\vert, \beta_{2e}\vert\}$ |
| 11  $\{\alpha_{1p}\vert\} \rightarrow \{\alpha_{2p}\vert\}$ |
| 12  $\{\alpha_{1e}\vert, \alpha_{2e}\downarrow\} \rightarrow \{\beta_{1e}\downarrow, \beta_{2e}\vert\}$ |

### *4.4.3  Performance Comparison and Feature Discovery*

Our miner (eFP) extends the FPgrowth* method [114] to identify the potential correlation from AMPK regulation. Table 4.7 presents a performance comparison between our miner and algorithms FPgrowth [126], dEclat [335] and MAFIA [34]. In the comparison, we use a synthetic sparse dataset *T40I10D100K* http://www.almaden.ibm.com/cs/quest/syndata.html and a dense dataset *connect-4* at http://www.cs.sfu.ca/~wangk/ucidata/dataset/connect-4/.

In the FI (frequent itemset) mining, the comparison shows that eFP outperforms FPgrowth, dEclat and MAFLA algorithms, and can still run for a small minimum support. It is observed that both dElcat and MAFIA suffer from high memory

**Table 4.7** Performance comparison in mining FI (frequent itemsets)

| Miner | Data set | Minimum support (%) | CPU Time(s) |
|---|---|---|---|
| eFP | T40I10D100K | $0.05 \leq minsupp \leq 2$ | [4.5, 390] |
| FPgrowth | T40I10D100K | $0.05 \leq minsupp \leq 2$ | [9.5, 390] |
| dEclat | T40I10D100K | $0.25 \leq minsupp \leq 2$ | [7.9, 400] |
| MAFIA | T40I10D100K | $0.75 \leq minsupp \leq 2$ | [60, 5936] |
| eFP | connect-4 | $20 \leq minsupp \leq 90$ | [0.04, 740] |
| FPgrowth | connect-4 | $20 \leq minsupp \leq 90$ | [0.04, 740] |
| dEclat | connect-4 | $20 \leq minsupp \leq 60$ | [1, 97] |
| MAFIA | connect-4 | $20 \leq minsupp \leq 80$ | [8.1, 593] |

consumption and low speed when a small minimum support is used. eFP has almost the same running time as FPgrowth in case of the dense dataset or very low levels minimum support, but shows a speedup when a sparser dataset is applied. eFP uses the compact FPtree [114], it not only spends less time on constructing and traversing the trees, than the time on TID-array intersections (dEclat) and bitvector and operations (MAFLA), but also needs less main memory space for storing FPtrees than that for storing diffsets or bitvectors. Thus eFP runs faster than the other three algorithms, and it performs well, even when giving very small minimum support.

In addition, our framework includes some novel features, by which to efficiently identify the association rules of interest. Preprocessing of experiment data is used to convert the qualitative data into quantitative data (non-negative integers). Particularly, filtering symbols are used to assist in pruning the untested items. They facilitate the identification of frequent itemsets. The constraint-based mining technique, namely top-N interesting itemsets, provides a flexible way for users to specify a set of constraints and allow them to search and control the interesting frequent patterns. The experiments discover a number of interesting frequent patterns that make sense biologically. They not only demonstrate former experiments but also predict some potential results that were unknown previously. These can benefit to the understanding of the signalling pathway of AMPK in regulating metabolism, and disease diagnosis and treatment.

### 4.4.4 Interpretation

AMP-activated protein kinase (AMPK) is a protein kinase which is ubiquitously expressed and functioned as a stress sensor of the cellular energy status. A functional AMPK exists as a heterotrimeric complex comprising one catalytic subunit and two regulatory subunits $\beta$ and $\gamma$. In mammals, each subunit is encoded by multiple genes ($\alpha_1$, $\alpha_2$, $\beta_1$, $\beta_2$, $\gamma_1$, $\gamma_2$, $\gamma_3$) [131]. AMPK activity is regulated not only by cellular AMP/ATP ratio, but also by upstream kinases. The skeletal muscle is one of most energy turnover tissue in mammals. AMPK was found to play an important role in the regulation of muscle metabolism. We have selected 45 experiments in relevant bio/ medical literatures in Medline by searching the NCBI using keywords

"*AMPK*" and "*human skeletal muscle*" (103 papers) and "*AMPK*" and "*endurance training*" (16 papers), respectively.

We try to find out potential relationships between the AMPK isoform expression and activity, and association between subunits. As mentioned above, this relationship is critical to assist biologists in further predicting AMPK pathways. These are usually hidden in experimental data and these pathways are not easy to identify by traditional statistics. From the experimental results in this study, we have selected 12 association rules to describe AMPK regulation in skeletal muscle, shown in Table 4.6. For example, as for rule 1 in Table 4.6, the items from the rule are mentioned in 27% of the relevant experiments, but only 2% or 0% for those items in other rules, such as $\{ng, t^-, nc, nd, I^{++}, T\}$ and $\{\alpha_{1a} \downarrow\}$ (2%), $\{ng, t^{++}, nc, nd, I^{++}, T\}$ and $\{\alpha_{1a} \downarrow\}$ (0%), $\{ng, t^+, nc, nd, I^{++}, T\}$ and $\{\alpha_{1a}|\}$ (2%), $\{ng, t^+, nc, nd, I^+, ut\}$ and $\{\alpha_{1a}|\}$ (0%), $\{ng, t^+, nc, nd, I^{++}, ut\}$ and $\{\alpha_{1a} \uparrow\}$ (2%) and $\{ng, t^{++}, nc, nd, I^{++}, ut\}$ and $\{\alpha_{1a} \uparrow\}$ (0%). In other words, the items in rule 1 occur much more frequently than those from other rules under the same indexes. The remaining rules can be explained in the same way. These can be secondary evidence to support the fact that our chosen rules are more important than the other ones.

The rules by 0.7 (minimum confidence) in Table 4.6 are a subset of the originally obtained rules. They not only show that in most of the experiments where stimuli were imposed the isoforms of AMPK can be activated, but also represent that specific correlations between the states of isoforms exist. For example, rule 4 in Table 4.6 states that in most of the cases where $\alpha_{1a}$ was highly expressed, $\alpha_{2a}$ was highly expressed too. The rest of the rules in the table can be interpreted in a similar manner. In particular, the rules that are not previously known will be highlighted.

Looking at Table 4.6 and the supplementary rules, it is seen that the expression of $\alpha$, $\beta$ and $\gamma$ varies from diverse exercise stimuli. In particular, skeletal muscle expresses predominantly the $\alpha_2$ and $\beta_2$ subunits. Referring to the rules by 0.6, we see $\beta_1$, $\beta_2$, $\gamma_1$ and $\gamma_3$ except $\gamma_{2e}$ are also activated (interacting with $\alpha$) in response to endurance training. This is due to $\beta$ and $\gamma$ that are two regulatory subunits, they are activated only when they are associated with $\alpha$ subunit. However, these rules have a slightly lower confidence than the cutoff threshold (70%), which would help explain their absence in the rules by 0.7. Synthetically, these factors/subunits/isoforms $\alpha_{1a}$, $\alpha_{2a}$, $\alpha_{1p}$, $\alpha_{2p}$, $\alpha_{1e}$, $\alpha_{2e}$, $\beta_{1e}$, $\beta_{2e}$, $\gamma_{1e}$ and $\gamma_{3e}$ are actively involved in regulating the metabolism in response to energy demand and supply in skeletal muscle. We seek more experiments to ascertain the characteristic of $\gamma_{2e}$ (in white muscle). In addition, we see a number of rules that state the latent correlation between the isoforms of AMPK. Most of them are new and make sense biologically. Furthermore, we can predict some latent associations that are selected for biologists to test in future experiments.

From our observations, most of the found rules except rule 2, 3, 4, 5 were unknown previously. They are important due to the identification of innovative correlations between AMPK subunits, which imply meaningful information for understanding their association and regulation in signalling pathways. Recent experimental results also demonstrate this [19, 92, 130]. We also view rule 1 as a type of specific rule using disjunctive normal form in the antecedent. This rule is able to integrate the knowledge from three sub-rules and lead to new knowledge using comparison amongst and between them. The details can be seen below.

Looking at rule 1 in Table 4.6, the activation of $\alpha_1$-AMPK usually has no change if the exercise intensity is not high enough and the duration is not extra long. Regardless of the status of training, glycogen, diabetes and nicotinic acid, $\alpha_1$ activity remains unchanged. Although some experiments suggested that AMPK can be substantially activated during maximal sprint-type exercise in humans [56, 100, 225]. Unfortunately, this rule cannot be generated at this stage due to insufficient experimental support. Rule 1 is a novel point since we only have seen $\alpha_1$ activity changes in very few experiments. In addition, it is innovative because the disjunction normal form of antecedents may simultaneously integrate information from multiple experiments. Thus, we determine that $\alpha_1$ activity cannot be significantly affected by the status of training, glycogen, diabetes and nicotinic acid because $\alpha_2$ instead of $\alpha_1$ predominantly localized in skeletal muscle. Such comparison cannot be achieved through traditionally isolated experiments. This can be tested in future experiments and aids in understanding the properties of $\alpha_1$. Thus, the regulation of AMPK in skeletal muscle is probably relied on $\alpha_2$ rather than $\alpha_1$. Furthermore, AMPK may be a critical mediator or exercise-induced changes in glucose uptake and fatty acid oxidation in human skeletal muscle, and the AMPK $\alpha_2$-containing heterotrimer is possible to be the predominant complex responsible for the regulation in both healthy and diabetic subjects.

Looking at rules 2, 3 and 4 in Table 4.6, $\alpha_{2a}$ is expressed in skeletal muscles from untrained to trained individuals. Nevertheless, $\alpha_{2a}$ is only highly expressed in skeletal muscle from well-trained individuals in both moderate-intensity and high-intensity training. Importantly, $\alpha_2$ activity is probably activated more easily in skeletal muscle from untrained individuals than well-trained individuals at the same relative intensity. These associations are in accordance with that of [236, 241, 321, 332]; $\alpha_{1a}$ is usually unchanged below high-intensity training, which is in agreement with the results of [103, 321]. A recent study also supports these rules [316]. These findings reveal that $\alpha_2$ and $\alpha_1$, may play different physiological roles in mediating metabolic events in skeletal muscle. Actually, AMPK $\alpha_2$ is predominantly localized in skeletal muscle, heart and liver, whereas $\alpha_1$ is widely distributed. In addition, the acute activation of $\alpha_2$-AMPK during exercise may result in not only a significant increased glucose disposal in muscle but also decreased malonyl-CoA contents, which might ameliorate insulin resistance and improve glycemia [235]. These may explain the above rules. Indeed, AMPK signaling was reduced by either overexpressing a kinase-dead $\alpha_2$-AMPK construct or knocking out the catalytic $\alpha_2$-isoform [166, 182]. Although an increase in $\alpha_2$ activity of subjects with type 2 diabetes was found during acute exercise, accompanying a significant decrease in blood glucose concentrations [235], we need more results to establish this rule.

Looking at rule 5, $\alpha$-AMPK phosphorylation on the $\alpha_1$ and $\alpha_2$ are increased in skeletal muscle from well-trained individuals with high-intensity and moderate duration training. This is because the phosphorylation of $\alpha_1$ and $\alpha_2$ is more relative to cell regulation by environment stress. In contrast, the expression of $\alpha_2$ tends to be gene regulation. This suggests that AMPK activity or upstream kinase(s) is being regulated by training, which is in agreement with the results of [62, 181, 261]. A newly published literature also defends this rule [63].

Looking at rules 6 and 7, both AMPK $\alpha_1$ and $\alpha_2$ expressed in skeletal muscle. There is no clear evidence that $\alpha_2$ activity is leaded by $\alpha_1$ since they are actually independent with each other. In [166], $\alpha_1$ protein expression was increased 2-3-fold in $\alpha_2$ knockout mice, while $\alpha_2$ protein level in $\alpha_1$ knockout mice is comparable with that observed in WT mice. Since $\alpha_1$ activity is usually unchanged while $\alpha_2$ activity is easily increased under the same exercises. $\alpha_1$ activity might change only under higher intensity exercises. In contrast, $\alpha_2$ activity will certainly go up under the same condition (higher intensity). That is why we get Rule 6. Looking at rule 8, in comparison with $\alpha_2$, $\alpha_1$ activity mostly remains unchanged, notwithstanding the high increase of phosphorylation of $\alpha_1$ because $\alpha_2$ phosphorylation should be higher and contributed to higher $\alpha_2$ activity after exercise. Actually, the phosphorylation of $\alpha$ is usually presented as a ratio of phosphorylated $\alpha$ divided by total $\alpha$. Although $\alpha_1$ phosphorylation may slightly increases, this cannot cause the increase of $\alpha_1$ activity. As to our knowledge, no literature in Medline previously points out the relationship between phosphorylation and expression of $\alpha_2$. The experimental results in [154] also match our computational discovery.

Rule 9 in Table 4.6 shows that $\alpha$ activity is co-expressed with expression of $\beta$ or $\gamma$. $\alpha_2$ activity rather than $\alpha_1$ activity appears to correlate with expression of $\beta$ or $\gamma$ subunits. Co-expression of $\alpha$ subunits with $\beta$ or $\gamma$ subunits modestly increases kinase activity accompanied by the formation of $\alpha/\beta$ or $\alpha/\gamma$ heterodimers. In addition to binding of each noncatalytic subunit to the $\alpha$ subunit, $\beta$ and $\gamma$ subunits bind to each other, possibly resulting in a more stable heterotrimeric complex [88]. The increase in kinase activity associated with expression of this heterotrimer is due both to an increase in enzyme-specific activity (units/enzyme mass) and to an apparent enhanced $\alpha$ subunit expression. Co-expression of the noncatalytic $\beta$ or $\gamma$ subunits is required for optimal activity of the $\alpha$ catalytic subunits. This may explain the possible and/or necessary co-expression of $\alpha$ with $\beta$ and $\gamma$ subunits. In the same way, we can explain Rule 10, which represents that if the expression of $\gamma_1$ and $\gamma_3$ are significantly increased, the expression of $\beta_1$, $\beta_2$ and $\gamma_2$ will increase too.

Rule 11 does not make sense in biology because there is no relationship between the phosphorylation of $\alpha_1$ and $\alpha_2$. Rule 12 shows the protein expression of $\alpha_1$ is co-expressed with the expression of $\beta_2$. This may imply that the tight relation between $\gamma_3$ and $\alpha_2$, $\gamma_3$ and $\beta_2$, $\gamma_1$ and both $\alpha_1$ and $\alpha_2$, and $\gamma_1$ and $\beta_2$. The new experimental results in [23,24] defend these rules. There are 12 theoretically possible AMPK heterotrimetric complexes. But in human skeletal muscle, there are only three detectable combinations exist $\alpha_2\beta_2\gamma_1$, $\alpha_2\beta_2\gamma_3$, and $\alpha_1\beta_2\gamma_1$ [24]. Our results predict that there maybe $\alpha_1\beta_1\gamma_1$ complex in human skeletal muscle as well.

Furthermore, we can predict some latent associations from the derived association rules. For example, if the training is not of high-intensity, we can predict deductively 1 activity in terms of rule 1 in Table 4.6. Besides, the newly found association rules can be used in the design of future experiments. For example, $\alpha_{2a}$ was not highly activated at rest status. If we want to activate it, we can regulate the intensity or duration of exercise as indicated in rules 2, 3 and 4 in Table 4.6. Therefore, the identified association rules may play important roles in three aspects:

- demonstrating former experiments via matching more experimental results;
- predicting potential results based on existing conditions; and
- guiding the design of future experiments.

From our experiments, we demonstrated that association rules can not only discover important biological patterns but also be used to reduce the cost of labor, resources and other associated activities. Experiments can be conducted based on the derived association rules, thereby reducing the number of experiments. For example, if $\alpha_2$ activity is increased with exercise in one experiment, we can predict that $\alpha_{1a}$ possibly has no change under the same condition based on rules 1 and 2 in Table 4.6. Similarly, if $\alpha_{1a}$ is highly increased with high intensity training, we can predict that $\alpha_{2a}$ is possibly highly increased either in light of rule 6. Therefore, it can save the experimental time by avoiding extra (unnecessary) stimuli. For example, rule 4 in Table 4.6 implies that high-intensity training can result in high expression of $\alpha_{2a}$. If we want to observe that $\alpha_{2a}$ is highly expressed in experiments, we can purposefully handle high-intensity stimuli rather than intense-intensity. Consequently, the rules are beneficial to understand the signalling pathway of AMPK in regulating metabolism and its potential benefits to disease treatment.

## 4.5 Discussion

In this study, we have proposed a framework by which to identify association rules of interest, either between the state of isoforms of $\alpha$, $\beta$ and $\gamma$ subunits of AMPK, or between stimulus factors and the state of isoforms, from AMPK regulation data. In particular, the item constraints are applied in the closed interpretation to the itemset generation. We have shown how to specify a threshold in terms of the amount of results instead of a fixed threshold for all itemsets.

Our approaches start with collecting hidden data from publications in Medline. The collected experimental data is qualitative and does not correspond with the data mining softwares [19]. Besides, we have shown that untested items in some experiments may result in many unrelated or even inaccurate rules. If the untested items are not pruned, it seemed to cause many inaccurate results, and the implementation of software became less efficient when identifying frequent patterns [8]. Consequently, we marked the untested items using the filtering symbols, which facilitate the pruning of frequent itemsets and avoid the generation of irrelevant frequent itemsets. To meet the criteria of softwares in [19], it is needed to conduct data preprocessing and convert the qualitative items into the form of quantitative items (non-negative integers), which benefit to the execution of software.

The traditional association rule mining typically requires a user to specify a minimum support threshold for the generation of all itemsets. It has been argued that without specific knowledge, it is difficult for users to obtain an optimal support threshold. It was showed that a better way is to identify top-$N$ interesting item-sets, instead of specifying a fixed threshold value for all itemsets of all sizes like [12,13,16]. However, a major problem is that not all top-$N$ itemsets are interesting. Some correlations might not make sense biologically at all. The item constraints in the closed interpretation are applied to the itemset generation. For example, in AMPK regulation, the relationships between the activity of *subunit isoforms* and *stimulus factors* such as intensity and duration are interesting but the relationships between *stimulus factors* are not. It provides a flexible way for users to specify a set of constraints and allow them to search and control the interesting frequent patterns.

In our selection of association rules, we adopt 0.7 as the minimum confidence because there is no sharp drop in rule output in contrast with 0.6. Although this helps us focus on the interpretation of significant rules, some rules that have a close confidence to 0.7 might be ignored. Extending the interpretation to those less important rules is therefore desirable, but it would require more computational resources and collaboration with biologists.

Bayesian network, a graphic model, has been widely used to identify metabolic pathways and construct genetic networks due to its statistical significance and inherited advantage in handling the information with uncertainty. Nevertheless, as an assumption-driven method, it relies on the quality and extent of the prior beliefs and is only as useful as this prior knowledge is reliable. However, the hidden and insufficient AMPK regulation data in the publications of Medline prevents us from obtaining reliable prior knowledge. Furthermore, some potential AMPK pathways are undetermined and might be ignored from the assumption. Considering the above difficulties, the authors turn to data mining, a data-driven method, in this study.

We have focused our attention here on human skeletal muscle. Also, our methods are eligible for other organisms, such as mouse, where the experimental indexes or criteria may be quite different. A modification with respect to data preprocessing may be adopted according to the criteria. Another interesting question is whether our methods can be used to explore the AMPK regulation on other tissues and organs, such as adipose tissue, heart and liver [4]. Intuitively, it is necessary to classify the data into different groups because different compositions may play a similar role on different tissues or organs. On the other hand, studying the potential metabolic pathways between AMPK regulations on different tissues or organs should be useful in disease prediction, diagnosis and treatment. We plan to seek answers for these questions in our future work. The results can enable biologists to understand AMPK pathways and extend it to the other kinases to form a full kinase interaction mapping.

## 4.6  Conclusion

AMPK has emerged as an important energy sensor in the regulation of cell metabolism. Recent experiments reveal that physical exercises are closely linked with AMPK activation in skeletal muscle. This chapter proposes a framework by which to identify association rules of interest from the published experimental data.

Unlike the conventional methods, the measurement of items from AMPK regulation data is taken into account. In addition, the items that have low occurrence in existing experiments are pruned prior to mining. Furthermore, we apply item constraints in the closed interpretation to the itemset generation so that a threshold is specified on the amount of results rather than a fixed threshold, thereby reducing the search space vastly.

Our framework was demonstrated by mining realistic AMPK regulation data set with respect to skeletal muscle. Many of the found rules make sense biologically, others suggesting new hypotheses that may warrant further investigation. Particularly, some of them were unknown previously. Moreover, they help us understand the characteristics of AMPK and relevant disease treatment. It is thus promising in the interpretation of AMPK regulation data.

# Chapter 5
# Mining Protein Kinase Regulation Using Graphical Models

Abnormal kinase activity is a frequent cause of diseases, which makes kinases a promising pharmacological target. Thus, it is critical to identify the characteristics of protein kinase regulation by studying the activation and inhibition of kinase subunits in response to varied stimuli. Bayesian network (BN) is a formalism for probabilistic reasoning that has been widely used for learning dependency models. However, for high-dimensional discrete random vectors the set of plausible models becomes large, and a full comparison of all the posterior probabilities related to the competing models becomes infeasible. A solution to this problem is based on the Markov Chain Monte Carlo (MCMC) method. This chapter proposes a BN-based framework to discover the dependency correlations of kinase regulation. Our approach is to apply MCMC method to generate a sequence of samples from a probability distribution, by which to approximate the distribution. The frequent connections (edges) are identified from the obtained sampling graphical models. Our results point to a number of novel candidate regulation patterns that are interesting in biology and include inferred associations that were unknown.

## 5.1 Introduction

Protein kinases (PKs, a protein enzyme) have been recognized as a metabolic master switch regulating the majority of cellular pathways. A protein kinase alters other proteins by chemically adding phosphate groups to them (phosphorylation). Phosphorylation usually leads to a functional alteration of the target protein by changing enzyme activity, cellular location, or association with other protein. They regulate many aspects that control cell growth, movement and death. Proteins may be modified by kinase activity, and kinases are known to regulate the majority of cellular pathways, especially those involved in signal transduction, the transmission of signals within the cell. Figure 5.1 shows a subclass of protein kinases and their different roles in specific tissues.

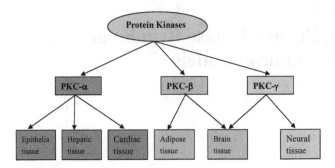

**Fig. 5.1**  An example of the protein kinase family and their corresponding roles

Since protein kinases have profound effects on a cell, their activity is highly regulated. Recent studies indicate that deregulated kinase activity is a frequent cause of diseases, such as cancer [277]. Approximately 50% of known genes that have been directly linked to induction of cancer encode protein kinases. Further, aberrant cell signaling through protein kinases has also been associated with cardiovascular disease [11, 210], diabetes [236], arthritis and other immune or neurological disorders. Over 400 human diseases have been connected to protein kinases [227]. The investigation into the regulation activity of kinases could be an efficient and promising way to diagnose disease genesis and create anti-disease drugs. Drugs which inhibit specific kinases have been in clinical use to treat several diseases [294].

It is thus important to understand the pathway properties of protein kinases. Figure 4.1 [47] depicts an example protein kinase $X$, which uses $IRS_i$, a regulatory subunit (a second protein molecule) to control the activity of a catalytic subunit $ICS_j$. Each subunit consists of several gene encoding isoforms (an alternative form of a protein resulting from differential transcription of the relevant gene either from alternative promoter or alternate splicing). Usually, the regulation of protein kinases can be determined by how an external stimulus might affect the catalytic subunit and regulatory subunit of protein kinases and by what isoforms are expressed or unexpressed in response to external stimuli.

In particular, AMP-activated protein kinase (AMPK) has recently emerged as a potential key signaling pathway, in the regulation of exercise-induced changes in glucose and lipid metabolism in skeletal muscle [37, 236], and in the regulation of stress-induced alterations in glucose uptake during low-flow ischemia and glycolysis, or protection from damage and apoptotic activity associated with ischemia and reperfusion in heart [130]. This enzyme is activated as a result of the alterations in cellular energy levels. The activation of AMPK also exerts long-term effects at the level of both gene expression and protein synthesis. Therefore, interpretation and analysis of AMPK regulation data and identification of regulation network from the data, may lead to a promising pharmacological target for diseases, such as type 2 diabetes and obesity.

There have been considerable efforts to investigate the metabolic pathways of protein kinases [261, 277, 294], such as AMPK [47] (AMP-activated protein kinases) that has been demonstrated to play an important role in regulating metabolism in Chapter 4. An investigation into the degree of activation and inhibition of kinases subunits under acute or chronic stresses can provide valuable data for understanding the pathways.

A number of articles describe results of experiments aimed at understanding kinase regulation have been publicly accessed over the Internet [56, 236]. Such biological data not only provides us with a good opportunity for understanding living organisms, but also poses new challenges. It has been recognized that the mere gathering of experimental data is insufficient for us to discover the potential correlations amongst them [47]. The biological interpretation and analysis of the data are imperative. Consequently, it is critical to have an intelligent way to analyze the data and extract useful pathway knowledge.

Recently, data mining techniques have emerged as a means of identifying patterns and trends from large quantities of data [339]. Association rule mining [82] was used to extract implicit, but potentially useful, frequent patterns from the AMPK regulation data [47]. The association rule method is generally inferior to Bayesian methods because the mined association rule cannot provide statistical significance and the selection of rules often need arbitrary manual intervention. Further, the prior knowledge in combination with previous knowledge should be used to obtain new knowledge.

Bayesian networks (BNs) is a probabilistic graphical model that represents a set of variables (nodes) and their probabilistic dependencies (arcs, links or connections), have been widely applied to discover the potential dependency and causality in databases [137]. BNs model the quantitative strength of the connections between variables, allowing probabilistic beliefs about them to be automatically updated as new evidence becomes available. For example, two connections might be '*moderate intensity*' $\rightarrow \alpha_{1a}|$ and '*moderate intensity*' $\rightarrow \alpha_{2a} \uparrow$ where $\alpha_{1a}|$ and $\alpha_{2a} \uparrow$ represent the activity of $\alpha$ subunits of AMPK. It shows that $\alpha_{1a}$ usually has no change in expression, and $\alpha_{2a}$ is highly expressed in most experiments where the exercise intensity (such as low 40±2% VO2 peak, medium 59±1% VO2 peak, and high 79±1% VO2 peak. The most accurate way to measure VO2 peak is to measure the amount of oxygen consumed during each minute of exercise while conducting a graded fitness test on a *treadmill*, *bike* or other piece of *cardio* exercise equipment.) is moderate [56]. We use one of the most popular *Markov Chain Monte Carlo* methods for structural learning in graphical models, called the *Metropolis-Hastings* (MH) [134] algorithm. Our aim is to apply this algorithm to learn the topology of the network from the protein kinase data set and identify the significant connections (dependency).

This chapter presents a BN-based framework to analyse the updated AMPK regulation data of Chapter 4. MCMC algorithm [9, 234] is used to learn the structure efficiently, and a voting-based solution is proposed to specify constraints on the generation of significant dependencies in terms of the frequency of connections. The main idea is to use MH algorithm to draw samples from $P(G|D)$ after specifying burn-in time ((number of steps to take before drawing samples) and the number of samples. Then a new graph $G'$ is kept if a uniform random variable takes a value greater than the bayes factor $P(D|G')/P(D|G)$. By comparing the frequency of connections in the derived graphs, we can determine which one is the strongest/most frequently found connection. Those suggesting new hypotheses may assure further investigation and complement relevant biological experiments. In particular, the weakly frequent connections that are not supported by adequate experiments in current data set will be reserved for future observation when more experimental data is available.

This chapter is organized as follows. In Section 5.2, the fundamental concepts are presented. Section 5.3 presents implementation of MCMC method for structure learning using kinase regulation data. Section 5.4 explains some significant connections from the created graphical models. Section 5.5 refers to our methodology and studies in the near future. Section 5.6 concludes this chapter.

## 5.2  Preliminaries

We use a four-step strategy to learn structure of BNs and discover the significant connections in terms of a voting criteria:

1. Normalizing the protein kinase regulation data derived from Medline
2. Learning the structure of BNs using MCMC sampling
3. Finding the approximate probability distribution in terms of the Bayes factor $P(D|G')/P(D|G)$ [111]
4. Identifying the strongest/frequent connections using a specified voting criteria

**Table 5.1** An instance of raw AMPK regulation data

| $\alpha_{1a}$ | $\alpha_{1e}$ | $\alpha_{1p}$ | $\alpha_{2a}$ | $\alpha_{2e}$ | $\alpha_{2p}$ | $\beta_{1e}$ | $\gamma_{1e}$ | Training | Diabetes | Intensity(Maximal oxygen uptake) |
|---|---|---|---|---|---|---|---|---|---|---|
| - | ↑ | - | - | ↓ | - | - | - | trained | normal | (70%) moderate intensity |
| ↓ | - | - | \| | - | - | - | - | untrained | normal | (75%) high intensity |
| ↓ | - | - | ↓ | - | - | - | - | untrained | normal | (50%) moderate intensity |
| ↓ | - | \| | \| | - | \| | - | - | trained | normal | (85%) high intensity |
| ↓ | - | ↑ | ↑ | - | ↑ | - | - | untrained | normal | (85%) high intensity |
| ↓ | - | ↑ | ↑ | - | ↑ | - | - | trained | normal | (65%) moderate intensity |

### 5.2.1  Data Preprocessing

This chapter focuses on the activity of subunit isoforms of AMPK in response to stimuli, such as physical training. The data set [54] includes 45 experiments in relevant bio/medical literatures in Medline by searching the NCBI using keywords "AMPK and human skeletal muscle" (103 papers) and "AMPK and endurance training" (16 papers), respectively. It comprises state data of stimuli and corresponding expression data of isoforms. The original data are only available as a textual description to the experimental results. Thus, the data need to be converted to numerical format for data analysis.

**Table 5.2** An instance of AMPK regulation data with discrete values

| $\alpha_{1a}$ | $\alpha_{1e}$ | $\alpha_{1p}$ | $\alpha_{2a}$ | $\alpha_{2e}$ | $\alpha_{2p}$ | $\beta_{1e}$ | $\gamma_{1e}$ | Training | Diabetes | Intensity |
|------|------|------|------|------|------|------|------|------|------|------|
| 4 | 7 | 12 | 16 | 17 | 24 | 27 | 33 | 50 | 70 | (70%) 91 |
| 1 | 8 | 12 | 14 | 20 | 24 | 27 | 33 | 51 | 70 | (75%) 92 |
| 1 | 8 | 12 | 13 | 20 | 24 | 27 | 33 | 51 | 70 | (50%) 91 |
| 1 | 8 | 10 | 14 | 20 | 22 | 27 | 33 | 50 | 70 | (85%) 92 |
| 1 | 8 | 11 | 15 | 20 | 23 | 27 | 33 | 51 | 70 | (85%) 92 |
| 1 | 8 | 11 | 15 | 20 | 23 | 27 | 33 | 50 | 70 | (65%) 91 |

Table 5.1 presents an example of the raw data set, in which the meaning of $\alpha_1$, $\alpha_2$, $\beta_1$, $\gamma_1$, the lowercase subscript '$a$', '$e$' and '$p$', and $-$, $|$, $\uparrow$ and $\downarrow$ can be found in Chapter 4. Each column of the table represents an attribute and each row represents an experiment. Nevertheless, the variables *Training*, *Diabetes* and *Intensity* are string variables and the data set cannot discriminate among states of different isoforms (for example, *no change* is always depicted by $\downarrow$) for all isoforms). In the similar manner, the textual description and state information need to be converted into discrete values for the purpose of data mining.

An example of the data set after formalization can be seen in Table 5.2, in which each attribute includes several integer values that correspond to the symbols and continuous values in Table 5.1. The conversion of discrete data into numerical data is to discriminate the categorical variables containing different states such as *expressed* and *no change*. 1 and 13 represent *no change* in corresponding items; 10, 14 and 22 represent *expressed*; 4, 8, 12, 16, 20, 24, 27 and 33 represent *no tested*; 50 and 51 represent *trained* and *untrained*, respectively; 70 represents *normal of diabetes*; 90, 91 and 92 represent the *maximal oxygen uptake* (VO(2)max) under 50%, VO(2)max between 65% and 75%, and VO(2)max between 80% and 100%, respectively. For example, 4 under the attribute $\alpha_{1a}$ corresponds to '*not tested*', namely '-' in Table 5.1. More details of the formalization from Table 5.1 to Table 5.2 can be seen in [54]. Nevertheless, BNT (Bayes Net Toolbox) [143] requires that each row corresponds to an attribute, and the column corresponds to an instance/samples. The complete data set can be accessed by [53] and [54]. The latter includes the normalized data used for structure learning.

### 5.2.2 Basics of Structure Learning of BNs

A Bayesian network can be viewed as a directed acyclic graph (DAG) that includes a set of nodes (variables) from the domain and a set of directed arcs (or links) that connect pairs of nodes.

The strength of variable is measured by conditional probability distribution associated with each node. Each node may take several values, such as discrete values $\{10, 11, 12\}$ with attribute $\alpha_{1p}$ and $\{13, 14, 15, 16\}$ with attribute $\alpha_{2a}$ in Table 5.2. Given a data set including a collection of variables and their corresponding values, we are able to learn the structure or topology of the network by capturing qualitative relationships between variables.

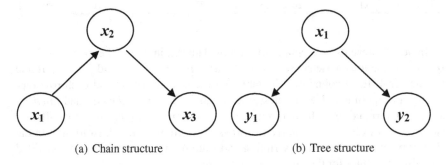

(a) Chain structure                              (b) Tree structure

**Fig. 5.2** The BN model with respect to $S$ and $ST$, in which $x_i \in ST$ and $y_i \in S$

A Bayesian network for a set of variables $X = \{X_1, \cdots, X_n\}$ consists of

- a network structure $S$ that encodes a set of conditional independence assertions about variables in $X$, and
- a set $P$ of local probability distributions associated with each variable.

Together, these components define the joint probability distribution for $X$. The network structure $S$ is a directed acyclic graph. The nodes in $S$ are in one-to-one correspondence with the variables $X$. We use $X_i$ to denote both the variable and its corresponding node, and $pa_i$ to denote the parents of node $X_i$ in $S$ as well as the variables corresponding to those parents. Arcs encode conditional independencies as the lack of an arc does not necessarily mean that the two unconnected variables are conditionally independent. In particular, given structure $S$, the joint probability distribution for $X$ is given by

$$p(x) = \prod_{i=1}^{n} p(x_i|pa_i)$$

where the local probability distributions $P$ are the distributions corresponding to the terms in the product of the above equation. Consequently, using the pair $(S, P)$, we obtain the joint distribution $p(x)$.

According to the definition of BNs in [136, 183], two nodes should be connected directly if one affects or causes the other, with the arc representing the direction of the effect. Suppose $EX = \{EX_1, ..., EX_n\}$ represents a collection of experiments. Each experiment includes a *state itemset* $(S_i)$, such as the expression of $\alpha_{1e}$, and a *stimulus itemset* ($ST_i$), such as *training* (exercise training, such as short term treadmill training on skeletal muscle) and *intensity* (exercise intensity), and $EX_i = (S_i, ST_i)$. $x \in ST_i$ is usually treated as the cause of $y \in S_i$. Moreover, it is also possible that $\exists\ x_1 \in ST_i$ that affects $\exists\ x_2 \in ST_i$. In that case, $x$ and $x_1$ are parent nodes of $y$ and $x_2$, respectively, and $y$ and $x_2$ are called child nodes. In Table 5.2, $\alpha_{1a}$, $\alpha_{1e}$, $\alpha_{1p}$, $\alpha_{2a}$, $\alpha_{2e}$, $\alpha_{2p}$, $\beta_{1e}$, $\gamma_{1e}$, *Training*, *Diabetes* and *Intensity* are viewed as a set of attributes that generate $S$, and a set of prior probability corresponding to each attribute creates $P$. For example, if there is an arc from $\alpha_{1a}$ to $\alpha_{1e}$, the child node $\alpha_{1e}$ is conditionally independent upon its parent node $\alpha_{1a}$. The BN model with $S$ and $ST$ is presented in Figure 5.2, in which Figure 5.2(a) depicts the determinism between the stimuli nodes and Figure 5.2(b) depicts the stimuli nodes cause the change of the state nodes.

### 5.2.3  Problems

Only limited studies have been conducted to deal with the valuable kinase regulation data. A method [47] was proposed to discover frequent patterns from an AMPK data set. However, many rules may contain more than two items, and may partially overlap with each other in conditions or conclusions. This makes it less intuitive and difficult to determine comprehensible and convicting relationship of *cause* and *effect*. Moreover, it is inflexible to use the obtained knowledge (prior knowledge) to reason about the posterior probability distribution for a set of query nodes (variables), given values for some evidence nodes.

In contrast, the probabilistic graphic models are well suited for composing different submodels in a principled and understandable fashion. A **v-structure** [314] is an ordered tuple $(X, Y, Z)$ such that there is an arc from $X$ to $Y$ and from $Z$ to $Y$, but no arc between $X$ and $Z$. For example, in Figure 5.3, a common cause **v-structure** can be identified as ($\beta_{2e} \uparrow$, *moderate intensity exercise*, $\gamma_{2e} \uparrow$), ($\beta_{2e} \uparrow$, *moderate intensity exercise*, $\alpha_{1a} \downarrow$) and ($\alpha_{1a} \downarrow$, *moderate intensity exercise*, $\gamma_{2e} \uparrow$), in which "*moderate intensity treadmill*" is the common cause of $\beta_{2e} \uparrow$, $\alpha_{1a} \downarrow$ and $\gamma_{2e} \uparrow$. MI is viewed as the evidence node and we can compute the posterior probabilities for $\beta_{2e} \uparrow$, $\alpha_{1a} \downarrow$ and $\gamma_{2e} \uparrow$ (query nodes) given evidence. If there is no evidence or information about "*moderate intensity exercise*" (evidence node), then learning that one effect is present will increase the chances of "*moderate intensity exercise*" which in turn will increase the probability of the other effect. However, if we already know about "*moderate intensity exercise*", then an additional positive $\gamma_{2e} \uparrow$ won't tell us anything new about the chances of $\beta_{2e} \uparrow$, and vice versa [183].

The data can contain significant pathway knowledge that is nevertheless hidden in the tremendous data. For example, a *moderate intensity treadmill training* can result in highly expression of activation of $\beta_2$ and $\gamma_2$ in white quadriceps. Thus, this connection can be described as two links $L_1 =$ "*moderate intensity treadmill*" $\rightarrow \beta_{2a} \uparrow$ and $L_2 =$ "*moderate intensity treadmill*" $\rightarrow \gamma_{2a} \uparrow$. It is derived from an

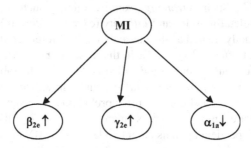

**Fig. 5.3** An example illustrating **v-structures** where *MI* is the abbreviation of *moderate intensity*

individual experiment and is not statistically reliable. Thus, the trusted links have to be identified from an experimental data set.

## 5.3   Structure Learning of BNs from Kinase Regulation Data

### 5.3.1   Initial Data Set

As mentioned in Chapter 4, the obtained data consists of two parts, stimulus factor *ST* (namely stimuli itemset) and subunit state *S*(namely state itemset). In reality, *S* = $\{\alpha_{1a}, \alpha_{1e}, \alpha_{1p}, \alpha_{2a}, \alpha_{2e}, \alpha_{2p}, \beta_{1e}, \beta_{2e}, \gamma_{1e}, \gamma_{2e}, \gamma_{3e}\}$ and *ST* = $\{training, glycogen, diabetes, nicotinic \ acid, intensity \ (maximal \ oxygen \ uptake), duration\}$. For example, each row in Table 5.1 corresponds to an experiment of AMPK regulation. They can be viewed as six initial rules in the table.

- $\{trained, normal, (70\%) \ moderate \ intensity\} \Rightarrow \{\alpha_{1e} \uparrow, \alpha_{2e} \downarrow\}$
- $\{untrained, normal, (75\%) \ high \ intensity\} \Rightarrow \{\alpha_{1a} \downarrow, \alpha_{2a} \downarrow\}$
- $\{untrained, normal, (50\%) \ moderate \ intensity\} \Rightarrow \{\alpha_{1a} \downarrow, \alpha_{2a} \downarrow\}$
- $\{trained, normal, (85\%) \ high \ intensity\} \Rightarrow \{\alpha_{1a} \downarrow, \alpha_{1p} \downarrow, \alpha_{2a} \downarrow, \alpha_{2p} \downarrow\}$
- $\{untrained, normal, (85\%) \ high \ intensity\} \Rightarrow \{\alpha_{1a} \downarrow, \alpha_{1p} \uparrow, \alpha_{2a} \uparrow, \alpha_{2p} \uparrow\}$
- $\{trained, normal, (65\%) \ moderate \ intensity\} \Rightarrow \{\alpha_{1a} \downarrow, \alpha_{1p} \uparrow, \alpha_{2a} \uparrow, \alpha_{2p} \uparrow\}$

Probabilistic graphic model is an option to model such biological system. To specify a model completely, we need to describe the conditional probability associated with each variable. However, it is not easy to determine the multivariate joint probability distributions in a high-dimensional space. Gelman et al [108] and Wakefield [317] both discuss the advantages of the simulation-based Bayesian approach to the analysis of sparse data with reference to nonlinear hierarchical models. The present study focuses on transition rate and half-response time estimates, and nonlinear functions of model parameters are involved. The need to obtain statistics on nonlinear functions would usually complicate the analysis, but presents no difficulty when using MCMC simulation. Thus, we use the reliable MCMC simulation to learn dependency model within a reasonable time.

### 5.3.2 MCMC Sampling Simulation

**Bayesian Model Score.** A graphical model [198] is generated by specifying local dependencies of each node of the graph in terms of its immediate neighbours. However, for high-dimensional discrete random vectors, the set of plausible models become large, and a full comparison of all the posterior probabilities associated to the competing models becomes infeasible. Metropolis-Hastings algorithm is the most popular MCMC method [134] and was proposed for model selection among graphical structures [214] since most practical MCMC algorithms can be interpreted as special cases or extensions of this algorithm [9, 111]. The basic idea of Monte Carlo simulation is to draw a set of samples $\{x^i\}_{i=1}^N$ from a target density distribution $p(x)$ defined on a high-dimensional space $X$. These $N$ samples can be used to approximate the target density.

The MCMC graphical model selection depends on the Bayesian graphical model scoring. Let a graph $G$ be represented by the pair $(V, E)$, in which $V$ and $E$ denote a set of vertices (each corresponds to a random variable or node) and a set of edges between the vertices. Conditional independence comes into play when we have multiple variables that can all be correlated. Suppose $A, B, C, E$ and $F \subset V$ are variables. The relationships between the variables can be expressed in Figure 5.4; nodes represent variables, and the directed edges show the dependencies. Variables not connected by edges are conditionally independent. For example, $B$ is conditionally independent of $F$ given $E$, namely $P(F|B, E) = P(F|E)$. In other words, the predictive value of $F$ is entirely mediated through the variable of $E$. If we already know whether or not $E$ occurs, knowing whether or not $B$ happens does not help further predict the occurrence of $F$. In the same way, we can generate other conditional independence in this figure. Thus, a graphical model is a family of probability distributions $P$, which are Markov (all conditional probabilities from $G$ hold in corresponding probability distribution) with respect to a graph $G$.

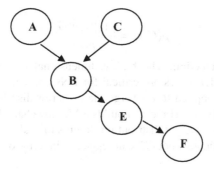

**Fig. 5.4** An example of the conditional independence

The object of inference will be a vector of discrete random variables, $X_V$, whose counts are arranged in a contingency table $\mathscr{I}$, with cells $i$. Let $\theta_G = (\theta(i), i \in \mathscr{I})$

be the vector of unknown cell probabilities in the table [137]. Given an observed sample from $P$, $X_V = x_V$, structure learning is to compare all possible graphs and determine the graph whose independency model best represents the mechanism that generated the data.

To carry out model selection, a bayesian *score* needs to be calculated for each considered model. The score $p(x|G)$ is the marginal likelihood of a model, and is denoted by

$$L(G) = p(x|G) = \int_{\theta_G} p(x|\theta_G, G)\pi(\theta_G)d\theta_G,$$

where $\pi(\theta_G)$ is the prior distribution of the parameter vector, conditionally on the graph $G$.

As mentioned in [111, 137], for DAG models, Dirichlet priors is commonly used in BNs to assess a prior distribution on the unknown cell probabilities for each node, conditionally on the configurations of its parents. Based on this approach, the marginal likelihood of a discrete DAG model is

$$L(g) = \prod_{i=1}^{n}\prod_{j=1}^{q_i} \frac{\Gamma(N'_{ij})}{\Gamma(N_{ij}+N'_{ij})} \prod_{k=1}^{r_i} \frac{\Gamma(N_{ijk}+N'_{ijk})}{\Gamma(N'_{ijk})},$$

where $\Gamma()$ is the Gamma function, which satisfies $\Gamma(x + 1) = x\Gamma(x)$ and $\Gamma(1) = 1$. The index $i$ indicates a node in the graph, $j$ a configuration of the parents of such nodes, and $k$ a realization of the considered node under each of such configurations. For each combination of the indexes, $N_{ijk}$ indicates the observed count and $N'_{ijk}$ the prior hyperparameter. It assumes complete model equivalence and takes a total prior precision of $N' = 1$ and, therefore, $N'_{ijk} = 1/(r_i * q_i)$, with $q_i$ the number of configurations of the parents and $r_i$ the number of realization of the node $i$.

Let $p(x) = \Sigma_{G \in \mathscr{G}} p(x|G)p(G)$ be the marginal likelihood of the data, with $\mathscr{G}$ the set of all considered models. Thus, $\forall\, G \in \mathscr{G}$, the Bayesian model score can be described as

$$p(G|x) = \frac{p(x|G)p(G)}{p(x)}$$

**Graphical Model Selection.** The highly dimensional integrals involved in the derivation of the model scores are critical for BNs approach [111]. In this chapter, Markov chain is applied to converge the posterior distribution of the models given the data. Usually, a MH method builds a Markov chain that has the posterior distribution $p(G|x)$ as its target distribution. It aims to evaluate, at each step of the chain, whether a candidate model $G'$ can replace $G$ in terms of specified acceptance probability.

Let $nbd(G)$ be the neighbourhood of $G$, which is a set of graphs that can be reached from $G$ in one step (adding or deleting arcs in DAGs), and let $q(G, G')$ be the transition probability that is equal to 0 if $G' \notin nbd(G)$ and $q(G, G') > 0$ if $G' \in nbd(G)$. The $nbd(G)$ must be constructed in a way that the transition matrix $q$

is irreducible. If the irreducibility is satisfied, the proposed move is accepted with probability $\alpha = min\{1, R_\alpha\}$ where

$$R_\alpha = \frac{\sharp(nbd(G))p(G'|x)}{\sharp(nbd(G'))p(G|x)}$$

where $\sharp(nbd(G))$ represents the cardinality of the neighbourhood of $G$. $\sharp(nbd(G))/\sharp(nbd(G'))$ is assumed to equal to 1 since $G$ and $G'$ differ in one single adjacency.

In the case of DAG models, the Bayes factor is computed according to

$$\frac{L(G',i)}{L(G,i)},$$

where the $L(G, i)$ represents the likelihood of $i$th variable.

$$L(G,i) = \prod_{j=1}^{q_i} \frac{\Gamma(N'_{ij})}{\Gamma(N_{ij}+N'_{ij})} \prod_{k=1}^{r_i} \frac{\Gamma(N_{ijk}+N'_{ijk})}{\Gamma(N'_{ijk})}$$

where $i$ refers to the random variable for which the parent set differs in $G$ and $G'$.

In addition to the previous types of move, the reversal of arcs for DAGs is used in a recent method [111] when the reversal does not lead to a directed cycle. Thus, when reversing an arc $j \to i$ in $G$, the Bayes factor becomes

$$\frac{L(G',i)L(G',j)}{L(G,i)L(G,j)},$$

Therefore, a new graph $G'$ is kept if the computed acceptance probability is greater than the Bayes factor.

### 5.3.3  Discovering Frequent Connections

We may obtain a number of graphical models, which depend on the burn-in time and the specified number of sample graphs to draw from the chain after burn-in. In that case, we may have to do some voting to the obtained connections (edges) between variables and identify those connections that have high support from the derived graphical models. A frequently occurred connection indicates that this is a frequently occurring patterns and is supported by most of the graphical models. Thus, it is identified as an interesting pathway of kinase regulation.

**Definition 5.1.** Let $\mathscr{G} = \{G_i \mid 1 \le i \le n\}$ be a set of generated graphical models, let $e$ be an edge of the graphical models, let $v(G_i, e)$ be the local voting of $G_i$ to $e$, let $v(\mathscr{G}, e)$ be the global voting of $\mathscr{G}$ to $e$ and let $E_{G_i}$ be the set of all edges of $G_i$.

$$v(\mathscr{G},e) = \sum_{i=1}^{n} v(G_i,e)$$

where $v(G_i, e) = 1$ if $e \in E_{G_i}$; otherwise $v(G_i, e) = 0$.

Let *minv* be a minimum voting threshold.

- if $v(\mathscr{G}, e) \geq minv$, $e$ is a connection of interest;
- otherwise, $e$ is viewed as an uninteresting connection.

Figures 5.5, 5.6, 5.7 show how to calculate the frequency of edges by splicing two obtained graphical models $G_1$ and $G_2$. In Figure 5.5 and Figure 5.6, the integers on each edge indicates the local voting. In contrast, Figure 5.7 depicts the global voting by combining the voting from $G_1$ and $G_2$ together. It is observed that the edges $A \rightarrow C$ and $C \rightarrow E$ are included in Figure 5.5 but are not presented in Figure 5.6. Thus, the edges $A \rightarrow C$ and $C \rightarrow E$ get only one mark in the splicing Figure 5.7, namely $v(\mathscr{G}, A \rightarrow C) = 1$ and $v(\{G_1, G_2\}, C \rightarrow E) = 1$, in comparison with the other edges.

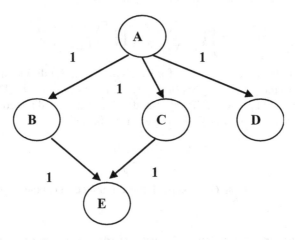

**Fig. 5.5** Graph model $G_1$

On the other hand, those links (connections) that do not make sense biologically are pruned. A valid connection should satisfy the given forms:

- $Link_1$: $A \Rightarrow B$, $A \subseteq S$ and $B \subseteq S$
- $Link_2$: $A \Rightarrow B$, $A \subseteq ST$ and $B \subseteq S$

The relation between only stimulus variables such as *intensity* and *time* is unmeaningful in biology at all. Moreover, state variables actually rely on stimulus variables; therefore, they should not be included in the cause and effect of a link simultaneously.

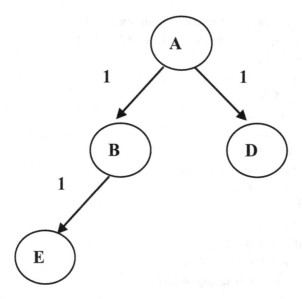

**Fig. 5.6**  Graph model $G_2$

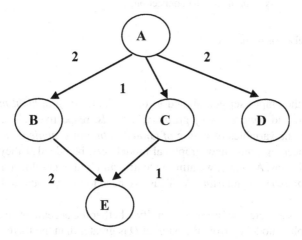

**Fig. 5.7**  Splicing of graphical model $G_1$ and $G_2$

### *5.3.4   Algorithm Design*

The presented algorithm identifies interesting connections from the obtained graphic models.

**begin**

*Input: D: AMPK data set; bf: Bayes factor; minv: minimum voting threshold; burn-in: burn-in time; nsample: number of samples; C: a valid connection using constraint C;*

(1) **let** $\mathscr{G} \leftarrow \emptyset$; $v(G_i, c) \leftarrow 0$; $v(\mathscr{G}, e) = 0$; $E_{G_i} \leftarrow \emptyset$, $E_{\mathscr{G}} \leftarrow \emptyset$;

(2) **forall** $G_i$ learned from $D$ using *burn-in* and *nsample* **do**

    **if** the computed acceptance probability of $G_i > bf$ **then**

        $\mathcal{G} = \mathcal{G} \cup G_i$;

  **end**

(3) **forall** $G_i \in \mathcal{G}$ **do**

    (3.1) **if** $\exists e \in E_{G_i}$ **then**

        $v(G_i, e) = 1$;

      **else** $v(G_i, e) = 0$;

    (3.2) $v(\mathcal{G}, e) = v(\mathcal{G}, e) + v(G_i, c)$;

    (3.3) $E_{\mathcal{G}} = E_{\mathcal{G}} \cup E_{G_i}$;

  **end**

(4) **forall** $e \in E_{\mathcal{G}}$ **do**

    **if** $e$ satisfied $C$ **then** {

      **if** $v(\mathcal{G}, e) \geq minv$ **then**

        $e$ is an interesting connection;

      **else**

        $e$ is an uninteresting connection;

    }

    **else** $e$ is pruned from $E_{\mathcal{G}}$;

  **end**

**end**

In step 1, the empty set is assigned to the variables of *graphical models, connections of* $G_i$ *and connection of graphical models*, respectively. The zero value is assigned to the variables of *voting of* $G_i$ *and voting of graphical models*. In the following processes, some new graphical models can be added if they satisfy the required conditions. Actually, we aim to identify all eligible graphical models $\mathcal{G}$ by virtue of $G_i$, *bf*, *burn-in* and *nsample*. Thus, we need to firstly find out the appropriate $G_i$.

Step 2 shows a cycle operations to identify whether the acceptance probability of a learned graphic model $G_i$ from the data set $D$ is greater than the Bayes factor *bf*. If a new graphic model $G_i$ satisfies this condition, it will be kept in the set of graphical models $\mathcal{G}$.

In Step 3, if the set of connection $E_{G_i}$ contains a connection $e$, then the voting to $e$ by $G_i$ is equal to 1, otherwise it is equal to zero (Step 3.1). The voting to the connection is then added together (Step 3.2). Step 3.3 combines the set of connections of $G_i$ into $E_{\mathcal{G}}$ using union operation.

Step 4 first selects those eligible connections from $E_{\mathcal{G}}$, which satisfied the format constraint $C$. If the voting of $\mathcal{G}$ to the connection $e$ is equal to or greater than the specified minimum voting threshold *minv*, it is viewed as an interesting connection, otherwise an uninteresting connection.

## 5.4 Results

As mentioned above, a preprocessing of experimental data is needed for data normalization that conforms to the required format of BNT toolbox. The normalization converts the raw data, a $45 \times 17$ matrix, into the standard data, a $17 \times 45$ matrix, which is column-based and each column represents a sample including its corresponding value to attributes. In particular, for one attribute, it allows only positive integers in order starting from 1.

For real usage, we need to set that *burn-in* steps to be at least 1000. Although the higher value, such as 10000, can in theory lead to better result, we specify its value as 8000 due to the computation time. As for the number of samples (*nsamples*), we select 100 as its value in this chapter. Moreover, a voting strategy is applied, by which we can identify the most significant/frequent links from the set of graphical models.

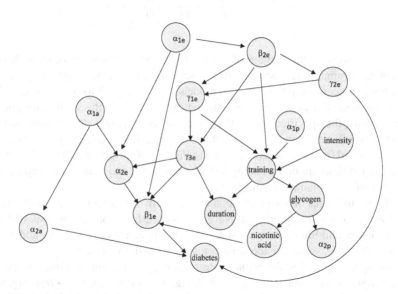

**Fig. 5.8** An example of the learned network

Figure 5.8 shows an example of the voting as a result of setting *burn-in* step as 8000, *nsamples* as 100 and *minv* as 60. The frequency threshold *minv* during the voting may affect the results. It may be too big to find anything, whereas a small one may degrade the system performance dramatically. It is observed that there is no significant difference in obtained graphical models when setting the *minv* from 0.6 to 1 in comparison with 0.5. Therefore, we select the results by 0.6 in contrast to the results by 0.5 in the following analysis. The readers can actually alter the value of *minv* and compare their difference in terms of different purposes.

There are 17 nodes including $\alpha_{1a}$, $\alpha_{1e}$, $\alpha_{1p}$, $\alpha_{2a}$, $\alpha_{2e}$, $\alpha_{2p}$, $\beta_{1e}$, $\beta_{2e}$, $\gamma_{1e}$, $\gamma_{2e}$, $\gamma_{3e}$, *training, glycogen, diabetes, nicotinic acid, intensity* and *duration* in the figure.

Each node represents a corresponding variable in the data set. Some connection are pruned due to weaker frequency than 60%, whereas they can be seen from the displayed matrix using `http://bioinformatics.gxu.edu.cn/bio/data/LNAI8335/8335-8.zip`. Some of them may be interesting but need to be confirmed by biologists. We repeatedly run the system for ten times by keeping the same configuration (*burn-in* and *nsamples*), and randomly select four learned model for analysis. The result can be seen by accessing `http://bioinformatics.gxu.edu.cn/bio/data/LNAI8335/8335-1.zip`.

**Table 5.3** The count of links in each running and their shared link

| Experiment | $EX_1$ | $EX_2$ | $EX_3$ | $EX_4$ |
|---|---|---|---|---|
| $EX_1$ | 29 | 9 | 8 | 6 |
| $EX_2$ | 9 | 35 | 9 | 14 |
| $EX_3$ | 8 | 9 | 29 | 8 |
| $EX_4$ | 6 | 14 | 8 | 30 |

Table 5.3 presents the number of obtained links and the number of their shared links in each running, respectively. It is observed that the experiments have close number of connections in the graphical models, 29 for $EX_1$, 35 for $EX_2$, 29 for $EX_3$, and 30 for $EX_4$. Furthermore, as mentioned in Section 5.3, the valid connections should satisfy the specified form. Thus, the connections that do not make sense biologically will be pruned from the obtained connections. For example, 9 connections are pruned from the graphical model in Figure 5.8 (originally, 29 connections). These pruned links are uninteresting in biological sense and thus do not impact the reliability of the remaining connections.

Table 5.3 indicates that we may obtain varied network structures due to different sampling in each learning process. Nevertheless, we focus on the analysis of $EX_1$ in this chapter and highlight some shared links between $EX_1$, $EX_2$, $EX_3$ and $EX_4$, respectively. Note, some uninteresting connections will not be discussed.

Looking at Figure 5.8, the connections *training → duration, training → glycogen, glycogen → nicotinic acid*, $\alpha_{1p}$ *→ training,* $\gamma_{1e}$ *→ training,* $\gamma_{2e}$ *→ training,* $\gamma_{2a}$ *→ diabetes* and *intensity → training* are pruned since they fail to satisfy the required forms.

Looking at the node $\alpha_{1a}$ without parents, this is consistent with the biological experimental results. In other words, the activation of $\alpha_{1a}$ usually has no change if the exercise intensity is not high enough and the duration is not extra long. Although some experiments suggested that AMPK can be substantially activated during maximal sprint-type exercise in humans [56, 100, 225], we determine that $\alpha_1$ activity cannot be significantly affected by the status of training, glycogen, diabetes and nicotinic acid because $\alpha_2$ is found predominantly in skeletal muscle.

Looking at all connections ending at node *diabetes*, they indicate the potential cause of diabetes in case of abnormal alteration of node $\alpha_{2a}$, node $\beta_{1e}$, node $\gamma_{2e}$ and node *intensity*. Although it does not conform to the specified form, these can be useful knowledge for disease diagnosis and treatment, and drug design. All the other nodes that link to them via the above nodes can be viewed as having indirect relation with diabetes, such as node $\alpha_{1a}$, node $\alpha_{1e}$, node $\alpha_{2e}$ and node $\beta_{2e}$.

Looking at the link *glycogen* $\to \alpha_{2p}$, it represents the density of glycogen can have an effect on phosphorylation of $\alpha_2$. This is because the phosphorylation of $\alpha_2$ is more relative to cell regulation by environment stress, which is in agreement with the recent results of [63, 181, 261]. Looking at the link *nicotinic acid* $\to \beta_{1e}$, it represents that the use of *nicotinic* can have an impact on $\beta_{1e}$.

Moreover, it is interesting to find Markov blanket from the graphical model. The Markov blanket of a node is the only knowledge that is needed to predict the behaviour of that node. The Markov blanket for a node $A$ in a BN is the set of nodes $\mathscr{A}$ composed of $A'$ parents, its children and its children's parents. For example, for node $\alpha_{2a}$, its Markov network $MB(\alpha_{2a})$ composes of its parents $\{\alpha_{1a}\}$, its children $\{diabetes\}$ and its children's parents $\{\beta_{1e}, \gamma_{2e}, intensity\}$. The Markov blanket of a node is interesting because it identifies all the variables that shield off the node from the rest of the network.

Looking at $EX_1$ and $EX_2$, the links $\alpha_{1a} \to \alpha_{2a}$ and $\alpha_{1p} \to \alpha_{2a}$ are supported by both of them. The two connections indicate that $\alpha_{2a}$ is the common effect of $\alpha_{1a}$ and $\alpha_{1p}$.

Looking at $EX_1$ and $EX_3$, $\beta_{2e} \to \gamma_{1e}$, $\gamma_{1e} \to \gamma_{3e}$, $\gamma_{3e} \to \alpha_{2e}$ and *glycogen* $\to \alpha_{2p}$ are supported by both $EX_1$ and $EX_3$. The former three constructs a potential pathway starting from $\beta_{2e}$, via $\gamma_{1e}$, $\gamma_{3e}$ to $\alpha_{2e}$, which has not been previously revealed by biological experiments. The latter represents the content of *Glycogen* has an impact on the alteration of $\alpha_{2p}$.

Looking at $EX_1$ and $EX_4$, $\alpha_{2e} \to \beta_{1e}$ and *glycogen* $\to \alpha_{2p}$ are their two shared connections. The link $\alpha_{2a} \to diabetes$ is removed since it does not conform to the required form. The first one enhances the correlation between $\alpha_{2e}$ and $\beta_{1e}$, and the second one shows that *Glycogen* can affect the activation of $\alpha_{2p}$.

Looking at $EX_2$ and $EX_3$, $\alpha_{1a} \to \alpha_{1e}$, $\alpha_{1p} \to \alpha_{2p}$, $\beta_{1e} \to \alpha_{1e}$, $\beta_{1e} \to \gamma_{3e}$, $\gamma_{1e} \to \gamma_{3e}$ and $\gamma_{3e} \to \gamma_{2e}$ are shared connections. $\alpha_{1p} \to \alpha_{2p}$ represents that the activation of $\alpha_{1p}$ can give rise to the change of $\alpha_{2p}$. $\beta_{1e} \to \alpha_{1e}$ and $\beta_{1e} \to \gamma_{3e}$ represent that $\beta_{1e}$ is the common cause of $\alpha_{1e}$ and $\beta_{3e}$. $\gamma_{1e} \to \gamma_{3e}$ and $\gamma_{3e} \to \gamma_{2e}$ and $\beta_{1e} \to \gamma_{3e}$ and $\gamma_{3e} \to \gamma_{2e}$ indicate two possible pathways from $\gamma_{1e}$, via $\gamma_{3e}$ to $\gamma_{2e}$ and from $\beta_{1e}$, via $\gamma_{3e}$ to $\gamma_{2e}$, respectively.

Looking at $EX_2$ and $EX_4$, $\alpha_{1a} \to \alpha_{1e}$, $\alpha_{1p} \to \alpha_{2p}$, $\alpha_{2e} \to \alpha_{1e}$, $\beta_{1e} \to \gamma_{1e}$, $\beta_{1e} \to \gamma_{3e}$, $\beta_{2e} \to \alpha_{1e}$, $\gamma_{3e} \to \gamma_{2e}$, *training* $\to \alpha_{1e}$ are shared connections. $\alpha_{1a} \to \alpha_{1e}$, $\alpha_{2e} \to \alpha_{1e}$, $\beta_{2e} \to \alpha_{1e}$ and *training* $\to \alpha_{1e}$ show that $\alpha_{1a}$, $\alpha_{2e}$, $\beta_{2e}$ and *Training intensity* are all possible cause of $\alpha_{1e}$. Similarly, $\beta_{1e} \to \gamma_{1e}$, $\beta_{1e} \to \gamma_{3e}$ represent that $\beta_{1e}$ is the common cause of $\gamma_{1e}$ and $\gamma_{3e}$. The remaining connections are consistent with $EX_2$ and $EX_3$.

Looking at $EX_3$ and $EX_4$, $\alpha_{1a} \to \alpha_{1e}$, $\alpha_{1a} \to \alpha_{2p}$, $\alpha_{1p} \to \alpha_{2p}$, $\alpha_{2a} \to \alpha_{1a}$, $\beta_{1e} \to \beta_{2e}$, $\beta_{1e} \to \gamma_{3e}$, $\gamma_{3e} \to \gamma_{2e}$ and *glycogen* $\to \alpha_{2p}$ are shared links. Their interpretation is skipped since they can be found in the above description.

It is observed that some specific pathways can not be found by using association rule mining [47]. For example, $\gamma_{1e} \to \gamma_{3e}$, $\gamma_{3e} \to \gamma_{2e}$, $\beta_{1e} \to \gamma_{3e}$ and $\gamma_{3e} \to \gamma_{2e}$ can be easily identified as a pathway in BNs, whereas association rule mining focuses on identifying frequent patterns instead of discovering patterns with direct or indirect dependency correlations.

## 5.5 Discussion

This chapter proposed a framework to learn the pathway network of protein kinases. We illustrate its performance using a AMPK regulation data set in skeletal muscle. A MCMC-based sampling algorithm is used to identify approximate graphical models in terms of the Bayes factor. The advantage of the Bayesian approach using MCMC is that one only has to consider the likelihood function conditional on the unobserved variables. In many cases, this implies that Bayesian parameter estimation is faster than classical maximum likelihood estimation.

Every biological experiment contains varied definitions and descriptions regarding experimental environments. However, some of them are subordinate and unuseful for data mining purposes. Thus, only the attributes that really make sense biologically are considered. Moreover, the qualitative data is needed to be normalized by transforming the value of attributes into non-negative integers in order as required.

Traditional Bayesian method depends on classical maximum likelihood estimation to search for the optimal solution. Although we use conditional independence to simplify probabilistic inference, exact inference in an arbitrary Bayesian network for discrete variables is NP-hard [68]. Even approximate inference such as Monte-Carlo methods is NP-hard [70]. The difficulty is arisen from undirected cycles in the Bayesian-network structure-cycles in the structure where we ignore the directionality of the arcs [136]. When a Bayesian-network structure includes many undirected cycles, inference is intractable. In many cases, however, structures are simple enough (or can be simplified sufficiently without sacrificing much accuracy) so that inference is efficient. Thus, it is an optional way to find an approximate solution using MCMC sampling because MCMC simulation is the only known general approach for providing a solution within a reasonable time [9]. In theory, if the sample space is big enough, we should be able to obtain a good approximation model that is statistically significant.

The *burn-in* time is specified as 8000 in this chapter. Certainly, it can be allocated a bigger value if the computation is acceptably fast. In theory, the accuracy of estimation and the value of burn-in time are in direct proportion, whereas, we have to consider the time consumption in practice. Similarly, the number of samples can be assigned different values in different cases. According to our experiences, 100 is a reasonable number of sampling.

Biological data are typically characterized by a small sample size, due to the high costs of the technology. The challenge is the common problem of sound statistical methods: a large number of variables with a small number of measurements. In the context of Bayesian networks, this situation leads to the inability to distinguish among the sets of possible models because the small amount of data is insufficient to identify a single most probable model. Thus, the choice of appropriate distributional assumptions may be critical.

We may obtain different approximate graphical models each time. It is possible that a connection is found in a graphical model but not in the others. This is possibly due to the discrepant sampling. This chapter generates four models and focuses on explaining one of them for brevity. To find more reliable connections from them, one option is to highlight the shared connections between models. However, by doing so, some meaningful links may be missed out. Thus, it is important to discover useful connections with the biologists' help.

Bayesian network, an assumption-driven method, has been widely used due to its statistical significance and inherited advantage in handling the information with uncertainty. Although the derived graphical model is intuitive, it depends on the quality and extent of the prior beliefs and is only as useful as this prior knowledge is reliable. This requires a sufficient sample space, whereas this can increase the computation complexity. In contrast, data mining, a data-driven method, may be more efficient in some cases. For example, some potential kinase pathways are undetermined and might be ignored from the assumption. As a result, it is reasonable to use different methods in terms of specific purposes.

There have been many studies to deal with kinase data. An electronic Kinase Inhibitor Database (eKID) is described in [190] and the KinMutBase [172] (a database of human disease-causing protein mutations) is a registry of mutations in human protein kinases related to disorders. They usually focus on collecting sequence data and discussing the kinase regulation from the aspect of genome. However, there are no efforts to deal with the kinase data regarding the expression of isoforms in response to specific stimuli. Further, the methods to analyze the kinase regulation data are underdeveloped. In [57], a web-based data analysis tool (B-Course) for Bayesian modeling is used to analyze the AMPK regulation data. Although the weighted dependency models are generated for AMPK regulation, the regulation of *burn-in* time and the configuration of pruning constraints are not allowed. This may result in missing interesting connections or generating redundant connections without the comparison between models.

We have focused our attention here on structure learning since this step is critical in constructing BNs. When more experimental data are available, it can be further used for Bayesian inference. This chapter analyses AMPK regulation data in human skeletal muscle. Certainly, it can be used for other organisms, such as mouse, and other tissues, such as adipose tissue, heart and liver. Intuitively, it is necessary to classify the data into different groups because different compositions may play a similar role on different tissues or organs. On the other hand, studying the potential metabolic pathways between kinase regulations on different tissues or organs should be useful in disease diagnosis and treatment. We plan to seek answers for these questions in our future work. The results can assist biologists in understanding kinases' pathways and extending it to the other kinases to form a full kinase interaction mapping.

## 5.6  Conclusion

To investigate the metabolic features of protein kinases, this chapter develops a BN-based method for structural learning from a discrete data set of protein kinases. It uses a Markov Chain Monte Carlo (MCMC) algorithm to search the space of all DAGs (directed acyclic graphics), and derive the approximate model $G'$ that can replace the current model $G$ at each step of the built Markov chain. We experimented on the AMPK regulation data, in which AMPK is activated by endurance training in human skeletal muscle. In particular, a voting strategy is applied to extract the connections with high frequency from the obtained graphical models. Our findings show that protein kinases is a metabolic master switch regulating the majority of cellular pathways, such as metabolic actions that are related to energy demand and supply. Those actions are adjusted via its subunit isoforms under specific activation. Thus, there are strong co-relationships between kinases subunit isoforms and external activation. Furthermore, the subunit isoforms are correlated with each other in some cases. The methods developed here could be used when predicting these essential relationships and enhance the understanding of the functions of protein kinases.

# Chapter 6
# Mining Inhibition Pathways for Protein Kinases on Skeletal Muscle

The former two chapters propose approaches to discover positive regulation patterns of protein kinases in signal transduction. However, a deep study into the degree of activation and inhibition of catalytic and regulatory subunits of protein kinases, assists in understanding their profound effect on a cell. Especially, the inhibitors of kinase activity are a frequent cause of diseases, where kinases participate many aspects that control cell growth, movement and death. Thus, it is critical to discover the inhibition pathways for protein kinases. This chapter aims to investigate the potential inhibitive correlation between the subunit isoforms of AMP-activated protein kinase (AMPK), and the stimulus factors by using negative association rule mining and mutual information, respectively. The obtained rules not only prompt a comprehensive understanding of signalling pathways of protein kinase and indicate an attractive pharmacological target for disease treatment.

## 6.1 Introduction

Being an important kinase enzyme, protein kinases become activated in situations of energy consumption and play an important role in diverse metabolic and cellular pathways. There have been a number of protein kinases, such as MAP (mitogen-activated protein) kinases. They perform key regulators of cell function and constitute one of the largest and most functionally diverse gene families [215]. It is already known that the human genome contains about 500 protein kinase genes. Up to 30% of all human proteins may be related to kinase activity, and kinases are known to regulate the majority of cellular pathways, especially those involved in signal transduction [189].

$5'$ AMP-activated protein kinase or AMPK or $5'$ adenosine monophosphate-activated protein kinase is an enzyme that plays a role in cellular energy homeostasis. It is formed by three subunits $\alpha$, $\beta$, $\gamma$ that together make a functional enzyme, conserved from yeast to humans. It is expressed in a number of tissues, including the liver, brain, and skeletal muscle, and is involved in the regulation of exercise-induced changes in glucose and lipid metabolism in skeletal muscle [37, 47].

For example, the activation of AMPK exerts long-term effects at the level of both gene expression and protein synthesis, such as positive effects on glucose uptake of heart, food intake of hypothalamus, and negative effects on insulin secretion of pancreas and cholesterol synthesis of liver [182].

There have been an increasingly growth of regulation data with respect to signal transduction pathways, which impact all areas of biology and medicine. The data are useful to generate understandable paradigms of cellular communication. For example, the analysis of kinase regulation data can determine how an external stimulus might affect the catalytic subunit and regulatory subunit of protein kinases, what isoforms are activated or inhibited in expression as a result of certain situations, and how they coordinate to perform complex functions [47, 87]. This demands for a systematic way to collect the abundant and valuable regulation data from biological experiments and needs advanced techniques for data analysis.

Many efforts have been devoted to analyze biological databases using association rule mining [48, 82, 298], whereas they mainly focus on exploring the positive association in regard to gene expression, genetic pathways and protein-protein interaction. We made an attempt to find positive regulation patterns of AMPK on skeletal muscle in Chapters 4 and 5, whereas the identification of hidden negative (also called *inhibitive* in this chapter) patterns have been largely overlooked and underdeveloped. In recent years, there have been increasing evidences to indicate that the inhibition activity of protein kinases is a frequent cause of disease and has a good prospect in drug design and disease treatment [185, 347]. Hence, the study into the correlations with respect to activation and inhibition of subunit isoforms of protein kinases will contribute to a greater understanding of signalling pathways.

Traditional associations have been extended to include negative associations as well as positive associations $X \Rightarrow Y$ [4, 44, 324]. Recent investigation indicates that frequent patterns can involve negative terms. Negative association rules assist in determining which alters can be ignored for a fair and efficient trading environment [324]. To our opinion, the negative associations are also prevalent in regulatory pathways. For example, as for AMPK regulation, a negative rule *low intensity* $\Rightarrow \neg \alpha_{2a} \uparrow$ may indicate that a low intensity exercise may inhibit the expression of $\alpha_{2a}$. If there is an evidence that the inhibited expression of $\alpha_{2a}$ is linked to a disease, this makes it an useful pharmacologic target.

Unlike association patterns, correlations mainly focus on describing the underlying dependency among variables. Further, it is not restricted to frequently co-occurring patterns. This is useful to avoid missing interesting patterns. A number of methods have been developed for correlations [220, 245]. In particular, mutual information is commonly recognized as one of the most effective and trusted measures for correlations. In *Quantitative Association Rule mining* [180], mutual information was employed to measure the strength of the relationships between two attributes, by which a strongly correlated mutual information graph was constructed. Based on mutual information, an unsupervised fuzzy c-means clustering was proposed, considering the significance of features and the relevance between features [329]. A number of mutual information measures have been developed under different scenarios, such as conditional mutual information, and provide disparate criteria of correlations. To identify inhibitory regulation patterns of protein kinases, it may be a good option to combine mutual information with negative association rule mining.

This chapter aims to identify negative patterns of AMPK regulation by extending the negative association rule mining algorithm. A data set of AMPK from Medline is applied in the experiment. Item constraints in the closed interpretation are proposed to specify general constraints on itemset generation. Further, the identification of top-N interesting negative itemsets, instead of specifying a fixed threshold value for all itemsets of all sizes like [59, 318] is also proposed. As a complement for identifying negative pattern, this chapter first applies correlation measure to extract significant items as initial dataset. Further, support constraints are applied to control the generation of interesting negative itemsets. The obtained negative rules reveal potential inhibitive associations with respect to AMPK regulation. Many of which make sense biologically. Those suggesting new hypotheses may warrant further investigation.

## 6.2 Preliminaries

### 6.2.1 Data Preprocessing

An AMPK regulation data set by searching the PubMed database of NCBI using the keywords *AMPK* and *human skeletal muscle* is applied in the experiment. As of June 2010, there are 413 articles in response to the search. A data set is generated by removing the records related to rat or genome regulation. In the same manner as Chapter 4, the obtained initial items are partitioned into state items and stimulus items. Each item corresponds to an attribute/value pair. Table 6.1 presents an example of raw data set of AMPK, in which $t$ and $t^-$ represent *moderate time* and *short time*, respectively; $I^-$, $I^{++}$ and $I^+$ represent *low intensity*, *high intensity* and *moderate intensity*, respectively; $nn$ indicates normal *Nicotinic acid*; $ng$ and $hg$ represent *normal glycogen* and *high glycogen*, respectively; $t$ and $ut$ indicate *trained* and *untrained*, respectively.

**Table 6.1** Activity, protein expression and phosphorylation of $\alpha_1$ of AMPK in skeletal muscle

| $a_{1a}$ | $a_{1e}$ | $a_{1p}$ | Training | Glycogen | Nicotinic acid | Intensity | Duration |
|---|---|---|---|---|---|---|---|
| $a_{1a}\downarrow$ | – | $a_{1p}\|$ | $t$ | $hg$ | $nn$ | $I^-$ | $t$ |
| – | – | – | $ut$ | $ng$ | $nn$ | $I^+$ | $t$ |
| $a_{1a}\|$ | – | – | $ut$ | $ng$ | $nn$ | $I^{++}$ | $t^-$ |
| $a_{1a}\uparrow$ | $a_{1e}\|$ | $a_{1p}\|$ | $ut$ | $ng$ | $nn$ | $I^{++}$ | $t$ |
| $a_{1a}\downarrow$ | – | – | $ut$ | $ng$ | $nn$ | $I^+$ | $t^-$ |

Incomplete, noisy, and inconsistent data are commonplace properties of real-world databases [127]. Data preprocessing may improve the quality of the data, and guarantee the efficiency and accuracy of mining algorithms. In AMPK regulation data, *activity*, *protein expression* and *phosphorylation* are used as testing indexes for $\alpha$, whereas only protein expression is used for $\beta$ and $\gamma$ [47]. Thus, we can generate the initial items including stimulus items after pruning unnecessary information such as publication. Further, the results derived from different experiments need to be integrated together, by which to generate a data set $I = S \cup ST$.

To generate negative association rules, we first need to identify frequent itemsets from the data according to Formula 4.2. To avoid missing valuable initial itemsets and ensure the correctness of patterns, it is necessary to distinguish high occurrence itemset from low occurrence itemset [47] in terms of the minimum occurrence $minoccur = 2/|E|$. Thus, a collection of initial interesting itemsets are obtained using the filtering symbols and given minimum occurrence.

### 6.2.2   Negative Association Rule Mining

In contrast to positive rule, a negative association rule is defined as the forms of $X \Rightarrow \neg Y$, $\neg X \Rightarrow Y$, and $\neg X \Rightarrow \neg Y$. For brevity, we use $\neg X \Rightarrow Y$ to represent negative association rules in this chapter. Suppose *minsup* and *mincof* represent *minimum support* and *minimum confidence*, respectively in usual sense. According to the definition in [324], the following criteria can be used to evaluate a negative association rule:

- $X$ and $Y$ are disjoint itemsets, namely, $X \cap Y = \emptyset$;
- $supp(X) \geq minsup$, $supp(Y) \geq minsup$ and $supp(X \cup Y) < minsup$;
- $supp(\neg X \Rightarrow Y) = supp(\neg X \cup Y)$;
- $conf(\neg X \Rightarrow Y) = \frac{supp(\neg X \cup Y) - supp(\neg X) * supp(Y)}{supp(\neg X) * (1 - supp(Y))} \geq mincof.$

In this chapter, the negative association rule mining is extended for analyzing kinase regulation data. Suppose $E = \{E_1, \cdots, E_n\}$ represents a collection of experiments. Each experiment includes an *eid* (experiment identifier) and two itemsets, $E_i = (eid, S_i, ST_i)$, in which $S$ and $ST$ represent state items and stimulus items, respectively. Let $I = \{x \mid x \in S_i \cup ST_i\}$, $1 \leq i \leq n\}$ be a set of items, and $X \subseteq I$ and $Y \subseteq I$ be itemsets. A rule $\neg X \Rightarrow Y$ has support, $s$, in the set of experiments if $s\%$ of experiments contains $X$ and $Y$. The rule has confidence, $c$, if $c\%$ of experiments containing $\neg X$, also contain $\neg X$ and $Y$.

The above confidence measure is specified in terms of the *CPIR* (*conditional-probability increment ratio*) function for a pair of itemsets $X$ and $Y$ [324], which is inferred by the statistical dependence $Dependence(X, Y) = \frac{P(Y|X)}{P(Y)}$ of Piatetsky-Shapiros argument [252]. If $Dependence(X, Y) = 1$, $X$ and $Y$ are independent. $Dependence(X, Y) > 1$ and $Dependence(X, Y) < 1$ indicate the *positive dependence* and *negative dependence*, respectively.

Apriori algorithm [4] is a popular strategy to mining frequent itemsets according to a uniform minimum support for all itemsets. Nevertheless, it is uneasy for users to specify an optimal support threshold for all itemsets of all sizes [59]. An inappropriate threshold may result in generating redundant results or missing interesting patterns. As a result, the constraint-based mining technique [318] in combination with negative association rules [324] is applied herein to provide a flexible identification and control of interesting negative patterns.

### 6.2.3  Mutual Information

Unlike association patterns, correlations mainly focus on describing the underlying dependency among the variables. Further, it is not restricted to frequently co-occurring patterns. This is useful to avoid missing interesting patterns. A number of methods have been developed for correlations [220, 245]. In particular, mutual information is commonly recognized as one of the most effective and trusted measures for correlations. In Quantitative Association Rule mining [180], mutual information was employed to measure the strength of the relationships between two attributes, by which a strongly correlated mutual information graph was constructed. Based on mutual information, an unsupervised fuzzy c-means clustering was proposed, considering the significance of features and the relevance between features [329]. A number of mutual information measures have been under different scenarios, such as conditional mutual information, and provide disparate criteria of correlations. To identify inhibitory regulation patterns of protein kinases, it may be a good option to combine mutual information with negative association rule mining.

This section presents another framework to capture biologically important negative regulation patterns from protein kinase data. It first applies correlation measure to extract significant items as initial dataset. Further, support constraints are applied to control the generation of interesting negative itemsets. The biological significance of obtained patterns is validated by known results in published literatures and comments from biological collaborators.

**Mutual Information.** In information theory, mutual information is a central concept and enables us to capture informative relationships between variables. The mutual information of two random variables $A$ and $B$, namely $I(A; B)$, is defined as:

$$I(A;B) = \sum_{v_A \in dom(A)} \sum_{v_B \in dom(B)} log \frac{p(v_A, v_B)}{p(v_A)p(v_B)} \tag{6.1}$$

A large $I(A;B)$ presents $A$ and $B$ share more information with each other. In contrast, $I(A;B) = 0$ means $A$ and $B$ share nothing, or indicates $A$ and $B$ are mutually independent. To capture the items with strong dependency correlations, mutual information measure needs to be extended and adapted as below. Given two items $a$ and $b$, the mutual information of $a$ and $b$ is defined as:

$$I(A;B) = P(a,b)log_2\frac{P(a,b)}{P(a)P(b)} + P(a,\bar{b})log_2\frac{P(a,\bar{b})}{P(a)P(\bar{b})} +$$
$$P(\bar{a},b)log_2\frac{P(\bar{a},b)}{P(\bar{a})P(b)} + P(\bar{a},\bar{b})log_2\frac{P(\bar{a},\bar{b})}{P(\bar{a})P(\bar{b})}$$

(6.2)

Given a minimum mutual information (*minmui*) threshold $\mu$, an item $\alpha$ is considered to be significant if there exists another item $c$ such that $I(a;c) \geq \mu$. Otherwise, the item $\alpha$ should be pruned owing to weak dependence on other items. For example, given an itemset $\{\alpha_{1a}|, \beta_{1e} \downarrow, low\ glycogen\}$, there are $I(\alpha_{1a}|; \beta_{1e} \downarrow) < \mu$ and $I(\beta_{1e} \downarrow; low\ glycogen) < \mu$. This indicates that *no change* of $\beta_{1e}$ has little correlation with *low glycogen* and the expressed $\alpha_{1a}$, and needs to be removed. This avoids the generation of uninteresting patterns. The remaining items are mutually dependent and contain biologically important information regarding protein kinase regulation.

### 6.2.4 Protein Kinase Regulation

As described in Chapter 4, AMPK contains catalytic subunit isoforms $\alpha_1$ and $\alpha_2$ and regulatory subunit isoforms $\beta_1$, $\beta_2$, $\gamma_1$, $\gamma_2$ and $\gamma_3$. The subunit isoforms congregate together to perform the functions of AMPK. Therefore, interpretation and analysis of AMPK regulation data and identification of inhibition pathways from the data, can enhance the understanding of its structure, function and expression. This chapter aims to discover negative patterns from a collection of AMPK regulation data.

Each experimental result consists of two types of items as described in Chapter 4, including *Stimulus item (ST)* and *State item (S)*. For example, *intensity*, *load* and *duration* are generally used to evaluate the exercise stimuli. +++, ++, + and - indicate that the stimulus is *"intense"*, *"high"*, *"moderate"* and *"low"*, respectively. ↑, | and ↓ are used to indicate *"highly expressed"*, *"expressed"*, and *"no change"* in expression, respectively. For example, $\beta_2$ and $\gamma_2$ isoforms of AMPK are found to be highly expressed in white quadriceps under the training of moderate intensity treadmill [86]. The initial rule for this experiment can be written as $X = \{moderate\ intensity\ treadmill\} \Rightarrow Y = \{\beta_{2a} \uparrow, \gamma_{2a} \uparrow\}$. Further, there might be hidden associations like $\{low\ intensity\ treadmill\} \Rightarrow \{\rightarrow \beta_{2a}|\}$, which indicates the negative regulation to $\beta_2$.

## 6.3 Inhibition Patterns Discovery Using Negative Association Rule

### 6.3.1 Item Constraints

As described above, it is quite subtle to set a minimum support: a too small threshold may result in the output of many redundant patterns, whereas a too big one may generate no answer or miss interesting knowledge. In addition, it is natural that the probability of occurrence of a larger size itemset is inherently much smaller than that of a smaller size itemset. A more flexible option is proposed in [47] to allow users to specify different thresholds in accordance with different itemsets and extract the *top-N interesting itemsets* as answers. This section aims to define *top-N interesting negative itemsets*.

**Definition 6.1. Interesting negative itemset.** Suppose $X = \{x_1, \cdots, x_m\}$ represents an itemset as usual. . Let $Y = \{\neg y_1, \cdots, \neg y_n\}$ be a set of negative items, $y_j \in X$, $1 \leq n \leq m$. Let $A = Y \cup (X - \{y_1, \cdots, y_n\})$. $A$ is an interesting negative itemset if $\forall x_i$, $supp(x_i) \geq minsup$, $supp(X) < minsup$, $supp(A) \geq minsup$.

**Definition 6.2. Top-N interesting negative $k$-itemset.** An *interesting negative k-itemset* represents an interesting negative itemset with $k$ items. The *interesting negative k-itemsets* are sorted in descending order by their supports. Let $s$ be the support of the $N$th *interesting negative k-itemset* in the sorted list. The *top-N interesting negative k-itemset* is defined as the set of *interesting negative k-itemset* whose supports are equal to or larger than $s$.

*Example 6.1.* Table 6.2 presents an example of interesting negative 2-itemsets and 3-itemsets. As a result, *top-2* interesting negative 2-itemsets = $\{A \rightarrow E, \neg AC, E \rightarrow F\}$, *top-1* interesting negative 2-itemsets = $\{\neg AC\}$, *top-2* interesting negative 3-itemsets = $\{BC \rightarrow F, BD \rightarrow F\}$.

**Table 6.2**  An example of interesting negative 2-itemsets and 3-itemsets

| itemset | support | itemset | support |
|---------|---------|---------|---------|
| $A, \neg E$ | 0.3 | $\neg B, E$ | 0.1 |
| $A, \neg F$ | 0.25 | $E, \neg F$ | 0.3 |
| $\neg A, C$ | 0.4 | $B, C, \neg F$ | 0.3 |
| $C, \neg E$ | 0.2 | $B, D, \neg F$ | 0.2 |

There are perhaps more than $N$ itemsets satisfy *top-N interesting negative k-itemset*. For exmaple, $A \rightarrow E$ and $E \rightarrow F$ have equal support in Example 6.1 and are included in the *top-2* interesting negative 2-itemsets. In this extreme case, it needs to be reported to the user, rather than returning all of them. In the similar manner, we can define *top-N interesting negative itemset*.

**Definition 6.3. Top-N interesting negative itemset** is the union of the *top-N interesting negative k-itemset* where $2 \leq k \leq k_{max}$ and $k_{max}$ is the upper bound of the size of itemsets we would like to find. An itemset is of interest if, and only if, it is in the *top-N negative k-itemset*.

*Example 6.2.* Suppose $k_{max} = 3$. According to Definition 6.3 and Table 6.2, *top-2* interesting negative itemset = $\{A \rightarrow E, \neg AC, E \rightarrow F\} \cup \{BC \rightarrow F, BD \rightarrow F\} = \{A \rightarrow E, \neg AC, E \rightarrow F, BC \rightarrow F, BD \rightarrow F\}$.

A number of *top-N* mining algorithms [59, 318] have been proposed to discover all *top-N* itemsets. This is often low efficient and results in many useless or uninteresting itemsets. A novel approach was developed [47] to divide a set of items, $I$, into several bins, where each bin $B_j$ contains a subset of items in $I$. Unfortunately, the above methods do not address the negative items.

In this chapter, the item constraint is applied in a similar way to the enumeration-based specification defined in [47, 66]. In the same way, the constraint can be expressed in a concise Formula 4.2, namely $IC_i(B_{i1}, \cdots, B_{im}) = N_i$, in which $B_{ij} \cap B_{ik} = \emptyset$, $1 \leq j, k \leq m, j \neq k$. $N_i$ represents the number of itemsets satisfying $IC_i$ in terms of a specified support. It explicitly indicates what particular items we focus on and which should be presented in the extraction of frequent patterns. For example, $B_1 = \{\alpha_{1a}, \alpha_{2a}\}$ and $B_2 = \{\gamma_{1a}, \gamma_{1p}\}$ indicate that the user is interested in activity of $\alpha$, rather than protein expression and phosphorylation, and only activity and phosphorylation of $\gamma_1$, rather than protein expression.

**Definition 6.4. Closed interpretation.** Let $B_{ij} \in IC_i$. An itemset $X = \{x_{i1}, \cdots, x_{im}\}$ satisfies a constraint $IC_i$ in the *closed interpretation* if $x_{ij} \in B_{ij}$ or $\neg x_{ij} \in B_{ij}$, and $\forall x_{ik} \in X, k \neq j, x_{ik} \notin B_{ij}, \neg x_{ik} \notin B_{ij}$.

Given $|IC_i| = k$, a collection of *interesting negative k-itemsets* can be generated in terms of closed interpretation. Suppose $\theta$ represents the $N_j th$ support according to the descending order of the support of itemsets. Consequently, all *interesting negative k-itemsets*, with support not less than $\theta$, are interesting under the constraint. We call them *top-$N_j$ interesting negative itemsets* of $IC_j$ in the closed interpretation. Users are allowed to specify several item constraints. It is flexible to obtain *top-$N_i$ interesting negative itemsets* for each $IC_i$ in the closed interpretation.

*Example 6.3.* Suppose, the items of regulation data are partitioned into the following bins: $B_1 = \{\alpha_{1a}, \alpha_{2a}\}, B_2 = \{\alpha_{1e}, \alpha_{2e}\}, B_3 = \{\alpha_{1p}, \alpha_{2p}\}, B_4 = \{\beta_{1e}\}, B_5 = \{\beta_{2e}\}, B_6 = \{high\ intensity,\ short\ duration,\ trained,\ diabetes\}$. Let $IC_1 = (B_1, B_2, B_3), |IC_1| = 3, IC_2 = (B_4, B_5), |IC_2| = 2$ and $IC_3 = (B_5, B_6), |IC_3| = 2$. Thus, the itemset $X_1 = \{\neg \alpha_{2a} \uparrow, \neg \alpha_{1e} \uparrow, \alpha_{1p} \uparrow\}, X_2 = \{\beta_{1e} \uparrow, \neg \beta_{2e}|\}$ and $X_3 = \{\neg \beta_{2e}|,\ high\ intensity\}$ correspond to bin patterns $(B_1, B_2, B_3), (B_4, B_5)$ and $(B_5, B_6)$, respectively. In other words, $X_1, X_2$ and $X_3$ satisfy the specified $IC_1, IC_2$ and $IC_3$, respectively in the closed interpretation. In contrast, $X_1' = \{\gamma_{1e} \uparrow, \neg \alpha_{1e} \uparrow, \alpha_{1p} \uparrow\}$ does not satisfy $IC_1$ in closed interpretation due to $\gamma_{1e} \notin B_1$.

As discussed above, the untested items in experiments need to be pruned while defining item constraints. Filtering symbols are specified to reduce the search space while identifying patterns from the initial interesting itemsets. The details can be seen at http://bioinformatics.gxu.edu.cn/bio/data/LNAI8335/8335-2.zip, in which 8, 12, 29 and 30 correspond to the untested items regarding $\alpha_{1e}, \alpha_{1p}, \beta_{1e}$ and $\beta_{2e}$, respectively. Further, in the data set, the non-negative integers 4, 8, 12 and 16 represent the specified filtering symbols for $\alpha_{1a}, \alpha_{1e}, \alpha_{1p}$ and $\alpha_{2a}$, respectively.

### 6.3.2 Negative Rules

The obtained *top-$N_i$ negative itemsets* in the closed interpretation are then used to identify negative association rules. Two options that depend on which antecedents or consequents of rules the item constraint *IC* are defined for rule generation. Let $X$ and $X'$ be top interesting itemsets from *IC* and *IC'*, respectively, and $X' \subset X = X' \cup \neg Y$.

- if $supp(X) / supp(X') \geq minconf$ and $supp(X' \cup Y) < minsup$, $X' \Rightarrow \neg Y$ is a negative rule of interest.
- if $supp(X) / supp(X - X') \geq minconf$ and $supp(Y \cup X') < minsup$, $\neg Y \Rightarrow X'$ is a negative rule of interest..

Further, those rules that are uninteresting from the aspect of kinase regulation need to be pruned. Usually, a negative rule is valid if it conforms to the rule of the forms below:

- *Rule*1: $\neg X \Rightarrow Y, X \subseteq S$ and $\forall y_i \in Y, y_i \in S$ or $\neg y_i \in S$ and
- *Rule*2: $\neg X \Rightarrow Y, X \subseteq ST$ and $\forall y_i \in Y, y_i \in S$ or $\neg y_i \in S$.

The relation between stimulus items such as *intensity* and *time* is not meaningful in biology at all. As a result, these rules are uninteresting and should be removed. Usually, if $X \Rightarrow Y$ is identified as a valid positive rule, it is impossible to obtain negative associations between $X$ and $Y$. However, we may obtain correlated positive and negative associations, which can be integrated to deduct new associations. For example, we can generate an association $X \Rightarrow \neg Z$ by integrating positive association $X \Rightarrow Y$ and negative association $Y \Rightarrow \neg Z$. Some authors may be concerned the associations may be dominated by positive associations or negative associations. In either cases, the positive associations and negative associations need to be considered together.

### 6.3.3 Experimental Results

This chapter identifies interesting negative itemsets by extending the algorithm in [324]. They are used to extract interesting negative association rules for protein kinase regulation in combination with specified item constraints using bins. As specified in Chapter 4, 17 bins corresponding to 17 attributes are specified in terms of the comments from our biology collaborators. Each attribute can contain several state measurements. Thus, each bin $B_i$ may contain more than one item. We specify item constraint $IC_i$ in the closed interpretation. Chapter 4 presents the formula 4.3, namely $IC_i(BV_1, \cdots, BV_k) = N_i, 0 \leq k \leq k_{max}$, in which $k_{max}$ is the upper bound of the size of itemsets that users want to find. More details can be seen in Chapter 4

**Rule Identification.** Unlike traditional association rule mining, the itemsets are allocated into specified bins and the extracted rules must satisfy the required forms described above. Further, the extraction of negative rule is complex in contrast to positive association rules due to its varied forms and additional conditions need to satisfy. Without exception, this may increase the complexity of discovering negative association rules. The procedure of identifying negative association rules mainly include four phases:

- Configure bin $B_j$ and item constraint $IC_i$.
- Generate initial interesting negative itemsets from initial items in terms of the specified bins.
- Sort out the itemsets that do not contain filtering symbols.
- Extract negative association rules using $IC_i$.

The obtained negative itemsets using item constraints are then sorted in descending order of supports, by which we can generate the *top-$N_i$* interesting negative itemsets for each corresponding constraint $IC_i$. This chapter focuses on identifying negative association rules on the basis of these *top-N* interesting negative itemsets. The search space is greatly reduced as a result of removing the itemsets with filtering symbols and sorting itemsets in bins in the closed interpretation.

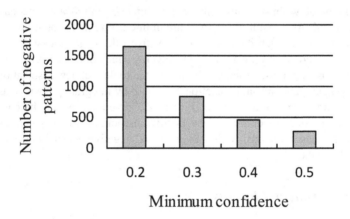

**Fig. 6.1** Negative interesting patterns using $\lambda = 25$

To see the variation of pattern output, the minimum confidence is varied from 0.2 to 0.5 by increasing 0.1 each time. Figure 6.1 shows the result of negative interesting patterns by using $\lambda = 25$ and including all attributes. There are 1648 and 843 negative association rules by minimum confidence 0.2 and 0.3, respectively. According to these rules, we can find many potential correlations between itemsets. Those rules that do not satisfy the forms of *Rule1* and *Rule2* in terms of the definition in Section 6.3.2 are removed. This can be achieved by using constraint while identifying negative patterns. Further, the rules that can overlap with each other need to be integrated.

**Algorithm and Performance.** This chapter focuses on identifying negative association rules from kinase regulation data. Thus, the algorithm for handling positive rules is not discussed herein. Those readers who want to learn more details can refer to the paper in [47].

> **begin**
>
> ***Input***: $D$: a data set of protein kinase; $IC$: item constraint, *mincof*: minimum confidence;
>
> (1) **let NL** $\leftarrow \emptyset$: set of infrequent itemsets of interest, $IS_i \leftarrow \emptyset$: frequent interesting itemsets from $IC_i$, **R** $\leftarrow \emptyset$: set of negative association rules;
>
> (2) **for** each $IC_i \in IC$ **do**
>
> >   **calculate** $minsup_i$ for each $IC_i$;
> >
> >   **call** *Apriori* algorithm to generate interesting itemsets $IS$ for each $IC_i$;
> >
> >   $IS_i \leftarrow IS_i \cup IS$;
> >
> > **end**
>
> (3) **for** each $IC_i \in IC$ **do**
>
> >   **for** each $X_{ij}, Y_{ij} \in IS_i$ from $IC_i$ **do**
> >
> >   **if** $X_{ij} \cap Y_{ij} = \emptyset, X_{ij} \cup Y_{ij} = A, supp(A) < minsup_i$ **then**
> >
> >   **NL** $\leftarrow A \cup$ **NL**;
> >
> > **end**
> >
> > **end**
>
> (4) **for** each infrequent itemset $X \cup Y = I \in$ **NL** from $IC_i$ **do**
>
> >   **if** $supp(Y \cup \neg X) \geq minsup_i$ **and** $conf(Y|\neg X) \geq mincof$ **then**
> >
> >   $R \leftarrow R \cup \neg X \Rightarrow Y$;
> >
> >   **if** $supp(\neg Y \cup X) \geq minsup_i$ **and** $conf(\neg Y|X) \geq mincof$ **then**
> >
> >   $R \leftarrow R \cup X \Rightarrow \neg Y$;
> >
> >   **if** $supp(\neg Y \cup \neg X) \geq minsup_i$ **and** $conf(\neg Y|\neg X) \geq mincof$ **then**
> >
> >   $R \leftarrow R \cup \neg X \Rightarrow \neg Y$;
> >
> > **end**
>
> **end**

Step 1 assigns an empty set for *NL*, $IS_i$ and *R*, respectively. An element will be added to the corresponding set if it satisfies requirements. They are used to store the infrequent itemsets, frequent itemsets and negative association rules, respectively.

Step 2 calculates the minimum support for each itemset constraint $IC_i$ in terms of the Formula 4.4. *Apriori* algorithm is used to identify all frequent interesting itemsets in corresponding $IC_i$. According to the obtained $IS_i$ in step 2, the infrequent itemset of interest *NL* is generated in step 3. Step 4 uses the derived infrequent itemsets of interest to extract frequent negative patterns according to their confidence. The identified negative association rules are stored into *R* for further interpretation.

The performance test is made by comparing our methods with the *Apriori* algorithm [4] and the algorithms from [59, 324]. The comparison is divided into two parts, including the capability of handling negative patterns and the efficiency of discovering negative association rules. As mentioned in [324], the results indicate that most existing algorithms focus on dealing with interesting positive itemsets. Although the method in [324] addresses the issue of mining negative association rules, it can generate abundant rules or missing interesting rules while analyzing regulation data.

The algorithm is implemented in a Lenovo PC, Pentium(R) Dual-core CPU E5400 @ 2.70GHz, 2.69GHz, 2.00GB memory. Our method is extended and adapted from the algorithms of [126, 324] (The software can be provided under request). They have made comparison with other algorithms with respect to identification of positive frequent itemsets. Thus, we do not repeat it again but focus on comparison of discovering negative rules. Table 6.3 presents the running time and number of corresponding output. It is observed that there are still 269 negative rules under the minimum confidence 0.5. Thus, it is uneasy for biologists to sort out the significant patterns and interpret them.

**Table 6.3** Running time and number of itemsets and patterns under *minconf* 0.5

| Output | time (seconds) | number |
|---|---|---|
| Frequent itemset | 481.593 | 40690 |
| Non-frequent itemsets | 481.593 | 465 |
| Interesting non-frequent itemsets | 485.316 | 125 |
| Negative patterns | 487.266 | 269 |

The *frequent itemsets* are generated by using *Apriori* algorithm and the remaining itemsets are generated in terms of the algorithm in [324]. The detailed comparison between them can be seen in the literature and is not repeated herein. Table 6.4 presents a brief comparison with respect to our miner tNP (*top negative pattern*), *Apriori* and NP [324]. It is observed that tNP and NP can be used for negative pattern mining, whereas only tNP is able to identify top negative patterns. Especially, the minimum support in tNP is computed in terms of different rule groups instead of specifying a fix value. Further, Table 6.5 presents the efficiency of pruning itemsets for all attributes, in which $fi$, $nfi$, $infi$ represent *frequent itemsets*, *non-frequent itemset* and *interesting non-frequent itemsets*, respectively. There is a major reduction from the frequent itemsets, non-frequent itemsets, to interesting non-frequent itemsets.

**Table 6.4** A comparison between tNP, Apriori and NP

| Miners | minsupp | non-frequent itemset | top negative patterns |
|---|---|---|---|
| tNP | no | yes | yes |
| Apriori | yes | no | no |
| NP | yes | yes | no |

As mentioned above, our method is able to identify top negative patterns by using constraints. It is convenient for users to specify the interesting attributes and efficiently identify the potential patterns. Figures 6.2 and 6.3 present the running

**Table 6.5** Efficiency of pruning itemsets for all attributes

| minconf | fi | nfi | infi |
|---------|-------|-----|------|
| 0.2 | 40690 | 465 | 330 |
| 0.3 | 40690 | 465 | 264 |
| 0.4 | 40690 | 465 | 187 |
| 0.5 | 40690 | 465 | 125 |

**Table 6.6** Efficiency of pruning itemsets with respect to $\alpha$, $\beta$, $\gamma$

| minconf | fi | nfi | infi |
|---------|------|-----|------|
| 0.2 | 4081 | 192 | 145 |
| 0.3 | 4081 | 192 | 124 |
| 0.4 | 4081 | 192 | 107 |
| 0.5 | 4081 | 192 | 100 |

efficiency of interesting non-frequent itemsets with respect to all attributes and the attributes of $\alpha$, $\beta$ and $\gamma$ subunits, respectively. In contrast to Table 6.5, Table 6.6 presents the pruning efficiency of interesting non-frequent itemsets by considering $\alpha$, $\beta$ and $\gamma$ only. Further, Figure 6.4 compares the identification of obtained negative patterns, in which *all* and *subunit* represent all attributes and the attributes regarding $\alpha$, $\beta$ and $\gamma$ subunits, respectively. From the observation, there is a significant reduction of negative patterns by using constraints. Certainly, this can be further reduced by specifying less bin and larger minimum confidence.

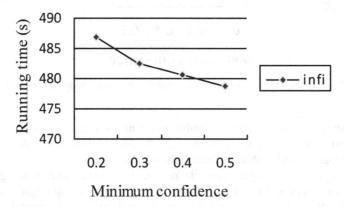

**Fig. 6.2** The change of running time for interesting non-frequent itemsets from all attributes using different minimum confidences

**Interpretation.** Many negative patterns can be generated by using the proposed framework in this chapter, whereas one of the most critical things is to sort out the patterns that make sense in biology and give corresponding biological interpretation. We have discovered a collection of positive association rules with respect to AMPK regulation on skeletal muscle [47]. Thus, this chapter focuses on explaining

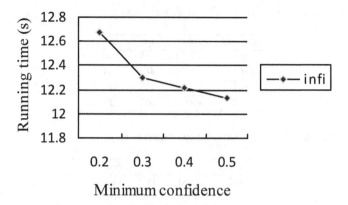

**Fig. 6.3** The change of running time for interesting non-frequent itemsets from attributes of $\alpha$, $\beta$ and $\gamma$ using different minimum confidences

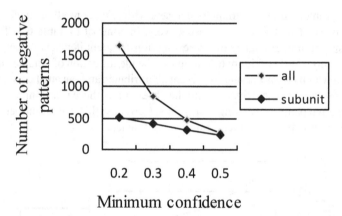

**Fig. 6.4** The comparison of number of negative patterns using different minimum confidences

the interesting negative patterns in combination with the previous positive patterns. Further, some relevant negative patterns, such as $\neg A \Rightarrow B$ and $\neg A \Rightarrow B, C$, will be combined together rather than explaining them separately.

Table 6.7 presents 23 negative association rules with respect to AMPK regulation in terms of *minconf* = 0.1 and $\lambda$ = 25. It is impractical to list all negative rules in this chapter due to limited space. From the observation, the rules contain at least one negative items and follow the specified rule formats as required. Unlike positive association rules, the negative patterns of pathway need to be explained from both aspects of activation and inhibition.

Looking at rules 1 and 2, they describe an inhibition relation between $\alpha_{1a}$ and $\alpha_{2a}$. The former means if the activity of $\alpha_{1a}$ has no change, it may result in an inhibition of highly expressed $\alpha_{2a}$. The latter indicates if $\alpha_{2a}$ is highly expressed, it may result in *no change* of the $\alpha_{1a}$ activity. Thus, the regulation of AMPK in skeletal

**Table 6.7** Selection of interesting negative patterns of AMPK regulation

| | negative patterns | confidence |
|---|---|---|
| 1 | $\alpha_{1a} \downarrow \Rightarrow \neg\, \alpha_{2a} \uparrow$ | 0.21 |
| 2 | $\alpha_{2a} \uparrow \Rightarrow \neg\, \alpha_{1a} \downarrow$ | 0.21 |
| 3 | $\alpha_{1a}| \Rightarrow \neg\, \beta_{1e}|$ | 1 |
| 4 | $\beta_{1e}| \Rightarrow \neg\, \alpha_{1a}|$ | 1 |
| 5 | $\alpha_{1a}| \Rightarrow \neg\, \beta_{2e}|$ | 1 |
| 6 | $\beta_{2e}| \Rightarrow \neg\, \alpha_{1a}|$ | 1 |
| 7 | $\alpha_{1a}| \Rightarrow \neg\, \gamma_{3e}|$ | 1 |
| 8 | $\alpha_{2a}| \Rightarrow \neg\, \beta_{1e}|$ | 0.2 |
| 9 | $\neg\, \alpha_{2a} \uparrow \Rightarrow \neg\, \beta_{1e}|$ | 0.24 |
| 10 | $\alpha_{2a}| \Rightarrow \neg\, \beta_{2e}|$ | 0.5 |
| 11 | $\alpha_{2a}| \Rightarrow \neg\, \beta_{1e}|$ | 0.2 |
| 12 | $\neg\, \alpha_{2a} \uparrow \Rightarrow \neg\, \beta_{2e}|$ | 0.2 |
| 13 | $\neg\, \alpha_{2a} \downarrow \Rightarrow \neg\, \gamma_{3e}|$ | 1 |
| 14 | $\beta_{1e}| \Rightarrow \neg\, \alpha_{2e} \downarrow$ | 1 |
| 15 | $\alpha_{2e} \downarrow \Rightarrow \neg\, \beta_{1e}|$ | 1 |
| 16 | $\{\neg ng, nd, nc\} \Rightarrow \alpha_{2a}|$ | 0.23 |
| 17 | $\{ng, nd, I\} \Rightarrow \neg\, \alpha_{2a} \uparrow$ | 0.39 |
| 18 | $\{\neg ng, nd\} \Rightarrow \neg\, \alpha_{2a} \uparrow$ | 0.13 |
| 19 | $\{ng, I^+\} \Rightarrow \{\neg\, \alpha_{1a} \downarrow, \alpha_{2a} \uparrow\}$ | 0.45 |
| 20 | $\{ut, nd\} \Rightarrow \{\neg\, \alpha_{1a} \downarrow, \alpha_{2a} \uparrow\}$ | 0.24 |
| 21 | $\{\neg nd, nc, I\} \Rightarrow \neg\, \alpha_{1a} \downarrow$ | 0.23 |
| 22 | $\{\neg ng, I\} \Rightarrow \neg\, \alpha_{1a} \downarrow$ | 0.17 |
| 23 | $\{\neg ut, I\} \Rightarrow \neg\, \alpha_{1a} \downarrow$ | 0.12 |

muscle is probably relied on $\alpha_2$ rather than $\alpha_1$ and the AMPK $\alpha_2$ is possible to be the predominant complex responsible for the regulation in both healthy and diabetic subjects. This is consistent to the results obtained in [47].

Looking at rules 3, 4, 5, 6, 7, they present the inhibitive relations between $\alpha_{1a}$ and $\beta_{1e}$, $\beta_{2e}$ and $\gamma_{3e}$. Rules 3 and 4 present $\alpha_{1a}$ and $\beta_{1e}$ may inhibit each other's expression or activity. There are similar relationships between $\alpha_{1a}$ and $\beta_{2e}$, $\gamma_{3e}$. However, it is uncertain that the expression or activity tends to be *no change* or *highly expressed*. This needs to be further verified in future experiments. Moreover, these rules present $\alpha_1$ activity is usually unchanged while $\alpha_2$ activity is easily increased under the same exercises. Actually, $\alpha_1$ activity might change only under higher intensity exercises. In contrast, $\alpha_2$ activity will certainly go up under the same condition (higher intensity). This is also demonstrated by [47].

Looking at rules 9, 10, 11, 12, 13, they show that $\alpha$ activity is co-expressed with protein expression of $\beta$ or $\gamma$. Although it is evident that $\alpha_1$ and $\alpha_2$ have different intrinsic activities, the observations in [26] show that regulation of their activity is highly dependent on the $\gamma$ isoform in the complex. This is consistent with rules 7 and 13. Further, it appears that $\alpha_2$ activity rather than $\alpha_1$ activity appears to correlate with protein expression of $\beta$ subunits. The other patterns may not be found previously, whereas they can be remained for test in future experiments.

Rules 14 and 15 describe the associations between protein expression of $\beta_{1e}$ and $\alpha_{2e}$. In other words, the expression of $\beta_{1e}$ may be co-expressed with the expression of $\alpha_{2e}$. Also, it is still unknown to us whether it tends to be *highly expressed* or *no change* at current stage. Nevertheless, this can be enhanced by combining positive association rules. For example, a positive rule found in [47] is $\alpha_{2e} \downarrow \Rightarrow \beta_{1e} \downarrow$. Thus, we can decide the protein expression of $\beta_{1e}$ may inhibit the protein expression of $\alpha_{2e}$ according to both positive and negative rules.

Rules 16 to 23 present the correlations between *stimuli* and $\alpha_{1a}$, $\alpha_{2a}$. Rule 16 indicates that the alteration of glycogen may inhibit the activity of $\alpha_{2a}$. Further, rule 17 presents the *normal glycogen, normal diabetes* and *low intensity* may inhibit the highly expressed $\alpha_{2a}$. This is consistent with the result in [103], in which a sprint activates both AMPK $\alpha_1$ and $\alpha_2$, whereas a *moderate* exercise normally activates $\alpha_2$. By considering rules 15 and 18 together, it is clear that the change of glycogen has a big possibility to lead to *expressed* $\alpha_{2a}$ rather than *no change*. As mentioned in [165], the final outcome of AMPK activation on glycogen metabolism seems to be a balance between increased availability of substrate and inhibition of glycogen synthase.

Rules 19 and 20 present the increasing intensity and untrained object may inhibit the highly expressed $\alpha_{2a}$. Rules 21, 22 and 23 present *diabetes*, alteration of *glycogen* and *training* may change the activity of $\alpha_{1a}$ notwithstanding the *low intensity*. This can be used as a secondary evidence that $\alpha_{1a}$ is usually unchanged in normal conditions.

The above selected rules not only reveal the hidden pathway knowledge regarding protein kinases and can be used to guide future experiments. Many interesting patterns can be generated according to the logical relationships between existing rules. For example, the combination of rules 13, 17 and 18 concludes *exercise training* decreases expression of the regulatory $\gamma_3$ subunit and attenuates $\alpha_2$ activity during exercise [26]. Further, the combination of positive and negative patterns is able to complement each other and is useful in determining the practical activity of subunits in response to certain stimuli, the activity or expression between subunits.

The presented study found that changes in AMPK $\alpha_2$ activity during exercise matched the changes in free cyclic AMP levels [287], which appears to regulate the secretory responses of the $\beta$-cell to glucose. Many type 2 diabetic patients rely on pharmacological treatments to improve glucose homeostasis, whereas the current treatments to enhance peripheral insulin sensitivity have limited efficacy. Thus, insight into novel methods capable of enhancing skeletal muscle glucose uptake could lead to new pharmaceutical strategies to improve treatment [78]. Hopefully, this can prevent peripheral insulin resistance in patients with type 2 diabetes.

## 6.4 Inhibition Patterns Discovery Using Mutual Information

### 6.4.1 Support Constraints

Traditional frequent pattern identification using a uniform minimum support either suffers from the combinatorial explosion, or misses potentially interesting patterns due to low support. A flexible solution is to apply support constraints to control itemset generation and extract significant patterns [204].

**Definition 6.5. Minimum support threshold.** Let $I = \{\alpha_1, \alpha_2, \cdots, \alpha_n\}$ be a set of distinct items, and $mins(\alpha_i)$ be the *minimum support* of item $\alpha_i \in I$. Suppose $X = B \cup \neg A$ represents a negative itemset, where $B \subset I$, $A \subset I$ and $A \cap B = \emptyset$. *Minimum support* threshold of $X$ is specified to be the lowest value of *minimum supports* of all items in $X$, namely $mins(X) = min(mins(x))$, $\forall x \in X$.

In the similar manner, minimum support threshold of itemset $B \cup A$ is also defined as the lowest value of *minimum supports* of all items in $B \cup A$. Obviously, we have $mins(B \cup \neg A) = mins(B \cup A)$ according to the above definition.

**Definition 6.6. Interesting negative itemset.** Given a negative itemset $X = B \cup \neg A$, in which $supp(A) \geq mins(A)$, $supp(B) \geq mins(B)$, and $supp(A \cup B) < mins(A \cup B)$, $X$ is called an interesting negative itemset if $supp(X) \geq mins(X)$.

According to Definition 6.5, different itemsets are required to satisfy different support thresholds depending on what items are included in the itemsets. For example, let $mins(\alpha_{1a} \uparrow) = 0.2$, $mins(\alpha_{2e} \uparrow) = 0.3$ and $mins(\beta_{1e} \downarrow) = 0.15$. The *minimum support* threshold of $\{\alpha_{1a} \uparrow \cup \beta_{1e} \downarrow\}$ by support constraint is 0.15, whereas the minimum support threshold of $\{\alpha_{1a} \uparrow \cup \neg \beta_{2e} \uparrow\}$ is 0.2. The validity of a generated negative itemset is determined by Definition 6.6. For example, $\{\alpha_{1a} \uparrow \cup \neg \beta_{2e} \uparrow\}$ is an interesting negative itemset if and only if $supp(\{\alpha_{1a} \uparrow \cup \neg \beta_{2e} \uparrow\}) \geq 0.2$.

The specification of support constraints is another key issue that needs to be addressed. Recently, a novel method regarding confidence and lift measures has been proposed to specify the minimum supports of items [203]. Although confidence and lift measures are useful in evaluating the interestingness of rules, their contributions are different. The former focuses on measuring the strength of a rule, whereas the latter aims to qualify the deviation of a rule according to independence. Due to the application of correlation measure, the above method is inappropriate for handling protein kinase regulation data. A similar method that integrates confidence measure into the specification of support constraints is thus proposed. Let $\theta = supp(\alpha_i) \times minc \times l$. The constraint is defined as:

$$mins(\alpha_i) = \begin{cases} \theta & if \quad \theta < 1 \\ 1 & otherwise \end{cases} \quad (6.3)$$

where $l$ is an integer equal or larger than 1 and used to adjust the *minimum supports* of items as a result of alteration of $supp(\alpha_i)$ and *minc*. Formula 6.3 not only determines the *minimum support* thresholds, but also guarantees the extracted negative itemsets are interesting. Although the selection of $l$ and *minc* may impact on support constraints of itemsets and result in distinguished negative patterns, this is not the main topic and will not be further discussed in the monograph.

### 6.4.2  Rule Generation

A methodology for negative association rule mining was proposed by Wu et.al [324]. In contrast to positive association rules, negative association rules are generated from interesting negative itemsets. The algorithm uses *downward closure property* as an optimization strategy to improve the efficiency. However, due to the application of support constraints, this property is inappropriate for our method. Thus, a strategy named *sorted closure schema* is proposed in this paper. Given an itemset, its contained items must be sorted in ascending order by their *minimum support* thresholds. The *minimum support* of the first item is specified as the *minimum support* of the corresponding itemset.

**Definition 6.7. Sorted closure schema.** Let $A = \{\alpha_1, \alpha_2, \cdots, \alpha_k\}$ be a sorted $k$-itemset, where $k > 1$ and $mins(\alpha_1) \leq mins(\alpha_2) \leq \cdots \leq mins(\alpha_k)$. $A$ is an infrequent itemset if and only if there exists a $k$-1 subset of $A$ that includes $\alpha_1$ and the subset is an infrequent itemset.

For example, there are three items $\alpha_{1a} \uparrow, \beta_{1e} \downarrow, \gamma_{1e} \uparrow$ with $mins(\alpha_{1a} \uparrow) = 0.2$, $mins(\beta_{1e} \downarrow) = 0.15$ and $mins(\gamma_{1e} \uparrow) = 0.4$. Let $(\alpha_{1a} \uparrow, \beta_{1e} \downarrow, \gamma_{1e} \uparrow)$ be a sorted 3-itemset. The subsets $(\alpha_{1a} \uparrow, \beta_{1e} \downarrow)$ and $(\beta_{1e} \downarrow, \gamma_{1e} \uparrow)$ by support constraints have the same *minimum support* 0.15, whereas $(\alpha_{1a} \uparrow, \gamma_{1e} \uparrow)$ has the *minimum support* 0.2. Thus, this sorted 3-itemset can be directly grouped into the set of infrequent itemsets since the support of $(\alpha_{1a} \uparrow, \beta_{1e} \downarrow)$ or $(\beta_{1e} \downarrow, \gamma_{1e} \uparrow)$, does not satisfy the specified threshold 0.15. Otherwise, it is essential to compute the support of the 3-itemset to determine whether the 3-itemset satisfies the corresponding support constraint or not. Obviously, the application of *sorted closure schema* greatly reduces the searching space.

The support constraints in combination with sorted closure schema assist in efficiently identifying infrequent itemsets for generating interesting negative itemsets. For example, suppose an infrequent itemset $\{\alpha_{1a}|, \beta_{1e}|\}$ is generated. Then, there may be three interesting negative itemsets including $\{\alpha_{1a}|, \neg \beta_{1e}|\}$, $\{\neg \alpha_{1a}|, \beta_{1e}|\}$ and $\{\neg \alpha_{1a}|, \neg \beta_{1e}|\}$ that need to be verified using support constraints. Further, if they all satisfy the constraints, corresponding association rules can be generated by using the evaluation criteria of negative association rules defined in Section 6.2.2. The algorithm for identifying interesting negative itemsets is described below:

#### Procedure AllNegativeItemsets

Input: $D$: AMPK dataset; $l$: a parameter related to the computation of support constraints of items; *minc*: minimum confidence threshold;

Output: *INS*: a set of interesting negative itemsets;

// find all interesting negative itemsets.

$FS$: a set of frequent itemsets; $NS$: a set of infrequent itemsets; $S$: a set of items with strong dependence obtained by mutual information measure;

**Condition 1: an itemset contains multiple state messages of an attribute;**

(1) **let** $FS \leftarrow \emptyset; NS \leftarrow \emptyset; INS \leftarrow \emptyset$;

(2) **let** $L_1 \leftarrow S; FS \leftarrow FS \cup L_1$;

(3) Scan $D$ to count the supports of items in $L_1$ and record the transactions in which each item $x$ occurs with $Rex(x) = \{t \mid x$ is included in transaction $t\}$;

(4) **for** $(k = 2; L_{k-1} \neq \emptyset; k{+}{+})$ **do**

    **begin** //Generate all possible frequent and negative itemsets of interest from $D$

(4.1) **let** $Tem_k \leftarrow \{\{x_1, \cdots, x_{k-2}, x_{k-1}, x_k\} \mid \{x_1, \cdots, x_{k-2}, x_{k-1}\} \in L_{k-1} \wedge \{x_1, \cdots, x_{k-2}, x_k\} \in L_{k-1}\}$;

    **let** $N_k \leftarrow \emptyset$

(4.2) Pruning strategy:

    **for** each itemset $A$ in $Tem_k$ **do**

        **if** $A$ satisfies **Condition 1 then**

            **let** $Tem_k \leftarrow Tem_k - \{A\}$;

(4.3) Optimization strategy:

    **for** each itemset $B$ in **do**

        **if** $B$ satisfies **Sorted closure schema then**

            **let** $Tem_k \leftarrow Tem_k - \{B\}$;

            **let** $N_k \leftarrow N_k \cup \{B\}$;

(4.4) // Calculate the supports of itemsets in $Tem_k$

    **for** each itemset $C = \{x_1, x_2, \cdots x_{n-1}, x_n\}$ in $Tem_k$ **do**

        Decompose $C$ into two itemsets $C_1 = \{x_1, x_2, \cdots x_{n-2}, x_{n-1}\}$ and $C_2 = \{x_1, x_2, \cdots x_{n-2}, x_n\}$

    **let** $Rec(C) \leftarrow \{t \mid Rec(C_1) \, Rec(C_2)\}$;

        **let** $supp(C) \leftarrow |Rec(C)|$

(4.5) **let** $L_k \leftarrow \{D \mid D \in Tem_k$ and $supp(D) \geq mins(D)\}$;

(4.6) **let** $N_k \leftarrow N_k \cup (Tem_k - L_k); NS \leftarrow NS \cup N_k$;

(4.7) **for** each itemset $E$ in $N_k$ **do**

    **for** each expression $X \cup Y = E$ and $X \cap Y = \emptyset$ **do**

        **if** $supp(\rightarrow X \cup Y) \geq mins(\rightarrow X \cup Y)$ **then**

        **let** $INS \leftarrow INS \cup (\rightarrow X \cup Y)$;

        **if** $supp(X \cup \rightarrow Y) \geq mins(X \cup \rightarrow Y)$ **then**

        **let** $INS \leftarrow INS \cup (X \cup \rightarrow Y)$;

        **if** $supp(\rightarrow X \cup \rightarrow Y) \geq mins(\rightarrow X \cup \rightarrow Y)$ **then**

        **let** $INS \leftarrow INS \cup (\rightarrow X \cup \rightarrow Y)$;

**end**

(5) output $INS$;

### 6.4.3  Experimental Results

**Rule Ordering.** An interesting negative itemset may generate more than one valid rule. In that case, it is necessary to highlight the most significant pattern. Given *rule* 1 and *rule* 2, *rule* 1 is more significant than *rule* 2, if and only if one of the following three conditions is satisfied: (1) the confidence of *rule* 1 is larger than the confidence of *rule* 2; (2) *rule* 1 and *rule* 2 have equal confidence, whereas the support of *rule* 1 is larger than *rule* 2; or (3) in some exceptions, if the confidences and supports of *rule* 1 and *rule* 2 are all equal, this will be reported to users. For example, $\neg \alpha_{1p}| \Rightarrow \{\alpha_{2e} \downarrow, \alpha_{1a} \downarrow\}$ has support 0.4 and confidence 0.6, but $\{\alpha_{2e} \downarrow, \alpha_{1a} \downarrow\} \Rightarrow \neg \alpha_{1p}|$ has support 0.3 and confidence 0.6, $\neg \alpha_{1p}| \Rightarrow \{\alpha_{2e} \downarrow, \alpha_{1a} \downarrow\}$ is more significant since it has larger support despite their equal confidence.

**Performance.** Our approach is extended and adapted from the negative association rule algorithm (called as NRA) in [324]. It uses correlation measure optimize the itemset generation. To evaluate the performance, we compare our proposed method (denoted as *nNRA*) with *NRA*. All experiments were performed on a Lenovo PC with Pentium(R) Dual-Cor CPU, 2.50 GHz CPU, and 4GB RAM. Algorithms were coded in VC++.

After removing the untested items, correlation measure is employed to extract the items that have strong dependency with each other. Figure 6.5 presents the pruning efficiency of mutual information measure under different *minimum mutual information* thresholds. It is observed that the application of correlation measure significantly reduces the number of insignificant items when *minmui* $\leq 0.7$. This facilitates the identification of AMPK regulation patterns.

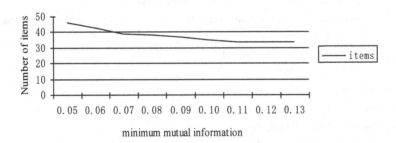

**Fig. 6.5** Number of items using different minimum mutual information

*NRA* uses a uniform support threshold to discover frequent itemsets and infrequent itemsets. Table 6.8 presents the number of corresponding output regarding different *minimum support* thresholds, in which *fn*, *fr* and *infr* denote the number of frequent 1-itemsets, frequent itemsets and infrequent itemsets, respectively. There are still a large number of itemsets generated in case of *mins* = 0.2. Table 6.9 presents the efficiency of itemset outputs in *nNRA* using different *minimum confidence* thresholds when *l* = 1 and *minmui* = 0.11. There is a significant reduction of frequent itemsets while the *minimum confidence* decreases. The comparison between Table 6.8 and Table 6.9 demonstrates our method outperforms *NAR*, even when a smaller *fn* is used in *NRA*. Table 6.10 presents the running efficiency of two algorithms in terms of different parameters. It shows that the presented method is faster than *NAR* by using support constraints.

**Table 6.8** Numbers of frequent 1-itemsets, frequent itemsets and infrequent itemsets in NRA regarding different mins

| *mins* | *fn* | *fr* | *infr* |
|---|---|---|---|
| 0.1 | 38 | 40690 | 4545 |
| 0.12 | 36 | 30007 | 3530 |
| 0.14 | 34 | 22620 | 3245 |
| 0.16 | 32 | 16264 | 2751 |
| 0.18 | 28 | 12009 | 1774 |
| 0.20 | 26 | 9076 | 1451 |

**Table 6.9** Numbers of frequent 1-itemsets, frequent itemsets and infrequent itemsets in nNRA using different mincs

| *minc* | *fn* | *fr* | *infr* |
|---|---|---|---|
| 0.3 | 34 | 10868 | 1622 |
| 0.4 | 34 | 7060 | 1155 |
| 0.5 | 34 | 4345 | 935 |
| 0.6 | 34 | 1645 | 527 |
| 0.7 | 34 | 1047 | 483 |
| 0.8 | 34 | 391 | 476 |

**Table 6.10** The comparison of running time between NRA and nNRA under different parameters

| nRNA | | NRA | |
|---|---|---|---|
| *minc* | *time(s)* | *mins* | *time(s)* |
| 0.3 | 45.95(*s*) | 0.10 | 569.01 |
| 0.4 | 22.22(*s*) | 0.12 | 334.17 |
| 0.5 | 11.52(*s*) | 0.14 | 210.92 |
| 0.6 | 3.61(*s*) | 0.16 | 123.83 |
| 0.7 | 2.5(*s*) | 0.18 | 75.45 |
| 0.8 | 1.92(*s*) | 0.20 | 48.74 |

Figure 6.6 shows a brief comparison between *IIN* and *INR*, in which *IIN* and *INR* represent the number of interesting infrequent itemsets and the number of itemsets for the generation of negative rules, respectively. It is observed that *INR* gets closer to *IIN* while the minimum confidence threshold decreases. Especially, when *minc* $\leq$ 0.5, *INR* is equal to *IIN*. This demonstrates that the interesting infrequent

itemsets specified by support constraints are effective in generating negative rules. This is because that the support constraints of items are specified in terms of confidence measure. Further, the minimum supports of items are computed with respect to the supports of items and parameter $l$. The comparison between the rules found by *nNAR* and the rules generated by *NAR* demonstrates our method is able to identify negative rules with low support but high confidence. Thus, the support constraints contribute to the identification of interesting negative itemsets. Suppose $conf_1 = supp(\neg A \cup B)/supp(A)$ and $conf_2 = CPIR(B| \neg A)$. Figure 6.7 presents the pruning efficiency of two confidence measures under different thresholds. It is observed that the number of rules is significantly reduced by $conf_2$. Further, the results by $conf_2$ are more useful for biologists.

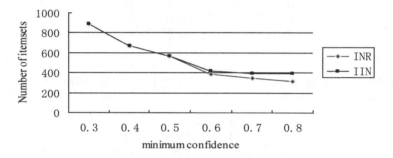

**Fig. 6.6** The comparison of the number of interesting infrequent itemsets and the number of itemsets for the generation of negative rules using different mincs

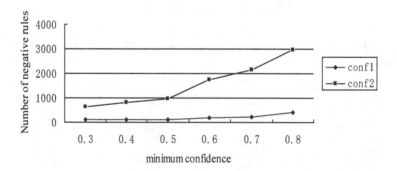

**Fig. 6.7** The pruning efficiency of two different confidence measures under different thresholds

To further assess the efficiency of our proposed algorithm, a dataset called mushroom from UC Irvine Machine Learning Repository is applied. Table 6.11 presents the running time and number of corresponding outputs of *NAR* and *nNAR* under different parameters, where $l = 1$. In contrast to *NAR*, *nNAR* has more *fn* but runs faster. Further, *nNAR* has much less *infr* than *NAR* while *minc* ≥ 0.5. NAR has more *fr* than nNAR under *mins* = 0.16. A further comparison shows that *nNAR* and *NAR* have 48 and 45 frequent 1-itemsets, respectively. It is observed that all frequent items in *NAR* have supports larger than 0.16, especially the supports of 2 items are larger than 0.978. However, the supports of frequent items in *nNAR* vary from 0.054 to 0.92. This is because *NAR* applies a uniform *mins* to control the generation of frequent items, but *nNAR* specifies the frequent items by mutual information measure. The latter focuses on capturing the dependent items and can remove the items with supports close to 1. Further, the support constraints in *nNAR* are computed in terms of the support of items. Thus, *NAR* only discovers the itemsets with high support. In contrast, *nNAR* is able to identify the itemsets with very low supports without generating a large number of uninteresting itemsets with high support items.

**Table 6.11** A performance comparison between NAR and nNAR in terms of the running time and the number of frequent itemsets and infrequent itemsets

| algorithm | threshold | fn | fr | infr | time(s) |
|-----------|-----------|-----|-------|------|----------|
| NAR(*mins*) | 0.16 | 45 | 74800 | 8839 | 16789.23 |
| NAR(*mins*) | 0.18 | 43 | 41268 | 5322 | 10703.04 |
| NAR(*mins*) | 0.2 | 41 | 39372 | 4581 | 9712.07 |
| nNAR(*minc*) | 0.4 | 48 | 53150 | 4603 | 7706.5 |
| nNAR(*minc*) | 0.5 | 48 | 39515 | 3030 | 6048.95 |
| nNAR(*minc*) | 0.6 | 48 | 17370 | 2028 | 3890.09 |

Note, different $l$ and *minc* can result in different *minimum supports* and different AMPK negative patterns. Several experiments that evaluate the values of $l$, *minc* and *minmui* have been conducted. As a result, the corresponding results by $l = 1$, *minc* = 0.6 and *minmui* = 0.11 better conforms to the requirement of our biology collaborators and are thus selected in the following analysis.

It is observed that we can obtain similar results by using mutual information in contrast to the methods described in Section 6.3.1. Thus, they are not further discussed and interpreted in the followings.

## 6.5 Conclusion and Discussion

Protein kinase is well known to play a central role in changing enzyme activity, cellular location, or association with other protein by regulating the cellular pathways with respect to signal transduction and transmission within the cell. Abnormal expression of protein kinases is strongly related to many human diseases, especially cancer. Drugs that inhibit specific kinases are being developed for disease treatment, and some have been in clinical use. The study on inhibitory regulation features of protein kinases could be an efficient and promising way for disease diagnosis and treatment. However, the negative correlations have been largely overlooked by traditional data mining techniques. There are insufficient works to identify inhibitory patterns in protein kinases. This chapter aims to develop a framework for discovering negative association rules from the derived regulation data of AMPK.

Unlike positive rule mining, the forms of negative rule are diverse and complex. Thus, the traditional support-confidence framework shows limitations in addressing the identification of negative patterns. It needs to identify not only frequent itemsets and unfrequent itemsets of interest, and evaluate the degree of dependence between itemsets. Further, the items that have low occurrence in existing experiments are pruned prior to mining. Item constraints in the closed interpretation are applied to the itemset generation so that a threshold is specified on the amount of results rather than a fixed threshold, thereby reducing the search space vastly.

This chapter proposes a framework to explore the inhibitory regulation patterns of protein kinase by using negative association rule and mutual information, respectively. A realistic data set regarding AMPK regulation on skeletal muscle derived from Medline is used in experiment. Support constraints are applied to identify a collection of interesting negative itemsets. Further, the subjective measures are considered to confirm the obtained rules are biologically significant. This avoids generating redundant rules and missing interesting rules. Many of the discovered negative patterns present interesting biological information of inhibition pathways. Some of them that were unknown previously suggest new hypotheses that may guide further investigation. In particular, some new knowledge are concluded by combining positive and negative patterns. Moreover, they assist in understanding the characteristics of AMPK regulation and relevant disease treatment. This demonstrates our method is useful in understanding regulatory networks of protein kinases.

# Chapter 7
# Modeling Conserved Structure Patterns for Functional Noncoding RNA

RNA regulation has been increasingly recognized as a potential and perhaps over-looked genetics of higher organisms. Noncoding RNAs (ncRNA) may play various catalytic and regulatory roles in the genetic operating system, such as RNAi (RNA interference) pathways for inhibiting gene expression and siRNAs silencing path-way leading to the degradation of the target mRNA. Thus, it is critical to develop methods and tools to investigate the featured patterns of RNA structures. Recent studies using comparative genomics and molecular genetics show evidence of the presence of varied ncRNAs. Unlike protein coding genes, there is a lack of com-parable information or outstanding signal for ncRNAs. Traditional computational linguistics show limitations in modeling complicated secondary structures and pre-vent us from identifying structure-function relationships of ncRNAs. This chapter presents a novel approach, based on a set of distance constraints, to model the pre-dicted RNA secondary structures. Further, a filtering schema is presented to identify matched models for the queried secondary structures.

## 7.1 Introduction

The genetic information was previously viewed as flowing from DNA to proteins via mRNA. It has been assumed that the genetic output is almost completely trans-acted by proteins in the past decade. This conclusion is true for prokaryotes, in which proteins comprise not only the primary functional and structural components of cells but also the main agents to regulate the cellular dynamics, in combina-tion with *cis*-regulatory elements and enviromental signals [224]. However, the pro-portion of protein-coding sequences that occupy only a small minority of genome of multicellular organisms is insufficient to perform complex cellular functions. It is thus critical to investigate if these functions of complexity are carried out by unknown noncoding RNAs.

As described in [159], structural genes encode proteins, and regulatory genes pro-duce ncRNA. Noncoding RNAs form transcripts that appear to be developmentally regulated instead of encoding protein. A variety of experimental techniques have been applied to identify the vertebrate transcriptomes, such as tiling arrays [24, 58, 173], cDNA cloning [247] and unbiased mapping of transcription factor biding sites [40]. The results unveil the involvement of ncRNA in the evolution and developmental programming of complex organisms. This demonstrates that these ncRNAs may fulfil some unexpected functions and constitute a critical hidden layer of gene regulation in mammalian biology. Most of the previous studies suggest that only a small fraction (1.2%) of the genome is transcribed and a large fraction (98%) of the transcriptome comprises noncoding RNAs [222, 223]. This demands us to understand the mechanisms of transition of genetic information in higher organisms.

A number of computational approaches have been developed to identify noncoding genes [12, 199, 202]. Some of these attempts look for signals that might suggest a functional RNAs in the molecule, such as the promising approach of using secondary structure as a signal [41, 71, 140, 201]. Other approaches aim to look for the transcription start and similar signals. However, they have had limited success because ncRNAs do not contain common signals that could be identified at the sequence level as protein coding genes.

Recent studies discovered that a large class of ncRNAs, such as rRNAs, tRNAs, small nuclear RNAs (snRNAs) and small nucleolar RNAs (snoRNAs), share characteristic structures that are functional and hence are well conserved through evolution [295]. The stabilizing selection of secondary structures results in corresponding substitution patterns in the underlying sequences. Consistent and compensatory mutations substitute one type of base pairs by another one in the helices of the molecule. Moreover, the discrepant distribution in the base composition and length between loops [212] and stems [1, 310] have been reported. Thus, studies of structural information on RNA can be an alternative to understand structure-function relationships in ncRNAs. A number of comparative methods based on conserved RNA structures over evolution have been developed. Moreover, some methods are to address the relatively easier problem of idenfiying subsequences that are similar in structure and sequence to query, rather than identifying novel ncRNA families. They have been used to find homologs of a specific RNA [345] and functional noncoding RNAs in human genome [295].

One of the biggest challenges in this field is to explore and discover the functional significance of this abundant non-coding transcription due to computational complexity and insufficient tools for modeling ncRNAs. Unfortunately, most ncRNA databases provide only sequence data [249] or separate sequence data from structure data [295]. The low quality data prevent us from applying advanced data mining techniques [127] to extract interesting knowledge of ncRNAs.

Linguistic methods have been successfully applied to the representation of biological sequences [279] since 1980. They use Chomsky-style grammars [60, 260] such as context free grammar and context sensitive grammar, to capture not only informational but also structural aspects of molecules. However, it has been criticized in representing complex cellular processes with overlapping, frameshifted coding regions such as the intersection of two stem-loop structures [254]. Although it has the advantage of flexibility, general-purpose parsers cannot compete in efficiency with programming that is customized to a particular domain such as data mining. Further, some flexible themes such as gene finding and gene structure need to specify variations and cannot greatly benefit from the capacity of grammars. Thus, it is critical to develop new methods to deal with complicated ncRNA data.

This chapter presents a framework to model predicted RNA secondary structures of vertebrate genome. It is able to convert the raw data into a compact data set, in which the sequence information and structure information are integrated together by using a collection of distance constraints. In particular, the *class* constraint is used to classify the data set into structure groups and the distance constraints with extra labels are applied to indicate the occurrence of loops and stacks. This leads to space reduction of searching matched models for the query. We randomly select a collection of consensus structures from RNAdb regarding RNAz as the training set, which were derived by comparatively screening to the most conserved regions for structural RNAs [295]. According to these constraint, we extract the consensus models for each set of predicted secondary structures among organisms, by which to search the matched patterns for the query.

## 7.2  Materials and Methods

### 7.2.1  NcRNAs Predicted from Structural Alignments

RNAdb [249] is a comprehensive database of mammalian ncRNAs, which are classified into several distinct datasets, such as miRNAs, snoRNAs and scaRNAs, ncRNAs predicted from structural alignments, and comprehensive antisense ncRNA dataset. Especially, the data set of *ncRNAs predicted from structural alignments* is derived from the results of a large scale comparative screen for structural RNAs in the human genome described in the manuscripts [249, 295]. Thousands of putative ncRNAs based upon structural features and alignments using novel comparative genomic tools, including RNAz, noncoding RNA search and Evofold, have been identified. Among them, RNAz combines a comparative approach (scoring conservation of secondary structure) with the observation that ncRNAs are thermodynamically more stable than expected by chance. According to the sequence conserved in at least human, mouse and rat, over 35000 structured elements were discovered in the human genome.

An initial set of alignments comprised all Multiz alignments corresponding to regions in the modified 'Most Conserved' track. Only those alignments that were conserved at least in the three mammals ('input alignments') are taken into account. The input alignment were screened for structural RNAs using RNAz. The resulting alignments were scored with RNAz using standard parameters. All alignments with classification scores $P$ (probability) $> 0.5$ and $P > 0.9$ were stored.

Eventually, overlapping hits (resulting from hits in overlapping windows and/or hits in both the forward and reserve strand) were combined into clusters.

The specificity of RNAz tested on shuffled alignments was divided to be $\approx 99\%$ and $\approx 96\%$, in terms of $P = 0.9$ and $P = 0.5$, respectively. The results can be downloaded as annotation tracks in BED format compatible with the UCSC genome browser [295]. The coordinates refer to the "hg17" assembly. The corresponding sequences can be downloaded in FASTA format. Note the FASTA files contain always the forward strand sequence since the predictions at this stage have no strand assignment. This chapter used the third data set that consisted of the annotation data of ncRNAs, which are conserved at least in human/mouse/rat/dog/chicken and fugu or zebrafish. They can be accessed at http://www.tbi.univie.ac.at/ papers/SUPPLEMENTS/ncRNA/. Further, we use the obtained alignments and detected structures in ncRNA, which show the input alignment, the RNAz results and a consensus secondary structure model. Figure 7.1 presents an example of the obtained structure in the cluster 58300. The detailed page for all detected structures can be reached at http://www.tbi.univie.ac.at/papers/ SUPPLEMENTS/ncRNA/structuresE.

```
>hg17. chr2/179216767-179216697
AUCAGAAAUGUAAGGCAUUGGUGAUGUUUGCAUUUACCCUCCUGUAAGCAACACUUUAACGUCUUACAUU
...... (((((((((((... ((((. (((((((((.........)))))))).)))).....))))))))))
>mm5. chr2/76598706-76598636
AUCAGAAAUGUAAGGCAUUGGUGAUGUUUGCAUCUACCCUCCUGUAAGCAACACUUUAACGUCUUACGUU
...... (((((((((((... ((((. (((((((((.........)))))))).)))).....))))))))))
>rn3. chr3/59301372-59301302
AUCAGAGACAUAAGGCAUUGGUGAUGUUUGCAUCUACCCUCCUGUAAGCAGCACUUUAACGUCUUAUGUU
...... (((((((((((... ((((. (((((((((.........)))))))).)))).....))))))))))
>galGal2. chr7/21153603-21153673
AUCAGAAAUGUAAGGCACUGGUGAUAUUUACAAUUACCCUCCUGUAAGUAUUACUUUAAUGUUUUACAUU
...... (((((((((((.. (((((((((((((((.........)))))))))))))....))))))))))
>danRer1. chrUn/522-438
ACAAGAAUUUAUGACUUGAAAUGUAAGACCUUGAGUGCUGUUUGCAUUUUACCCUCAUGUAAGCAGGACAACUGGGUCUUGUGUU
. ((((.........)))) ((.. (((((((((... ((. ((((((((((.........)))))))))).))....)))))))))..))
>fr1. chrUn/124298735-124298805
ACUGUGAACUUAAGACCCUGAGUGCUGCUUCCAUCACCCUCAUGGAAGCAGCAGGAACCGGUCCUGAGCU
........ (((((. ((((..... (((((((((((((...,..))))))))))))).......)))).))))..
>consensus
AUCAGAA_____AUGUAAGGCAUUG_GUGAUGUUUGCAUCU_ACCCUCCUGUAAGCAGCACUUUAACGUCUUACGUU
.................. (((((((((..... (((. (((((((((.........)))))))).)))......))))))))).
```

**Fig. 7.1** Selected example (#110235) of RNAz output from *human* (hg17), *mouse* (mm5), *rat* (rn3), *chicken* (galGal2), *zebrafish* (danRer1) and *fugu* (fr1), respectively, detected with $P > 0.9$. A consensus of these alignments is presented at the bottom of the figure.

In addition to the consensus alignments, predicted consensus structures with annotation of consistent and compensatory mutations are also presented. Figure 7.2 show the predicted secondary structure #148166, in which variable positions are marked with circles (one circle: consistent mutation, two circles: compensatory mutation). This chapter focuses on modeling the predicted RNA secondary structures in terms of the RNAz results.

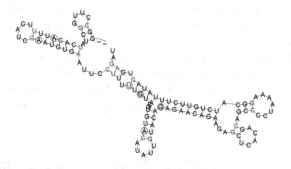

**Fig. 7.2** Secondary structure graph for structure #148166

## 7.2.2 Methods

The developed framework in this chapter aims to deal with the modeling of RNA structures. In other words, given a RNA sequence with predicted secondary structure, model the conserved secondary structure by using a set of distance constraints, in which the sequence information and structure information are combined together. Especially, we provide a mechanism to choose the optimal representation of conserved secondary structures by multiple organisms. There are four stages in this framework:

1. Collect a training set of predicted RNA secondary structures of vertebrate organisms.
2. Decompose the secondary structures into substructures (substrings) including various loops and stack regions.
3. Compute the distance constraints for the decomposed structures including both base-paired and base-unpaired regions.
4. Assign additional labels to the constraints and generate class labels for every secondary structures.

Before introducing our methods, we want to explain the reason why the structure similarity of homologous organisms is highlighted to obtain an initial set of candidate patterns of conserved secondary structures. A sequence alignment is able to identify regions of similarity that may be a consequence of functional, structural or evolutionary relationships between the sequences. In RNA sequence alignment, the conservation of base pairing can indicate a similar functional or structural role. Figure 7.3 shows an example of multiple sequence alignment [295]. It belongs to one cluster that may comprise a number of overlapping hits by browsing the database of predicted structures. Each annotated feature in the track corresponds to a cluster of RNAz hits. It not only detects signals for structural RNAs but in the process of classification constructs an explicit model from the aligned sequences. This assists in searching a database for sequences with high homology.

Recently, many evidences have indicated that the sequence similarity with the query string is insufficient to get the candidate regions. A number of cases show complete conservation of structure, but low sequence similarity [345]. It is impractical for a tool using sequence similarity to be effective in identifying RNA homologs. Therefore, the structure similarity is viewed as the basis of modeling RNA secondary structures. The sequence similarity will be used as a secondary evidence to evaluate homologs. We do not discuss the conservation of secondary structure in comparison with sequence similarity in this chapter.

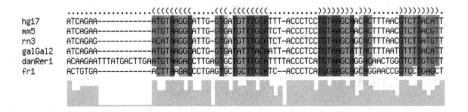

**Fig. 7.3** Selected example (#110235) of alignments from *human* (hg17), *mouse* (mm5), *rat* (rn3), *chicken* (galGal2), *zebrafish* (danRer1) and *fugu* (fr1), respectively

The secondary structure of a RNA is usually presented as a tree like shape and may consist of various stems and loops (bugle, interior loops, multiloops) regions. Each stem in this tree contains energetically favorable stacked base-pairs. In addition to the most energetically favorable Watson-Crick base-pairing (A $\leftrightarrow$ U, C $\leftrightarrow$ G), the other pairings such as the wobble base-pair (G $\leftrightarrow$ U) are possible as well. Each stem comprises a pair of substrings. These pairs are nonintersecting. Although intersected stacks, or pesudoknots (such as the pairs $e$ and $e'$, and $g$ and $g'$ in Figure 7.4), they can be ignored since we focus on modeling the predicted RNA secondary structures.

**Definition 7.1.** Given a nucleotide sequence $s$ with length $|s| = n$. We define a $(k, l)$ stack as a pair of indices $(i, j)$ if $(j - i) \leq 1$, $s[i \cdots i + k -1]$, and $s[j \cdots j + k - 1]$ can form an energetically favorable base-pair stack.

For example, suppose the indices of the substring $(a, a')$ in Figure 7.4 is at most $l$ bases apart. They form a $(5, l)$ stack according to Definition 7.1. It is observed that the string length of a possible stack is varied. Furthermore, given a random sequence of length $n$, for a randomly chosen pair of bases, the probability $p$ of paring is $p = 3/8$ due to the three possible base-paring ways of Waston-Crick ($A \leftrightarrow U, C \leftrightarrow G$) and wobble ($G \leftrightarrow U$). According to the specification in [345], the expected number of hits in a random string of length $n$ is $E(\sum_{i=1}^{n} \sum_{j=i+k}^{i+l} X_{ij}) = \sum_{i=1}^{n} \sum_{j=i+k}^{i+l} E(X_{ij}) \leq nlp^k$, where $(i, j)$ is a pair of indices. $X_{ij}$ is the indicator valuable with $X_{ij} = 1$ if and only if $(i, j)$ forms a $(k, l)$ stack. The probability that $(i, j)$ forms a $(k, l)$ stack is $p^k$.

It also demonstrates that a large $k$ and small $l$, a simple model can perform very well. As an example, typical tRNA structures have a clover-leaf shape with the

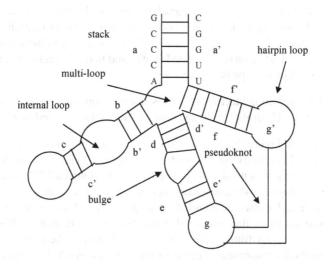

**Fig. 7.4** A RNA structure that comprises stacked based-pairs, bulges, hairpin, multiloops, and pseudonots

outermost stem having a seven base-pair stack [345]. More than 90 percent of the starting position from consideration can be eliminated by using a (7, 70) model. In contrast, nearly 98 percent of the starting position can be removed by using the constraint of at least 50 bases ($50 \leq l \leq 70$) in all tRNA.

### 7.2.3 Model Design

The defined $(k, l)$ stack of nucleotide string can be used as the foundation for modeling predicted secondary structures. However, two genetic mutations (insertion or deletion) that may decrease the effective value of $k$, and the variability of $l$ that may increase the effective value of $l$. Thus, more complicated models are needed in practice. Further, we need to identify models for the consensus structures of homologous organisms with similar RNAz hits.

**Definition 7.2.** Nested stacks. Suppose $S_1 = (i_1, j_1)$ and $S_2 = (i_2, j_2)$ are two $(k, l)$ stacks. Stack $S_1$ is said to be nested within stack $S_2$ if $i_1 \geq i_2 + k$ and $j_2 \geq j_1 + k$.

According to this definition, we can define $(k, l, h)$ as a set of $(k, l)$ nested stacks $S_1, S_2, \cdots, S_h$ such that, for all $i \in [1, h - 1]$, $S_{i+1}$ is nested in $S_i$. For example, in Figure 7.4, the substrings $(a, a')$, $(b, b')$ and $(c, c')$ constitute a $(k, l, 3)$ nested stack.

**Definition 7.3.** Parallel stacks. Suppose $S_1 = (i_1, j_1)$ and $S_2 = (i_2, j_2)$ are two stacks. Stack $S_1$ is said to be parallel to stack $S_2$ if $i_2 > j_1 + k$ or $i_1 > j_2 + k$.

In the similar manner, a $(k, l, h)$ parallel stack can be defined as a collection of stacks $S_1, S_2, \cdots, S_h$ such that any two of them are parallel to each other. For example, in Figure 7.4, $(b, b')$, $(d, d')$ and $(f, f')$ is a $(k, l, 3)$ parallel stack in terms of the definition. In addition to the nested stacks and parallel stacks, it is necessary to define the stacks for loops in Figure 7.4.

**Definition 7.4.** Multiloop stacks. $(k, l, h)$ is a multiloop stack if its configuration contains a $(k, l, h - 1)$ parallel stack and each of the stacks is nested in a $(k, l)$ stack.

For example, in Figure 7.4, $(a, a')$, $(b, b')$, $(d, d')$ and $(f, f')$ consist of a $(k, l, 4)$ multiloop stack. In contrast, $(a, a')$, $(b, b')$, $(c, c')$, $(d, d')$ and $(f, f')$ are not a multiloop stack since there is no $(k, l, 4)$ parallel stack. Although a RNA structure may contain various loops, we do not discuss them separately due to modeling purposes.

The above nested, parallel and multiloop stacks can be observed in all families of ncRNA. There are particular conserved structural features in every ncRNA family that give rise to correct folding. Thus, it is feasible to use the nested and multiloop stacks to model conserved secondary structures in ncRNA. Usually, each stack comprises a pair of substrings corresponding to a fixed length. However, the distance between stacks is varied due to the various loop (bulge, interior loops, multiloop) regions. As a result, we have to use distance constraints to specify a variety of $(k, l)$ stacks.

Given a model with $n$ $(k, l)$ stacks, there are $2n$ substrings each with a $2n - 1$ distances with its adjacent substring. If the distance between the first and the last substring is taken into account, we can obtain a $2n$ dimensional vector $\overrightarrow{l}$ to specify the model. The vector actually comprises the allowed range intervals for each of the considered distances. Suppose $l_0, \cdots, l_{2n-1}$ represent a set of distance ranges, in which $l_0$ is the range between the first and the last substrings, and $l_j, j > 0$ is the range in the substrings ordered from left to right. We have $\overrightarrow{l} = \{l_0, \cdots, l_{2n-1}\}$. As a result, the nested, parallel and multiloop stacks can be redefined by a set of distance ranges. A model that satisfies the distance constraint can be written as $(k, \overrightarrow{l}, h)$.

**Definition 7.5.** Suppose $(k, \overrightarrow{l}, n)$ is a multiloop stack, in which the distance vector $\overrightarrow{l} = \{l_0, \cdots, l_{2n-1}\}$. Let $l_j = [l_{j,l}, l_{j,u}]$ where $l_{j,l}$ and $l_{j,u}$ represent the lower limit and upper limit of $l_j$, respectively. Let $|s_i|$ $(1 \leq i < n)$ be the length of the stack $s_i$. $(s_2, \cdots, s_n)$ is a $(k, l, n - 1)$ parallel stack and is nested in a $(k, l)$ stack $s_1$. We have

$$l_0 = [\sum_{i=1}^{2n-1} l_{i,l} + \sum_{i=2}^{n} |s_i|, \sum_{i=1}^{2n-1} l_{i,u} + \sum_{i=2}^{n} |s_i|] \tag{7.1}$$

Figure 7.5 presents a $(k, \overrightarrow{l}, 3)$ multiloop stack with appropriate distance constraints, in which the stacks $s_2$ and $s_3$ comprise a $(k, \overrightarrow{l}, 2)$ parallel stack and they are nested in the stack $s_1$. The intervals $[2, 6]$, $[4, 13]$, $[0, 7]$, $[4, 15]$ and $[3, 7]$ correspond to the distance ranges of $l_1$, $l_2$, $l_3$, $l_4$ and $l_5$, respectively. For example, for $l_1$ and $l_2$, we have $l_{1,l} = 2$, $l_{1,u} = 6$, $l_{2,l} = 4$ and $l_{2,u} = 13$. To obtain $l_0$, it is necessary to include the base-pair stacks $s_2$ and $s_3$ in Figure 7.5. Therefore, we can compute

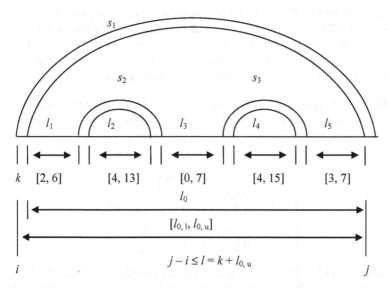

**Fig. 7.5** A $(k, 3)$ multiloop stack with a distance constraint vector $= \{[2, 6], [4, 13], [0, 7],$ $[4, 15], [3, 7]\}$, in which $i$ and $j$ represent the starting position of each side of outermost stem, respectively

$l_{0,l} = 2 + |s_1| + 4 + 0 + |s_2| + 4 + 3 = 13 + |s_1| + |s_2|$ and $l_{0,u} = 6 + 13 + 7 + 15 + 7 + |s_1| + |s_2| = 48 + |s_1| + |s_2|$.

The multiloop stack $(k, \overrightarrow{l}, h)$ with the vector $\overrightarrow{l}$ can be used to establish the model. However, there might be discrepant model configurations for ncRNA structures conserved by homologous organisms. Thus, it is critical to determine a candidate model for a set of conserved structures.

## 7.2.4 Selection of Candidate Model

Given a conserved secondary structure, we might obtain varied models for different organisms. For example, in Figure 7.1, although the alignment detects conserved secondary structures of *human*, *mouse*, *rat*, *chicken*, *zebrafish* and *fugu*, they are in fact discrepant with each other. This will cause difficulty to model these conserved structures.

To determine a candidate model that contains the most possible $(k, l, h)$ multiloop stack for the observed secondary structures, the model is one that has the maximum $kl$ and $k$ must be as low as possible in terms of the expected number of hits mentioned above. Although, it is possible that $kl$ may be very close between two different models, in that case, the $kl$ has priority to determine the final model in contrast to $k$. Thus, it is possible that $k$ might not be the minimum but $kl$ must be the maximum within all models. For example, suppose (4, 80) and (5, 60) are two stacks. Eventually, (4, 80) is selected as the candidate model due to $4 < 5$ and $4 \times 80 > 5 \times 60$. Nevertheless, as to (5, 60) and (4, 55), and (5, 60) and (4, 75), it would be indirect to choose the optimal model in the usual sense. In that case, we may have to find another way to decide the most representative model.

**Definition 7.6.** Suppose $k_i l_i$ and $k_j l_j$ are two stacks corresponding to conserved secondary structures of two organisms. Let $k_{ma} l_{ma} = \max(k_i l_i, k_j l_j)$, $k_{mi} l_{mi} = \min(k_i l_i, k_j l_j)$. Thus, we have

$$
y = \begin{cases}
k_j l_j & \text{if } k_j l_j > k_i l_i \text{ and } k_j \leq k_i \\
k_i l_i & \text{if } k_j l_j < k_i l_i \text{ and } k_j \geq k_i \\
k_m l_m & \text{if } k_j l_j = k_i l_i \text{ and } k_m = \min(k_i, k_j) \\
k_{ma} l_{ma} & \text{if } k_{ma} \geq k_{mi} \text{ and } \frac{k_{ma} l_{ma}}{k_{mi} l_{mi}} > \frac{k_{ma}}{k_{mi}} \\
k_{mi} l_{mi} & \text{if } k_{ma} \geq k_{mi} \text{ and } \frac{k_{ma} l_{ma}}{k_{mi} l_{mi}} \leq \frac{k_{ma}}{k_{mi}}
\end{cases}
\tag{7.2}
$$

In the Formula 7.2, $\frac{k_{ma} l_{ma}}{k_{mi} l_{mi}} \geq \frac{k_{ma}}{k_{mi}}$ means that the growth rate from $k_{mi} l_{mi}$ to $k_{ma} l_{ma}$ is equal to or larger than the growth rate from $k_{mi}$ to $k_{ma}$. As a result, $k_{ma} l_{ma}$ is selected as the candidate filtering model rather than $k_{mi} l_{mi}$. As to the (5, 60) and (4, 55), according to the formula 7.2, (5, 60) is the candidate model owing to $(5 \times 60 / 4 \times 55) > 5 / 4$. In another example of (5, 60) and (4, 75), (4, 75) is chosen as the final model due to $5 \times 60 = 4 \times 75$ and $4 < 5$ according to the Formula 7.2.

*Example 7.1.* Figure 7.1 includes the RNAz output of six organisms. They can be represented by using the multiloop stacks (10, 54), (10, 54), (10, 54), (11, 53), (12, 54) and (9, 51), respectively. According to Definition 7.6, the multiple stack (10, 54) is selected as the candidate model for the structure in Figure 1.8(b).

Further, given two candidate models $(k_i, l_i)$ and $(k_j, l_j)$ $(i \neq j)$ that correspond to two group of conserved secondary structures. $(k_i, l_i)$ and $(k_j, l_j)$ are said to be matched if $k_i = k_j$. $l_i$ and $l_j$ are used to include members as much as possible. Thus, it is not surprised to see $l_i < l_j$ or $l_i > l_j$. Nevertheless, the specificity with respect to inner structures (loops and stacks) can be measured by using the distance constraints. This can guarantee the reliability of matched models for the query.

The formula assists us in selecting the candidate model from a collection of conserved secondary structures of organisms. Further increase in applicability of the model can be achieved by taking into account more conserved secondary structures of the ncRNA family. Section 7.4 presents the experimental results on six queried RNA secondary structures. The identified candidate model assists in increasing the characteristics of a model while admitting a large fraction of members. It enables efficient searching for the query in conjunction with the specified distance constraints.

## 7.3 Identification of Matched Models for the Query

### 7.3.1 Modeling Conserved RNA Secondary Structures

Suppose the queried secondary structure is represented as a stack (multiloop or nested) $S_q = (k_q, l_q, h_q)$ that consists of a set of indices of the substrings $\{(a_{q1}, a'_{q1}), (a_{q2}, a'_{q2}), \cdots, (a_{qn}, a'_{qn})\}$. According to the Definition 7.4, the multiloop stack can be viewed as a configuration of a $(k_q, l_q, h_q - 1)$ parallel stack $\{(a_{q2}, a'_{q2}), \cdots, (a_{qn}, a'_{qn})\}$ in which each of the stacks is nested in the $(k_q, l_q)$ stack of the index of the substring $(a_{q1}, a'_{q1})$. It is assumed that there are $m$ models detected from the ncRNA database. The set of models are represented by using $S_f = \{S_{f1}, S_{f2}, \cdots, S_{fm}\}$. We aim to identify the most appropriate model that satisfies the queried secondary structure from the $S_f$. Each index of $\{(a_{q1}, a'_{q1}), (a_{q2}, a'_{q2}), \cdots, (a_{qn}, a'_{qn})\}$ can be viewed as an attribute of ncRNA database. Thus, the identification of matched model is converted to a classification issue of the query.

**Table 7.1** Consensus RNA secondary structures predicted by using UCSC genome browser

| $a_0$ | $a_1$ | $a_2$ | $a_3$ | $a_4$ | $a_5$ | $a_6$ | $a_7$ | $a_8$ | $a_9$ | $a_{10}$ | $a_{11}$ | $a_{12}$ | $a_{13}$ | S_ID | Class |
|---|---|---|---|---|---|---|---|---|---|---|---|---|---|---|---|
| 9 | 5 | 3 | 1 | 8 | 11 | null | null | null | null | null | null | null | null | #110235 | nested |
| 7 | 1 | 3 | 4 | 11 | 2 | 4 | 70 | null | null | null | null | null | null | #110236 | multiloop |
| 5 | 8 | 5 | 1 | 6 | 6 | 9 | 4 | 7 | 5 | null | null | null | null | #110238 | multiloop |
| 13 | 3 | 5 | 6 | 11 | 1 | 9 | 4 | null | null | null | null | null | null | #110241 | multiloop |
| 4 | 11 | 1 | 3 | 5 | 1 | 5 | 8 | 10 | 1 | 4 | 2 | 6 | 6 | #110288 | multiloop |

Table 7.1 presents a collection of identified consensus conserved secondary structure of vertebrate organisms. For simplicity, we just present part of the structures in several cases. In this example, each column represents an attribute variable. Each row presents a predicted RNA secondary structure that is expressed by a collection of attribute variables. The attribute values represent the size of stacks or loops from the starting position $i$ to the end position $j$ along the structure tree. For example, 9, 5, 3 and 8 in the first row indicate the length of the first base-paired region, the first gap region, the second base-paired region and the first loop, respectively in terms of the structure in Figure 1.8(b). It is observed that there might be different attribute variables to describe varied conserved RNA secondary structures. For example, the first structure is expressed by 6 attribute variables only in contrast to 14 variables of the fifth structure. Further, it is unclear where a loop or a stack starts. These may cause unexpected difficulty to find matched structure models.

In this chapter, the embedded nested stacks is ignored to established the initial models of predicted secondary structures. We need to indicate the exact configurations of the stacks and loops rather then simple *nested* and *multiloop* in Table 7.1. Moreover, the class labels are used to divide the data set into different groups. Table 7.2 presents the improved Table 7.1, in which the $l_m$ indicates this is a multiloop stack. We replace the *nested* and *multiloop* with specific configuration such as $(k, \overrightarrow{l}, 3)$. The superscript '+' indicates the start of a new stack; '++' presents the parallel stacks that are nested in its neighborhood stack labeled with '+'; '+++' shows the stack that is nested in its previously adjacent '++' stack. Moreover, the number with superscript '-' means a gap between or within stacks and the number with '*' indicates a loop to link the base pairs of a stack. In particular, the number of '-' and the number of '*' indicate the layer of the gap and loop in the structure tree, respectively. For example, $11^{***}$ presents a loop in the third layer of nested stacks. In the similar manner, we can describe other conserved RNA secondary structure of the database. It is observed that there might be no gap between stacks, such as $11^{++}$ ($a_1$) of the fifth row in Table 7.2 that has no gap with $a_0$.

**Table 7.2** Class-labeled training tuples converted from Table 7.1

| $a_0$ | $a_1$ | $a_2$ | $a_3$ | $a_4$ | $a_5$ | $a_6$ | $a_7$ | $a_8$ | $a_9$ | $a_{10}$ | $a_{11}$ | $a_{12}$ | $a_{13}$ | $S\_ID$ | Class |
|---|---|---|---|---|---|---|---|---|---|---|---|---|---|---|---|
| $9^+$ | $5^-$ | $3^{++}$ | $1^{--}$ | $8^{+++}$ | $11^{***}$ | $1^{--}$ | $6^-$ | null | null | null | null | null | null | #110235 | $(k, l, 3)$ |
| $7^+$ | $1^-$ | $3^{++}$ | $4^{**}$ | $11^{--}$ | $2^{++}$ | $4^{**}$ | $70^-$ | null | null | null | null | null | null | #110236 | $(k, \vec{l}, 3)$ |
| $5^+$ | $8^-$ | $5^{++}$ | $1^{--}$ | $6^{+++}$ | $6^{***}$ | $9^{--}$ | $4^{++}$ | $7^{**}$ | $5^-$ | null | null | null | null | #110238 | $(k, \vec{l}, 3)$ |
| $13^+$ | $3^-$ | $5^{++}$ | $6^{**}$ | $11^{++}$ | $1^{--}$ | $9^{+++}$ | $4^{***}$ | null | null | null | null | null | null | #110241 | $(k, \vec{l}, 3)$ |
| $4^+$ | $11^{++}$ | $1^{--}$ | $3^{+++}$ | $5^{***}$ | $1^{---}$ | $5^{+++}$ | $8^{***}$ | $10^{--}$ | $1^-$ | $4^{++}$ | $2^{--}$ | $6^{+++}$ | $6^{***}$ | #110288 | $(k, \vec{l}, 3)$ |

There are actually 31998 (from *structure*80001 to *structure*111998) conserved RNA secondary structures in the database. Considering the diverse configurations of stacks, it may be slow to search all these structures for the query. Thus, it is critical to apply the above constraints (class and distance) to identify matched models. This can assist us in reducing the searching space greatly. For example, the class label $(k, \vec{l}, 3)$ in Table 7.2 would eliminate 20 percent of the secondary structures from consideration, and the class label $(k, \vec{l}, 3)$ and $a_0 = 5$ would eliminate 80 percent of the secondary structures.

Nevertheless, in Table 7.2, we may observe that those attributes may present different configurations in different columns. For example, the attribute $a_1$ in the first four columns indicates a gap between $a_0$ and its adjacent nested stack, but presents a starting nested stack in the last column. The issue is arisen since there is no gap between $a_0$ and its adjacent nested stack in the column. The regions of base pair (such as $9^+$ and $3^{++}$ of the first structure in Table 7.2) are ignored since we focus on matching models from the aspect of structures. In this regard, the data in Table 7.2 can be transferred into a well compact form of Table 7.3. Note, in this case, each attribute variable is described by a single value instead of an interval since the data is from an organism only. The users can still see the comprehensive structures by combining the data in Table 7.2 and Table 7.3 together.

There might be sub-nested stacks with respect to an attribute $a_i$. For example, in the first row of Table 7.3, the attribute $a_3$ actually indicates a sub-nested stack between attributes $a_2$ and $a_4$. They need to be integrated together for filtering purposes. Further, the values of attribute variables may be varied in different organisms. In this matter, it is infeasible to describe the structures by using a collection of single values. Thus, we use the mentioned distance constraints and transfer the discrete

**Table 7.3** Class-labeled training tuples converted from Table 7.2

| $a_1$ | $a_2$ | $a_3$ | $a_4$ | $a_5$ | $a_6$ | $a_7$ | $a_8$ | $S\_ID$ | Class |
|---|---|---|---|---|---|---|---|---|---|
| $5^-$ | $1^{--}$ | $11^{***}$ | $1^{--}$ | $6^-$ | null | null | null | #110235 | $(k, l, 3)$ |
| $1^-$ | $4^{**}$ | $11^{--}$ | $4^{**}$ | $70^-$ | null | null | null | #110236 | $(k, l_m, 3)$ |
| $8^-$ | $1^{--}$ | $6^{***}$ | $9^{--}$ | $7^{**}$ | $5^-$ | null | null | #110238 | $(k, \vec{l}, 3)$ |
| $3^-$ | $6^{**}$ | $1^{--}$ | $4^{***}$ | $1^{--}$ | $4^-$ | null | null | #110241 | $(k, \vec{l}, 3)$ |
| $0^-$ | $1^{--}$ | $5^{***}$ | $1^{---}$ | $8^{***}$ | $10^{--}$ | $2^{--}$ | $6^{***}$ | #110288 | $(k, \vec{l}, 3)$ |

data into quantitative attribute variables by using intervals. In Table 7.4, considering *human*, *rat* and *mouse*, the structure #110235 can be represented by using a set of labeled intervals $\{[42, 46], [4, 5]^-, 28_I^{++}, [5, 6]^-\}$, in which $l_0$ is computed in terms of the formula 7.1. In particular, the attribute value with the subscript $I$ show that this is an integrated stack. In other words, the stack may include embedded loops or stacks.

**Table 7.4** Conserved RNA secondary structures presented by using intervals

| $C\_model$ | $l_0$ | $l_1$ | $l_2$ | $l_3$ | $l_4$ | $l_5$ | $S\_ID$ | Class |
|---|---|---|---|---|---|---|---|---|
| $(9, 54)$ | $[42, 46]$ | $[2, 5]^-$ | $[28, 42]_I^{++}$ | $[2, 6]^-$ | null | null | #110235 | $(k, l, 3)$ |
| $(7, 108)$ | $[89, 100]$ | $1^-$ | $4^{**}$ | $[10, 11]^{--}$ | $4^{**}$ | $[58, 69]^-$ | #110236 | $(k, \vec{l}, 3)$ |
| $(5, 16)$ | $[65, 68]$ | $[8, 10]^-$ | $20_I^{++}$ | $[6, 9]^{--}$ | $[5, 7]^-$ | null | #110238 | $(k, \vec{l}, 3)$ |
| $(13, 108)$ | $[92, 93]$ | $[3, 4]^-$ | $6^{**}$ | $[0, 1]^{--}$ | $17_I^{++}$ | $[29, 30]^-$ | #110241 | $(k, \vec{l}, 3)$ |

A group of conserved RNA secondary structures corresponding to a specified $S\_ID$ actually come from several organisms. Thus, it is needed to generate a candidate model for these structures. The attribute $C\_model$ in Table 7.4 presents the candidate models of the conserved RNA secondary structures. However, the derived candidate model

The search starts from dividing the conserved secondary structure into groups in terms of the *class* constraint by using the transferred data in Table 7.4. After determining the group for the query, we need to identify the structure models that the queried secondary structure may satisfy by checking the available models in the group one by one. The details of matching models can be seen in Section 7.4.

## 7.3.2 Algorithm Design

The presented algorithm aims to covert the raw data of predicted RNA secondary structures to the form of compact data set, and identify the consensus pattern of conserved secondary structures of homologous organisms by using a set of distance constraints.

**begin**

**Input**: *D: ncRNA training set; Org: a set of homologous organisms; c: distance constraints; g: a group of ncRNA of the organisms; sid: structure identifier of ncRNA in the database; Cons: consensus secondary structure; Cmodel: candidate model*;

(1) **let** $g_{ij} \leftarrow \emptyset$;

(2) **forall** $g_i$ extracted from $D$ using *sid* **do**

    (2.1) **forall** $j \in Org$ **do**

        **if** the structure $s \in g_i$ is from the organism $j \in Org$ **then**

            $g_{ij} = g_{ij} \cup s$;

        **end**

    **end**

(3) **forall** $g_{ij} \in D$ **do**

    (3.1) **decompose** $g_{ij}$ into a set of distance constraints $c_{ij}$;

    (3.2) **assign** additional marks to corresponding loops and stacks;

    **end**

(4) **forall** $g_i \in D$ **do**

    (4.1) **forall** $j \in Org$ **do**

        Compute $Cons_i$ by integrating the distance constraints of $g_{ij}$;

        Compute $Cmodel_i$ in terms of Formula 7.2 and $(k_{ij}, l_{ij})$ of $g_{ij}$;

        **end**

    **end**

**end**

In step 1, the empty set is assigned to the variables of $g_{ij}$, which is the set of conserved secondary structures corresponding to the structure identifier $i$ and the organism $j$.

Step 2 presents a cycle operation to collect a set of secondary structures in terms of the given $i$ and $j$.

In step 3, the secondary structure $g_{ij}$ is decomposed by using a collection of distance constraints from (3.1). Further, the step (3.2) adds additional labels to the obtained distance constraints to indicate the occurrence of specific loops and stacks.

Step 4 uses another cycle operation to compute the consensus structure model (by integrating their distance constraints together) and compute the candidate model (by checking $(k_{ij}, l_{ij})$) for $g_{ij}$ . The obtained models are then used for classification analysis of searching matched models for the queried secondary structures.

## 7.4 Experiments

### 7.4.1 Preprocessing of ncRNA Data

This chapter aims to extract models for conserved secondary structure of ncRNA, by which to search matched patterns for the query in terms of specified constraints.

The experiment is implemented on the published experimental results of a large scale comparative screen in vertebrate genomes for structural noncoding RNAs, which evaluates conserved genomic DNA sequences for signatures of structural conservation of base-pairing patterns and exceptional thermodynamic stability. The data set includes 30,000 predicted structured RNA elements in the human genome, in which nearly 1,000 of which are conserved across all vertebrates. The raw data can be reached by using `http://www.tbi.univie.ac.at/papers/SUPPLEMENTS/ncRNA/structuresE`. We select 500 predicted structures as the training set to learn the consensus structure patterns of ncRNAs, which can be seen by using `http://bioinformatics.gxu.edu.cn/bio/data/LNAI8335/8335-10.zip`. Ultimately, 100 candidate models are learned from the given training set, which can be accessed by `http://bioinformatics.gxu.edu.cn/bio/data/LNAI8335/8335-9.zip`.

Nevertheless, the original data separate the sequence data from the structure data that are represented by the graph of consensus secondary structures). Figure 7.1 and Figure 7.3 present an example of sequence data with respect to structure #110235 in the data set. Figure 1.8(b) and Figure 7.2 presents the corresponding structure data to the structure #110235 and #148166. To extract the correct structure models, we need to combine the sequence and structure information together and convert them into the data format by following the processes from Table 7.1 to Table 7.4. The conversion depends on the class and distance constraints. In the training set, the sequence data are represented by using the distance constraints (attribute variables). The detailed nucleotide sequences are ignored since we focuses on finding matched patterns for consensus secondary structures rather than comparing the sequence similarity. The initial sequence data of each organism are expressed by using a set of nonnegative integers, such as $\{9^+, 5^-, 3^{++}, 1^{--}, 8^{+++}, 11^{***}, 1^{--}, 6^-\}$ in Table 7.2.

The separated structure data using graphs are unfit for data mining application and need to be combined with sequence data for computation purpose. To achieve this goal, we normalize the structure data by adding additional labels to the attribute values of loops and stacks. As mentioned above, the union of '+' indicates the start of a new stack; the union of '*' represents different layers of loop; and the union of '-' indicates different layers of gap. Actually, the first indicates the region of paired bases in the stacks, whereas the last two indicate the region of unpaired bases. For example, in the first row of Table 7.2, $9^+$ ($a_0$) represents a region of paired bases that is the start of the multiloop stack, $5^-$ ($a_1$) represents a region of unpaired bases between $a_0$ and $a_2$, and $3^{++}$ ($a_2$) is a region of paired bases and represents the stack that is nested in the multiloop stack. In the similar manner, more structure data can be normalized and explained.

In summary, the normalization of conserved RNA secondary structures comprises four steps.

- Initialize the data set converted from the raw data of predicted RNA secondary structure like Table 7.1.
- Combine the structure data and normalize the data by using distance constraints with extra labels '+', '-' and '*' like Table 7.2.

- Remove the regions of paired bases like Table 7.3.
- Compress the data set by integrating the child structures of nested stacks in a multiloop stack like Table 7.4.

The generated data can be used for data mining analysis. If users want to find the matched models for a query, the search however will follow the reverse direction of the above data preprocessing. In other words, it first works on the data without considering child structures of nested stacks, and then checks further the data with detailed structures if necessary.

## 7.4.2  Searching Matched Patterns for the Query

Unlike traditional methods, our method starts with dividing the data set into different groups in terms of the *class* constraint rather than going through all structure models. However, we may obtain more than one matched model that has the same *class* label. Thus, it is necessary to sort out the most appropriate models in terms of the distance constraints of the queried secondary structure. This chapter focuses on the primary structures and discards the embedded loops or stacks of nested stacks.

**Table 7.5** Queried RNA secondary structures

| S_ID | Organism | C_model | Class | $l_0$ | $l_1$ | $l_2$ | $l_3$ | $l_4$ | $l_5$ | $l_6$ | $l_7$ |
|---|---|---|---|---|---|---|---|---|---|---|---|
| #110235 | human | (9, 53) | $(k, l, 3)$ | 44 | $3^-$ | $28_I^{++}$ | $5^-$ | null | null | null | null |
| #110538 | dog | (6, 90) | $(k, \vec{l}, 3)$ | 84 | $3^-$ | $5^{**}$ | $6^-$ | $35_I^{++}$ | $8^-$ | null | null |
| #110575 | rat | (8, 85) | $(k, \vec{l}, 4)$ | 77 | $0^-$ | $21_I^{++}$ | $1^-$ | $12_I^{++}$ | $0^-$ | $4^{**}$ | $5^-$ |
| #110886 | chicken | (4, 9) | $(k, l, 1)$ | $5^*$ | null | null | null | null | null | null | null |
| #111036 | mouse | (6, 63) | $(k, \vec{l}, 3)$ | 57 | $0^-$ | $26_I^{++}$ | $2^-$ | $5^{**}$ | $0^-$ | null | null |
| #111933a | human | (5, 49) | $(k, l, 4)$ | 44 | $7^-$ | $26_I^{++}$ | $6^-$ | null | null | null | null |

To demonstrate our methods, six predicted RNA secondary structures regarding *human*, *mouse*, *rat*, *dog* and *chicken* are selected as the queries. They are obtained from the results of a comparative screen (on the program RNAz) for structural RNAs in the vertebrate genome described in the manuscript [295]. Table 7.5 presents the six secondary structures that are represented by using distance constraints. The details of the structures can be reached by http://bioinformatics.gxu.edu.cn/bio/data/LNAI8335/8335-13.zip.

- '*Human: 110235*' — the predicted secondary structure in the *human* genome for structure #*110235*,
- '*Rat: 110575*' — the predicted secondary structure in the *rat* genome for structure #*110575*,
- '*Dog: 110538*' — the predicted secondary structure in the *dog* genome for structure #*110538*,

- 'Chicken: 110886' – the predicted secondary structure in the *chicken* genome for structure #110886,
- 'Mouse: 111036' – the predicted secondary structure in the *mouse* genome for structure #111036,
- 'Human: 111933a' – the predicted secondary structure in the *human* genome for structure #111933.

To measure the performance of applied constraints, we need to calculate the support of models to the queried structures by using a support function below.

**Definition 7.7.** Let $R = \{r_i \mid 1 \leq i \leq n\}$ be a set of models of RNA secondary structures, let $s(r_i, l_{kj}, q_k)$ be the support of $r_i$ to a queried structure $q_k$ with respect to its constraints $c_{kj}$ (class and distance), let $s(l_{kj})$ be the support of $R$ to the queried secondary structure $q_k$ regarding $l_{kj}$, and let $L_{r_i}$ be the set of distance constraints of $r_i$.

$$s(c_{kj}) = \sum_{i=1}^{n} s(r_i, c_{kj}, q_k) \qquad (7.3)$$

where $s(r_i, c_{kj}, q_k) = 1$ if $l_{kj} \in L_{r_i}$ ; otherwise $s(r_i, c_{kj}, q_k) = 0$.

The results of these queried structures are presented in Table 7.6, in which the attribute *class* are used to calculate the percentage of the models that match the groups of the queried structures, and the attributes $l_i$ are applied to compute the percentage of the models that satisfy the distance constraints of the queries. We use a binary variable that has two states: 0 or 1, where 0 means that the variable is dissatisfied, and 1 means it is satisfied.

**Table 7.6** Query results of matched models of secondary structures

| S_ID | Organism | C_model | s(Class) | s($l_0$) | s($l_1$) | s($l_2$) | s($l_3$) | s($l_4$) | s($l_5$) | s($l_6$) | s($l_7$) |
|------|----------|---------|----------|--------|--------|--------|--------|--------|--------|--------|--------|
| #110235 | human | 6 | 11 | 9 | 33 | 6 | 26 | 0 | 0 | 0 | 0 |
| #110538 | dog | 15 | 31 | 11 | 33 | 16 | 17 | 1 | 8 | 0 | 0 |
| #110575 | rat | 9 | 7 | 9 | 13 | 9 | 31 | 1 | 6 | 2 | 2 |
| #110886 | chicken | 11 | 28 | 16 | 0 | 0 | 0 | 0 | 0 | 0 | 0 |
| #111036 | mouse | 15 | 31 | 7 | 13 | 9 | 37 | 13 | 6 | 0 | 0 |
| #111933a | human | 14 | 7 | 9 | 13 | 16 | 0 | 0 | 0 | 0 | 0 |

## 7.4.3 Results and Interpretation

Although most of predicted RNA secondary structures include the sequence and structure data, they are usually separated and expressed in different ways, such as nucleotide sequence in Figure 7.1 and graphs in Figure 7.2. However, it is critical to take into account the sequence and structure data together while searching the structure databases for a queried secondary structure. The search will be low efficient if the data are not processed and divided into different groups in terms of the structural features. Further, it is difficult to apply advanced data mining techniques such as classification and clustering, to extract interesting patterns from the tremendous data set of predicted RNA secondary structures in a systematic way.

We search the learned models of RNA secondary structures for the queries by following the order from *class* constraints to *distance* constraints. In the same manner, each query presented above can give rise to a collection of models of secondary structures, which include the patterns that satisfy both class and distance constraints. It is perhaps that we cannot obtain 100 percentage matched models, whereas our methods bring out the most possible models. The details can be seen in the following figures that present the statistic results of matched models in response to the increasingly applied constraints or extra candidate models.

To measure the reduction of searching space, we count the visited models in terms of Definition 7.7. In this way, the smaller the number is, the less searching space is needed. Table 7.6 presents the percentage of the accessed models with respect to each constraint. For example, the percentage of possibly searched models regarding attribute *Class* in the first column is 11 in contrast to 31 in the second column. In either case, the search is limited to a small group in contrast to the search without group separation. Nevertheless, it is still insufficient to filter the irrelevant models by relying only on the *Class* constraint due to the complexity of secondary structures. The distance constraints assist us in reducing the searching space further. For example, considering *Class* and $l_0$ together, the percentage of satisfied models becomes 3% in contrast to 12% using *Class* only.

The constraints allow users to reduce the searching space gradually. A comparison between 'without constraints' (*class* and *distance*) and 'with constraints' was conducted. In the case of 'without constraints', the search will have to go through detailed structures of all available models. Suppose each record in the data set is a minimum $k$-dimensional structure, the queried secondary structure is a $m$-dimensional structure and the size of data set is $n$. To find a match pattern, the search space becomes $m^{nk}$ at least. Obviously, this will be a NP problem in case of a large $n$ or $k$. In other words, the space shows an exponential growth if the data set is tremendous and the structures are complex.

From Figure 7.6 to Figure 7.11, they show the comparison between "without constraints" and "with constraints" with respect to the queried RNA secondary structures in Table 7.6, respectively. Further, a comparison between "no candidate model" and "candidate model" is performed. In some cases, the application of candidate model show significant reduction of searching space. On the whole, more or less, it speeds up the search for the queried structure.

Suppose $q$ is the query, $D$ is the database of models of RNA secondary structures, and $r$ represents a model of secondary structure. Let $c_i(r) = \{r \text{ in } D | r \text{ satisfies } c_i\}$. The statistics of matched models of RNA secondary structures in the data set with specified constraints is implemented by using a function below.

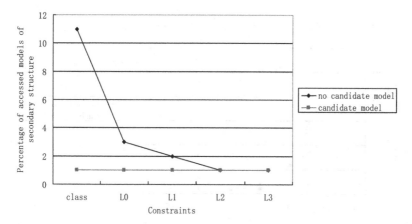

**Fig. 7.6** The statistics of accessed models of secondary structures regarding the queried structure *Human*: 110235

$$Y_{supp}(c_i) = \frac{|\bigcap_{j=0}^{i} c_j(r)|}{|D|} \tag{7.4}$$

In Figure 7.6, the applied *class* (primary structure) constraint assists in filtering out 88% of models from the data set. This leads to significant reduction of searching space for the queried structure. Further, the distance constraints help determine whether the queried substructures are satisfied. The identification starts from comparing $l_i$ of the queried structure with the corresponding $l_i$ of the remaining structures that satisfy the *class* constraint. For simplicity, if the queried $l_i$ is matched, the value 1 is returned, otherwise 0 is returned. It is observed that there is a sharp drop between $l_0$ and $l_1$. This proves that the *class* and $l_0$ constraint play a dominant role in reducing the searching space. For clarity, we calculate the percentage of matched $l_i$ for each compared structure in the data set. This measures the structure similarity between the query and the compared structure in an intuitive way. Moreover, we compare the results between "*no candidate model*" and "*candidate model*". It is observed that there is a sharp drop of the satisfied models with respect to *class* after applying candidate model. And then, the matched models become unchanged. This presents, in this case, the candidate model has a low occurrence and shows a dominant role in identifying matched models. In the same way, the results of other queries can be explained.

Figure 7.7 presents the searching results with respect to a predicted RNA secondary structure of *Dog*. Although the curve is strictly decreasing on the whole, there is a slight difference between the results of $l_2$ and $l_3$ and there is no change between $l_3$ and $l_4$. This indicates that the search is close to the queried target, whereas it is still necessary to check the remaining distance constraints to confirm the matched models. Unlike Figure 7.6, the number of matched models keeps going down gradually and becomes stable until $L_2$ even the application of candidate model. This indicates this is a prevalent candidate model in the database.

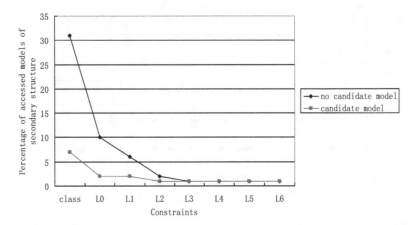

**Fig. 7.7** The statistics of accessed models of secondary structures regarding the queried structure *Dog*: 110538

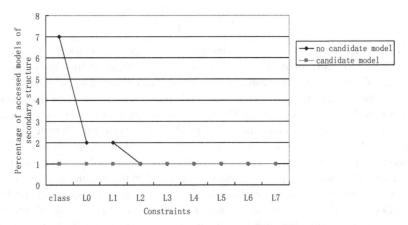

**Fig. 7.8** The statistics of accessed models of secondary structures regarding the queried structure *Rat*: 110575r

In Figure 7.8, there is no change between $l_2$ and the remaining $l_3$, $l_4$, $l_5$, $l_6$ and $l_7$. In this matter, most unvisited models have been filtered out since $l_2$. On the other hand, this query uses four constraints including *class*, $l_0$, $l_1$ and $l_2$ before reaching the minimum set of matched models (1%). In contrast, the other queried structures use less constraints to reach the stable situation. This indicates that it is a more complex (multiple loops with nested stacks) structure than other queried structures, and thus requires more constraints to describe it. Similar to Figure 7.6, the candidate model is unfrequent in the database and have a good performance in reducing the searching space.

Figure 7.9 presents the results with respect to a queried structure of *Chicken*. This is actually a simple structure that comprises a paired base region and an inner

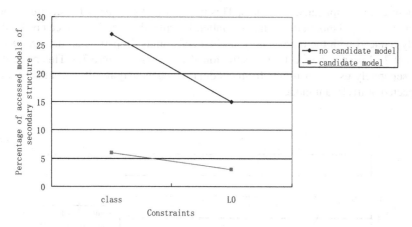

**Fig. 7.9** The statistics of accessed models of secondary structures regarding the queried structure *Chicken*: 110886c

loop. However, nearly 30% structure models satisfy it. This indicates that it is one of widely occurred secondary structure of ncRNAs. Thus, there is a high matched number of models and a small set of constraints are sufficient to find the appropriate models for the query. The slopes from *class* to $L_0$ is smaller than the other figures, whereas there is still a small decrease of matched models. In this regard, the candidate model assists in reducing the searched models more or less even for a simple queried structure.

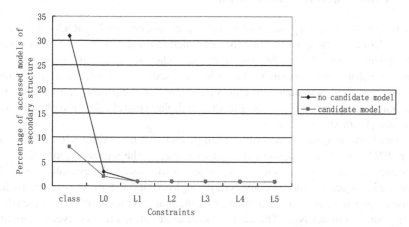

**Fig. 7.10** The statistics of accessed models of secondary structures regarding the queried structure *Mouse*: 111036

Figure 7.10 and Figure 7.11 present similar results. The former becomes stable from the $l_1$ in contrast to the $l_0$ in the latter. Moreover, only a small percentage of models satisfy the queried structures. It may indicate they are either rarely occurred structures or complicated structures. This presents that the queried structure in the former may need more efforts than the latter. Usually, the search space can be gradually reduced with the increasingly applied constraints. In particular, the curves in Figure 7.11 do not intersect. Such situation also occurs in Figure 7.9. This presents the separately used constraints from candidate models may result in obtaining unexpected or irrelevant models.

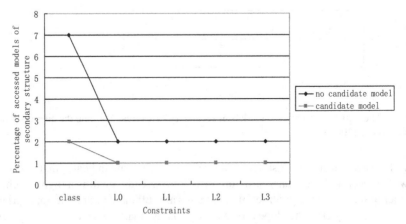

**Fig. 7.11** The statistics of accessed models of secondary structures regarding the queried structure *Human*: 111933a

## 7.5    Conclusion and Discussion

As a potential regulation genetics of higher organisms, nonconding RNAs have been explored for characteristic structure that are functional and hence are well conserved over evolution. The stable selection on the secondary structures gives rise to characteristic substitution patterns in the underlying sequence. Thus, the investigation of conserved RNA secondary structures can benefit to the prediction of functional noncoding RNAs in genome of organisms, and play central roles in pathway construction of biology systems.

There have been many works to search genome for noncoding RNA. However, the ncRNA signals in a genome are not as strong as the signals for protein coding genes. A natural way to solve this problem is to consider the evidence for RNA structure in sequences that are conserved through evolution. A variety of experimental techniques have been used to uncover the human and mouse transcriptomes that mainly consists of ncRNAs. The identified conserved structures however are not fitted for further data mining application due to complex substructures and separation of sequence information from structure information.

This chapter aims to model the predicted RNA secondary structures by using *class* constraints and *distance* constraints. The former divides the initial data set into groups in terms of the primary structure, and the latter specifies the detailed substructures by quantifying the inner loops and stacks using intervals. Further, the candidate model considers the outermost stem and avoid unexpected models. These greatly reduce the searching space for the query. The experimental results demonstrate that our methods are useful for ncRNAs modeling and further data mining application.

The learned models of conserved secondary structures show potential data mining applications. The users can classify a collection of predicted secondary structures in terms of the similarity of their constraints, conduct clustering for structures by measuring the distance between constraints and combine the sequence similarity with the structure similarity together for accurate identification of functional ncRNAs.

# Chapter 8
# Interval Based Similarity for Function Classification of RNA Pseudoknots

Many raw biological sequence data have been generated by the human genome project and related efforts. The understanding of structural information encoded by biological sequences is important to acquire knowledge of their biochemical functions in varied pathways but remains a fundamental challenge. Recent interest in RNA regulation has resulted in a rapid growth of deposited RNA secondary structures in varied databases. However, a functional classification and characterization of the RNA structure have only been partially addressed. Chapter 7 proposes methods for modelling conserved structure patterns of ncRNAs, whereas does not provide a intuitive way to evaluate structure similarity. This chapter aims to introduce a novel interval-based distance metric for structure-based RNA function assignment. The characterization of RNA structures relies on distance vectors learned from a collection of predicted structures. The distance measure considers the intersected, disjoint and inclusion between intervals. A set of RNA pseudoknotted structures with known function are applied and the function of the query structure is determined by measuring structure similarity. This not only offers sequence distance criteria to measure the similarity of secondary structures and aids the functional classification of RNA structures with pesudoknots.

## 8.1 Introduction

The origin, structure and function of living systems have been explored throughout history in biology [151]. The knowledge of living organisms derived from relevant research is critical but complex for us to comprehend owing to potential correlations of components with respect to inheritance, variation and selection. The discovery of DNA's structures and the unraveling of the genetic code is a revolution in science and the increasing studies of the molecular biology of cell give rise to the development of bioinformatics that combine biological knowledge and information technology [47, 51, 98]. The effective computational methods are able to not only manage the tremendous biological data and extract interesting biological knowledge.

Many studies have been conducted for data storage and retrieval, genome sequence analysis, protein sequence analysis and structure prediction [47, 66, 279, 281]. They focused on genome sequencing to localize the useful region, identify the exact position of genes, extract the sequence of the encoded molecules, understand the mechanism of their expression and predict secondary structures. This brings out abundant data for discovering potential function. In particular, the investigation of structures has drawn biologists' attention since increasing evidences indicate that the structure information as well as the sequence information of a molecular is critical for determining its functions [264, 345]. In other words, the identification of a characterized structure pattern of a molecular can assist us in predicting its function.

Secondary structures are the general three-dimensional form of local segments of protein and nucleic acids (DNA/RNA) and have been viewed as a critical element in biochemistry and structural biology [1]. They have been found to be correlated with diverse and important functions in biological systems [253, 293, 349]. The prediction and analysis of secondary structures such as non-coding RNA (ncRNA) is an important research field in functional genomic [41, 71, 140, 201]. A number of new classes of functional secondary structures such as *miRNA*, *splicing factors* [3], and *snoRNA* have been reported [249]. However, unlike the cluster of gene expression data, the analysis of secondary structure data is insufficient due to the complexity of modeling the structures and difficulty of choosing fitted distance metrics. Figure 8.1 presents two alternative secondary structures. The first describes the so called dumbbell structure, in which the two inverted repeats base-pair separately and the second is an intermediate cloverleaf structure. A variety of secondary structure data have been publicly accessed on Internet [249, 311]. They provide useful and abundant resource for understanding structural features and potential structure-function relationships.

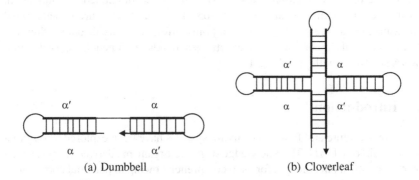

(a) Dumbbell                    (b) Cloverleaf

**Fig. 8.1** Two alternative secondary structures

There have been increasing efforts for characterization and deep analysis of secondary structures. Much of the work concerned with the formal characterization of the language of nucleic acids regarding the processes of transcription and translation from strings of one kind to strings of a different kind [279, 281]. Computational linguistics have been applied to biological sequence such as gene regulation, gene structure and expression, other forms of mutation and rearrangement and in particular as the basis for computational analysis of sequence data. Nevertheless, other biological phenomena indicate that the language of nucleic acids may be beyond context free. For example, pseudoknots that are forms of secondary structure that require context-sensitive expression in the general case. Although it may be possible to describe more complex higher-order structure in certain organisms, this requires significantly more complex grammar and may result in unperfect matching and unexpected difficulty in classification.

There are two types of classification procedures: supervised classification and unsupervised classification. They all depend on distance functions that determine how the similarity of two elements is calculated. Thus, an appropriate distance metric is critical to achieve correct and efficient classification. Usually, a distance function or a metric is a function to define a distance between elements of a set. There have been many metrics developed for different purposes, such as *Euclidean metric* for translation and rotation invariant, *taxicab metric* for translation invariant, *graphic metric* defined in terms of distance of a certain graph, and *Fubini-Study metric* on complex projective space. *Euclidean distance* is the most widely used distance measure for similarity search [43, 96] since it is simple to use and easy to compute. A disadvantage of the *Euclidean distance* is its sensitivity to the scales of measurements. It is often a few variables to dominate the distance measure owing to large differences in scale. For example, a time series may vary within small amplitude 10 and 20, while another may vary within larger amplitude between 20 and 40. In that case, the *Euclidean distance* will be large.

A weighted distance that reflects the importance of the variables is thus preferable if the scales of measurements are uncommon for all variables. This requires normalizing the data before applying the distance operator. An extension of the system of weights that also takes into account the covariances among the variables is the *Mahalanobis* distance, which is called a multivariate measure of distance because it considers the covariance structure among the variables. Another alternative distance is the *Manhattan metric*, which uses the absolute values of the difference among the coordinates. In contrast to the *Euclidean distance*, the *Manhattan* metric is much less sensitive to the outliers. Although all these distances have been widely used in clustering algorithms, they show limitation with respect to time consumption and the criterion of separating the cluster. In most of case they need to be extended and adapted in terms of the features of practical data and specific issues.

In this chapter, an interval-based distance metric is proposed to evaluate the similarity of secondary structures that are modeled by a set of distance vectors. Unlike the traditional scale issue, our method considers the specific situations in more details, in which an interval might be a single value, two intervals might be non-overlapped, or one interval is a subset of another one. We define different distance functions in terms of different situations to ensure the correctness of clusters. The identified group of secondary structures that belong to a same cluster center indicates similar functional role in biology and assists in searching matched structure patterns for the query in an intuitive way.

## 8.2  Motivations

There have been an increasing growth of biological data due to the application of new experiment technology, such as microarray, in conjunction with efficient computational methods, such as machine learning. In particular, the study of structure data has been highlighted in functional genomic owing to its potential correlation to critical biological functions. For example, the studies of structural information on RNA have been an alternative to understand structure-function relationship in biology [345]. Further, RNA regulation has been increasingly recognized as a potential and perhaps overlooked genetics of higher organisms [224]. The previous investigation focuses on the prediction of secondary structures by improving the accuracy and correctness of results. A number of valuable structure data can be publicly accessed on Internet such as PseudoBase [310] and RNAdb [249], and have been widely used for diverse research projects.

The data have been used to identify structure-function relationships by finding clusters of similar structures. Unfortunately, the complexity and diversity of secondary structures make it difficult to normalize those structures and may result in incorrect results while generating clusters. Further, a given RNA secondary structure includes not only sequence information and contains structure information. Traditional computational linguistics has been applied in the computational biology toward abstracted, hierarchical views of biological sequences [279], whereas they show limitations in modeling complicated secondary structures [254]. The generated set of all ideal strings using grammar is inappropriate to analyze using advanced data mining techniques and prevents us from discovering structure-function relationships. Thus, this requires us to develop methods to characterizing these complicated secondary structures and propose novel distance functions to finding similar structures.

Usually, the distance means the shortest while talking about distance. For example, a point $A$ is said to have a distance $d$ to a point set $P$. We generally assume that $d$ is the distance from $A$ to the nearest point of $P$. It seems that the same logic can be applied for polygons. Suppose $A$ and $B$ present two point sets, their distance is commonly viewed as the shortest one between any point $a$ of $A$ and any point $b$ of $B$. The distance between $A$ and $B$ can be presented as

$$d(A,B) = \min_{a \in A}\{\min_{b \in B}\{d(a,b)\}\} \tag{8.1}$$

The above definition of distance has showed its limitation for some applications because the shortest distance does not take into account the whole shape. Further, the shortest distance does not account for the position of the objects. Thus, *Hausdorff* distance is proposed as the maximum distance of a set to the nearest point in the other set [263]. *Hausdorff* distance from *A* to *B* is a maximum function and can be more formally defined as

$$h(A,B) = \max_{a \in A}\{\min_{b \in B}\{d(a,b)\}\} \qquad (8.2)$$

where *a* and *b* represent points from *A* and *B*, respectively, and $d(a, b)$ represents *Euclidian* distance between *a* and *b*. This is also known as directed *Hausdorff Distance* from *A* to *B*.

In the similar way, the distance from *B* to *A* is defined as

$$h(B,A) = \max_{b \in B}\{\min_{a \in A}\{d(b,a)\}\} \qquad (8.3)$$

The concern was the insensitivity of the shortest distance to the position of the sets. Actually, the disposition of the sets is not considered at all in the shortest distance. From the above observation, *Hausdorff* distance is better in contrast to the shortest distance. It not only gives an interesting measure of their mutual proximity by indicating any point of one set to the other set and has the advantage of being sensitive to position.

## 8.3 Materials and Method

### 8.3.1 Data

**Pseudoknot Data.** Suppose $S_1$, $S_2$, $L_1$, $L_2$ and $L_3$ represent *stem 1, stem 2, loop 1, loop 2* and *loop 3*, respectively; *A, G, C* and *U* represent base *adenine, guanine, cytosine*, and *uracil*, respectively; the abbreviation *vr, vt, vf, v3, v5, vo, rr, mr, tm, ri, ap, ot* and *ar*, denote *viral ribosomal readthrough signals, viral tRNA like structures, viral ribosomal frameshifting signals, other viral 3'-UTR, other viral 5'-UTR, viral others, rRNA, mRNA, tmRNA, ribozymes, aptamers, artifical molecules* and *others*, respectively; and *ss, tc* and *fs* represent *self-splicing, translation control* and *viral frameshifting*, respectively.

The data here is collected from PseudoBase that includes the whole pesudoknot data from the publications in Medline, and can be reached at http://www.ekevanbatenburg.nl/PKBASE/PKBGETCLS.HTML. Originally, each pseudoknot is recorded by 12 data items, such as *PKB number, EMBL number* and *reference*, whereas some of them are unuseful for data mining application. Thus, only *organism, RNA type* and *bracket view of structure* are considered in this chapter. Furthermore, the structural information is classified by two stems and three loops, including their corresponding nucleotide sequence and size.

After removing 8 unusual pseudoknots, 7 reductant pseudoknots [1] and 5 pseudoknots that have loop lengths $\geq 200$, a dataset consisting of 284 H-pseudoknots is obtained. The authors have developed methods for the characterization of pseudoknot structures, whereas the modeling and clustering of the structures are underdeveloped. Although the most studied type of pseudoknot is with coaxial

**Table 8.1** An example of pseudoknot data

| C | $S_1$ | Sequence | $S_2$ | Sequence | $L_1$ | Sequence |
|---|---|---|---|---|---|---|
| Vt | 3 | CCC | 6 | UCCUGC | 2 | CC |
| V3 | 3 | CCU | 5 | GUCUC | 1 | U |
| V3 | 3 | CUU | 4 | GGCU | 1 | U |
| Vf | 6 | GGGGGG | 3 | GCG | 5 | ACUUA |

stacking of stems, *loop* 2 is reserved here as a secondary evidence to enhance the similarity comparison.

Table 8.1 presents an example of the structures, classes and functions of pseudoknots in PseudoBase. Each row in the table represents a RNA pseudoknot. The non-negative integers denote the number of nucleotides. It can be seen at http://bioinformatics.gxu.edu.cn/bio/data/LNAI8335/8335-12.zip in more details.

### 8.3.2 Hausdorff Distance

*Haudorff* distance has been widely used in computer vision for finding a given template in an arbitrary target image. The area in the target image with the minimal *Haudorff* distance to the template will be viewed as the best candidate for locating the template in the target. Also, it is often used in computer graphics for changing the resolution of a mesh. This distance is actually oriented or we can say asymmetric as well. A more general definition of *Haudorff* distance would be defined as

$$H(A,B) = \max\{h(A,B), h(B,A)\} \tag{8.4}$$

Although it is an extremely useful mathematical concept, the traditional *Haudorff* distance is intended for two sets that are totally separated from each other and also works when $B$ is inside $A$. However, it won't work if $A$ is inside $B$, or when $A$ and $B$ are partially intersecting. It can be defined in a general metric space to compute the distance between point sets rather than polygons by extension or adaption. Further, the distance is too fragile for practical tasks. For example, a single point in $A$ that is far from anything in $B$ will cause $h(A, B)$ to be large. A natural way to deal with this problem is to regulate the distance in terms of specific requirements. As a result, the distance needs to be modified to make it suitable for handling complicated secondary structure data that are represented by using a collection of interval-based distance vectors.

**Table 8.2** An example of normalized structure data

| Group | interval_1 | interval_2 | interval_3 | interval_4 | interval_5 | interval_6 |
|-------|-----------|-----------|-----------|-----------|-----------|-----------|
| 1 | [42, 46] | [2,5] | [28,42] | [2,6] | null | null |
| 2 | [79,90] | [3,4] | [3,3] | [5,5] | [21,39] | [0,1] |
| 3 | [65,66] | [0,1] | [14,14] | [0, 1] | null | null |
| Query | [84,84] | [3,3] | [5,5] | [6,6] | [35,35] | [8,8] |

## 8.4 Identification of Top Similar Structure Patterns

### 8.4.1 Problem Definition

Table 8.2 presents 3 groups of interval and a query of interval with respect to RNA secondary structures. We need to find out which cluster center these instances belong to. Then, we are able to determine into which group the query falls. As a result, it is important to have a novel metric to correctly measure the distance between structure patterns and identify the top similar patterns to the targeted structures. There are three key issues need to be solved in this chapter:

- Definition of distance functions for two intervals. In particular, the situations of *overlapped*, *containing* and *disjoint* sets need to be considered and appropriate functions are required for each specific case;
- Definition of the distance between a query of intervals and a group of intervals. Given a group of target structures, it is critical to efficiently identity the top-similar structures for the queried structure;
- Identification of similar structures by removing the structures that are actually dissimilar in substructures.

### 8.4.2 Modeling RNA Pseudoknots

As mentioned above, a variety of secondary structures might be obtained from structure prediction. Figure 8.1 and Figure 8.2 present instances of those diverse secondary structures. Also, there has been quite a bit of focus on pseudoknots in ncRNA. Figure 8.3 presents two types of pesudoknot fold. In particular, Figure 8.3(a) presents a classical RNA pseudoknot with two stems and two loops. Many consensus structures might be derived from identifying the structures with high similarity among homologous species. There are a number of cases where pseudoknots exist and perform an important role.

The modeling schema described in Chapter 7 is applied to model RNA pseudoknots. For example, suppose the indices of the substring (UCCGUGA, AGGCGCU) in Figure 8.2 is at most $l = 57$ bases apart from $5'$ to $3'$. They form a (7, 57) stack according to Definition 7.1. It is observed that the string length of a possible stack is varied.

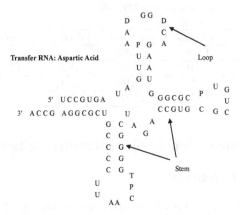

**Fig. 8.2** Stem-loop secondary structure of a transfer RNA(tRNA) molecule in a simple two-dimensional form. There is some pairing between G and U as well as the more usual A-U pairing. Further, it often includes a few unusual bases designated P, D and T.

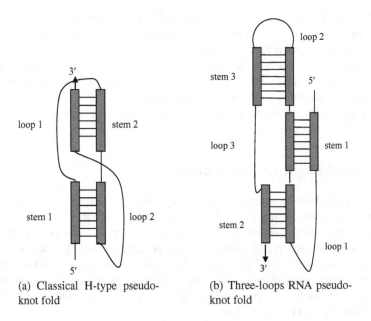

(a) Classical H-type pseudo-knot fold

(b) Three-loops RNA pseudo-knot fold

**Fig. 8.3** RNA pseudoknot architecture

The defined $(k, l)$ stack of nucleotide string can be used as the foundation for modeling predicted secondary structures. However, two genetic mutations (insertion or deletion) that may decrease the effective value of $k$, and the variability of $l$ that may increase the effective value of $l$. Thus, more complicated models are needed in practice. Further, we need to identify models for the consensus structures of homologous organisms with similar RNAz hits. The definitions of nested stack and intersected stack can be seen in Section 7.2.3. Thus, they are not repeated herein.

According to the definition, we can define $(k, l, h)$ as a set of $(k, l)$ nested stacks $S_1, S_2, \cdots, S_h$ such that, for all $i \in [1, h - 1]$, $S_{i+1}$ is nested in $S_i$. For example, in Figure 8.2, the substrings (UCCGUGA, AGGCGCU) and (CGGGG, GCCCC) constitute a $(k, l, 2)$ nested stack. In the same way, a $(k, l, h)$ intersected stack can be defined as a collection of stacks $S_1, S_2, \cdots, S_h$ such that there are more than two stacks that are intersected. According to the nested stacks and intersected stacks, it is ready to define the stacks for RNA pseudoknots with stems and loops.

**Definition 8.1.** Pseudoknot stacks. $(k, l, h)$ is a pseudoknot stack if its configuration contains an $(k, l, h)$ intersected stack and each of the stacks is nested in a $(k, l)$ stack.

For example, in Figure 8.4, $s_0$ consists of a $(k, l, 2)$ pseudoknot stack. Although an RNA pseudoknot may contain additional structures, they are not discussed here owing to the purpose of modeling.

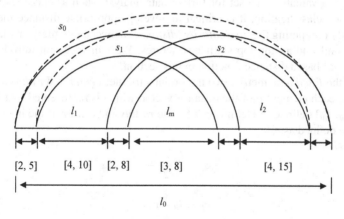

**Fig. 8.4** A $(k, 2)$ multiloop stack with a distance constraint vector $= \{[2, 5], [4, 10], [2, 8], [4, 15]\}$, in which $i$ and $j$ represent the starting position of each side of outermost stem, respectively

The mentioned nested, intersected and pseudoknot stacks can be observed in most families of RNA. They can be used to model varied RNA secondary structures. Usually, each stack comprises a pair of substrings corresponding to a fixed length. However, the distance between stacks is varied due to the various loop (bulge, interior loops, multiloop) regions. As a result, we have to use distance constraints to specify a variety of $(k, l)$ stacks.

Suppose $(k, \overrightarrow{l}, m)$ is a pseudoknot stack, in which the distance vector $\overrightarrow{l} = \{l_0, \cdots, l_{2m}\}$. Let $l_j = [l_{jl}, l_{ju}]$ where $l_{jl}$ and $l_{ju}$ represent the lower limit and upper limit of $l_j$, respectively. Let $|s_i|$ $(1 \leq i < m)$ be the length of the stack $s_i$. We use the Formula 7.1, namely $l_0 = \sum_{i=1}^{2m-1} l_{il} + \sum_{i=1}^{m} |s_i|, \sum_{i=1}^{2m-1} l_{iu} + \sum_{i=1}^{m} |s_i|$ to compute $l_0$.

Figure 8.4 presents a $(k, \overrightarrow{l}, 2)$ pseudoknot stack with appropriate distance constraints, in which the stacks $s_1$ and $s_2$ form a $(k, \overrightarrow{l}, 2)$ intersected stack and they are nested in the stack $s_0$. The intervals [2, 5], [4, 10], [2, 8], [3, 8] and [4, 15] correspond to the distance ranges of *stem 1*, $l_1$, *stem 2*, $l_m$ and $l_2$, respectively. For example, for $l_1$, we have $l_{1l} = 2$, $l_{1u} = 5$. To obtain $l_0$, it is necessary to include the base-pair stacks $s_2$ and $s_3$ in Figure 8.4. Therefore, we can compute $l_{0l} = 2 + 4 + 2 + 3 + 2 + 4 + 2 = 19$.

The pseudoknot stack $(k, \overrightarrow{l}, h)$ with the vector $\overrightarrow{l}$ can be used to establish the model. However, there might be discrepant model configurations for different pseudoknot structures. Thus, it is critical to develop distance function to compute their similarity for structure-function relationships.

### 8.4.3   Distance Function between Intervals

The complicated secondary structures can be transformed into the concise form of a set of distance vectors by using the above modeling schemes. This normalization gives rise to a valuable data set for further data analysis such as classification. To achieve good classification, it is critical to develop appropriate distance measures for correctly computing the *dissimilarity (distance)* between the query and targeted structures and finding the top similar structures. We will focus on introducing a novel interval-based distance function in this section.

Unlike the *Euclidean* metric, two important attributes *center* and *radius* are used to describe each element $l_i$ of the distance vector, which is represented by using an interval $[l_{il}, l_{iu}]$ defined in Definition 7.5. The *radius* and *center* of the interval $l_i = [l_{il}, l_{iu}]$ are defined as:

$$r_{l_i} = \frac{l_{iu} - l_{il}}{2} \tag{8.5}$$

$$c_{l_i} = l_{il} + r_{l_i} \tag{8.6}$$

where $l_{iu} = r_{l_i} + c_{l_i}$ in terms of the definitions of *center* and *radius*.

*Example 8.1.* The *center* and *radius* of the intervals $l_i = [5, 8]$ and $l_j = [0, 7]$ is $r_{l_i} = \frac{8-5}{2} = 1.5$, $r_{l_j} = \frac{7-0}{2} = 3.5$, $c_{l_i} = 5 + r_{l_i} = 6.5$, and $c_{l_j} = 0 + r_{l_j} = 3.5$.

The radio between the overlapped area and the area of $l_i$ could be defined as: $\frac{O(l_i, l_j)}{2r_{l_i}}$. This represents the similarity intensity from $l_i$ to $l_j$. Since we want to combine the overlapped area with the *Hausdorff* distance, and expect that the bigger the overlapped area is, the lower $d(l_i, l_j)$ should be. As a result, we use $1 - \frac{O(l_i,l_j)}{2r_{l_i}}$ to represent the overlapped-area-based dissimilarity intensity, by which to generate $d(l_i, l_j)$. However, it is possible that $l_i$ is a single value. In other words, $r_{l_i} = 0$. In that case, it is more appropriate to change the dissimilarity intensity to $1 - \frac{O(l_i,l_j)}{2r_{l_i}+1}$. According to the definition of two attributes, the distance between two intervals $l_i = [l_{il}, l_{iu}]$ and $l_j = [l_{jl}, l_{ju}]$ is defined as:

$$d(l_i, l_j) = H(l_i, l_j) * (1 - \frac{O(l_i,l_j)}{2r_{l_i}+1}) \tag{8.7}$$

where $H(l_i, l_j)$ represents the Haudorff distance between $l_i$ and $l_j$.

## 8.5 Analysis of Distance Function

The distance function defined in Equation 8.7 combines the *Hausdorff* distance and the overlapped area method. The overlapped area coefficient represents the dissimilarity intensity of two intervals according to their overlapped area, and it is symmetric. Since the *Hausdorff* distance is asymmetric, the distance function defined in Equation 8.7 is asymmetric. Given two intervals $a = [a_1, a_2]$ and $b = [b_1, b_2]$, they have three possible relationships:

- Perfect Match;
- Partially Overlapped;
- Non-Overlapped;

It is necessary to define distance measures by taking these situations into account. This is critical to ensure correct results of search for the queried structure.

**Perfect Match.** Given interval $a = [a_1, a_2]$ and $b = [b_1, b_2]$, if both $b_1$ and $b_2$ are in $[a_1, a_2]$ or both $a_1$ and $a_2$ are in $[b_1, b_2]$, then it is called a perfect match. They can be seen in Figure 8.5(a) and Figure 8.5(b), respectively.

In the perfect match situation, $|c_a - c_b|$ must be less than $|r_a - r_b|$. Given $a_i \in a$ and $b_i \in b$, it is observed that the minimum distances $min(a_i, b) = 0$ and $min(b_i, a) = 0$ in either cases. According to the definition of Hausdorff distance, we have $h(a, b) = h(b, a) = 0$. According to Equation 8.4, $H(a, b) = max(h(a, b), h(b, a)) = 0$. Thus, we have $d(a, b) = 0$.

It is not difficult to compute the distance of perfect match intervals, whereas it becomes more complicated when the intervals are partially overlapped. In that case, the minimum distance of any point that is not in the overlapped area from one interval to the other one is not zero. Thus, we need to compute the Hausdorff distance by determining the maximum distance between two point sets.

**Partially Overlapped.** Given interval $a = [a_1, a_2]$ and $b = [b_1, b_2]$, if only $a_1$ or $a_2$ is in $[b_1, b_2]$, or only $b_1$ or $b_2$ is in $[a_1, a_2]$, it is called *partially overlapped*.

Figures 8.6(a), 8.6(b), 8.7(a), 8.7(b) present instances with respect to partially overlapped. Note not all possible situations are included in these figures.

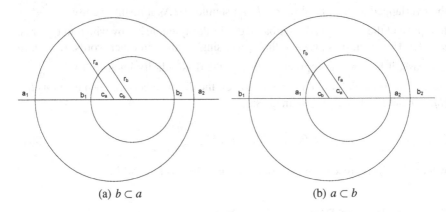

(a) $b \subset a$                              (b) $a \subset b$

**Fig. 8.5** The perfect match between intervals

Although the position of $c_a$ and $c_b$ might be altered in different cases, such as $c_a < b_1$ in Figure 8.6(a) and $c_a > b_1$ in Figure 8.6(b), this does not impact on computing the distance since we always have $h(a, b) = b_1 - a_1$ and $h(b, a) = b_2 - a_2$. Thus, $H(a, b)$ $= \max\{h(a, b), h(b, a)\} = \max\{b_1 - a_1, a_2 - b_2\}$ according to the Equations 8.2, 8.3 and 8.4. No matter which case occurs, we actually obtain $b_1 - a_1 = c_b - c_a + r_a - r_b$ and $b_2 - a_2 = c_b - c_a + r_b - r_a$ in terms of Equations 8.5 and 8.6. It is observed that the two distances all have $c_b - c_a$. We just need to compare $r_a - r_b$ and $r_b - r_a$. Thus, we have

$$H(a,b) = \begin{cases} c_b - c_a + r_a - r_b \text{ if } r_a \ge r_b \\ \\ c_b - c_a + r_b - r_a \text{ if } r_b > r_a \end{cases} \tag{8.8}$$

The distance can be worked out by multiplying the dissimilarity intensity coefficient $(1 - \frac{O(a,b)}{2r_a+1})$. The $d(a,b)$ approximates the *Hausdorff* distance while the value of the overlapped area decreases. From the figures, $O(a, b) = a_2 - b_1 = c_a - c_b + r_a + r_b$. As a result, we have $d(a, b) = H(a, b) * (1 - \frac{|c_a - c_b| + r_a + r_b}{2r_a+1})$ in a more general form.

**Non-overlapped.** Given intervals $a = [a_1, a_2]$ and $b = [b_1, b_2]$, if neither $a_1$ or $a_2$ is in $[b_1, b_2]$, or neither $b_1$ or $b_2$ is in $[a_1, a_2]$, then we call it is non-overlapped.

Figures 8.8(a) and 8.8(b) present two possibilities of non-overlapped, respectively. Similar to the partially overlapped, they all have $h(a, b) = b_1 - a_1$ and $h(b, a) = b_2 - a_2$. Nevertheless, *Hausdorff* distance is their maximum. In the same way, we have

$$H(a,b) = \begin{cases} c_b - c_a + r_a - r_b \text{ if } r_a > r_b \\ \\ c_b - c_a + r_b - r_a \text{ if } r_b > r_a \end{cases} \tag{8.9}$$

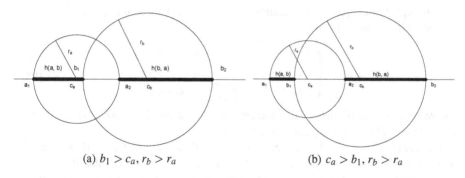

(a) $b_1 > c_a$, $r_b > r_a$       (b) $c_a > b_1$, $r_b > r_a$

**Fig. 8.6** The partially overlapped between intervals, $r_b > r_a$

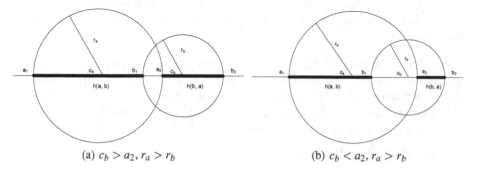

(a) $c_b > a_2$, $r_a > r_b$       (b) $c_b < a_2$, $r_a > r_b$

**Fig. 8.7** The partially overlapped between intervals, $r_a > r_b$

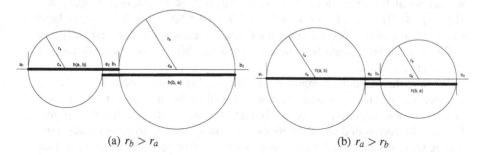

(a) $r_b > r_a$       (b) $r_a > r_b$

**Fig. 8.8** The non-overlapped between intervals

It is similar to the partially overlapped situation. The selection depends on the comparison of the radius of point sets, namely $r_b$ and $r_a$. Further, unlike the *partially overlapped*, there is a *gap* between two intervals $a$ and $b$. Especially, the *gap* is viewed as a negative overlapped area in this chapter, namely $O(a, b) = - gap = -(b_1 - a_2) = a_2 - b_1 = c_a + r_a - (c_b - r_b) = c_a - c_b + r_a + r_b$. Thus, we have $d(a, b) = H(a, b) * (1 - \frac{c_a - c_b + r_a + r_b}{2r_a + 1}) = H(a, b) * (1 + \frac{(c_b - c_a) - (r_a + r_b)}{2r_a + 1})$.

Although the expressions to compute distance are varied, the distance can be presented in a concise form below:

$$d(a,b) = \begin{cases} 0 & \text{iff } a \subseteq b \text{ or } b \subseteq a \\ |c_a - c_b| & \text{if } r_a = r_b = 0 \\ H(a,b) * (1 - \frac{O(a,b)}{2r_a+1}) & \text{otherwise} \end{cases} \qquad (8.10)$$

where $O(a, b)$ can be further divided into two situations in response to *partially overlapped* and *non-overlapped*, respectively.

Formula 8.10 is derived by merging *Hausdorff* distance with the overlapped area method. In case of the *perfect match*, situation $|c_a - c_b| \leq |r_a - r_b|$, the distance is defined as 0. A special case is both $a$ and $b$ are single values. In other words, there is no overlapped area between them at all. In that case, we just consider the *Hausdorff* distance, $|a - b|$. Otherwise, we use $1 - \frac{O(a,b)}{2r_a+1}$ as a coefficient to indicate the dissimilarity intensity. The distance is derived by multiplying the *Hausdorff* distance by the coefficient.

*Example 8.2.* Suppose $a = [2, 7]$ and $b = [0, 5]$ represent two intervals. They are partially overlapped. Thus, their distance can be calculated in terms of the formulas 8.5, 8.6 and 8.8. $r_a = \frac{7-2}{2} = 2.5$, $c_a = 2 + r_a = 4.5$, $r_b = \frac{5-0}{2} = 2.5$, $c_b = 0 + r_b = 2.5$. Thus, we have $h([2, 7], [0, 5]) = 2$ and $h([0, 5], [2, 7]) = 2$, and $H([0, 5], [2, 7]) = 2$. In the similar manner, we can compute $1 - \frac{O([0,5],[2,7])}{2r_{[0,5]}+1} = 1 - \frac{3}{2*2.5+1} = 0.5$ and

$$d(a, b) = H([0, 5], [2, 7]) * (1 - \frac{O([0,5],[2,7])}{2r_{[0,5]}+1}) = 0.5.$$

Suppose $a = [4, 7]$ and $b = [0, 5]$ are the same as Example 8.2. In the similar way, we can calculate their distance. Thus we have $h([0,5], [4,7]) = 4$, $h([4,7], [0,5]) = 2$, $H([0, 5], [4, 7]) = \max(4, 2) = 4$, $d([0,5], [4,7]) = 4 * 5/6 = 3.3$. Actually, the latter case has more overlapped area than the former by comparing $[2,7]$ and $[4,7]$. The different in the latter could be more distinguished. Thus, it has a larger distance in contrast to the former.

We have discussed the computation of distance between intervals. Nevertheless, it is necessary to have distance function to calculate the distance between a query of intervals and a group of intervals. In that case, we firstly calculate the distance between the corresponding $i$-th intervals in the query and the group; secondly, summarize those distances and use the sum as the distance between the query and the group. The distance between interval $q = \{a_1, a_2, \ldots, a_m\}$ and $g = \{b_1, b_2, \ldots, b_n\}$ is defined as follows:

$$d[q,g] = \Sigma_{i=1}^{l} d(a_i, b_i) \qquad (8.11)$$

where $l = \min(m, n)$.

## 8.6  Experiments

The experiments start from learning the structure patterns in terms of the available data of PesudoBase. The patterns with respect to classes are studied in this chapter. There are 13 categories of pesudoknots in PseudoBase, including *vr, vt, vf, v3, v5, vo, rr, mr, tm, ri, ap, ot* and *ar*. Further, they are mainly involved in the functions of *frameshifting* [238, 288, 304], *translation control* and *self-splicing*. Thus, it is critical to develop techniques to deal with the increasing and varied pseudoknot structures and study their potential correlations. We aim to identify the top-similar structure patterns for the query, by which to separate the classes with high similarity to the query from those with low similarity and predict its potential function. Six of the learned structure patterns with respect to classes are presented in Table 8.3. More patterns can be seen by accessing http://bioinformatics.gxu.edu.cn/bio/data/LNAI8335/8335-11.rar.

**Table 8.3** Structure patterns of classes

| Class | Stem 1 | Stem 2 | Loop 1 | Loop 2 | Loop 3 |
|-------|--------|--------|--------|--------|--------|
| Ap | [3, 7] | [3, 7] | [1, 3] | [0, 6] | [3, 30] |
| Ar | [3, 3] | [5, 5] | [4, 4] | [0, 0] | [6, 6] |
| Mr | [4, 19] | [5, 33] | [0, 13] | [0, 4] | [1, 83] |
| Ot | [4, 22] | [6, 9] | [3, 8] | [0, 1] | [4, 29] |
| Ri | [5, 7] | [4, 8] | [8, 158] | [2, 261] | [10, 41] |
| Rr | [3, 10] | [3, 8] | [1, 32] | [0, 6] | [0, 8] |

According to the proposed method, it is observed that the single values may occur in the collection of intervals of structures. In that case, they are still viewed as a special interval that has equal upper limit and lower limit. Thus, the single value is allowed in our framework and our methods are able to evaluate the similarity between varied secondary structures.

The queried pseudoknot structures are obtained by searching the keyword *pseudoknot* in Rfam database [104]. We found 65 unique results for the query in 3 sections of the database, including 37 hits with Rfam, 56 hits with Wikipedia and 4 hits with Literature. To demonstrate the performance of the proposed framework, 7 pseudoknot structures from the database are selected to find the classes that have similar structure features to the query. Although the *loop* 2 is included in the presented patterns for clarity, they are ignored while computing similarity since it is often absent in most pseudoknots. Nevertheless, it can be taken into account to complement the similarity comparison when it presents in the queried structure and structure patterns.

Table 8.4 describes the distance from the structures, RF00523, RF00165, RF00507 and RF00381 to the classes. According to the results, we are able to conduct an initial classification for the queried structures. If two structures have an equal or close distance to a class, it is necessary to further compare the detailed distance of stems and loops in combination with their frequency in the class.

**Table 8.4** Examples of distance from structures to classes

| Class | RF00523 | RF00165 | RF00507 | RF00381 |
|-------|---------|---------|---------|---------|
| Ap | 6 | 194 | 980 | 56 |
| Ar | 10 | 23 | 41 | 16 |
| Mr | 0 | 28 | 640 | 0 |
| Ot | 0 | 137 | 740 | 12 |
| Ri | 770 | 24 | 34 | 0 |
| Rr | 60 | 21 | 32 | 78 |
| Tm | 0 | 20 | 309 | 20 |
| V3 | 40 | 96 | 772 | 55 |
| V5 | 44 | 28 | 40 | 60 |
| Vo | 0 | 10 | 421 | 0 |
| Vr | 49 | 410 | 1086 | 93 |
| Vt | 0 | 155 | 888 | 35 |
| Vf | 0 | 330 | 706 | 0 |

Figure 8.9 presents the distance with respect to specified stems and loops in more details. It has zero distance to *stem* 1, *stem* 2 and *loop* 3 of *Ap* in contrast to *loop* 1 of *Ar*. This results in more accuracy while performing similarity comparison. Thus, this not only facilitates the measure of similarity between structures in an intuitive way and enhances the correctness by comparing substructures if required. The similarity measure would eliminate 54 percent and 69 percent of the structure patterns from consideration for the queries RF00523 and RF00381, respectively. Further, RF00523 and RF00381 have zero distance to multiple classes. To distinguish them, the frequency of stems and loops of RF00523 and RF00381 in corresponding classes is applied. Figures 8.10 and 8.11 present the frequency distribution of RF00523 and RF00381, respectively. It is not difficult to sort out the most fitted classes Vf and Mr in answer to RF00523 and RF00381, respectively. Although there might be a high frequency in one stem or loop, such as Ot and Tm in Figure 8.10, they have very low frequency in other substructures. Thus, they are not viewed as a similar structure pattern to the query herein.

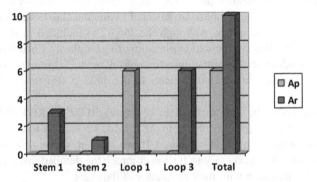

**Fig. 8.9** Distance from RF00523 to Ap and Ar

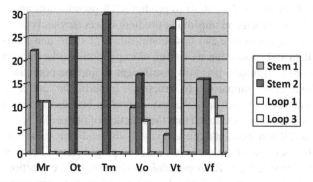

**Fig. 8.10** Frequency distribution of stems and loops of RF00523

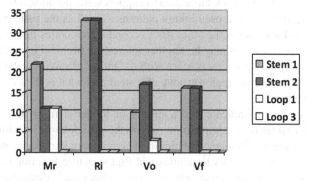

**Fig. 8.11** Frequency distribution of stems and loops of RF00381

It is observed that there may be a large distance from the query to all available classes, such as the structures RF00165 and RF00507. In other words, the database has no similar structure patterns to the query. In that case, it will be reported to users rather than choosing them randomly. Although the distance from the query to a class might be very close to 0, such as the distance 10 from RF00165 to Vo, it is not considered in this chapter.

## 8.7 Conclusion and Discussion

As an important functional structure, the pseudoknot is more highly constrained by non-local base pairs and presents specific three dimensional geometries. Such non-local contacts make pseudoknot problem NP-complete. A number of pseudo-knot algorithms [80, 260] have been developed but searched for only a subset of pseudoknots.

There have been many algorithms to predict RNA pseudoknots and characterize them. However, they focus on improving prediction accuracy and extracting the information with respect to size and base composition of stems and loops. Although the obtained data and knowledge are useful, most previous works study pseudoknots from the aspect of sequence. It is still insufficient to find the potential relation between pseudoknots by comparison of structures. In particular, unlike general data, the genome data contain not only the sequence data but also structural information. More evidences have indicated that the function of molecules is determined by structures. Thus, it is important to develop methods to address these critical issues.

We have focused our attention here on developing distance functions for measuring the similarity between RNA pseudoknots in terms of a collection of distance vectors. The distance vector is derived from modeling the pseudoknots. If more pseudoknot data are available, the constructed models will become more stable. Moreover, we also need to seek more data to support some pseudoknots with lightly weak similarity from current pseudoknot patterns as well as the patterns with high similarity. We did not discuss the other RNA secondary structures like *dumbbell* and *cloverleaf* in this chapter. It may be another interesting problem to collect data for them, such as why a loop interacts more with the minor groove of a stem, or why a loop interacts less with the major groove of a stem and what is their correlation to the structure features.

The previous results indicate that a shorter or longer stem or loop, or a stem or loop with irregular base composition may make pesudoknots non-functional or have reduced function efficiency. We aim to generate more knowledge with respect to a variety of RNA secondary structures and find structure-function relationships by searching similar structure patterns for query. This idea is desired to extend to generate more trusted search results, whereas this would require a large dataset and evaluation of their soundness.

This chapter aims to model increasingly available RNA pseudoknot data, by which to find similar structure patterns to the queried structure. The satisfied patterns present the similar pseudoknots in structure and imply common functional roles in RNA molecules. Further, the patterns with lower similarity to the query are reserved for future analysis when more data are available in the future. The identified similar structures may share common function, which help us build up pathways with correct function annotation.

# Chapter 9
# Discovery of Structural and Functional Features Bind to RNA Pseudoknots

The identification of RNA secondary structures has been among the most exciting recent developments in biology and medical science. It has been recognized that there is an abundance of functional structures with frameshifting, regulation of translation, and splicing functions. However, the inherent signal for secondary structures is weak and generally not straightforward due to complex interleaving substrings. This makes it difficult to explore their potential functions from various structure data. In particular, an RNA pseudoknot consists of nonnested double-stranded stems connected by single-stranded loops as mentioned in Chapter 8. There is increasing recognition that RNA pseudoknots are one of the most prevalent RNA structures and fulfill a diverse set of biological roles within cells, and there is an expanding rate of studies into RNA pseudoknotted structures as well as increasing allocation of function. These not only produce valuable structural data but also facilitate an understanding of structural and functional characteristics in RNA molecules. Although Chapter 7 and Chapter 8 develop approaches to model RNA structures and measure their similarity, the deep analysis of important structural and functional features in substructures is ignored.

To capture the features of RNA pseudoknots, we present a novel framework based on a collection of predicted RNA secondary structures and quantitative association rule mining to analyze the pseudoknot data. Our approach, allows users to efficiently capture interesting characteristic relations in RNA and bring out the top-ranked rules for specified association groups. The derived rules are classified into specified association groups regarding structure, function, and category of RNA pseudoknots. The discovered association rules assist biologists in filtering out significant knowledge of structure-function and structure-category relationships. Our results not only point to a number of interesting associations and include a brief biological interpretation to them. It assists biologists in sorting out the most significant characteristic structure patterns and predicting structure-function relationships in RNA.

## 9.1 Introduction

Accurately predicting the functions of biological macromolecules is one of the biggest challenges in functional genomics. However, the protein folding problem is difficult because the local secondary and non-local tertiary contacts both contribute to the stability of the final native folds in RNA. It is secondary structure (base-pairing interactions) that has more influences on the final fold rather than tertiary contacts. Secondary structures are viewed as essential elements of the topology of many structural RNAs such as ribosomal RNAs or ribozymes. They have been found in most organism and comprise functional domains within ribozymes, self-splicing introns, ribonucleoprotein complexes, viral genomes, and many other biological systems [1, 71]. Thus, studies of structural information on RNA can be an alternative to understand structure-function relationships in biology.

A number of new classes of functional RNA structures such as miRNA and riboswitches, have been reported [90]. Recent studies indicate that they perform many important regulatory, structural, and catalytic role in the cell. For example, rRNA is the catalytic component of the ribosomes, and miRNA can block the mRNA from being translated, or accelerate its degradation. Further, many reports indicate that the transactional complexity of mammalian genomes has been significantly underestimated. As described in [159], a large class of ncRNAs (noncoding RNAs) such as rRNAs, tRNAs, small nuclear RNAs (snRNAs) and small nucleolar RNAs (snoRNAs), share characteristic structures that are functional and hence are well conserved through evolution. They may constitute a critical hidden layer of gene regulation in higher organisms. It is suggested that perhaps a large fraction of the significance of RNA secondary structures are currently unrevealed. Thus, it is critical to mining the valuable predicted RNA secondary structure data for prediction of structure-function relationships in RNA.

RNA molecules play a central role in a number of biological functions within cells, from the transfer of genetic information from DNA to protein, to enzymatic catalysis. To perform diverse functions, the simple linear nucleotide sequence of RNA forms a variety of complex three-dimensional structures. One of the most prevalent structures adopted by RNA molecules is a commonly-occurring structural motif known as the pseudoknot that was first recognized in the turnip yellow mosaic virus in 1982 [259]. It is known that the RNA pseudonots perform varied roles in biology such as efficient frameshifting in many retroviruses [259]. An RNA pseudoknot is formed when bases outside a hairpin structure pair with bases within the hairpin loop to create a second stem and loop structure. The secondary structure of an RNA shows a tree like shape that comprises various loops and stack regions as described in Figure 7.4. The variation of the size of stems and loops and their base composition lead to a diverse set of functions. Thus, the understanding of the base pairing pattern of the stems and loops provide better insight into the structural features and potential structure-function relationships.

As described in Chapter 8, pseudoknot is a RNA structure that involves base pairing between a loop, formed by an orthodox secondary structure, and some region outside this loop [311]. Although several distinct folding topologies of pseudoknots exist, the simplest or classical pseudoknot is the H-pseudoknot (Figure 8.3(a)) that is formed by the pairing of a region in the hairpin loop with the bases outside the hairpin. The H-pseudoknot minimally consists of two stems (*stem* 1 and *stem* 2) and two loops (*loop* 1 and *loop* 2). If the two stems form a quasi-consecutive helix, the base stacking at the junction becomes possible, otherwise an additional loop (*loop* 3 in Figure 8.3(b)) might be created. The single stranded loop regions may contain hundreds of nucleotides and often interact with adjacent stems and hence a relatively simple fold can yield complex and stable RNA structures. Moreover, due to the variation of the lengths of loops and stems and their base composition, as well as each other's interactions, pseudoknots show a diverse set of roles in biology. Thus, a comprehensive understanding of the functions of RNA molecules requires knowledge of their structures.

RNA pseudoknots are viewed as essential elements of the topology of many structural RNAs such as ribosomal RNAs or ribozymes. They have been found in most organism and comprise functional domains within ribozymes, self-splicing introns, ribonucleoprotein complexes, viral genomes, and many other biological systems [1, 71]. The in-depth knowledge of a psuedoknot's structure provides a better insight into understanding their psuedoknot's functions in varied organisms.

A great deal of studies have been put into predicting the secondary structure from the nucleotide sequence. The prediction of RNA secondary structures [27, 349] mainly consists of comparative RNA analysis [105, 260, 264] and approximating the free energy of any given structure [307]. Many techniques using the Tinoco model [212, 348] or thermodynamics-based energy minimization algorithm [349] such as well-accepted parameters of D. Turner et al [99], aim to discover the structure of optimal score. Recently, there have been many computational methods developed to efficiently identify functional RNA structures by using comparative genomic. They present a characteristic substitution pattern in their stem-paring regions such that only substitutions that maintain the pairing capability between paired bases will be allowed in evolution [264, 345].

Regardless of continued work to increase the prediction accuracy [42, 211, 293] by improving on the parameters, the accuracy of predictions using the Tinoco model can never reach 100% and the constraint on nested secondary structures is applied. However, the problem of RNA structure prediction can be attributed to inaccurate thermodynamic parameters but also pseudoknot formation. Although more than 95% of the base pairs do not contain any pseudoknots at all, nearly all RNA molecules have one or more pseudoknots. As a result, there have been multiple known algorithms to predict RNA pseudoknots, such as heuristic modelling [72] and RNA sampler [327] for generating accurate structural information in RNA molecules.

A variety of RNA secondary structure data have been publicly accessed. Among them, PseudoBase [253] is the only online database containing structural, functional and sequence data of RNA pseudoknots, allowing us to investigate deeply into structure-function relationships in RNA molecules. Unfortunately, the analysis of this valuable data set is underdeveloped due to the difficulty in modelling and complexity in computing. It is difficult to predict structural and functional features of pseudoknots by only analysing individual experimental result. Thus, association rule mining that has been successfully used to discover valuable information from a large amount of data [339] can be used to analyse this data set.

Recently, many applications using data mining have been reported in analysing various biological data sets [47, 51, 66]. Most of them [125, 292] however show limitations in handling the data with multi-valued variables including categorical multi-valued valuables (such as color {red, blue, green}) and quantitative multi-valued variables (such as weight {[40, 50], [50, 75]}). A model is proposed in [339] to identify quantitative association rules, in which the domain of multi-valued variables is partitioned into intervals. An association rule is represented as $X \Rightarrow Y$ along with a conditional probability matrix $M_{Y|X}$ according to Bayesian rules.

In the present study, we develop a framework based on association rule mining to identify potential top-$k$ covering rule groups in RNA pseudoknots, including the relationships with respect to structure-function and structure-category, significant ratios of stems and loops, base composition and organisms. The relationships are captured by using an intuitive conditional probability matrix. It allows users to regulate $k$ and the *minsupp* threshold and compare between rules in the same group. The domain of quantitative attributes are divided by a novel point-based partition schema. Further, the performance evaluation demonstrates the advantages of our miner in handling high dimensional data. The results by 0.1 (*minsupp*) in contrast to the results by 0.2 are presented in the analysis. The identified distributions (sizes and nucleotide composition) of stems and loops indicate the interactions between loops and stems and account for the reproduction of a variety of pseudoknots. The identified distributions (sizes and nucleotide composition) of stems and loops indicate the interactions between loops and stems and account for the reproduction of various pseudoknots. In particular, the identified ratios imply the role of pseudoknots in the promotion of function efficiency. We also observe that there is discipline of sizes and base composition (stems and loops) in specific organisms. A brief interpretation of the obtained rules is presented. Furthermore, a deep study builds connections between these rules and enhances the understanding of structure-function relationships in RNA pseudoknots of various organisms.

## 9.2  Motivations

Traditional association rule mining has been widely and successfully used to identify frequent patterns from general datasets. However, it is unfit for the data that contains multi-valued variables [339]. It has been argued that the former mining approach depended on two thresholds and a conditional probability matrix can be helpful for association studies due to its impressive expressiveness. However, if the item variable $X$ impacts on variable $Y$ at only a few point values, item-based association mining and quantitative association rule mining may be more appropriate and efficient than this method.

The previous techniques can only identify rules among simple variables, such as *tea* → *sugar* or *state* → *united*. They have limitations in discovering rules among multi-valued variables from large databases and for representing them. For example, in Figure 8.3, *stem* and *loop* are categorical multi-valued variables. They have a range of categories of {*stem* 1, *stem* 2} and {*loop* 1, *loop* 3}, respectively. The sizes of stems and loops are quantitative multi-valued variables that are represented as a collection of intervals such as {(0, 1], (1, 2], (2, 3]}. The size distribution of stems and loops are discrepant. For example, the size of *stem* 1 in PseudoBase varies between 0 and 22 only, whereas the size of *loop* 3 is between 0 and 890. Thus, it is necessary to generate a common partition. Therefore, this urges us to develop new methods to address the relationships among these multi-valued variables.

Usually, we may obtain a number of rules in traditional association rule mining. However, it is not easy to sort those rules that are ranked higher than the others. Furthermore, some interesting rules might be missed or redundant rules were generated due to an unappropriate threshold. Thus, this chapter extends and adapts traditional association rule mining by representing a rule as the form of $X \rightarrow Y$ in conjunction with a probability matrix $M_{Y|X}$ in terms of Bayesian rules. This captures the relationship that the presence of $X$ results in the occurrence of $Y$. $M_{Y|X}$ is defined as

$$M_{Y|X} \triangleq P(Y=y|X=x) =$$

$$= \begin{pmatrix} p(y_1|x_1) \ p(y_2|x_1) \ \cdots \ p(y_n|x_1) \\ p(y_1|x_2) \ p(y_2|x_2) \ \cdots \ p(y_n|x_2) \\ \cdots \\ p(y_1|x_m) \ p(y_2|x_m) \ \cdots \ p(y_n|x_m) \end{pmatrix}$$

where $p(y_j \mid x_i)$ represents the conditional probability, $i = 1, 2, \cdots, m$, and $j = 1, 2, \cdots, n$. $x_i$ and $y_j$ represent a categorical item and a quantitative item, such as *stem* 1 and a size interval (1, 2], respectively. The matrix comprises a group of association rules that correspond to a specified characteristic relationship of RNA pseudoknots. Each column consists of a subgroup of the rules corresponding to a categorical attribute variable $x_i$. Thus, this assists us in extracting the most significant rules in each subgroup separately rather than identifying the rules from the whole group.

A high dimensional dataset can result in many redundant rules and long mining process [66], and makes it difficult to sort out interesting information from databases. These challenges block the analysis of the pseudoknot data. To address this critical problem, we propose a novel mining method to identify the most significant top-$k$ covering rule groups. As mentioned in [66], it is easier and semantically clearer to choose $k$ than minimum confidence. Moreover, it avoids missing interesting rules and generating too many redundant rules. A natural alternative to our model is to set different values of $k$, and compare each other's results.

## 9.3    Materials and Methods

### 9.3.1    Partition of Attributes

The used data can be referred to Section 8.3.1. After removing 8 unusual pseudo-knots, 7 reductant pseudoknots [1] and 5 pseudoknots that have loop lengths $\geq 200$, a dataset consisting of 225 H-pseudoknots is obtained. Within the 225 unique H-pseudoknots, 170, or 76%, have $L_2 = 0$; 22, or 10% have $L_2 = 1$; 8, or 4% have $L_2 = 2$; 1, or 0.4% has $L_2 = 3$. In particular, *loop* 2 is ignored here since the most studied type of pseudoknot is with coaxial stacking of stems so that *loop* 2 is absent.

Suppose $\{class, function, stem, loop, base, ratio, length\}$ denotes the domain of attributes of PseudoBase. The first six elements are viewed as categorical attributes, and the last one is a quantitative attribute. We thus propose a novel partition in conjunction with the properties of pseudoknot data and top-$k$ rule groups. A categorical attribute has a number of categories, such as hair color including *blonde*, *brown* and *black*. According to the specification in PseudoBase, the partition of domain of categorical attributes *class*, *function*, *stem*, *loop*, *base* and *ratio* is defined as

* $class = \{vr, vt, vf, v3, v5, vo, rr, mr, tm, ri, ap, ot, ar\}$
* $function = \{ss, tc, fs\}$
* $stem = \{S_1, S_2\}$
* $loop = \{L_1, L_2, L_3\}$
* $base = \{A, C, G, U\}$
* $ratio = \{S_1/S_2, L_1/L_3, S_1/L_1, S_2/L_1, S_1/L_3, S_2/L_3\}$

Unlike the categorical attributes, the domain of quantitative attribute has to be partitioned into intervals. The partition usually needs to determine (1) the number of intervals and (2) the size of each interval. Although PseudoBase provides an initial partition of base length for each stem and loop, they are actually inconsistent with each other. For example, in the initial partition, (14, 15] is included in *stem* 1, *stem* 2 and *loop* 1 but not in *loop* 3. Nevertheless, as mentioned in [339], a unified partition is required to generate the probability matrix.

The equi-depth partitioning model proposed by Agrawal [292] is an alternative method for causality mining. The number of partitions is defined as *Number of Intervals* $= \frac{2n}{m(K-1)}$, in which $n$ represents the number of quantitative attributes, $m$ represents the minimum support, and $K$ represents the partial completeness level. However, it is inappropriate for sparse datasets and might include much unnecessary information. For example, the size of *stem* 1 in PseudoBase varies between 0 and 22 only, whereas the size of *loop* 3 is between 0 and 890. Thus, traditional partition schemas like equal interval width and equal frequency might lead to inaccurate or uninteresting results of data mining. We thus propose a novel partition in conjunction with the properties of pseudoknot data and top-$k$ rule groups.

**Definition 9.1.** Suppose a quantitative attribute $y$ is divided into a set of intervals $\{y_1, \ldots, y_n\}$ (called base intervals) using the categorical item $x_i$ such that for any base interval $y_j$, $y_j$ consists of a single value for $1 \leq j \leq n$.

- $|y_i| = 1, 1 \leq i \leq n$; and
- for $\forall\, l \neq k$, and $1 \leq l, k \leq n$, $y_l \cap y_k = \emptyset$.

Note, the values of ratio attribute are non-zero real number rather than integers. Thus, the condition $|y_i| = 1$ in Definition 9.1 can be regulated to $|y_i| = 1$ or $|y_i| = 0.5$. This aims to avoid missing interesting knowledge.

Suppose $y_{1i}, \ldots$ and $y_{mi}$ represent the partition using the categorical item $x_i$ in ascending order of their maximum sizes. The partition starts from the categorical item with the minimum of maximum sizes, and integrates it with the next one until all items are gone through. The partition using $x_i$ is defined as $\{(y_{1i}, max(y_{2i})], \ldots, (max(y_{m-1i}), max(y_{mi})]\}$. Table 9.1 presents the distribution of sizes of *stem 1* and *stem 2* of pseudoknots in PseudoBase.

**Table 9.1** Distribution of stem sizes of pseudoknots

| Stem 1 | Number | Stem 1 | Number | Stem 2 | Number |
|--------|--------|--------|--------|--------|--------|
| 0 | 0 | 10 | 5 | 0, 1, 2 | 0 |
| 1 | 0 | 11 | 7 | 3 | 5 |
| 2 | 0 | 12 | 3 | 4 | 33 |
| 3 | 77 | 13 | 6 | 5 | 66 |
| 4 | 42 | 14 | 6 | 6 | 69 |
| 5 | 24 | 16 | 3 | 7 | 36 |
| 6 | 14 | 17 | 3 | 8 | 9 |
| 7 | 8 | 18 | 3 | 9 | 5 |
| 8 | 10 | 19 | 3 | 10 | 1 |
| 9 | 10 | 22 | 1 | 33 | 1 |

The initial partition for each attribute variable actually comprises a collection of ranges. It simply includes one element in each range since each point-value may imply an important structural feature of pseudoknots. For example, according to Definition 9.1, the partition starts from stem 1 and is presented in Table 9.1 as $Y_1 =$ $\{0, (0, 1], (1, 2], (2, 3], (3, 4], (4, 5], (5, 6], (6, 7], (7, 8], (8, 9], (9, 10], (10, 11],$ $(11, 12], (12, 13], (13, 14], (14, 15], (15, 16], (16, 17], (17, 18], (18, 19], (19, 20],$ $(20, 21], (21, 22]\}$. Nevertheless, it is observed that $(19, 20]$ and $(20, 21]$ are not recorded with *stem* 1. They will be combined with $(21, 22]$ if we cannot find them in the partition of other attribute variables. Thus, the final partition needs to consider all attribute variables and integrate their partitions together.

**Definition 9.2.** Suppose $Y_i = \{y_{1i}, \ldots, y_{mi}\}$ and $Y_{i+1} = \{y_{1i+1}, \ldots, y_{ni+1}\}$ are two adjacent partitions. Let $Y = \emptyset$. The integration of them is defined as

- $Y = Y \cup x$, if $x \in Y_i \cup Y_{i+1}$, and $|x| = 1$;
- $Y = Y \cup x \cup \cdots \cup x_c$, if $|x| = 0$, $|x_c| = 1$, $x \in Y_i$ and $x \notin Y_{i+1}$, $max(x) < max(x_c)$ $\leq max(y_{mi})$;
- $Y = Y \cup x \cup \cdots \cup x_c$, if $|x| = 0$, $|x_c| = 1$, $x \in Y_{i+1}$ and $x \notin Y_i$, $max(x) < max(x_c)$ $\leq max(y_{ni+1})$;

where $x_c$ is the closest point value to $x$ that includes one element in the range, and $max()$ represents the function of maximum. There might be more than one categorical item that has the equivalent maximum size with one another. In this extreme case, it will be reported to the user, rather than selecting them randomly. Suppose $Y = \{y_1, \cdots, y_k\}$ is the final partition after integration. The partition $y_k$ might be a large interval that includes unfrequent or missing structures (no record). For example, there is just one record of *stem* 1 of size 22 and there is no record of *stem* 1 from size 20 to 21 at all. In that case, it is reasonable to combine these point-values to a partition instead of listing all of them one by one.

In the similar manner, we can obtain the partition for stem 2 as $Y_2 = \{0, (0, 1], (1, 2], (2, 3], (3, 4], (4, 5], (5, 6], (6, 7], (7, 8], (8, 9], (9, 10], (10, 11], (11, 12], (12, 13], (13, 14], (14, 15], \cdots, (31, 32], (32, 33]\}$ where 33 denotes the maximum size of *stem* 2. This will be integrated with the partition of stem 1 in terms of Definition 9.2. As a result, the integrated partition of $Y_1$ and $Y_2$ is $\{0, (0, 1], (1, 2], (2, 3], (3, 4], (4, 5], (5, 6], (6, 7], (7, 8], (8, 9], (9, 10], (10, 11], (11, 12], (12, 13], (13, 14], (14, 15], (15, 16], (16, 17], (17, 18], (18, 19], (19, 22], (22, 33]\}$. Note there might be more than one categorical item that has equal maximum size with one another.

The partition scheme of *length* in this study adopts the point-based decomposition of quantitative attributes. In the similar way, we can generate partition for loop lengths. Table 9.2 presents the distribution of size of *loop* 1 and *loop* 3. It seems that *loop* 3 has wider range of size than *loop* 1. Their partition can be combined as $\{0, (0, 1], (1, 2], (2, 3], (3, 4], (4, 5], (5, 6], (6, 7], (7, 8], (8, 9], (9, 10], (10, 11], (11, 12], (12, 13], (13, 15], (15, 16], (16, 17], (17, 18], (18, 19], (19, 20], (20, 24], (24, 26], (26, 27], (27, 28], (28, 29], (29, 30], (30, 31], (31, 32], (32, 34], (34, 41], (41, 47], (47, 51], (51, 58], (58, 61], (61, 67], (67, 83], (83, 158], (158, 177], (177, 185]\}$. More details can be seen in Section 9.4. In comparison, the values of ratio attribute are positive real number rather than integers. Thus, the condition $|y_i| = 1$ in Definition 9.1 needs to be changed to $|y_i| = 1$ or $|y_i| = 0.5$. Accordingly, $|x| = 1$ and $|x_c| = 1$ in Definition 9.2 are changed to $|x| = 1$ and $|x_c| = 1$ or $|x| = 0.5$ and $|x_c| = 0.5$. These aim to avoid missing interesting knowledge.

**Table 9.2** Distribution of loop sizes of pseudoknots

| Loop 1 | Number | Loop 1 | Number | Loop 3 | Number | Loop 3 | Number | Loop 3 | Number |
|--------|--------|--------|--------|--------|--------|--------|--------|--------|--------|
| 0 | 1 | 11 | 1 | 0 | 1 | 11 | 5 | 29 | 1 |
| 1 | 72 | 12 | 1 | 1 | 1 | 12 | 3 | 30 | 1 |
| 2 | 43 | 13 | 1 | 2 | 16 | 15 | 6 | 31 | 3 |
| 3 | 39 | 19 | 6 | 3 | 55 | 16 | 1 | 32 | 1 |
| 4 | 29 | 20 | 1 | 4 | 12 | 17 | 2 | 34 | 1 |
| 5 | 12 | 24 | 1 | 5 | 9 | 18 | 7 | 41 | 1 |
| 6 | 2 | 32 | 1 | 6 | 31 | 19 | 1 | 51 | 1 |
| 7 | 0 | 47 | 1 | 7 | 17 | 24 | 2 | 58 | 1 |
| 8 | 3 | 158 | 1 | 8 | 9 | 26 | 1 | 61 | 2 |
| 9 | 4 | 177 | 2 | 9 | 15 | 27 | 3 | 67 | 2 |
| 10 | 4 | 185 | 1 | 10 | 4 | 28 | 2 | 68,69,75,83 | 8 |

## 9.3.2 Rule Groups

Based on the partitioned variables, we then work out the conditional probabilities for $X$ and $Y$ in the probability matrix below. Therefore, we can determine the conditional probability of $Y = y_i$, given $X = x_i$, as $p(y_i|x_i) = p(x_i|y_i) * p(y_i)/p(x_i)$.

For example, $x$ and $y$ represent *stem* 1 of pseudoknots, and the size interval (3, 4] of *stem* 1, respectively. By Table 9.1, we have $n = 225$ and $p(x = stem\ 1) = 225/225 = 1$. Additionally, the number of pseudoknots containing *stem* 1 with 4 nucleotides is equal to 42, we have $p(y = (3, 4] \wedge x = stem\ 1) = 42/225 = 0.19$. In the same way, we have $p(y = (3, 4] \mid x = stem\ 1) = p(y = (3, 4] \wedge x = stem\ 1) / p(x = stem\ 1) = 0.19$. As a result, we are able to compute the entire conditional probabilities of *stem* 1, namely $[p(y_1 \mid stem\ 1) p(y_2 \mid stem\ 1) \ldots p(y_n \mid stem\ 1)]$, where $y_j$ denotes the *j*th size interval by partition.

Suppose $x$ and $y$ represent *loop* 1 of pseudoknots, and the size interval (2, 3] of *loop* 1, respectively. By Table 9.2, we have $n = 225$ and $p(x = loop\ 1) = 225/225 = 1$. Additionally, the number of pseudoknots containing *loop* 1 with 3 nucleotides is equal to 39, we have $p(y = (2, 3] \wedge x = loop\ 1) = 39/225 = 0.17$ and $p(y = (2, 3] \mid x = loop\ 1) = p(y = (2, 3] \wedge x = loop\ 1) / p(x = loop\ 1) = 0.17$. Then, we are able to compute the entire conditional probabilities of *loop* 1, namely $[p(y_1 \mid loop\ 1) p(y_2 \mid loop\ 1) \ldots p(y_n \mid loop\ 1)]$, where $y_j$ denotes the *j*th size interval by partition.

In a similar manner, the conditional probabilities of *stem* 2 and *loop* 3, can be computed. Thus, we have

$$M_{Y|X} =$$

$$= \begin{pmatrix} p(y_1|stem1) & p(y_2|stem1) & \ldots & p(y_n|stem1) \\ p(y_1|stem2) & p(y_2|stem2) & \ldots & p(y_n|stem2) \\ p(y_1|loop1) & p(y_2|loop1) & \ldots & p(y_n|loop1) \\ p(y_1|loop3) & p(y_2|loop3) & \ldots & p(y_n|loop3) \end{pmatrix}$$

In the similar manner, some matrixes with respect to the associations of organisms and ratios can be created as follows.

$$M_{Y|X} = $$

$$\begin{pmatrix} p(y_1|vr) & p(y_2|vr) & \ldots & p(y_n|vr) \\ p(y_1|vt) & p(y_2|vt) & \ldots & p(y_n|vt) \\ \ldots & \ldots & \ldots & \ldots \\ p(y_1|ot) & p(y_2|ot) & \ldots & p(y_n|ot) \\ p(y_1|ar) & p(y_2|ar) & \ldots & p(y_n|ar) \end{pmatrix} \tag{9.1}$$

$$M_{Y|X} = $$

$$\begin{pmatrix} p(y_1|S_1/L_1) & p(y_2|S_1/L_1) & \ldots & p(y_n|S_1/L_1) \\ p(y_1|S_1/L_3) & p(y_2|S_1/L_3) & \ldots & p(y_n|S_1/L_3) \\ p(y_1|S_2/L_1) & p(y_2|S_2/L_1) & \ldots & p(y_n|S_2/L_1) \\ p(y_1|S_2/L_3) & p(y_2|S_2/L_3) & \ldots & p(y_n|S_2/L_3) \end{pmatrix} \tag{9.2}$$

We can generate other matrixes in terms of different associations. As mentioned above, there must be enough point-pairs $(x_i, y_j)$ in the conditional probability matrix $M_{Y|X}$ that satisfy the conditions of valid rules. In contrast to traditional *minimum confidence*, this chapter uses a flexible way to allow users to have the ability to control the number of rules in each rule group.

Suppose $M_{Y|X}$ corresponding to an association *AS* consists of a set of rows $\{r_1, ..., r_n\}$. Let $A = \{A_1, ..., A_m\}$ be the complete set of antecedent items of *AS*, and $C = \{C_1, ..., C_k\}$ be the complete set of consequent items of *AS*, then each row $r$ includes an antecedent item from $A$ and a set of consequent items from $C$. As a mapping between rows and items, given a row $r_i$, we define **PS** (Point-paris Support Set) as the set of point-pairs whose conditional probabilities are not equal to zero, namely $PS(x) = \{(x, y_j) \mid y_j \in C, p(y_j|x) \neq 0\}$.

**Definition 9.3. Rule group.** Let $G_x = \{x \rightarrow C_j \mid (x, C_j) \in PS(x)\}$ be a rule group with an antecedent item $x$ and consequent support set $C$.

It is observed that the rules from different rule groups might have different supports and confidences. Moreover, there might be different numbers of valid rules derived from different groups. The top-$k$ covering rule groups are thus applied to encapsulate the most significant association of the dataset while enabling users to control the number of rules in a convenient manner.

**Definition 9.4.** Let $R_i: X \rightarrow Y_i$ and $R_j: X \rightarrow Y_j$ be two valid rules with respect to a given categorical item $X$. **Top-k covering rule group** is the subset of the union of rule groups where $1 \leq k \leq k_{max}$ and $k_{max}$ is the upper bound of the number of rules we would like to find. A rule is of interest if, and only if, it is in the **top-k covering rule group**. $R_i$ is ranked higher than $R_j$ if $p(Y_i|X) > p(Y_j|X)$.

*Example 9.1.* In Table 9.1, we have $k_{max} = 21$ due to 21 intervals of *stem* 1. As a result, **top-1 covering rule group** = $\{stem\ 1 \rightarrow (2, 3], stem\ 2 \rightarrow (5, 6]\}$ and **top-2 covering rule group** = $\{stem\ 1 \rightarrow (2, 3], stem\ 1 \rightarrow (3, 4], stem\ 2 \rightarrow (5, 6], stem\ 2 \rightarrow (4, 5]\}$. The rule *stem* 1 $\rightarrow$ (2, 3] is given higher ranking than *stem* 1 $\rightarrow$ (3, 4] due to its higher support in the conditional probability matrix.

*Example 9.2.* In Table 9.2, we have $k_{max} = 39$ due to 39 intervals of combination of *loop* 1 and *loop* 3. Then, **top-1 covering rule group** = $\{loop\ 1 \rightarrow (1, 2], loop\ 3 \rightarrow (2, 3]\}$ and **top-2 covering rule group** = $\{loop\ 1 \rightarrow (1, 2], loop\ 1 \rightarrow (2, 3], loop\ 3 \rightarrow (2, 3], loop\ 3 \rightarrow (5, 6]\}$.

### 9.3.3  Algorithm Design

The algorithm presents the procedure to identify top-$k$ rules from the specified characteristic relations described above.

**begin**

**Input:** *D: RNA pseudoknot data set; minsupp: minimum support threshold; k: constraint of rule groups; $G_x$: rule groups; $G_x^k$: top-k covering rule groups;*

(1) **let** $IG_x \leftarrow \emptyset$; $G_x^k \leftarrow \emptyset$;

(2) **forall** $C_i \in C$ (consequent support set of $G_x$) **do**

    **if** the computed conditional probability of

    $p(C_i|x) > minsupp$ **then**

        $IG_x = IG_x \cup \{(x, C_i)\}$;

    **end**

(3) **for** $(i = |IG_x|, i > 1; i - 1)$ **do**

    **for** $(j = 1; j \leq i - 1; j + 1)$ **do**

      (3.1) **if** $p(C_j|x) < p(C_{j+1}|x)$ **then**

          swap$(C_j, C_{j+1})$;

    **end**

    **end**

    $G_x = IG_x$;

(4) **for** $(i = 1, i \leq k; i + 1)$ **do**

    (4.1) **forall** $g_i \in G_x$ **do**

        $G_x^k = G_x^k \cup \{(x, C_i)\}$;

    **end**

    **if** $p(C_k|x) = p(C_{k+1}|x)$ **then**

      *This is reported to users;*

    **end**

**end**

In step 1, the empty set is assigned to the variables of the initial rule groups $IG_x$ and the top-$k$ rule groups $G_x^k$, respectively.

Step 2 presents a cycle operations to compute the conditional probability of rules of probability matrix for all elements in the consequent set of a specified rule group. If the conditional probability of a rule is equal to or larger than a given minimum support threshold, it will be added to the set of $IG_x$.

In Step 3, the process is used to sort the elements in the obtained $IG_x$ in terms of their conditional probabilities. Step (3.1) is a *swap* operation to make the element with a bigger probability value move forward. The sorted $IG_x$ is then assigned to $G_x$.

Step 4 first selects those eligible elements from $G_x$, which satisfied the minimum support constraint *minsupp* and were already sorted in ascending order. Only those top-$k$ rules are derived from $G_x$ and are saved to $G_x^k$ eventually. If we observed subsequent elements that share an equal probability value to the $k$th rule, this will be reported to the users rather than select it randomly.

## 9.4   Experiments

### 9.4.1   Rule Group Generation

After partition, we need to construct the matrix in terms of the conditional probability of point-pairs, such as (*stem* 1, (0, 1]). Each association $AS_i$ consists of $|A| \times |C|$ initial rules, in which $|A|$ and $|C|$ represent the cardinality of antecedent set $A$ and consequent set $C$, respectively. Nevertheless, some of them have weak statistic significance. Further, this may result in uninteresting or redundant rules. Thus, top-$k$ covering rule groups are applied to search for the most significant rules and brought into comparison with other rules in the same group.

To identify top-$k$ covering rule group, we need to set up the values of parameters. According to the assumed associations, $k_{max1} = 46$ is the maximum of $k$ of the size domain. According to Definition 9.1, we have $k_{max2} = 8$ for the association of base composition. In the similar way, we have $k_{max3} = 27$ for the association of ratios between stems or loops. We can obtain different numbers of rule by regulating the values of $k_1 \leq k_{max1}$, $k_2 \leq k_{max2}$ and $k_3 \leq k_{max3}$. Note, the $k_{max}$ regarding organisms (size and base composition) has been considered in $k_{max1}$ and $k_{max2}$. The valid rules are determined by $k_1$, $k_2$ or $k_3$ in combination with minimum supports *minsupp* that specify the minimum frequencies of occurring associations [339]. In practice, we may need to vary *minsupp* and $k$ in terms of different associations. For simplicity, we only discuss the results by $k = 4$ in this chapter. Moreover, given $k$, we compare the difference in case of varied *minsupp*.

By comparison, we observe that there is no sharp drop in rule output when assigning the *minsupp* from 0.1 to 0.2. Thus, the corresponding results by 0.1 in contrast to the results by 0.2 are selected in the following analysis. Based on the selected $k$, there are 13 rules in $AS_1$ (sizes of stems and loops) and 16 rules in $AS_2$ (base composition of stems and loops). Moreover, $AS_3$ (classes and sizes), $AS_4$ (classes and base composition), $AS_5$ (functions and sizes), $AS_6$ (function and base composition) and $AS_7$ (ratios of stems and loops) consist of sub-associations in terms of different classes and functions of pseudoknots.

Table 9.3 presents a random example of the significant ratios between stems and *loop* 3. The distributions of *stem* 1/*loop* 1 and *stem* 2/*loop* 1, *stem* 1/*loop* 3 and *stem* 2/*loop* 3, and *stem* 1/*stem* 2 and *loop* 1/*loop* 3 are showed in Figure 9.1, Figure 9.2 and Figure 9.3, respectively. Such structure features have not been reported before and may play an important role in prompting the efficiency of functions.

**Table 9.3** Top-2 rule group of *stem* 1/*loop* 3 and *stem* 2/*loop* 3

| Ratio | Interval | Percentage |
|-------|----------|------------|
| *Stem* 1/*Loop* 3 | [1, 1.5] | 34 |
| *Stem* 1/*Loop* 3 | [0.5, 1) | 32 |
| *Stem* 2/*Loop* 3 | [0, 0.5) | 22 |
| *Stem* 2/*Loop* 3 | [2, 2.5) | 19 |

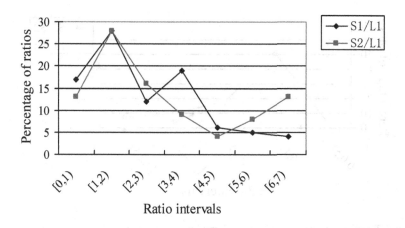

**Fig. 9.1** The distributions of stem 1/loop 1 and stem 2/loop 1

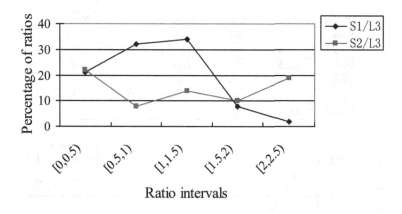

**Fig. 9.2** The distributions of stem 1/loop 3 and stem 2/loop 3

Table 9.4 presents a random example of the top-$k$ rule group between stems and lengths and between loops and lengths. Note that there are only two rules with respect to *loop* 3 due to the constraints (*minsupp* and $k$). The distributions of lengths of *stem* 1 and *stem* 2, and *loop* 1 and *loop* 3 are shown in Figure 9.4 and Figure 9.5, respectively, which not only demonstrate the previous results in [1] and provide more accurate and intuitive understanding to them. The distributions of base composition can be seen in Figures 9.6, 9.7, 9.8 and 9.9 below. It is possible that there is no base distribution with respect to some intervals of the stems or loops. This may arise from the application of *minsupp*, whereas we still can see base distribution in the intervals that have smaller support than *minsupp*. The detailed interpretation for the identified rules are presented in Section 9.4.3.

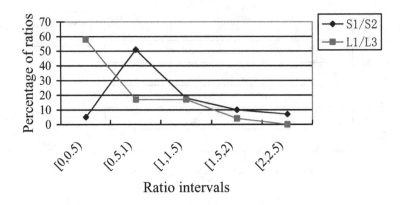

**Fig. 9.3** The distributions of stem 1/stem 2 and loop 1/loop 3

**Table 9.4** Top-3 rule group of sizes of stems and loops

| Structure | Size | Number | Structure | Size | Number |
|-----------|------|--------|-----------|------|--------|
| *Stem* 1 | (2, 3] | 84 | *Loop* 1 | (0, 1] | 72 |
| *Stem* 1 | (3, 4] | 42 | *Loop* 1 | (1, 2] | 45 |
| *Stem* 1 | (4, 5] | 24 | *Loop* 1 | (2, 3] | 43 |
| *Stem* 2 | (5, 6] | 70 | *Loop* 3 | (2, 3] | 59 |
| *Stem* 2 | (4, 5] | 69 | *Loop* 3 | (5, 6] | 31 |
| *Stem* 2 | (3, 4] | 36 | | | |

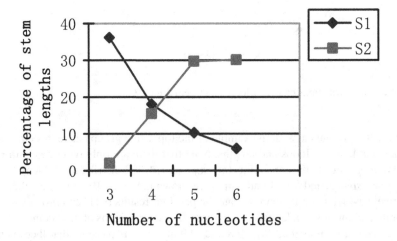

**Fig. 9.4** The distributions of top stem lengths

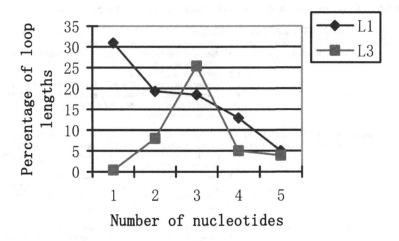

**Fig. 9.5** The distributions of top loop lengths

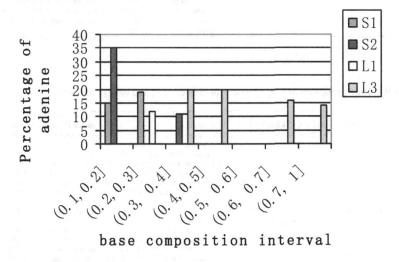

**Fig. 9.6** The distributions of adenine

We also identify some new correlations that have been unknown previously. Table 9.5 shows the rule groups about functions, including self-splicing, translation control and frameshifting, and Table 9.6 presents part of the rule groups about pseudoknot classes.

Furthermore, the significant ratios with respect to stems and loops indicate structure features of RNA. They have not been reported before and may imply an important role of RNA pseudoknots in prompting the efficiency of varied functions. Further, Table 9.6 presents several instance of the rule groups with respect to pseudoknot classes, which have been unknown previously. These rules not only enhance

**Table 9.5** Rule groups regarding pseudoknot functions, size and base composition

| Functions | size of stems | size of loops | base composition of stems | base composition of loops |
|---|---|---|---|---|
| self-splicing | stem 1 = 7, 60%<br>stem 2 = 8, 40% | loop 1 = 3, 20%<br>loop 3 = 7, 20% | $0.2 <$ adenine of stem $1 \le 0.3$, 40%<br>$0.3 <$ adenine of stem $2 \le 0.4$, 40%<br>$0.1 <$ cytosine of stem $1 \le 0.2$, 40%<br>$0.2 <$ cytosine of stem $2 \le 0.3$, 40%<br>$0.2 <$ guanine of stem $1 \le 0.3$, 40%<br>$0.3 <$ guanine of stem $2 \le 0.4$, 40%<br>$0.1 <$ uracil of stem $1 \le 0.2$, 50%<br>$0.3 <$ uracil of stem $2 \le 0.4$, 40% | $0.2 <$ adenine of loop $1 \le 0.3$, 60%<br>$0.2 <$ cytosine of loop $1 \le 0.3$, 60%<br><br><br>$0.2 <$ guanine of loop $1 \le 0.3$, 40%<br>$0.1 <$ guanine of loop $3 \le 0.2$, 40%<br>$0.2 <$ uracil of loop $1 \le 0.3$, 40% |
| translation control | stem 1 = 3, 39%<br>stem 2 = 5, 32% | loop 1 = 1, 35%<br>loop 3 = 3, 28% | $0.2 <$ adenine of stem $1 \le 0.3$, 21%<br>$0.1 <$ adenine of stem $2 \le 0.2$, 38%<br>$0.3 <$ cytosine of stem $1 \le 0.4$, 23%<br>$0.1 <$ cytosine of stem $2 \le 0.2$, 30%<br>$0.3 <$ guanine of stem $1 \le 0.4$, 29%<br>$0.1 <$ guanine of stem $2 \le 0.2$, 32%<br>$0.3 <$ uracil of stem $1 \le 0.4$, 29%<br>$0.1 <$ uracil of stem $2 \le 0.2$, 29% | $0.3 <$ adenine of loop $1 \le 0.4$, 11%<br>$0.4 <$ adenine of loop $3 \le 0.5$, 21%<br>$0.1 <$ cytosine of loop $3 \le 0.2$, 16%<br><br>$0.7 <$ guanine of loop $1 \le 1$, 14%<br>$0.1 <$ guanine of loop $3 \le 0.2$, 21%<br>$0.7 <$ uracil of loop $1 \le 1$, 25%<br>$0.3 <$ uracil of loop $1 \le 0.4$, 31% |
| frameshifting | stem 1 = 5, 28%<br>stem 2 = 4, 28% | loop 1 = 2, 44% | $0.1 <$ adenine of stem $1 \le 0.2$, 16%<br>$0.1 <$ adenine of stem $2 \le 0.2$, 20%<br>$0.1 <$ cytosine of stem $1 \le 0.2$, 28%<br>$0.4 <$ cytosine of stem $2 \le 0.5$, 36%<br>$0.7 <$ guanine of stem $1 \le 1$, 32%<br>$0.2 <$ guanine of stem $2 \le 0.3$, 28%<br>$0 <$ uracil of stem $1 \le 0.1$, 20%<br>$0.1 <$ uracil of stem $2 \le 0.2$, 32% | $0.4 <$ adenine of loop $1 \le 0.5$, 24%<br>$0.7 <$ adenine of loop $3 \le 1$, 20%<br>$0.4 <$ cytosine of loop $1 \le 0.5$, 32%<br>$0.1 <$ cytosine of loop $3 \le 0.2$, 44%<br>$0.4 <$ guanine of loop $1 \le 0.5$, 20%<br>$0.1 <$ guanine of loop $3 \le 0.2$, 36%<br>$0.1 <$ uracil of loop $3 \le 0.2$, 28% |

**Table 9.6** Rule groups regarding pseudoknot classes, size and base composition

| Classes | size of stems | size of loops | base composition of stems | base composition of loops |
|---|---|---|---|---|
| other viral 3'-UTR | stem 1 = 3, 47%<br>stem 2 = 6, 46% | loop 1 = 1, 52%<br>loop 3 = 3, 45% | $0.2 <$ adenine of stem $1 \le 0.3$, 23%<br>$0.1 <$ adenine of stem $2 \le 0.2$, 39%<br>$0.3 <$ cytosine of stem $1 \le 0.4$, 33%<br>$0.1 <$ cytosine of stem $2 \le 0.2$, 40%<br>$0.3 <$ guanine of stem $1 \le 0.4$, 37%<br>$0.1 <$ guanine of stem $2 \le 0.2$, 37%<br>$0.3 <$ uracil of stem $1 \le 0.4$, 35%<br>$0.3 <$ uracil of stem $2 \le 0.4$, 29% | $0.5 <$ adenine of loop $3 \le 0.6$, 30%<br>$0.1 <$ cytosine of loop $3 \le 0.2$, 25%<br><br><br>$0.7 <$ guanine of loop $1 \le 1$, 25%<br>$0.1 <$ guanine of loop $3 \le 0.2$, 16%<br>$0.7 <$ uracil of loop $1 \le 1$, 37%<br>$0.3 <$ uracil of loop $3 \le 0.4$, 53% |
| viral tRNA like structure | stem 1 = 3, 65%<br>stem 2 = 5, 41% | loop 1 = 3, 41%<br>loop 3 = 3, 43% | $0.2 <$ adenine of stem $1 \le 0.3$, 12%<br>$0.1 <$ adenine of stem $2 \le 0.2$, 29%<br>$0.7 <$ cytosine of stem $1 \le 1$, 33%<br>$0.3 <$ cytosine of stem $2 \le 0.4$ 24%<br>$0.3 <$ guanine of stem $1 \le 0.4$, 31%<br>$0.1 <$ guanine of stem $2 \le 0.2$, 33%<br>$0.3 <$ uracil of stem $1 \le 0.4$, 33%<br>$0.3 <$ uracil of stem $2 \le 0.4$, 31% | $0.3 <$ adenine of loop $1 \le 0.4$, 18%<br>$0.3 <$ adenine of loop $3 \le 0.4$, 33%<br>$0.3 <$ cytosine of loop $1 \le 0.4$, 12%<br>$0.3 <$ cytosine of loop $3 \le 0.4$, 16%<br>$0.4 <$ guanine of loop $1 \le 0.5$, 12%<br>$0.2 <$ guanine of loop $3 \le 0.3$, 10%<br>$0.3 <$ uracil of loop $1 \le 0.4$, 16%<br>$0.3 <$ uracil of loop $1 \le 0.4$, 29% |
| mRNA | stem 1 = 6, 22%<br>stem 2 = 7, 44% | loop 1 = 1, 33%<br>loop 3 = 4, 22% | $0.1 <$ adenine of stem $1 \le 0.2$, 75%<br>$0.1 <$ adenine of stem $2 \le 0.2$, 50%<br>$0.3 <$ cytosine of stem $1 \le 0.4$, 33%<br>$0.1 <$ cytosine of stem $2 \le 0.2$, 57%<br>$0.1 <$ guanine of stem $1 \le 0.2$, 44%<br>$0.2 <$ guanine of stem $2 \le 0.3$, 44%<br>$0.2 <$ uracil of stem $1 \le 0.3$, 33%<br>$0.2 <$ uracil of stem $2 \le 0.3$, 71% | $0.7 <$ adenine of loop $1 \le 1$, 43%<br>$0.2 <$ adenine of loop $3 \le 0.3$, 50%<br>$0.2 <$ cytosine of loop $3 \le 0.3$, 67%<br>$0.6 <$ guanine of loop $1 \le 0.7$, 67%<br>$0.1 <$ guanine of loop $3 \le 0.2$, 56%<br>$0.2 <$ uracil of loop $1 \le 0.3$, 40%<br>$0.2 <$ uracil of loop $3 \le 0.3$, 38% |

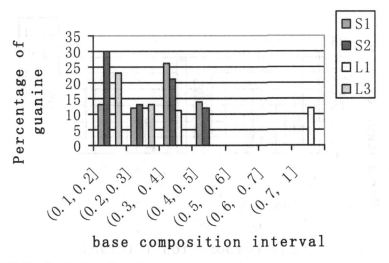

**Fig. 9.7** The distributions of guanine

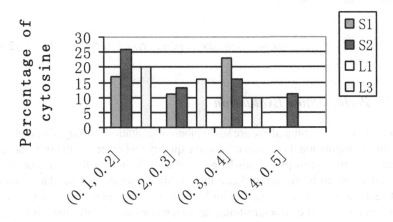

**Fig. 9.8** The distributions of cytosine

the understanding of structural features of RNA pseudoknots and prompt the exploration of structure-function relationships in RNA.

The derived rules assist us in understanding the structure-function relationship in pseudoknots. The rule groups not only confirm the previously observed results ($AS_1$) in [1] but also discover interesting pseudoknot properties such as $AS_3$, $AS_4$ and $AS_7$ that have not been reported before.

The details can be seen in the following interpretation. As for the other rule groups, such as the rules regarding pseudoknot functions, the details can be reached

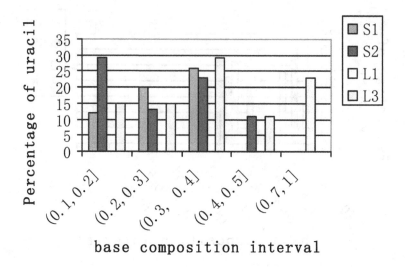

**Fig. 9.9** The distributions of uracil

by http://bioinformatics.gxu.edu.cn/bio/data/LNAI8335/
8335-6.zip.

### 9.4.2 Performance Evaluation

In contrast to data mining, there are some inherent limitations to Bayesian methods, including computational complexity and the quality and extent of the prior beliefs. It is only useful as this prior knowledge is reliable. Thus, the Bayesian method is assumption-driven in the sense that a hypothesis is formed and validated against the data. However, the learning of prior belief is a NP-complete problem in case of enormous dataset. The structure-function correlations are usually hidden in pseudoknot data with multi-valued variables. These prevent us from obtaining reliable prior knowledge. Furthermore, some associations are not obvious (undetermined) and might be ignored from the assumption. This may result in missing interesting knowledge of RNA pseudoknots. Therefore, we turn to association rule mining, a data-driven method, in terms of the available pseudoknot data and the potential structure-function correlations commented on by our collaborators.

Many algorithms can be used for association rule mining, such as support-confidence framework and FP tree [339]. There have been many extension or adaption from the previous methods. Further, they are classified into quantitative association rule and qualitative association rule for different purposes. Nevertheless, not all of them can deal with top-ranked rule group and use discretization to divide the attribute values. A data partition schema is proposed in [339], whereas it cannot identify the top-$k$ rules. In contrast, a top-$k$ rule mining algorithm is presented in

[66], whereas it does not provide solution to partition the attribute values. Thus, an algorithm for association rule mining is presented in this chapter by combining their ideas.

All tests reported herein were performed on a 1.86GHz Intel Core(TM)2 PC. The parameters including *applicability, Top-k rule group, minsupp, frequent patterns* and *CPU Times*(s) are selected as the comparison metric, so as to assess the efficiency of algorithms while using the same data set. The comparison is implemented among three related algorithms. Although there may be other algorithms such as FPtree [126] to identify associations, they are not included since they are inappropriate to identify rule groups.

Our miner (kTOP) extends the LCD (Local Causal Discovery) method [67] to discover association rules among multi-valued variables from PseudoBase. Moreover, we adapt the proposed method in [339] using top-$k$ covering rule group instead of enumerating all potential correlations. This is able to avoid not only the huge number of rules owing to the high-dimensional pesudonkot dataset, but also a long mining process due to large number of rules. Table 9.7 shows a performance comparison between our miner and algorithms LCD [67] and PPM (Probability Partition Matrix) [339]. In the comparison, we identify the rules regarding the lengths of stems and loops using a dataset OPMV from PseudoBase at http://bioinformatics.gxu.edu.cn/bio/data/LNAI8335/8335 -7.zip. Note that the number of rules in Table 9.7 include all possible rules in theory. Some of them can be pruned if the minimum support or $k$ is applied. Figure 9.10 presents the derived frequent patterns under different minimum supports.

**Table 9.7** Performance comparison in identification of rules

| Miner | Data set | Applicability | Top-k rule group | minsupp | Frequent patterns | CPU Time(s) |
|-------|----------|---------------|------------------|---------|-------------------|-------------|
| *kTOP* | *OPMV* | *Yes* | *Yes* | [0.01, 0.05] | 16 | [4.5, 380] |
| *LCD* | *OPMV* | *No* | *No* | N/A | N/A | N/A |
| *PPM* | *OPMV* | *Yes* | *No* | [0.01, 0.05] | [19, 49] | [9.5, 380] |

The comparison shows that kTOP has better performance than LCD and PPM methods, and can still have a short process for a small minimum support. In Table 9.7, the number of obtained frequent patterns from kTOP is 16 in comparison with the number (varied from 19 to 49) of PPM even using a small minimum support. The derived patterns assist in understanding structure-function relationships in RNA pseudoknots. The relevance of the obtained rules to the problems need to solve are described in the late interpretation and Section 9.5. Thus, kTOP assists biologists in sorting out the most significant or interesting biological knowledge. From the observation, both LCD and PPM show limitations in high dimensional data, which may lead to the long process and huge number of rules even with rather high minimum support and confidence threshold. kTOP has almost the same running time as PPM in case of the low dimensional data and a low level minimum support within [0.01, 0.05], but shows an acceleration when a high dimensional dataset is used.

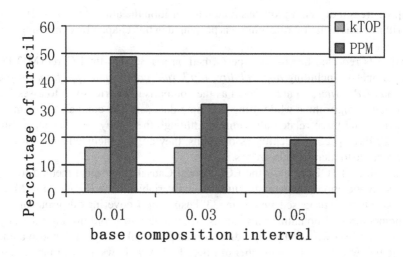

**Fig. 9.10** The frequent patterns by using different *minsupp*

As mentioned above, this chapter uses a point-based decomposition for quantitative attributes in contrast to the optimization-based partition of PPM [339]. The latter has to find the bad quantitative items that result in missing valid rules, decompose these item variables and compose the good item variables. This is complex because it aims to find an optimized partitions for the domain of all attributes (*categorical* and *quantitative*). However, the categorical attributes in pseudoknot data are already partitioned. Thus, the partition of categorical attributes in PMM should be ignored to deal with the pseudoknot data. However, even so, PMM may generate reductant rules or miss interesting rules. In terms of the personnel data set at a university in [339], the domain of *Education* can be divided into {*Doctor, Master, UnderMaster*} or {*Doctor, Master*}. We use the same configuration of *minsupp* = 0.6. In either cases, kTOP can obtain the same results by regulating *k*. However, the rule *Education* = *Doctor* → *2100* ≤ *Salary* < *3500* is removed by PMM but reserved by our miner. The top-*k* rules enable a flexible comparison between rules in the same group.

The miner kTOP requires users to specify the minimum support threshold and the number of top covering groups, *k*, only. Such improvement is useful because it is not easy to select an appropriate confidence threshold while the choice of *k* is semantically clear. It provides users the flexibility to control the output and balance between two extremes [66]. Usually, only a rule from each row can be obtained by the rule induction algorithms like a decision tree, which could miss interesting rules. And too many redundant rules covering the same rows can be found by traditional association rule mining algorithms. Moreover, our method includes some extra processes to facilitate the identification of association rules. The experiments found a number of interesting rules regarding structure-function relationship of pseudoknots. Most of them were unknown previously. These can benefit to the understanding of the occurring structure motifs in RNA, such as RNA folding, and a number of RNA functions, such as ribosomal frameshifting, translation control and splicing.

### 9.4.3 Interpretation

Table 9.8 presents a subset of the originally derived association rules by using 0.1 (*minimum support*) and 4 (*number of top covering rule*). The rules are selected from rule groups and have dominant support in each subgroup. For example, *rules* 1 and 2 are from $AS_1$ and present the top-2 rules in the subgroup with respect to the length of *stem* 1; and the rules 6, 7, 8 and 9 are from $AS_2$ and indicate the most significant rules of the subgroups regarding *adenine*, *guanine*, *cytosine* and *uracil*, respectively.

These rule not only present that in most of simple pseudoknots their stems and loops favor different numbers of nucleotides and different base compositions, but also indicate that potential associations may exist between category and pseudoknot structure, between organisms (classes) and pseudoknot structures, and between function and pseudoknot structure. Moreover, several significant ratios regarding stems and loops are reported. For example, rule 12 shows that in most of cases, the number of nucleotides of pseudoknot of *mRNA* (messanger RNA that is transcribed from a DNA template, and carries coding information to the sites of protein synthesis: the ribosomes) may peak at 6 base pairs. In the similar manner, the remaining rules in Table 9.8 can be interpreted. The rules in fact unveil the structural features of RNA pseudoknots and potential structure-function relationship.

The rules about $AS_1$ and $AS_2$ demonstrate previous work in a more comprehensive and accurate way. Especially, the rules ($AS_3$, $AS_4$, $AS_5$, $AS_6$, $AS_7$) that were unknown previously will be highlighted, and specific comparisons will be conducted between stems, between loops, between different classes and between different functions, respectively.

Moreover, this chapter provides a novel facility to predict some potential correlations by combining several association rules together, which can be left for biologists to examine in the future experiments. By doing so, it is able to generate new biological knowledge. Some recent studies [242, 299] also mention such information but did not provide semantically clear interpretation for the potential correlations.

Looking at *rule* 1, *rule* 3, *rule* 4 and *rule* 5, there are discrepant leading numbers of nucleotides between *stem* 1 and *stem* 2 and between loop 1 and loop 3. These characteristics (asymmetry) may arise from the difference in tertiary interactions between stems and loops [299]. The difference of the sizes of stems and loops, as well as the types of interaction between them, mean that pseudoknots represent a structurally diverse group. It is corresponding that they play diverse roles in biology such as forming the catalytic core of various ribozymes [257] and self-splicing introns [3], and altering gene expression of many viruses by inducing ribosomal frameshifting [288]. The generated leading rule is a novel point of this chapter because this assists in not only understanding the properties of stems and loops, but also providing an intuitive and quantified comparison to their difference. *Rule* 2 can be a supplement to demonstrate the difference between *stem* 1 and *stem* 2. Looking at rules 6-11, there is apparent biases of base composition in the loops

**Table 9.8** Selected rules from the above rule groups

| Association rules |
|---|
| 1. *stem* 1 → *stem* 1 = 3 with support 34% |
| 2. *stem* 1 → *stem* 1 = 4 with support 19% |
| 3. *stem* 2 → *stem* 2 = 6 with support 31% |
| 4. *loop* 1 → *loop* 1 = 1 with support 32% |
| 5. *loop* 3 → *loop* 3 = 3 with support 24% |
| 6. *stem* 1 → 0.2 < *adenine* ≤ 0.3 with support 19% |
| 7. *stem* 1 → 0.3 < *guanine* ≤ 0.4 with support 26% |
| 8. *stem* 1 → 0.3 < *cytosine* ≤ 0.4 with support 23% |
| 9. *stem* 1 → 0.3 < *uracil* ≤ 0.4 with support 26% |
| 10.*loop* 1 → 0.7 < *uracil* ≤ 1 with support 23% |
| 11. *loop* 3 → 0.3 < *adenine* ≤ 0.4 with support 20% |
| 12. *mRNA* → *stem* 1 = 6 with support 22% |
| 13. *mRNA* → *stem* 2 = 7 with support 44% |
| 14. *mRNA* → 0.1 < *adenine* in *stem* 1 ≤ 0.2 with support 75% |
| 15. *mRNA* → 0.1 < *guanine* in *stem* 1 ≤ 0.2 with support 44% |
| 16. *mRNA* → 0.3 < *cytosine* in *stem* 1 ≤ 0.4 with support 33% |
| 17. *mRNA* → 0.3 < *uracil* in *stem* 1 ≤ 0.4 with support 33% |
| 18. *translation control* → *stem* 1 = 3 with support 41% |
| 19. *translation control* → 0.2 < *adenine* in *stem* 1 ≤ 0.3 with support 21% |
| 20. *other viral 3′-UTR* → *stem* 1 = 3 with support 47% |
| 21. *other viral 3′-UTR* → *stem* 2 = 6 with support 46% |
| 22. *other viral 3′-UTR* → 0.2 < *adenine* in *stem* 1 ≤ 0.3 with support 23% |
| 23. *other viral 3′-UTR* → 0.3 < *guanine* in *stem* 1 ≤ 0.4 with support 37% |
| 24. *other viral 3′-UTR* → 0.7 < *cytosine* in *stem* 1 ≤ 1 with support 33% |
| 25. *other viral 3′-UTR* → 0.3 < *uracil* in *stem* 1 ≤ 0.4 with support 33% |
| 26. $S_1/L_1$ → 1 ≤ $S_1/L_1$ < 2 with support 28% |
| 27. $S_1/L_3$ → 1 ≤ $S_1/L_3$ < 1.5 with support 34% |
| 28. $S_1/S_2$ → 0.5 ≤ $S_1/S_2$ < 1 with support 51% |
| 29. $S_2/L_1$ → 1 ≤ $S_2/L_1$ < 2 with support 16% |
| 30. $S_2/L_3$ → 0 ≤ $S_2/L_3$ < 0.5 with support 22% |
| 31. $L_1/L_3$ → 0 ≤ $L_1/L_3$ < 0.5 with support 58% |

of H-pseudoknots. The facts of *adenine*-rich in *loop* 3 and *uracil*-rich in *loop* 1 is coherent with results of [1, 242] and [2], respectively.

The remaining rules in Table 9.8 are novel and can be classified into two categories in terms of different purposes. *Rules* 12 and 13 describe the correlations between pesudoknot categories and the size of stems. *Rules* 14, 15, 16 and 17 describe the associations between pseudoknot classes and the base composition in *stem* 1. Especially, the associations between size and class, the associations between base composition and class, and the ratios between stems or loops have not been reported by previous pseudoknot studies.

Looking at *rule* 12 and *rule* 13, the pseudoknots of *mRNA* favor 6 base pairs in *stem* 1, but peak at 7 base pairs in *stem* 2. Such rules can be viewed as a secondary evidence in determining pseudoknots' categories, predicting the size distribution of specific class of pseudoknots and understanding the association between structure and function. Looking at *rules* 14, 15, 16 and 17, they show that *stem* 1 of *mRNA* has a high percentage of *adenine* rather than *cytosine, guanine* and *uracil*.

In a similar way, we can predict the size distribution and base composition for other pseudoknot categories, such as *other viral 3'-UTR* and *viral tRNA like structure* in Table 9.6. The pseudoknots of *other viral 3'-UTR* favor 3 base pairs, 6 base pairs, 1 base pair and 3 base pairs in *stem* 1, *stem* 2, *loop* 1 and *loop* 3, respectively. Such rules can be viewed as a secondary evidence in determining pseudoknots' categories, predicting the size distribution of specific class of pseudoknots and understanding the association between structure and function. Looking at its dependencies regarding base composition, they show that stem 1 of *other viral 3'-UTR* has a high percentage of guanine rather than adenine, cytosine and uracil. Although the *other viral 3'-UTR* has the same percentages of uracil and cytosine as guanine, the support of guanine in the dependency is a little higher than the percentage of uracil and cytosine in *stem* 1. Thus, we determine that the *stem* 1 of *other viral 3'-UTR* is guanine rich. The observation is consistent with reports that GC-rich *stem* 1 (many DNA sequences carry long stretches of repeated G and C which often indicate a gene-rich region) present resistance to chemical cleavage. This makes *stem* 1 appear to be remarkably stable. On the other hand, there is a preference for the G in the 5' end of the stem [304] and a number of the pseudoknots with G-rich stretch may be more effective in frameshifting [238]. Looking at the dependencies regarding base composition of loops, we cannot obtain the rules between $L_1$ and adenine and between $L_1$ and cytosine due to insufficient support from the current data set.

Looking at the dependencies of *viral tRNA Like structure*, it also peaks at 3 base pairs of *stem* 1 and 3 base pairs of *loop* 3 as *other viral 3'-UTR*, whereas it favors 3 base pairs of *loop* 1 and 5 base pairs of *stem* 2. As to the base composition of *viral tRNA Like structure*, it has a high percentage of cytosine of stem 1, high percentage of uracil of *stem* 2, high percentage of uracil of *loop* 1 and high percentage of adenine of *loop* 3. As mentioned above, *stem* 1 is stabilized due to abundant G-C base pairs. A stable pseudoknot structure is important for both amino-acylation and transcription. Moreover, GC rich *stem* 1 rather than A-U rich may increase the transcription efficiency. It was reported that the mutation in *stem* 1 by changing specific G-C base pair into an A-U base pair reduced the transcription efficiency [76]. These features may help explain the reports of flexible tertiary contacts between stems and loops. Thus, the results in this chapter not only discover the structural properties of RNA pseudoknots in specific organisms, but also aid in understanding structure-function relationships in RNA molecules.

Looking at the rules 18 and 19 in Table 9.8, most *stem* 1 in a pseudoknot that plays a role in translation regulation usually, has 3 base pairs by *rule* 18. This may indicate that efficient translation control depended upon the presence of a close 3 base pair; pseudoknots with a shorter or longer stem 1 were either non-functional or had reduced translational efficiency. *Rule* 19 represents the percentage of adenine of *stem* 1 in a pseudoknot for translational regulation peaks at 20% to 30%. In comparison with the compositions of guanine, uracil and cytosine in *stem* 1, such *stem* 1 has a high percentage of uracil.

These observations also indicate that RNA pseudoknots are critical for specific protein binding. A number of proteins bind to a pseudoknot in its mRNA, which result in autoregulation [284]. In the rule groups of mRNA, we can see GC-rich is prevalent. Usually, the major loop is likely to be flexible. However, the stable structures with a flexible major loop also indicates the possibility that it can fold in a precise pattern when in contact with a protein. This may imply a motif in the pseudoknot that may show to interact with specific mRNA. For example, the CUGGG motif in the human prion pseudoknot was also found in the loop of HIV TAR RNA have been proved to interact with human prion mRNA [276]. Moreover, the structural flexibility (flexible loop and neutral interaction) at helical junctions due to U-rich *loop* 1 and A-rich *loop* 3 may be important for proper telomerase function and regulation of protein binding.

In particular, Figure 9.1, Figure 9.2 and Figure 9.3 present novel and significant ratios of stems and loops, which may have relation to functions. We observe that the ratio of $S_1/L_1$ peaks at the interval $[1, 2)$. Its number decreases in the consequent intervals. This phenomenon can be seen in both frameshifting-related and translation control-related RNA pseudknots. We also observe similar discipline with respect to $S_2/L_1$, $S_1/L_3$ and $S_2/L_3$. These are consistent with the rules 26, 27, 28, 29, 30, 31. Thus, they are not repeated herein. As we know, the folding of a RNA pseudoknot requires that loops span the helix of stems. If we altered the length of *stem* 1 or loop 1, it is possible that the consequent change in ratio of stem length to stem helix length may have an effect on function efficiency. A further understanding of these ratios needs to be demonstrated in future biological experiments.

Furthermore, we can predict some novel correlations from the obtained association rules. For example, as for *rule* 18, if we find any pseudoknot whose *stem* 1 peaks at 3 base pairs, we may predict its functions according to *rule* 18 in Table 9.8. Thus, the newly generated association rules can be used to complement the prediction of pseudoknots' functions. We may also predict the function of pseudoknots in terms of the rules like *rule* 19. For example, if we found a pseudoknot whose *stem* 1 is cytosine rich and favors 20% to 30% percentage of adenine, it may be translational regulation relevant. In practice, we may need to consider the composition of other bases together to enhance its reliability. The experimental results demonstrate that our approach not only can discover meaningful biological patterns but also can facilitate the analysis for biologists by purposely controlling the number of interesting patterns.

## 9.5    Conclusion and Discussion

A number of RNA structures including tRNA, miRNA, snoRNAs have been found to play important regulatory, structural and catalytic roles in cell. In particular, recent evidences of ncRNA in the evolution and development programming of complex organisms RNA may perform many unexpected functions and participate many complex gene regulations that haven been unknown to us. Thus, there have been considerable efforts to study the RNA structures such as secondary structure prediction for detecting interesting functional signals of RNA.

As an important functional structure, pseudoknot is more highly constrained by non-local base pairs and presents specific three dimensional geometries. Such non-local contacts make pseudoknot problem NP-complete. Traditional association rule mining has been widely and successfully used to identify frequent patterns from general datasets. However, it is unfit for the data that contains multi-valued variables [339]. It has been argued that the former mining approach depended on two thresholds and a conditional probability matrix can be helpful for association studies due to its impressive expressiveness. However, if the item variable $X$ impacts on variable $Y$ at only a few point values, item-based association mining and quantitative association rule mining may be more appropriate and efficient than this method.

A high dimensional dataset can result in many redundant rules and long mining process [66], and makes it difficult for biologists to filter out interesting information from databases. These challenges block the analysis of the pseudoknot data. It is easier and semantically clearer to choose $k$ than minimum confidence [66]. Moreover, it avoids missing interesting rules and generating too many redundant rules. A natural alternative to our model is to set different values of $k$, and compare their different results.

In this chapter, we analyse RNA pseudoknot data from PseudoBase for extracting interesting patterns with respect to structures, functions and classes. Top-ranked rule groups are applied to identify these characteristic relations in RNA pseudoknots and especially highlight the potential structure-function and structure-class relationships in RNA molecules. Moreover, the interpretation of rules demonstrates their significance in the sense of biology.

Further, we attempt to combine several rules from different rule groups together for inference of novel biological knowledge. In this way, a further understanding of pseudoknot's structure and function can be achieved. Moreover, we may need to seek more data to support some rules with lightly weak support from current pseudoknot data. We did not touch the biased base composition at the end ($3'$ side) of the loop 3 and at the start ($5'$ side) of loop 3. It may be an interesting problem to interpret the tertiary interactions between loops and the grooves helices, such as why a loop interacts more with the minor groove of a stem, or why a loop interacts less with the major groove of a stem. We do not identify the rules between functions and pseudoknots in this chapter. It is perhaps that a shorter or longer stem or loop, or a stem or loop with irregular base composition may make pesudoknots non-functional or have reduced function efficiency. We generate new knowledge by considering this interesting correlation. Extending this idea to more complex and more realistic scenario is therefore desirable, but it would require a larger dataset and evaluation of their soundness.

# Chapter 10
# Mining Featured Patterns of MiRNA Interaction Based on Sequence and Structure Similarity

MicroRNA (miRNA) is endogenous small non-coding RNA which plays an important role in gene expression through the post-transcriptional gene regulatory pathways. There are many literatures focusing on predicting miRNA target and exploring gene regulation network of miRNA family. We suggest, however, the study to identify the interaction between miRNAs is insufficient. This chapter presents a framework to identify relationships of miRNAs using joint entropy, to investigate the regulatory features of miRNAs. Both the sequence and secondary structure are taken into consideration to make our method more relevant from the biological viewpoint. Further, joint entropy is applied to identify correlated miRNAs, which are more desirable from the perspective of the gene regulatory network. A dataset of Drosophila melanogaster and Anopheles gambiae is used in experiment. The results demonstrate that our approach is able to not only find known miRNA interaction and identify novel patterns of miRNA regulatory network.

## 10.1 Introduction

MiRNAs are post-transcriptional regulators that bind to complementary sequences on target messenger RNA transcripts (mRNAs), usually participating translational repression and gene silencing. MiRNA genes are firstly transcribed as primary miRNAs(pri-miRNAs), and then are processed to precursor miRNAs(pre-miRNAs). These are of 70nt long and hairpin structures, and mature to miRNAs via the endonuclease Dicer [170, 200]. MiRNAs play important roles in many biological processes including, cell proliferation, differentiation, growth, metabolism, apoptosis, and diseases [30, 169]. For example, many experiments prove that miR-10 regulates a number of Hox genes and is relevant to diseases such as melanoma and breast cancer. In zebrafish embryos, three prime untranslated regions (3UTR) of the HoxB1a and HoxB3a genes related to embryonic development are targeted by miR-10 [322].

Since the first miRNA was found in Caenorhabditis elegans, there has been considerable effort to identify unknown miRNAs. Due to the proliferation of high throughput techniques, miRNA research has experienced rapid growth. Several databases have been established to provide various retrieval services. For example, miRbase is the online database containing mature sequence, pre-miRNA, and structure of identified miRNAs [119]. MiRNAmap is an integrated database of miRNAs, which compiles the known miRNAs, the putative miRNAs, the miRNA targets and the regulatory relationships between the miRNAs and the coding genes in humans, mice, rats, and dogs [142]. Plant microRNA (PMRD) is a large database for PMRD, consisting of sequence and their target genes, secondary structure, and so on [346].

Since the first miRNA was found in *C.elegans*, a number of experiments have been conducted to identify unknown miRNAs. Due to the application of high throughput techniques, miRNAs are increasingly generated. Several databases are established for miRNA and provide various retrieval services. For example, miR-base (http://www.mirbase.org) is the online database containing mature sequence, pre-miRNA and structure of identified miRNAs. MiRNAmap is an integrated database for miRNAs, which compiles the known miRNAs, the putative miRNAs, the miRNA targets and the regulatory relationships between the miRNAs and the coding genes in humans, mice, rats and dogs. PMDB is a large database for plant microRNAs, consisting of sequence and their target genes, secondary dimension structure and so on.

According to the knowledge that miRNAs regulate genes expression by binding to complementary sites in the target messenger RNA (mRNA) [271], several approaches have been developed to predict miRNA target or explore the relationship between miRNA and messenger RNA (mRNA). For example, Bayesian network structure learning with splitting-averaging strategy is employed to discover all strong and subtle interaction of miRNA-mRNA [205]. Probabilistic graphical models are applied to explore microRNA regulatory modules [169].

Unfortunately, most of these methods are concerning on the relationship between miRNA and mRNA. The interactions between miRNAs, including cross-species (two miRNAs in different species) and within-species (two miRNA in same species), have been largely ignored and the efforts for mining miRNA relation are insufficient. Since genes formed regulatory network in biological evolution and all the miRNAs cooperate with other functionally associated genes [150], it is reasonable to speculate that the miRNA's function may depend on the miRNA interaction. Hence, the deep analysis of miRNA interaction can contribute to predict miRNA functions and understand the regulation mechanism of miRNAs.

This chapter presents a framework to study the interaction between different miR-NAs. It evaluates the similarity of two miRNAs in terms of sequence and secondary structure. The latter has been proved to be more conserved than the former in biological evolution [196]. Further, joint entropy is applied to measure the interaction and a *min_entropy* (*minimum entropy*) threshold is used to prune less important miRNAs. A data set from miRbase is applied in the experiment. The results demonstrate that our method is useful in discovering interesting patterns regarding miRNA interaction.

## 10.2 Related Work

Recently, there has been an increasing number of studies focusing on RNA secondary structure which has proved to be more closely related to RNA function than sequence [52, 196]. A variety of methods have been developed to predict RNA secondary structure, primarily including phylogenetic sequence analysis, such as stochastic context free grammars and methods based on thermodynamics to find the minimum free energy structure [345]. A modified nucleotide cyclic motif with scoring strategy is used to predict mature miRNA structure [124].

Without an intelligent and systematic method, the deep analysis of expansive, complex, and varied miRNA data is time-consuming and may result in abundant or missing patterns. Thus, it requires us to develop new methods for analyzing the rapid growth of miRNA data and discovering biological knowledge. Data mining has been viewed as a popular approach to extract patterns representing valuable knowledge implicitly stored in large or high-dimensional databases. A number of successful applications help solve various issues arising from the management and analysis of biological data [48]. A tool based on sequence and structure alignment is developed to identify new miRNA genes [319]. Clustering is proposed to discover the patterns of structure conservation among human precursor miRNAs [170]. Graph theory is employed to explore functional miRNA-mRNA regulatory modules [209].

The above research works deal with some important problems with respect to miRNAs. However, the investigation of miRNA interaction is still insufficient. This chapter proposes a joint entropy-based framework to explore featured patterns of miRNA interaction according to sequence and structure similarity.

## 10.3 Methods

### 10.3.1 Secondary Structure Modeling

Most research focuses on the prediction of secondary structure of miRNA, whereas the deep analysis of miRNA secondary structure has been largely unexplored. One of the most critical issues is to transform complex miRNA secondary structures into an appropriate data format for further data analysis.

To normalize loop-stem miRNA structure, in the similar way as Chapter 7, $S_1$, $S_2$, $S_3$, $L_1$ and $L_2$ are used to indicate *stem* 1, *stem* 2, *stem* 3, *loop* 1 and *loop* 2, respectively [48]. For example, dme-mir-1 with stem-loop structure is shown in Figure 10.1. Two characters linked by vertical indicate stem region, the remainder presents loop region. Nucleotides with uppercase characters are mature sequence of dme-mir-1. In this figure, the mature sequence of dme-mir-1 is UGGAAUGUAAA-GAAGUAUGGAG and it contains three stems and two loops in dme-mir-1 secondary structure. The mature sequence corresponding to *stem* 1, *loop* 1, *stem* 2, *loop* 2 and *stem* 3 can be represented as U, G, GAAUGUAA, A and GAAGUAUG-GAG, respectively. We focus on the number of nucleotides included in each stem and loop. As a result, the dme-mir-1 mature sequence can be modeled by $S_1 = 1$, $L_1$ = 1, $S_2 = 8$, $L_2 = 1$ and $S_3 = 11$. The numbers of loops and stems are not the same for all miRNAs. Some miRNAs may have less loops or stems. It is reasonable to give zero for those absent structures. For instance, dme-mir-5 only has $S_1$; $L_1$, and $S_2$. The missing structures, $L_2$ and $S_3$ of dme-mir-5 are assigned zero.

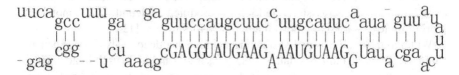

**Fig. 10.1** The stem-loop structure of dme-mir-1. The uppercases stand for dme-mir-1's mature sequence. The stem regions are represented by vertical line.

An example of sequences and normalized structures of miRNA is presented in Table 10.1. Three miRNAs are modeled in term of stems and loops. Each row in the table represents a miRNA. The integers denote the number of nucleotides contained in corresponding stems or loops. In particular, the loop size of some miRNAs can be zero, such as $L_2$ of dme-mir-2a-2. This means that no nucleotide exists in that region.

**Table 10.1** An example of miRNA data

| miRNA | $S_1$ | Sequence | $L_1$ | Sequence | $S_2$ | Sequence | $L_2$ | Sequence | $S_3$ | Sequence |
|-------|-------|----------|-------|----------|-------|----------|-------|----------|-------|----------|
| dme-mir-1 | 1 | U | 1 | G | 8 | GAAUGUAA | 1 | A | 11 | GAAGUAUGGAG |
| dme-mir-2a-2 | 11 | UAUCACAGCCA | 2 | GC | 8 | UUUGAUGA | 0 | - | 2 | GC |
| dme-mir-6-3 | 5 | UAUCA | 0 | - | 3 | CAG | 2 | UG | 12 | GCUGUUCUUUUU |

## 10.3.2 Similarity Measure

The distance metric is a critical issue in clustering. A good distance function is able to correctly identify genuinely similar objects. A number of distance functions have been developed for similarity measure, such as *Euclidean distance* to measure the similarity of two objects, *Mahalanobis distance* to compute the similarity between two sample sets, and *Hausdorff distance* to determine the similarity of two points in image. In recent years, there have been many applications by using metrics to measure the similarity in biology. For example, an interval-based distance metric was presented to evaluate the similarity of RNA secondary structures [52].

To measure the level of affinity between two miRNAs with the same elements in two structures, a popular metric for structural similarity *Root Mean Square distance (RMS)* [158] is proposed to measure structure similarity. Suppose $g_1$ and $g_2$ represent two miRNAs. According to the above modeling strategy, the RMS for $g_1$ and $g_2$ can be represented as:

$$RMS(g_1, g_2) = \sqrt{\frac{(s_{11} - s_{21})^2 + (l_{11} - l_{21})^2 + \cdots + (s_{1n} - s_{2n})^2 + (l_{1m} - l_{2m})^2}{m + n}}$$

(10.1)

where $n$ and $m$ represent the number of stems and loops of $g_1$ and $g_2$, respectively. $\{s_{11}, s_{12}, \cdots, s_{1n}\}$ denotes the set of number of nucleotides in stem region of miRNA $g_1$; $\{l_{11}, l_{12}, \cdots, l_{1n}\}$ denotes the set of number of nucleotides in loop region of miRNA $g_1$; $\{s_{21}, s_{22}, \cdots, s_{2n}\}$ denotes the set of number of nucleotides in stem region of miRNA $g_2$; $\{l_{21}, l_{22}, \cdots, l_{2n}\}$ denotes the set of number of nucleotides in loop region of miRNA $g_2$. For example, the dme-mir-1 and dme-mir-6-3 presented in Table 10.1 include two stems and three loops. According to Equation 10.1, we have

$$RMS(dme - mir - 1, dme - mir - 6 - 3) = \sqrt{\frac{(1-5)^2 + (1-0)^2 + (8-3)^2 + (1-2)^2 + (11-12)^2}{5}}$$
$$\approx 2.97$$

It is observed that if two miRNAs are perfectly matched in structure, the RMS score will be zero. On the contrary, the RMS score will increase. Since distance is inversely proportion to similarity, the structure similarity (*str_sim*) measure is defined as

$$str\_sim(g_1, g_2) = \frac{1}{RMS(g_1, g_2)}$$

(10.2)

where $str\_sim(g_1, g_2)$ denotes the structure similarity of two miRNAs $g_1$ and $g_2$. The $str\_sim(g_1, g_2)$ value becomes lower if the RMS score is higher. In other words, two miRNAs are dissimilar in structure. In case of $RMS(g_1, g_2) = 0$, we define $str\_sim(g_1, g_2) = 1$. This means that $g_1$ and $g_2$ are identical in structure. For example, the similarity between dme-mir-1 and dme-mir-6-3 using our similarity measure is equal to $str\_sim$(dme-mir-1, dme-mir-6-3) = 1/2.97 ≈ 0.34.

Considering the situation where two miRNAs might not have a high sequence similarity even if they have high structure similarity, it may be a more feasible way to evaluate their similarity by combining sequence and structure similarity. To tackle this problem, this paper proposes *average similarity*, which is defined as

$$ave\_sim(g_1, g_2) = \sqrt{seq\_sim(g_1, g_2) * str\_sim(g_1, g_2)}$$

(10.3)

where $seq\_sim(g_1, g_2)$ and $str\_sim(g_1, g_2)$ represent sequence similarity and structure similarity between $g_1$ and $g_2$, respectively. There might be other options to compute the average similarity, whereas it is not the main topic herein and will not be further discussed.

### 10.3.3　Joint Entropy-Based Measure

Information entropy is widely applied in communication engineering to measure how much information is contained in the communication system. In recent years, information entropy has been widely applied in many fields, such as data mining and pattern recognition. Joint entropy is a measure of the uncertainty associated with a set of variables by which to evaluate how much information is contained between two variables. Suppose $X$ and $Y$ represent two random variables and $H(X; Y)$ is their joint entropy. In information theory, $H(X; Y)$ is defined as

$$H(X;Y) = -\sum_{i=1}^{n}\sum_{j=1}^{m} p(x_i,y_j)logp(x_i,y_j) \tag{10.4}$$

where $p(x_i,y_j)$ is the joint probability of random variables $X$ and $Y$. One important property with respect to $p(x_i,y_j)$ is defined as

$$\sum_{i=1}^{n}\sum_{j=1}^{m} p(x_i,y_j)logp(x_i,y_j) = 1 \tag{10.5}$$

The greater $H(X; Y)$ is, the more information $X$ and $Y$. If $H(X$ contain; $Y) = 0$, it means that $X$ and $Y$ do not contain any shared information at all. In general, joint entropy is less than the entropy sum of variables $X$ and $Y$. If they are equal, this indicates that the variables $X$ and $Y$ are mutually independent.

Traditional data mining methods measure the relationship between two objects in terms of object similarity such as *K-mean*. Although they show simplicity and efficiency in many applications, they have limitations in handling biology structure data. One primary reason is due to the complex relationships in gene regulatory network. A simple measure of gene similarity cannot correctly evaluate the interaction between genes and discover their hidden and complicated relationships. This chapter uses joint entropy to identify the relationship between miRNAs [342]. Figure 10.2 presents the structure of related miRNAs based on joint entropy, where $C_1$ and $C_2$ present two species. $g_1$ and $g_2$ represent miRNA of species $C_1$ and $C_2$, respectively. $R_1 = \{g_{11}, g_{12}, \cdots, g_{1n}\}$ represents a set of miRNAs that belong to species $C_1$ and is associated with $g_1$. $R_2 = \{g_{21}, g_{22}, \cdots, g_{2n}\}$ denotes a set of miRNAs that belongs to species $C_2$ and is associated with $g_2$. The link between two miRNAs means they share some information with each other, such as $g_1$ and $g_2$. The value of joint entropy will become bigger if two miRNAs contain more information. As for within-species, $C_1$ and $C_2$ present two conceptual clusters in the same species. $g_1$ and $g_2$ represent miRNA of conceptual cluster $C_1$ and $C_2$, respectively. $\{g_{11}, g_{12}, \cdots, g_{1n}\}$ represents a set of miRNAs that belongs to conceptual cluster $C_1$ and is associated with $g_1$. $\{g_{21}, g_{22}, \cdots, g_{2n}\}$ denotes a set of miRNAs that belongs to conceptual cluster $C_2$ and is associated with $g_2$.

The joint entropy [342] of $g_1$ and $g_2$ is defined as:

$$H(g_1,g_2) = H(g_1) + H(g_2) \tag{10.6}$$

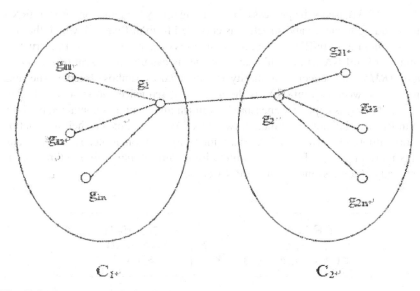

**Fig. 10.2** The structure of related miRNAs based on joint entropy

$$H(g_1) = -\sum_{i=1}^{n} p(g_1, g_{1i}) log p(g_1, g_{1i}) \qquad (10.7)$$

$$p(g_1, g_{1i}) = \frac{ave\_sim(g_1, g_{1i})}{\sum_{i=1}^{n} ave\_sim(g_1, g_{1i})} \qquad (10.8)$$

where $H(g_1, g_2)$ denote the information exchange of two miRNAs $g_1$ and $g_2$; $ave\_sim(g_1, g_{1i})$ indicates the average similarity of two miRNAs $g_1$ and $g_{1i}$ which belong to the same class $C_1$. In the same way, $H(g_2)$ can be worked out. The structure similarity measures the affinity degree between two miRNAs in a class or species, and the entropy measures the interaction between two clusters in two classes or species.

To identify the most significant miRNAs, a minimum threshold *min_entropy* is defined to prune those less important miRNAs.

$$H(g_1, g_2) \geq min\_entropy \qquad (10.9)$$

A pair of miRNA is important if their $H(g_1, g_2)$ is equal to or larger than *min_entropy*. The greater their joint entrpoy is, the closer association two miRNAs has. Moreover, *min_entropy* assists in improving the efficiency and avoiding the generation of uninteresting patterns. For example, suppose there are $N$ miRNAs in $C_1$ and $M$ miRNAs in $C_2$. $N * M$ related miRNAs are generated in our method. However, some of the obtained miRNAs may have low joint entropy. They have less important interactions with each other and need to be pruned.

Figure 10.3 presents the process of identifying miRNA interaction. First, miRNA data including sequence and structure is collected from miRbase, in which the secondary structures of miRNA are modeled in terms of stems and loops. The structure similarity of miRNA pairs within same species is calculated in term of *root mean square* (*RMS*) and sequence similarity is computed by Emboss-Needle. The final similarity between two miRNAs is the average of sequence and structure similarity. Joint entropy is applied to measure how much information is contained between two miRNAs. The more information two miRNAs contain means their association is more important. If two miRNAs share more information, it means their association is more important. Further, minimum joint entropy (*min_entropy*) threshold is employed to filter less interesting miRNA pairs.

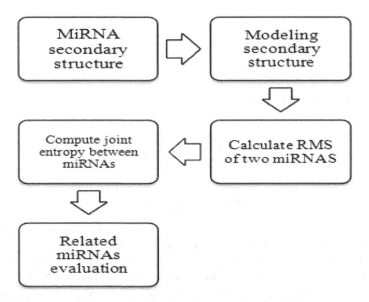

**Fig. 10.3** The computation procedure for identifying interacted miRNAs

Suppose there is a relationship between dme-mir-1 and aga-mir-13b, we model all miRNA secondary structures of *Drosophila melanogaster* and *Anopheles gambiae*. Then the *RMS* between dme-mir-1 and other miRNAs in *Drosophila melanogaster* is calculated. Emboss-Needle is employed to compute sequence similarity (*seq_sim*). Similar calculations are implemented between aga-mir-13b and other miRNAs in *Anopheles gambiae*. Further, we compute total entropy between dme-mir-1 and other miRNAs in *Drosophila melanogaster* in term of Formula 10.8. For example, $pseq\_sim(dme-mir-1, dme-mir-6-3) = 0.37$ and

$$ave\_sim(dme-mir-1, dme-mir-6-3) = \sqrt{0.34*0.37} = 0.355 \text{ then}$$

$$p(dme - mir - 1, dme - mir - 6 - 3)$$

$$= \frac{ave\_sim(dme - mir - 1, dme - mir - 6 - 3)}{\sum_{g_i \in dme} ave\_sim(dme - mir - 1, g_i)}$$

$$= \frac{0.335}{42.3} \approx 0.0083$$

and

$$H(dme - mir - 1) = \sum_{g_i \in dme} p(dme - mir - 1, g_i) * log p(dme - mir - 1, g_i)$$

$$= 1.88$$

In the similar way, the total entropy is calculated between aga-mir-13b and other miRNAs in *Anopheles gambiae*.

$$H(aga - mir - 13b) = -\sum_{g_i \in aga} p(aga - mir - 13b, g_i) * log p(dme - mir - 1, g_i)$$
$$= 1.52.$$

The joint entropy of dme-mir-2a-2 and aga-mir-13b by Formula 10.8.

$$H(dme - mir - 1, aga - mir - 13b) = H(dme - mir - 1) + H(aga - mir - 13b)$$
$$= 3.4.$$

The formula 10.8 is finally applied to determine whether the relationship between dme-mir-1 and aga-mir-13b is important or not.

## 10.4 Experiment

### 10.4.1 Data Preparation

The miRNA dataset is downloaded from miRbase (http://www.miRbase.org). There are 15172 precursor miRNAs and 17341 mature miRNAs in the database. *Drosophila melanogaster* and *Anopheles gambiae* are selected in the experiment. There are 167 precursor miRNAs producing 204 mature miRNAs of *Drosophila melanogaster* and 67 precursor miRNAs producing 68 mature miRNAs of *Anopheles gambiae*, respectively. There are 23 and 96 literature references associated with *Anopheles gambiae* and *Drosophila melanogaster*, respectively. Some precursor miRNAs can generate two mature miRNAs, for example, precursor miRNA of dme-mir-2a-1 forms two mature miRNAs (dme-miR-2a-1-5p and dme-miR-2a-3p). Therefore, the number of mature miRNAs is higher than precursor miRNAs in two species. The retrieved

**Table 10.2** The result of searching Drosophlia melanogaster and Anopheles Gambiae in miRbase

| Species | Section | Number of hits |
|---------|---------|----------------|
| D.melanogaster | MiRNA name | 176 |
| A.gambiae | MiRNA name | 67 |
| D.melanogaster | Mature name | 204 |
| A.gambiae | Mature name | 68 |
| D.melanogaster | Dead entry | 1 |
| A.gambiae | Dead entry | 0 |
| D.melanogaster | Gene symbol | 0 |
| A.gambiae | Gene symbol | 0 |
| D.melanogaster | Description | 0 |
| A.gambiae | Description | 0 |
| D.melanogaster | Comments | 0 |
| A.gambiae | Comments | 0 |
| D.melanogaster | PubMed ID | 0 |
| A.gambiae | PubMed ID | 0 |
| D.melanogaste | Literature reference | 0 |
| A.gambiae | Literature reference | 23 |

result of *Drosophila melanogaster* and *Anopheles gambiae* in miRbase database is presented in Table 10.2.

## 10.4.2   Results and Interpretation

According to knowledge that genes have a mutual relationship like network [150], an experiment is conducted in *Drosophila melanogaster* and *Anopheles gambiae* to explore the interaction between miRNAs. To discover interesting association between miRNAs, there are two primary processes. First, we investigate the relationship of cross-species miRNAs in terms of the data set from *Drosophila melanogaster* and *Anopheles gambiae*. Second, we focus on *Drosophila melanogaster* to discover the correlation of within-species.

To study the relation of cross-species, the joint entropy between Drosophila melanogaster and Anopheles gambiae is calculated. To observe association between minimum joint entropy and interacting miRNAs, the minimum joint entropy is changed from 3.45 to 3.47 by increasing 0.005 each time. Figure 10.4 shows the result of different minimum joint entropies. Total 13,872 (204 ∗ 68) related miRNAs are identified by our method. From the observation, the number of related miRNAs is significantly changed from 3.45 to 3.465. This is perhaps caused since many unimportant related-miRNAs have low joint entropy. In contrast, there is no a sharp drop of the number of related miRNAs while changing the minimum joint entropy from 3.465 to 3.47. Therefore, 3.465 is selected as minimum joint entropy threshold to filter less important or unexpected miRNAs for enhancing accuracy. For example, for the first 1,500 related miRNAs, 161 related miRNAs are eventually identified. The accuracy of 3.455 and 3.46 is 21 and 49 percent, respectively, which are calculated in terms of the following formula [52]:

$$acc = sen * \frac{pos}{pos+neg} + spe * \frac{neg}{pos+neg} \qquad (10.10)$$

where *pos* and *neg* represent the number of positive related miRNA and the number of negative related miRNAs, respectively; *sen*(sensitivity) and *spe*(specificity) denote true positive rate and true negative rate, respectively.

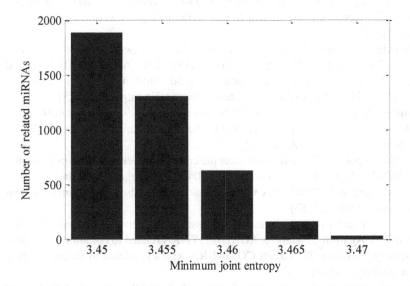

**Fig. 10.4** Number of related miRNAs of cross-species with respect to different minimum joint entropies

Table 10.3 presents the first seven associated miRNAs between *Drosophila melanogaster* and *Anopheles gambiae*. According to miRNAMap [142], patterns identified by our method are proved to be true..

**Table 10.3** Top seven patterns between *Drosophlia melanogaster* and *Anopheles gambiae*

| ID | Patterns | |
|----|----------|---|
| $CS_1$ | dme-mir-13a | aga-mir-13b |
| $CS_2$ | dme-mir-2c | aga-mir-2-1 |
| $CS_3$ | dme-mir-7 | aga-mir-7 |
| $CS_4$ | dme-mir-92b | aga-mir-92b |
| $CS_5$ | dme-mir-9a | aga-mir-9c |
| $CS_6$ | dme-mir-263a | aga-mir-263a |
| $CS_7$ | dme-mir-283 | aga-mir-283 |

Looking at patterns $CS_1$, it presents the association between *dme-mir-13a* and *aga-mir-13b*. According to miRanda [25], *aga-mir-13b* targets *AAEL002004-RA* which is related to serine protease activity. Dme-mir-13a targets CG9453-PA and CG12172-PA which are proved to have molecular function with active serine protease too. [341].

Looking at pattern $CS_2$, it indicates the relationship between *dme-mir-2c* and *aga-mir-2-1*. *Aga-mir-2-1* targets AGAP007740-RA which has association with 26S proteasome non-ATPase regulatory subunit. Dme-mir-210 targets CG4087-RA which is proved to have molecular function of 60S acidic ribosomal protein P1 [25, 120].

Looking at pattern $CS_3$, it demonstrates the correlation between dme-mir-7 and aga-mir-7. Aga-mir-7 targets AGAP008999-RA related to serine protease. Dme-mir-7 targets CG10882 which has relationship to serine-type protease activity [25, 83].

Looking at pattern $CS_4$, it shows the relation between dme-mir-92b and aga-mir-92b. Aga-mir-92b targets AGAP003307-RB, AGAP003307-RA, and AGAP003530-RA which have association with odorant-binding protein. Dmemir-92b targets CG15505-RA which is related to odorantbinding protein [25].

Pattern $CS_5$ presents the relationship between dme-mir- 9a and aga-mir-9c. Aga-mir-9c targets AGAP009913-RA related to Actin. Dme-mir-9a targets CG18290-RA which is connected to Actin [25].

Looking at pattern $CS_6$, it demonstrates the correlation between dme-mir-263 and aga-mir-263a. Aga-mir-263a targets AGAP004592-RA related to serine protease. Dme-mir-7 targets CG10851-RA which is associated with serine-arginine protein 55 protease activity [25, 83].

Looking at pattern $CS_7$, it presents the association between dme-mir-283 and aga-mir-283. Aga-mir-283 targets AGAP011177-RA related to ubiquitin ligase protein activity. Dme-mir-277 targets CG5841-RA which is related to ubiquitin ligase protein activity too [25].

Recently, many studies have proved that genes have interaction with each other by forming a network [150]. To illustrate the identification of interaction within-species, we apply our method in *Drosophila melanogaster*; 20,808 (204 ∗ 204) related miRNAs are discovered. By removing repeated data, a total of 20,706 related miRNAs are selected as a training set. According to the comparison in Figure 10.5, it indicates that the number of related miRNAs withinspecies, using 3.83, becomes stable. Thus, it is used as minimum joint entropy.

Table 10.4 presents the first seven patterns of within-species. Pattern WS2 in Table 10.4 presents the correlation between dme-mir-289 and dme-mir-11. According to PicTar [120], CG7417_RA is targeted by dme-mir-289. There is experimental evidence that CG7417_RA is associated with DNA binding transcription factor activity [243]. Dme-mir-11 also relates to depression of protein-activity [10, 243].

Pattern $WS_3$ describes the relationship between dmemir-2a and dme-mir-2b. According to [120, 270], dme-mir-2a is associated with protein tyrosine kinase activity. Dme-mir-2b also links to protein tyrosine kinase activity [91, 120].

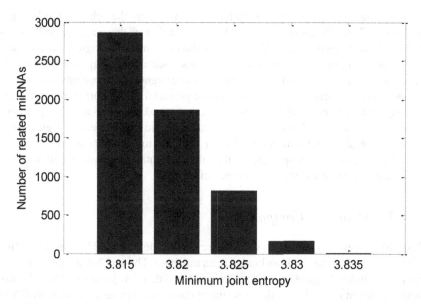

**Fig. 10.5** Number of related miRNAs of within-species with respect to different minimum joint entropies

**Table 10.4** The selected top seven patterns of within-species

| ID | Patterns | |
|---|---|---|
| $WS_1$ | dme-mir-287 | dme-mir-2c |
| $WS_2$ | dme-mir-11 | dme-mir-289 |
| $WS_3$ | dme-mir-310 | dme-mir-33 |
| $WS_4$ | dme-mir-287 | dme-mir-4 |
| $WS_5$ | dme-mir-315 | dme-mir-283 |
| $WS_6$ | dme-mir-92b | dme-mir-286 |
| $WS_7$ | dme-mir-287 | dme-mir-5 |

Pattern $WS_4$ presents a relation between dme-mir-287 and dme-mir-4 [120]. According to PicTar [120], FBgn0010583 is targeted by dme-mir-287. FBgn0010583 has axon guidance molecular function [290]. Dme-mir-4 is related to axon guidance, which is reported in [120, 323].

Pattern $WS_5$ in Table 10.4 describes a relationship between dme-mir-287 and dme-mir-3. By [28, 120], dme-mir-287 is associated to axon guidance. According to [120], Dme-mir-3 correlates with axon guidance of Drosophila melanogaster.

Pattern $WS_6$ shows an association between dme-mir-92b and dme-mir-286. Dme-mir-92b has a close relation to zinc ion binding [120, 175]. According to [120]and Helfrich-Forster and Homberg [138], dme-mir-286 has similar function in zinc ion binding of *Drosophila melanogaster*.

Some new interesting patterns are also discovered from the experimental results. For example, looking at pattern WS1 in Table 10.4, it indicates that dme-mir-287 has correlation with dme-mir-2a. Pattern WS7 uncovers the relationship between dme-mir-287 and dme-mir-5. The biological function of these related miRNAs is still unveiled. It can be left for biologist to validate by using biological experiments.

For those patterns discovered within-species, their relationships are not obvious and cannot be directly found by existing sequence alignment algorithms. In contrast, our method can discover patterns which have potential and important relationships. The experimental results demonstrate that our method is able to not only correctly identify the related miRNAs but also facilitates users to predict new biological functions. The obtained patterns can be further explored to enhance our understanding of biological evolution of species. Further, their potential correlations with diseases can benefit to the development of biomedicine.

### 10.4.3  Algorithm Comparison

Table 10.5 shows a comparison with respect to our algorithm (BJE) and miRAlign [319].The miRNA data is downloaded from miRbase. The miRNA data used by miRAlign excludes *A. gambiae*. We select miRNA data of *A. gambiae* whose homologue existed in miRAlign as the experiment data, which includes total 38 miRNAs in *A. gambiae* (http://mirnamap.mbc.nctu.edu.tw/php/search_kw. php?species=aga&choice=miRNA). The parameter of miRAlign is set by standard definition (*deltalen* = 15, *minseqsim* = 70, *MFE* = -20kcol=mal). There are 26 and 29 miRNAs, which have related miRNAs (in different species but belong to same miRNA family), detected by miRAlign and BJE, respectively. The comparison shows that our method is slightly better than miRAlign in accuracy.

**Table 10.5**  The comparison between BLAST and miRAlign

| Method | Species | Alignment |
|---------|-----------|-------------|
| BJE | A gambiae | 76%(29/38) |
| miRAlign | A gambiae | 68%(26/38) |

To evaluate the sensitivity of our method, an experiment is conducted on a real world data set derived from Kdnuggets [184]. The algorithm is implemented on Windows XP, Intel(R) Core(TM) 2 Duo Cu T6670@ 2.20GHZ, 2.0-GB memory and C++. Figure 10.6 presents the relationship between average transaction length and running time. It is observed that there is no significant change in running time while increasing average transaction length. In other words, our method is not sensitive to the transaction length.

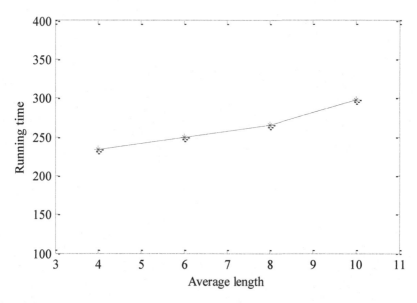

**Fig. 10.6** The influence of average transaction length. The vertical axis and horizontal axis represent running time and average transaction length, respectively.

## 10.5   Conclusion

There is much evidence that miRNA plays an important role in gene regulation [120, 169]. Although there has been considerable efforts to investigate the regulatory mechanisms of miRNA [209, 271], the study for miRNA interaction of cross-species or within-species is still insufficient. Usually, structure is more conserved than sequence in biological evolution. Thus, structure similarity has been widely used to study miRNA. However, there is limited literature reported on the relationships between miRNAs.

This chapter employs structure similarity in combination with sequence similarity to explore the relationships of miRNAs. Further, joint entropy is used to measure the importance of related miRNAs. The related miRNAs that have higher joint entropy are viewed as more important. The experiment is conducted by using a *Drosophila melanogaster* and *Anopheles gambiae* data set collected from miRbase. The results demonstrate that our method is able to correctly identify interacting miRNAs and distinguish them by importance.

# Chapter 11
# Discovering Conserved and Diverged Patterns of MiRNA Families

MicroRNAs (miRNAs) have been recognized as important regulators of post-transcriptional gene expression. They additionally perform crucial functions in a wide range of biological processes. Many efforts have been made to explore miR-NAs, however the investigation of structural features regarding conservation and divergence through evolutionary time has been largely overlooked and underdeveloped. This chapter presents a novel association rule framework to capture interesting conserved and divergent patterns, by which to explore the regulatory roles of miRNAs, and a framework to investigate conservative positions of miRNAs using information redundancy. A structural schema is proposed to model miRNA data. Support constraints are used to control the generation of frequent itemsets. Further, a correlation measure is applied to identify strongly correlated infrequent itemsets. In addition, the single base information redundancy and the adjacent base related information redundancy are applied to measure the importance of miRNA sites. Two thresholds are employed to prune the sites without biological meaning. The derived rules and positions not only unveil important structural features of miRNAs, but also promote a comprehensive understanding of the regulatory roles of miRNAs.

## 11.1 Introduction

MicroRNAs (miRNAs) are endogenous small non-coding RNA of $\sim$22 nt in length that play an important role in post-transcriptional regulation. These miRNAs act across thousands of genes by base pairing with target mRNAs. In plants, miRNA genes are first transcribed as primary miRNA sequences, and are subsequently processed into precursors (pre-miRNAs) with secondary hairpin structure by a Dicer-like enzyme. Finally, mature miRNAs are derived from either the $5'$ or $3'$ arm of the pre-miRNAs. The maturation process of miRNAs in animals is similar to that in plants.

Since the first miRNA was discovered [199], significant efforts have been made to study miRNAs from different aspects. Discovery of miRNAs and their target genes are fundamental to investigate their functional roles and regulatory features. Many evidences prove that miRNA is important in various biological processes of most organisms, such as developmental timing, cell proliferation, differentiation, growth, apoptosis, etc. Recent studies show that miRNA is also associated with many cancers and other diseases. For example, miRNA-151 relates to liver cancer by facilitating tumor cell migration and spread [79]. As a result, a substantial number of computational methods have been developed to identify either novel miRNA genes or possible target genes of known miRNAs [113, 331]. This gives rise to abundant and valuable miRNA data. Several databases have been established for their storage and various retrieval services, including miRBase, miRNAmap and PMRD.

The vast majority of miRNA families exhibit high conservation across different species, however, individual species also contain highly specific, recently evolved miRNA genes. Further, many miRNAs in different species have evolved from a common ancestor, cases have been shown where these have diverged across time and space. Identifying conserved patterns and divergent patterns of miRNAs throughout evolutionary time could provide novel insight into miRNA regulation.

Secondary structures have been recognized as crucial elements of the topology of many structural RNAs. As an important class of regulatory RNAs, miRNA precursors have characteristic hairpin structures, which are thought to provide deeper insight into biological function [221]. Moreover, miRNA genes are more conserved in secondary structure than primary sequence. Consequently, a large number of effective approaches for miRNA study take sequence and secondary structure information into account. As an example, homologous miRNAs were investigated by combining sequence and secondary structure analysis [45]. Based on both sequence and structure alignment, MiRAlign presents better performance than other reported homology search methods [319].

The study of important sites of miRNAs has become a hot issue in recent years. Many evidences demonstrate that those positions of miRNA, which play central roles in biological evolution and gene regulation like target binding and miRNA's formation, are more conserved [35]. For example, RNA editing in specific position of pri-miR results in complete blockage of its cleavage. There have been methods developed to identify important position of miRNA. For example, information entropy is applied to find the sequence conversion and base correlation degree of mature miRNA and precursor miRNA. It focuses on sequence level, but ignores miRNA secondary structure. Further, there is insufficient effort to find mature miRNA positions related to gene expression.

In contrast to animal genomes, plant genomes have fewer but larger miRNA gene families, and the members derived from the same miRNA family have nearly identical sequence. These miRNAs often share common targets, but are distributed in different plants and exhibit species-specific functional characteristics. An investigation into the structural features of plant miRNA families in evolution may facilitate a comprehensive understanding of their regulatory roles. Current research has focussed on identifying new miRNAs and predicting target genes of known miRNAs. The study of characterized conserved and divergent patterns of secondary structure is however insufficient since it is uneasy to predict miRNAs in species with unsequenced genomes. This prevents us from developing new experimental approaches for understanding miRNA origins, evolution and divergence.

Association rule mining, as a pattern extraction algorithm, has been widely applied to handle various biological data types [47, 66]. Most focus is paid to finding frequent patterns. In contrast, the infrequent patterns have been largely ignored. Actually, the infrequent patterns may contain valuable but hidden biological information for exploring the evolutionary mechanism of miRNAs as described in Chapter 6. For example, an infrequent pattern *miR399, ath* → *S1_A5* may demonstrate the structure of *miR399* with 5 *adenine* in *stem* 1 is only distributed in plant *Arabidopsis thaliana* and may result in diverse regulatory functions. Thus, the frequent pattern combined with the infrequent pattern may contribute to a greater understanding of miRNAs' function. A method based on joint entropy can explore the relationship between ncRNA. Thus, information redundancy is applied to evaluate the importance degree of miRNA postition.

This chapter uses association rules to identify structure patterns that are conserved and divergent in plant miRNA families, and applies information redundancy for discovery of mature miRNA conservation sites. Two data sets including five miRNA families and the species Drosophila melanogaster from miRbase, respectively are applied in the experiment. Support constraints are used to identify interesting itemsets. This avoids generating redundant rules and missing interesting rules. Further, the interesting infrequent itemsets are extracted by using a novel correlation measure. Information redundancy is employed to measure the conservative degree of miRNA site. Further, two thresholds are used to sort out more important miRNA sites. The derived patterns present significant structure-category relationships in miRNAs. This not only reveals the highly conserved property of miRNAs in evolution, but also indicates the divergent species-specific functional features.

## 11.2 Preliminaries

### 11.2.1 Structure Normalization

Figure 11.1 presents a miRNA precursor. The sequence contains *adenine* (A), *uracil* (U), *cytosine* (C) and *guanine* (G). The regions with vertical lines are called stems and the rest is viewed as loops. The nucleotides labeled in boldface are miRNA (or called mature miRNA ), and their complements on the other arm of the stem-loop structure are miRNA$^\star$. In particular, some miRNA precursors are proved to have two complementary mature miRNAs, located in the 3$'$ and 5$'$ arm of the stem-loop structure, respectively. For simplicity, we call them 3$'$ miRNA and 5$'$ miRNA.

The number of loops and stems are not the same for all miRNAs. Some miRNAs may have less loops or stems. According to statistics, the applied miRNAs in this chapter contain at most five stems and four loops. A substructure scheme for mature miRNA is presented as *stem* 1 (*S1*), *loop* 1 (*L1*), *stem* 2 (*S2*), *loop* 2 (*L2*), *stem* 3 (*S3*),

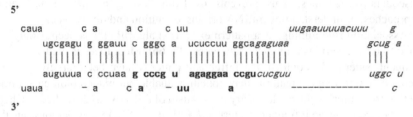

**Fig. 11.1** The secondary structure of the *sbi-miR399f* precursor. The miRNA sequence is located in the 3' arm, labeled in boldface. *LA* is defined as the sequence length of the nucleotides in italics.

*loop* 3 (*L3*), *stem* 4 (*S4*), *loop* 4 (*L4*) and *stem* 5 (*S5*). For example, the 3' miRNA in Figure 11.1 is represented by *S*1(ugcc), *L*1(a), *S*2(aaggaga), *L*2(uu), *S*3(u), *L*3(-), *S*4(gccc), *L*4(a) and *S*5(g). To normalize the miRNA structures, 3' miRNAs are sorted due to the precursors that have two mature miRNAs. Table 11.1 presents a raw data set of miRNA structure, in which the structure attribute $S1\_A$ represents adenine in *stem* 1 and the integers denote its corresponding size of base composition. Each row describes structure information of a specific miRNA. For brevity, only *stem* 1 is presented. In the same manner, the base composition of the flanking region (*FR*) can be normalized. 40 structure attributes are obtained including $S1\_A$, $S1\_U$, $S1\_C$, $S1\_G$, $S2\_A$, $S2\_U$, $S2\_C$, $S2\_G$, $S3\_A$, $S3\_U$, $S3\_C$, $S3\_G$, $S4\_A$, $S4\_U$, $S4\_C$, $S4\_G$, $S5\_A$, $S5\_U$, $S5\_C$, $S5\_G$, $L1\_A$, $L1\_U$, $L1\_C$, $L1\_G$, $L2\_A$, $L2\_U$, $L2\_C$, $L2\_G$, $L3\_A$, $L3\_U$, $L3\_C$, $L3\_G$, $L4\_A$, $L4\_U$, $L4\_C$, $L4\_G$, $FR\_A$, $FR\_U$, $FR\_C$ and $FR\_G$.

**Table 11.1** An example of raw data regarding stem 1 of miRNA structures

| *miRNA* | $S1\_A$ | $S1\_U$ | $S1\_C$ | $S1\_G$ |
|---------|-----|-----|-----|-----|
| ath-mir399f | 1 | 1 | 2 | 1 |
| ath-mir399d | 1 | 1 | 2 | 1 |
| osa-mir399d | 1 | 1 | 2 | 1 |
| osa-mir395b | 2 | 1 | 0 | 2 |

The location feature, namely *LA*, indicates the position of miRNAs in the stem-loop structure. It is defined as the number of nucleotides between the miRNA and miRNA\* (or the complementary mature miRNA) illustrated in Figure 11.1, in which the value of *LA* is 38. A total of 41 structure attributes are considered in the structure modeling. To simplify the process, 10 nucleotides are selected as the flanking region.

## 11.2.2  *Data Preparation*

Hundreds of miRNA families have been identified in plants. However, it is observed that some families only contain one or two miRNA members. In this study, we use five highly abundant miRNA families collected from miRBase as experimental data. They are *miR399, miR395, miR165, miR171* and *miR169*, widely distributed in plant species. To identify interesting structure patterns, some miRNAs are removed from each family due to underrepresentation in some species. Further, the selected members in the five families need to be derived from the same plant species. As a result, the dataset of plant species contain *ath, osa, mtr, sbi, zma, aly, ptr, tcc, vvi* and *rco*. These species can be classified into *Eu* and *Mo*, in which *Eu* contains *ath, aly, mtr, ptr*, and *vvi*. They can be classified into *Eu* and *Mo*, in which *Eu* contains *ath, aly, mtr, ptr* and *vvi*, and *Mo* includes *osa, sbi* and *zma*, respectively. The abbreviation *Eu* and *Mo* denote *eudicotyledons* and *monocotyledons*, respectively; *ath, osa, mtr, sbi, zma, aly, ptr, tcc, vvi* and *rco* represent *Arabidopsis thaliana, Oryza sativa, Medicago truncatula, Sorghum bicolor, Zea mays, Arabidopsis lyrata, Populus trichocarpa*, and *Vitis vinifera*, respectively. After removing 25 unusual pre-miRNAs that only contain stem 1 in the mature sequence and 30 that have no nucleotide in all loops, a dataset consisting of 460 precursor sequences is generated.

The second dataset is related to the species *Drosophila melanogaster* (*dme*), which is the same as Section 10.4.1. In the experiment, Table 11.2 presents the retrieval results using the keywords dme. There are 238 matching precursor miRNAs and 434 matching mature miRNAs.

**Table 11.2** The result of searching *Drosophila melanogaster* in miRBase

| Section | Description | Number of hits |
|---------|-------------|----------------|
| *miRNA name* | *match the accession or ID of a hairpin precursor entry* | 238 |
| *Previous ID* | *match the previous ID of a hairpin precursor entry* | 7 |
| *Mature name* | *match the accession or ID of a mature miRNA sequence* | 434 |
| *Dead entry* | *match the accession or ID of a dead entry* | 3 |

## 11.3 Identification of Featured Patterns of miRNAs

### 11.3.1 Partition of Attributes

Table 11.3 presents an example of the raw data set of miRNA samples in which the category attributes include miRNA family, taxonomic group and species. Their corresponding partitions, namely category items, are defined as:

- *miRNA family* = {*miR399, miR395, miR165, miR171, miR169*},
- *taxonomic group* = {*Eu, Mo*},
- *species* = {*ath, osa, mtr, sbi, zma, aly, ptc, vvi*}.

Unlike the category attributes, the structure attributes are quantitative and need to be partitioned into intervals. By statistics, the size of base composition in stems,

**Table 11.3** An example of raw data set of miRNA samples

| miRNA family | Taxonomic group | species | S1_A | S1_U | S1_C | S1_G |
|:---:|:---:|:---:|:---:|:---:|:---:|:---:|
| mir399 | Eu | aly | 2 | 1 | 1 | 1 |
| mir399 | Mo | osa | 2 | 2 | 2 | 2 |
| mir395 | Eu | ptr | 2 | 1 | 0 | 2 |
| mir171 | Mo | osa | 2 | 4 | 2 | 4 |
| mir165 | Mo | osa | 3 | 1 | 1 | 2 |

loops and the flanking region varies from 0 to 10 and only peaks at limited points. In the same manner as Section 9.3.1, the point-based decomposition of quantitative attributes may imply important structural features of miRNAs. For example, the partition of $S1\_A$ is represented as $D(S1\_A)=\{0, (0, 1], (1, 2], (2, 3], (3, 4], (4, 5], (5, 6], (6, 7], (7, 8], (8, 9], (9, 10]\}$ by using this approach, in which each range of partition only contains one element. For the interval $(0, 1]$ of $S1\_A$, it can be written as $S1\_A1$. This is viewed as a structure item herein, and indicates the number of adenine in *stem* 1 is 1. The domain of *LA* shows an extensively varied range. The partition based on equal width is suitable. Thus, its partition is defined as $D(LA) = \{(0, 20], (20, 40], (40, 60], (60, 80], (80, 100], (100, 120], (120, 140]\}$. Each miRNA data sample used in this chapter comprises a collection of structure items and category items.

## 11.3.2  Discovery of Conserved Patterns

The secondary structure of miRNAs comprises various stems and loops, which are functional and hence are well conserved through evolution. The investigation on the base composition of stems, loops and flanking region facilitates the recognition of characteristic structural features of miRNAs. Thus, this section applies association rule mining [4] to capture conserved structure patterns from the modeled miRNA data. Usually, it is difficult to select an appropriate support threshold for mining the frequent pattern. A larger threshold may miss interesting patterns, whereas a lower one may result in redundant patterns. Further, the support of a large size itemset is inherently lower than a small size itemset [318]. A flexible way is to specify constraints in terms of the itemset generation.

**Definition 11.1. Support Constraint.** Suppose $I = \{a_1, a_2, \cdots a_n\}$ is the set of all category items and structure items, and $mins(a_i)$ denotes the *minimum support* of item $a_i \in I$. Given an itemset $A = \{b_1, b_2, \cdots b_k\}$, $b_i \in I$, $1 \leq i \leq k$, $A \subset I$, the *minimum support* threshold of $A$, namely $mins(A)$, is defined as the minimum of the *minimum supports* of items in $A$. $A$ is an interesting frequent itemset if $supp(A) \geq mins(A)$.

According to Definition 11.1, different itemsets are required to satisfy different *minimum supports*. For example, suppose $mins(S1\_A2) = 0.2$, $mins(S1\_C1) = 0.3$

and $mins(S1\_G2) = 0.15$. The minimum support threshold of $\{S1\_A2, S1\_G2\}$ by support constraint is 0.15, whereas the minimum support threshold of $\{S1\_A2, S1\_C1\}$ is 0.2. Further, the large size of interesting itemsets can be identified by using the support constraint.

The determination of *minimum support* of each item is another critical issue that needs to be addressed. A method involving confidence and lift measures was proposed to specify *support constraint*, which is able to make the obtained rules strong and interesting [207]. However, it fails to remove the items with relatively low occurrence while identifying interesting 1-itemsets, such as the item whose frequency is 1. Thus, this approach needs to be extended and adapted. Suppose $\lambda = supp(a_i) \times minc$, $1 \leq i \leq n$. The minimum support of item $a_i$ can be defined as:

$$mins(a_i) = \begin{cases} \lambda & \lambda > MS, \\ MS & \text{otherwise.} \end{cases} \tag{11.1}$$

where $MS$ denotes the minimum support constraint of all items and is used to prune the low occurrence items, namely infrequent items. Formula 11.1 specifies the support constraints of items and ensures the generated itemsets are interesting. Note, the higher an item's support is, the larger the item's *minimum support* will be. Further, the *minimum support* threshold of each item in $I$ is sensitive to the alteration of *minimum confidence*, which may result in varied patterns.

The interesting itemsets can be identified by using the above support constraints. As a result, conserved structure patterns can be generated from the identified itemsets. For example, suppose $\{ath, S1\_A2, S1\_U3\}$ is an interesting itemset. The corresponding conserved pattern can be $ath \rightarrow S1\_A2, S1\_U3$.

## 11.3.3 Discovery of Divergent Patterns

Due to the variation of base composition in stems and loops, miRNAs shows diverse roles in biology. Therefore, the identification of divergent patterns in miRNAs facilitates the exploration of species-specific functional characteristics. Different from traditional association rules as well as negative association rules [324], our divergent pattern mining focuses on the infrequent structure items that do not satisfy the specified $MS$. As a result, the original support measure is inappropriate. A new method is needed for capturing strongly correlated items with low occurrence.

Recently, many approaches have been proposed to identify correlations between items [220, 245]. Especially, a correlation method, named *h-confidence* has emerged in a variety of applications, including item clustering, copy detection, and collaborative filtering. It enables the degree of affinity among items to be measured and is effective in capturing patterns of low occurrence. Further, like the support, it also has the downward closure property on which the association rule algorithm heavily relies. Nevertheless, it cannot be directly applied to identify the itemsets that have a high affinity. Thus, a correlation measure similar to the definition in [326] is incorporated into the infrequent pattern mining.

Suppose $X = \{x_1, x_2, \cdots, x_m\}$ is an itemset that comprises category items and infrequent structure items, $x_i \in I$, $1 \leq i \leq m$. The measure can be expressed as:

$$h - confidence(X) = \frac{sup(X)}{max\{sup(\{x_i\}), x_i \subset \{X - C\}\}} \tag{11.2}$$

where $C$, $\{X - C\}$ and $max\{supp(\{x_i\}), x_i \subset \{X - C\}$ represent the set of category items, the set of infrequent structure items, and the maximum support of items in $X$ - $C$, respectively. If $X$ satisfies $h - confidence(X) \geq MHC$, in which $MHC$ denotes the predefined *minimum h-confidence*, the itemset is called an interesting infrequent itemset and the structure items $\{X - C\}$ have a high correlation under specific category $C$. Suppose the *minimum h-confidence* threshold is 0.6. Given a generated itemset $\{ath, S1\_A3, S2\_U2\}$ where items $S1\_A3$ and $S2\_U2$ are infrequent. If $h$-confidence ($\{ath, S1\_A3, S2\_U2\}$) $\geq$ 0.6, the itemset is interesting and might generate a divergent pattern $ath \rightarrow S1\_A3, S2\_U2$ indicating that 3 *adenine* in *stem* 1 and 2 *uracil* in *stem* 2 may be an evolutionarily divergent property across species *Arabidopsis thaliana*.

### 11.3.4  Rule Groups

The discovered rules can be classified into different association groups that have disparate biological meanings. For example, a rule shows a shared structure feature of *miR399* $\rightarrow$ *S1\_A2* across all plant species that we selected, whereas another rule *ath, miR399* $\rightarrow$ *S1\_A2, S1\_U1* presents an association of *miR399* only in the plant, *Arabidopsis thaliana*. This assists in further understanding the biological evolution of miRNAs.

**Definition 11.2. Rule group.** Let $RG_X = \{X \rightarrow Y\}$ be a rule group, where $X$ represents a category itemset and $Y$ denotes a set of structure itemsets.

Suppose *MF*, *TG* and *SS* represent *miRNA family*, *taxonomic group* and *species*, respectively. $CC1 = \{MF, TG\}$, $CC2 = \{MF, SS\}$ and $CC3 = \{MF, MF\}$ denote three different combinations of category attributes. The category attributes as well as the combinations form a collection of category itemsets of rule groups. Thus, biologically important rules are generated in terms of *MF*, *TG*, *SS*, *CC1*, *CC2* and *CC3*. According to Definition 11.2, the rules $\{ath \rightarrow S1\_A3, S2\_U3\}$ and $\{ath \rightarrow L1\_U1\}$ are derived from the same rule group $\{ath \rightarrow Y\}$ that present the structure patterns of miRNAs in the plant *Arabidopsis thaliana*.

## 11.4 Identification of Conserved Sites

### 11.4.1 Information Redundancy

Information entropy proposed by C.E Shannon in 1948 and based on probability theory and statistics is a metric of information uncertainty. Due to the advantage of information entropy in information quantitative measurement, information entropy is widely applied in many fields, such as image processing, voice identification, data mining and bioinformatics. For example, a method based on joint entropy and mutual information is used to explore the relationship between non-coding RNA.

Information redundancy is a core concept of the information theory, which measures the reiteration of information. In communication system, the bigger the information redundancy, the more useless information it is. In information entropy, the information redundancy is the number of bits used to transmit a message minus the number of bits of actual information in the message. Suppose $X$ denotes a random variable, the information redundancy $\gamma$ is defined as:

$$\gamma = 1 - \eta = 1 - \frac{H(X)}{H_0(X)} \tag{11.3}$$

where $H(X)$ denotes the practical information entropy of $X$; $H_0(X)$ is the ideal information entropy of equal probability; $\eta$ represents the relative entropy.

Since the advantage of information entropy in quantitatively measuring how much useful information contained in system, it has been widely used in many areas. It is viewed as a criterion for feature selection and feature transformations in machine learning, and a significant function for the computation of collocation in corpus linguistics. For example, information redundancy is employed to correctly select discriminative genes from microarray data [217].

This section employs information redundancy to measure conservation degree of every site. It contains two kind information redundancies: single base information redundancy and adjacent base information redundancy. The single base information redundancy is used to measure how much information contains in special site. The miRNA site that has higher information redundancy is viewed as more conservation. The single base information redundancy of site ($i$) is defined as:

$$R_0(i) = 1 - \frac{H_0(i)}{H_{0max}} \tag{11.4}$$

$$H_0(i) = -\sum_{\alpha}\sum_{\chi} p_i(\alpha\chi) log p_i(\alpha\chi) \tag{11.5}$$

where $\alpha$ denotes a kind of A, U, G and C; $\chi$ denotes stem or loop; $p_i(\alpha\chi)$ denotes the probability of special base with stem or loop appearing on site ($i$); $H_0(i)$ represents the single base information entropy of site ($i$); $H_{0max}$ represents the maximum information entropy. For a miRNA sequence, when the probability of every kind of nucleotide with stem or loop appearing on one site is equal, the value of information entropy is max. In other words, if $p_i(\alpha\chi) = 1/8$, the maximum value of information entropy is generated, namely $H_{0max} = 3$.

Increasing evidences indicate that there is certain relation between neighboring bases in biological sequence. In order to find the relationship of contiguous nucleotide, the adjacent base information redundancy is defined as:

$$R_1(i) = 1 - \frac{H_1(i)}{H_{1max}} \tag{11.6}$$

$$H_1(i) = -\sum_\alpha \sum_\beta p_i(\alpha\beta) log p_i(\alpha\beta) \tag{11.7}$$

where $\alpha$ and $\beta$ denote A, U, G and C. $p_i(\alpha\beta)$ denotes the probability of $\alpha$ base appearing on site $(i)$ and $\beta$ base appearing on site $(i+1)$. $H_1(i)$ denotes the adjacent base information entropy. $H_{1max}$ denotes the maximum information entropy. Similar to $H_{0max}$, given a miRNA sequence, when $p_i(\alpha\beta) = 1/16$, the information entropy is the maximum value $H_{1max} = 4$.

In order to find more important conservation site, we define two thresholds: $min\_R_0$ for single base information redundancy and $min\_R_1$ for adjacent base information redundancy.

$$R_0(i) \geq min\_R_0 \tag{11.8}$$

$$R_1(i) \geq min\_R_1 \tag{11.9}$$

Each site which satisfies with two inequalities are viewed as significant and interesting. In addition, the thresholds $min\_R_0$ and $min\_R_1$ assist in enhancing the running efficiency and accuracy of our method. In RNA world, some RNAs have a long nucleotide sequence. For example, in prokaryotes, the rRNA (ribosomal RNA) include 5S16S and 23S which contains 250 nucleotides, 1540 nucleotides and 2900 nucleotides, respectively. In eukaryotes, the rRNA (ribosomal RNA) contains four rRNA species (5S, 5.8S, 18S and 28S which contain 120 nucleotides, 160 nucleotides, 1900 nucleotides and 4700 nucleotides, respectively). However, some of these RNA sites have low information redundancy. These RNA sites are less conservative and need to be pruned.

## 11.5    Results of miRNA Structure Patterns

### 11.5.1    Experimental Results

It is observed that conservation and divergence patterns are determined by different parameters. Suppose the *minimum confidence* in conserved patterns and divergent patterns are denoted by $minc_1$ and $minc_2$, respectively. To identify the structure patterns of one miRNA family in a plant species, a low *MS* is preferred. This is because the number of one miRNA family across a plant species in the collected dataset mainly falls within the range of [15, 30]. Compared with 460 miRNAs collected from miRBase, the number is small. Further, since the support of category itemset (antecedent) is much larger than infrequent structure itemset (consequent) in divergence patterns, a low $minc_2$ is applied. Thus, $MS = 0.015$ and $minc_2 = 0.1$ are used herein and we focus on comparing the difference by varying $minc_1$ and *minimum h-confidence*, respectively.

Figure 11.2 presents the number of frequent itemsets under varied $minc_1$. There are 2122 frequent itemsets generated by $minc_1 = 0.5$, which is in the middle of the five cases. The corresponding results by $MS = 0.015$ and $minc_1 = 0.5$ are included in the following analysis. In contrast to conserved patterns, the identification of divergent pattern requires another parameter (*MHC*) to specify the strong dependence among items. A comparison of interesting infrequent itemset output regarding different *minimum h-confidence* is presented in Figure 11.3, where $MS = 0.015$. There is no sharp drop in itemset output while varying *MHC* from 0.6 to 0.7. Thus, 0.6 is used as the *minimum h-confidence* to identify divergent patterns.

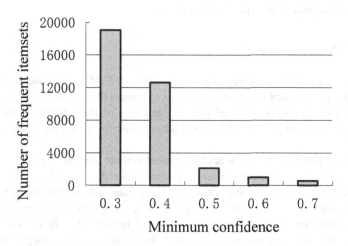

**Fig. 11.2** The comparison of number of frequent itemsets using different minimum confidences

According to the specified rule groups, the generated associations of *MF* present the structure features of one miRNA family or shared structure features of all families; the associations of *TG* show the structure features of miRNAs across *eudicotyledons* and *monocotyledons*, respectively; the associations of *SS* presents the structure features of miRNAs across a plant species; the associations of *CC*1 presents the structure features of one family across *eudicotyledons* and *monocotyledons*, respectively; the associations of *CC*2 presents the structure features of one family

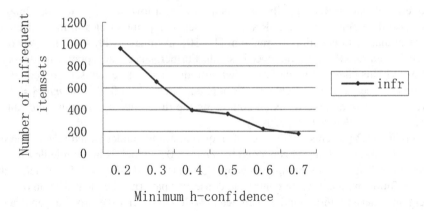

**Fig. 11.3** The change of number of interesting infrequent itemset using varied *minmum h-confidence*

across a species; the associations of *CC3* presents the structure features of two different miRNA families. These discovered structure-category correlations help us understand the biological evolution of miRNAs.

### 11.5.2  Performance

In contrast to the traditional association rule mining (*TAM*), our conserved pattern identification (*CPI*) adopt support constraints to control the frequent itemset output. Further, the constraint is specified not only in terms of the supports of items but also the *minimum confidence*. This guarantees the discovery of interesting structure features.

Table 11.4 presents the efficiency of frequent itemset obtained by *CPI* and *TAM* in terms of different parameters. There is a significant reduction of frequent itemsets in *CPI* by using constraints. Algorithm *TAM* generates a large number of itemsets in case of *mins* = 0.04 (occurrence frequency is no less than 18.4), whereas some interesting structure patterns cannot be discovered. In particular, the results by *mins* = 0.1 have no biological meanings, in which the occurrence frequency of itemsets is larger or equal to 46. Compared with *TAM*, our method can efficiently identify all interesting structure features. Table 11.5 presents the running efficiency of the two algorithms. The comparison demonstrates that the presented method is faster by using support constraints. All experiments were performed on a Lenovo PC with Pentium(R) Dual-Core 2.0 GHz CPU, and 1GB RAM. Algorithms were coded in VC++.

**Table 11.4** Number of frequent itemsets generated by two algorithms

| CPI | | TAM | |
|---|---|---|---|
| *minc* | *fr* | *mins* | fr |
| 0.4 | 12651 | 0.04 | 14810 |
| 0.5 | 2122 | 0.06 | 3805 |
| 0.6 | 991 | 0.08 | 1401 |
| 0.7 | 565 | 0.10 | 585 |
| 0.8 | 177 | 0.12 | 334 |

**Table 11.5** Running time of two algorithms under different parameters

| CPI | | TAM | |
|---|---|---|---|
| *minc* | *time(s)* | *mins* | *time(s)* |
| 0.4 | 186.56 | 0.04 | 309.36 |
| 0.5 | 20.92 | 0.06 | 69.86 |
| 0.6 | 15.29 | 0.08 | 31.1 |
| 0.7 | 13.71 | 0.10 | 17.85 |
| 0.8 | 12.89 | 0.12 | 13.15 |

### *11.5.3 Interpretation*

This section identifies interesting conserved patterns as well as divergent patterns in terms of specified rule groups. Due to large number of mining results, several patterns that have the higher supports in each specified group are selected for interpretation. Table 11.6 presents 6 structure patterns for all miRNA families that have dominant support, where ALL represents the five miRNA families. Table 11.7 shows 7 conserved patterns pertaining to *miR399*. 4 divergent patterns listed in Table 11.8 are also correlated with *miR399*. These rules facilitate the understanding of structure-function relationships for *miR399* family in a more comprehensive and accurate manner.

**Table 11.6** 6 conserved patterns across all families

| | | |
|---|---|---|
| 1 | *ALL* → *S1_A2* | with support = 0.2 |
| 2 | *ALL* → *S2_A2* | with support = 0.31 |
| 3 | *ALL* → *S3_A1* | with support = 0.21 |
| 4 | *ALL* → *S1_U1* | with support = 0.56 |
| 5 | *ALL* → *S1_C2* | with support = 0.36 |
| 6 | *ALL* → *S1_G1* | with support = 0.22 |

Looking at rules 1, 2 and 3, they show leading numbers of *adenine* in *stem* 1, *stem* 2 and *stem* 3 across all miRNA families. The comparison between the three rules can be a supplement to demonstrate the differences between stems. Considering rules 1, 4, 5 and 6, they present the distribution of base compositions in *stem* 1. These unveil the conserved property of secondary structures through evolution, which has

**Table 11.7** Conserved patterns of miR399 family regarding different categories

| 7  | $mir399 \rightarrow S1\_A2, S1\_U1, S1\_C2, S1\_G1, L1\_A1$ |
|----|---|
| 8  | $Eu, mir399 \rightarrow S1\_A2, S1\_U1, S1\_C2, S1\_G1, L1\_A1, S3\_G3$ |
| 9  | $Mo, mir399 \rightarrow S1\_A2, S1\_U1, S1\_C2, S1\_G1, L1\_A1$ |
| 10 | $mtr, mir399 \rightarrow S1\_A2, S1\_U1, S1\_C2, S1\_G1, S3\_C3, S3\_G1$ |
| 11 | $ath, mir399 \rightarrow S1\_A2, S1\_U1, S1\_C2, S1\_G1, L1\_A1, S2\_A2, S3\_U2$ |
| 12 | $rco, mir399 \rightarrow S1\_A2, S1\_U1, S1\_C2, S1\_G1, S2\_G2, S3\_C3$ |
| 13 | $mir399 \rightarrow LA[40, 59]$ |

**Table 11.8** Diverged patterns regarding *miR399*

| 14 | $mir399, ath \rightarrow S3\_C2, L3\_U1$ |
|----|---|
| 15 | $mir399, ath \rightarrow S2\_A1, S3\_C2$ |
| 16 | $mir399, rco \rightarrow L1\_G1, S3\_G2, FR\_A1$ |
| 17 | $mir399, rco \rightarrow FR\_C4$ |

been proved in relevant studies of secondary structure. Figure 11.4 presents the size distributions of $S1\_A$, $S1\_U$, $S1\_C$ and $S1\_G$, respectively. It shows the structures $S1\_A2$, $S1\_U1$, $S1\_C2$ and $S1\_G1$ that have higher frequency are more conserved than others. Likewise, other derived rules regarding base composition present leading numbers of base composition in other stems, loops and flanking region. This not only assists in understanding the properties of stems, loops and flanking region in evolution, but also provides an intuitive way to distinguish them. Further, the difference between stems and between loops may indicate different regulatory roles in biology.

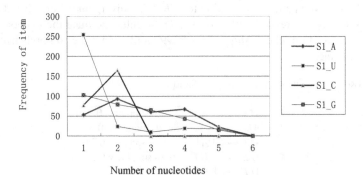

**Fig. 11.4** The size distributions of *adenine, uracil, cytosine* and *guanine* in *stem* 1. For example, the frequency of occurrence of the structure ($S1\_A1$) that has 1 *adenine* in *stem* 1 is 58. If the supports of the structure items dissatisfy the support constraints, the frequencies of structure items (such as $S1\_C3$) are set as 0 in the figure.

Rule 7 shows that the numbers of *adenine, uracil, cytosine,* and *guanine* in *stem* 1, and *adenine* in *loop* 1 may peak at 2, 1, 2, 1 and 1, respectively, in *miR399* family.

Such structure characteristics may be functional and hence are conserved across various species. This is also demonstrated by [338]. Further, this structure is located on the nucleus positions of mature miRNAs that are identified to be conserved in [305]. Thus, *stem* 1 may be the key site that recognizes the shared target genes for miR399 family. This helps us understand the structure-function correlations of miRNAs.

Rule 8 presents an association of *miR399* family across *eudicotyledons*. It uncovers the mechanism of evolutionary conservation. While rule 7 demonstrates the conserved structure feature across all species of *miR399*, rule 8 shows a conserved pattern only across *eudicotyledons*. This reflects the structural variation of genes in evolutionary process and might result in different regulatory functions. For example, *miR399* family was validated to be involved in the seeding development of *eudicotyledons* plants [337]. Looking at rule 9, it describes a conserved structure pattern of miR399 family across *monocotyledons*. Compared with rule 7, the structure pattern has no change, indicating relatively weak structural variation. The comparison between rules 7, 8 and 9 indicates that plant miRNAs are conserved between *monocots* and *eudicots*. This has been discovered in [119, 167].

Rule 10 describes a structure rule composed of $S1$, $S3\_C3$ and $S3\_G1$ in species *Medicago truncatula*. Especially, the combination of rules 8 and 10 indicates that such *stem* 1 are conserved across *eudicotyledons* but another two structure compositions are diverged through evolution. This unveils that distinct plants in *eudicotyledons* may be subject to different structure constraints. As a result, different species belonging to the same *taxonomic group* show distinguished evolutionary patterns. It may lead to functional specialization. This needs to be further validated.

Looking at rule 11, it presents a conserved structure rule in respect of $S1$, $L1$, $S2$ and $S3$ in species *Arabidopsis thaliana*. 5 *adenine*, 3 *uracil*, 2 *cytosine*, and 1 *guanine* occur in the structure model. Interaction between target gene AT3G20940.1 and *ath-mir399a* from PMRD presents 14 matches involving 5 *adenine*, 5 *uracil*, 3 *cytosine* and 1 *guanine* on *ath-mir399a* sequence. The observed target sites can be considered as a specific example of target sites in rule 11. In contrast, rules 14 and 15 show two diverged patterns with respect to $S2\_A1$, $S3\_C2$, and $L3\_U1$. These structural features can distinguish *Arabidopsis thaliana* from other species and may imply specific-species target sites. Further, the combination of the two rules may indicate diverse functional features of miRNAs in biological systems.

Looking at rule 12, it presents a conserved structure rule in terms of $S1$, $S2$ and $S3$ in *Ricinus communis*. Compared with rule 7, it highlights 2 *guanine* in *stem* 2 and 3 *cytosine* in *stem* 3 are evolutionarily conserved in species *Ricinus communis*, and shows species-specific structure characteristics. This may indicate *miR399* has diverse functional specifications in *Ricinus communis*. This result was proved in [337]. Rules 16 and 17 present diverged structure patterns across species *Ricinus communis*. The structure features $FR\_A1$ and $FR\_C4$ are useful in separating the precursors of *Ricinus communis* from the precursors of other species and may lead to different regulatory patterns for the mature miRNAs.

Rule 13 describes most mature miRNAs in the *miR399* family have a specific position on stem-loop structure, namely the number of nucleotides between miRNA and miRNA* is within the range of [40, 59]. This could provide an important spatial clue about at which position the enzyme prefers to cleave the precursor sequences and facilitates the understanding of biogenesis of miRNAs.

These rules present important evolutionary patterns for the *miR399* family. Further, the comparison between the rules as well as their combination can provide better insight into the evolutionary and functional mechanisms of miRNAs. Other miRNA families could also be analyzed in a similar manner. In addition, such structure rules can be viewed as a secondary evidence in determining the category of miRNAs. Thus, the investigation into structural features of miRNAs assists in understanding miRNAs functions. Further, the obtained conserved patterns may have potential use to explore distant homology.

## 11.6    Interpretation of Conserved miRNAs Sites

To find out the miRNA conservation site, we model the Drosophila melanogaster data with our method which is presented previous. Then, the dataset modeled by our method is counted. The information entropy is calculated with the result of statistics. There are 29 sites of longest miRNA (dme-miR-284) and 20 sites of shortest miRNA (dme-miR-307). In this chapter, we choose the first 20 sites. The sites (21-29) are removed from our experimental results.

Figure 11.5 presents the top eight single base information redundancy $R_0(i)$ of Drosophila melanogaster with $min\_R_0(i) \geq 0.4$. The site (1) with $R_0(1) = 0.52$ is the highest single base redundancy of information of the 20 sites. It demonstrates that the site 1 is more conservative than other sites. Looking at site(17), (19), (20), those sites have lower single nucleotide redundancy of information $R_0(17) = 0.42, R_0(19) = 0.44$ and $R_0(20) = 0.46$). In addition, it is observed that single base information redundancies of the sites (3), (5), (6), (7) are approximately equal, namely $R_0(3) = 0.42, R_0(5) = 0.41$ and $R_0(7) = 0.41$. It indicates that those sites are less conservative than sites (1), (17), (19), (20), but they are more conservative than other sites.

In Figure 11.6, the adjacent base information redundancy $R_1(i)$ of Drosophila melanogaster is showed by $min\_R_1(i) \geq 0.29$. The site 1 has maximum adjacent base information redundancy with $R_1(i) = 0.41$. It indicates that the adjacent base correlation degree of site 1 is stronger than other 20 sites. Looking at sites (2), (3), (4), (5), (6), (7), those sites are neighboring bases. Their adjacent base information redundancies are roughly equal, namely $R_0(2) = 0.32, R_0(3) = 0.31, R_0(4) = 0.3, R_0(5) = 0.298, R_0(6) = 0.297$ and $R_0(7) = 0.299$. Furthermore, the site (19) which belongs to end of mature miRNA has a relatively high adjacent nucleotide redundancy of information $R_1(19) = 0.29$.

According to the results of single base information redundancy $R_0(i)$ and adjacent base information redundancy $R_1(i)$, the site (1) has maximum value both in the single base information redundancy $R_0(1) = 0.52$ and adjacent base information redundancy $R_1(1) = 0.41$. It is demonstrate that the site (1) is more conservative than other 20 sites. The occurrence probability of U is 0.74 (0.56 in stem, 0.18 in loop) which is far greater than average probability as described in Table 11.9. The site (1)

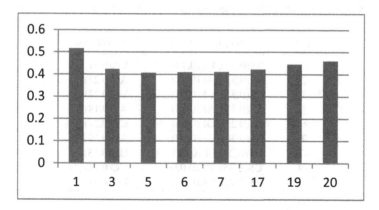

**Fig. 11.5** The top eight single base information redundancies of Drosophila melanogaster with $min\_R_0(i) \geq 0.4$

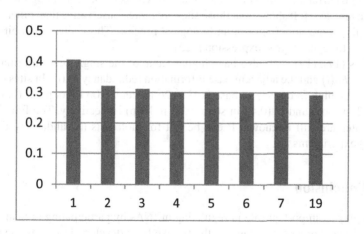

**Fig. 11.6** The top eight single base information redundancies of Drosophila melanogaster with $min\_R_1(i) \geq 0.29$

is the splicing sites of precursor miRNA. It demonstrates that the enzyme Dicer usually plays important roles in the stem of precursor miRNA and special base [179]. In addition, the site (1) has significant correlation of contiguous bases. The probability of adjacent bases: UA is up to 0.31.

The result of experiment shows that the single base information redundancy $R_0(i)$ in sites (3), (5), (6), (7) and the adjacent base information redundancy $R_1(i)$ in sites (2), (3), (5), (6), (7) are mostly equal. The dominant base in sites (2), (3), (5), (6), (7) is A, U, A, G, G, respectively. The content of those bases in corresponding site is 0.44 (0.33 in stem, 0.11 in loop), 0.44 (0.37 in stem, 0.07 in loop), 0.37 (0.32 in stem, 0.05 in loop), 0.30 (0.25 in stem, 0.05 in loop) and 0.32 (0.3 in stem, 0.02 in loop) respectively. Further, those sites also have a higher value of base correlation,

**Table 11.9** The probability of high frequency base in important site

| Site | Single base | Adjacent base |
|------|-------------|---------------|
| 1 | US(0.56), UL(0.18) | UA(0.31) |
| 2 | AS(0.33), AL(0.11) | AU(0.25) |
| 3 | US(0.37), UL(0.07) | UC(0.22) |
| 5 | AS(0.32), AL(0.05) | AC(0.18) |
| 6 | GS(0.25), GL(0.05) | CA(0.27) |
| 7 | GS(0.30), GL(0.02) | AG(0.19) |
| 17 | US(0.26),UL(0.06) | UG(0.13) |
| 19 | CS(0.35), CL(0.02) | CC(0.14) |
| 20 | US(0.42), UL(0.05) | UG(0.11) |

in which the content of AU, UC, AC, CA and AG in site 2, 3, 5, 6, 7 is 0.25, 0.22, 0.18, 0.27 and 0.19 respectively. In addition, we notice that the site (4) has a high value of base correlation, in which the content of CA is 0.25, even though $R_1(i)$ is lower than $min\_R_1(i)$. It shows that those sites are more conservative than other sites and may play more important role in biological process. Those sites often bind to target genes to regulate gene expression [325].

The sites (17), (19), (20) also have higher value of the single base information redundancy $R_0(i)$ and the adjacent base information redundancy $R_1(i)$. In sites (17), (19), (20), the high frequency of base is U (0.26 in stem, 0.06 in loop), C (0.35 in stem, 0.02 in loop) and U (0.42 in stem, 0.05 in loop) respectively. The functions of those sites are still unknown. It can be left for biologists to validate by using biological experiments.

## 11.7    Conclusion

MiRNAs play an important role in regulating mRNAs by participating in many essential biological processes. Many methods have been developed to study the regulatory characteristics of miRNAs in biology and medical sciences. The difference in the size of loops and stems and their base compositions through evolution results in various functions. This chapter thus extends the traditional association rule by considering infrequent patterns to identify significant evolutionary patterns in one family and across different families. A structure model is proposed to describe the secondary structure of miRNAs. Based on collected and normalized miRNA data, a number of conserved and divergent structural patterns are generated from different aspects of biology. The obtained rules not only provide an insight into the potential structure-function relations in miRNAs, but also unveil the regulatory mechanisms of miRNAs in biological evolution.

Many researchers discovered that conservative sites have more important functions in gene regulation and biological evolution. A number of approaches have been developed to research miRNA site. However, there are insufficient studies on important sites of mature miRNAs. This chapter employs single nucleotide information redundancy and adjacent nucleotide information redundancy for discovering interesting sites. The site with bigger value of information redundancy is regarded as more conservative. The results demonstrate that our methods not only verify some known biological knowledge of important position, but also discover some interesting features of previous overlooked position.

# Chapter 12
# Bioinformatics-Based Drug Discovery for Protein Kinases

Protien kinases have been implicated in a number of diseases, where kinases participate many aspects that control cell growth, movement and death. The deregulated kinase activities and the knowledge of these disorders is of great clinical interest of drug discovery. The most critical issue is the development of safe and efficient disease diagnosis and treatment for less cost and in less time. It is important to develop innovative approaches that aim at the root cause of a disease, not just its symptoms. Bioinformatics including genetic, genomic and computational technologies, has become the most promising option for effective drug discovery, and has showed its potential in early stage of drug-target identification and target validation. It is essential that these aspects are understood and integrated into new methods used in drug discovery for diseases arisen from deregulated kinase activity. This chapter reviews bioinformatics techniques for protein kinase data management and analysis, kinase pathways and drug targets and describes their potential application in pharmaceutical industry.

## 12.1 Introduction

Protein kinases are regarded as the second most important group of drug targets after G-protein-coupled receptors [65]. There are several groups of protein kinases, and each group is then classified into families or subfamilies [129]. Protein kinases are clinically relevant and abnormal kinase activity is a frequent cause of a number of human diseases. Nearly 400 human diseases have been reported to be connected to protein kinases, such as cancer [265, 289], cardiovascular [262, 333], neurological disorders [121, 272], diabetes [269, 283], rheumatoid arthritis [285, 336], and asthma [115, 313, 328]. Kinase activity is highly regulated by phosphorylation, by combining activator proteins or inhibitor proteins [219], or by changing their cellular location. Kinase activity has a significant effect on up to 30% of all human proteins. Further, the statistic data indicate that nearly 2% of human genes, including 500 protein kinase genes, are contained in the human genome [215]. Thus, the investigation of features of kinase activity is an attractive therapeutic and pharmaceutical strategy for drug design and the treatment of human diseases.

Traditional approach for drug discovery relies on trial-and-error of new chemical entities on cultured cells or animals, and matching the apparent effects to treatments. Ligand-based drug design (indirect drug design) and structure-based drug design (direct drug design) are two major types [163]. However, the drug developed from traditional methods might not be appropriate for all patients. Some patients may be at risk of suffering serious side effects from new drug. Further, traditional methods that largely depends on organism level experimentation are time consuming and high cost.

Bringing a new drug to market from scratch typically takes 15 years and costs about $500 million. The pharmaceutical industry are constantly searching for a better understanding of fundamental disease mechanisms, tools for early diagnosis and even pre-diagnosis disease [148]. The successful sequencing of the genomes of human and other organisms in the past few years has opened the way to an entirely new approach to drug design. A wealth of information on the ingredients of patients at the genetic level is available due to the usage of bioinformatics. A number of algorithms and tools from data mining, machine learning, artificial intelligence, statistics have been successfully used for gene identification and classification, secondary structure prediction and function annotation [66, 90]. In particular, some of them have been applied in complementing disease diagnosis and treatment [272]. They will surely to play an essential role in drug target discovery.

Recent studies have shown that the structural variations [97] of genome are implicated in a number of diseases and medical conditions, ranging from genetic disorders to cancer, and are seen as increasingly important in pharmaceutical research and development and medical diagnostics [244]. The genome approach offers a blueprint for efficient and personalized drug development. The tremendous genome data make computational biology a central aspect for developing more advanced and highly customized therapies [85]. In addition, the technology may increase efficiency and effectiveness of tests for diagnosis of disease and patient-specific risk factors, and tools for identification of individual patients likely to suffer from side effects from taking certain drugs.

There have been an explosion of knowledge about signal transduction pathways, impacting virtually all areas of biology and medicine. Protein Kinases are key regulators of cell function that constitute one of the largest and most functionally diverse gene families [145]. Further, many diseases, such as cancer, diabetes and neurodegeneration, indicate underlying gene correlations to the disease phenotype. The study of in-depth knowledge of kinase pathways and possible role to disease state is a big challenge [187]. There is still a long way to go by combining the molecular biology, biochemistry, genetics and bioinformatics for modern drug development [47].

Many valuable genome data are generated owing to high throughout biology techniques. Their management becomes a critical issue for drug design. This may include gene data collection, gene annotation, structure data modeling, standardization and normalization of data, database establishment, and so forth. Further, the communication between heterogenous biological databases would be another key issue and often requires data integration by removing inconsistent and noisy data [51]. In addition, many protein kinase databases have been created to explore the genomics, function and evolution of protein kinases. However, the relevant data analysis and knowledge extraction for modern drug discovery have been underdeveloped. Obviously, it is impractical to handle this arduous and challenging problem by just relying on traditional biological experiments. In this regards, bioinformatics [151] that include aspects of computer science, mathematics and molecular biology has become integral to process in that field.

Bioinformatics has been widely applied to investigate the regulatory mechanisms of protein kinase, including their structural and functional features [47]. Further, some researchers attempt to build human protein kinase gene family and repository, by which to identify kinases that have a high probability of impacting human disease based on data analysis [308]. This is able to discover useful information from existing valuable data resources and greatly benefit to the pharmaceutical industry in the aspect of increasing accuracy and reducing cost. Although there have been many successful cases of bioinformatics application in kinases and drug discovery, the bioinformatics is still frequently underestimated in both its importance and its resource requirement [280]. This article aims to provide a literature review for recent application and development of bioinformatics in protein kinase for drug discovery.

## 12.2 Protein Kinase and Diseases

Edmond H. Fischer and Edwin G. Krebs were awarded the 1992 Nobel Prize in Physiology and Medicine for discovering reversible protein phosphorylation as a biological regulatory mechanism. Consistent with the complex role of the post-translational modification in the cell, protein kinases can be regulated by activator proteins, inhibitor proteins, ligand binding to regulatory subunits, cofactors, and phosphorylation by other proteins or by themselves (autophosphorylation) [144]. To ensure effective and correct drug design for varied diseases, it is critical to understand the correlations between kinase, disease and drug target. Figure 1.2 presents the protein kinase regulatory network with respect to target discovery.

Protein kinases have been viewed as a very attractive target class for therapeutic interventions in many disease states such as cancer, diabetes, obesity, autoimmune disorders, inflammation, vascular diseases, and arthritis owing to their families key function in signal transduction for all organisms. In this regard, protein kinases represent as much as 30% of all protein targets under investigation by pharmaceutical companies. Recent successful launches of drugs with kinase inhibition as the mode of action demonstrate the ability to deliver kinase inhibitors as drugs with the appropriate selectivity, potency, and pharmacokinetic properties [65, 315]. In particular, protein kinases are novel and excellent drug targets of post genomic era.

There are various kinases that are related to different diseases, such as cancer and diabetes. To explore the functions, evolution and diversity of protein kinases, it is necessary to transfer our focus to their relevant sequenced genome. This assists us in

**Table 12.1** An example of kinase-gene associations

| Gene | Species | Kinase Classification |
|------|---------|-----------------------|
| AKT1 | Human | AGC: Akt |
| AKT2 | Human | AGC: Akt |
| ATK3 | Human | AGC: Akt |
| BARK1 | Human | AGC: GRK: BARK |
| MAST1 | Human | AGC: MAST: MAST |

obtaining a deep and comprehensive understanding of kinase pathways with respect to drug discovery. It has been commonly recognized that gene mutation, including deletion, insertion and duplication, can result in diseases. Not matter which case occurs, the protein made by the gene may not function properly. In other words, the mutation can alter the function of the resulting protein. Thus, the investigation of disease relevant kinase gene families, including sequences and structure is critical.

The gene family encoding protein kinases is the most commonly mutated in human cancer. Moreover, mutated and activated protein kinases have proved to be tractable targets for the development of new anticancer therapies. At http://www. sanger.ac.uk/genetics/CGP/Kinases/, it examined the full coding sequence of the protein kinase genes (518 protein kinases, more than 1.3Mb of DNA per sample) in primary cancers and cancer cell lines. Targeting receptor protein tyrosine kinases (RPTKs) as a cancer chemotherapy has continued to become a compelling approach for a long time. Preclinical and clinical data strongly support the involvement of specific RPTKs in the formation and progression of a subset of solid and liquid tumors. Table 12.1 presents a list of genes with respect to specified kinase categories. Suppose one gene is found to be related to a kinase group, or its families or subfamilies, we are able to link genes and diseases via kinases. For example, in Table 12.2, AGC kinase group is a frequent cause of many diseases. Kinase types can be viewed as the key, by which a comprehensive regulatory networks for protein kinases, genes and diseases can be generated.

A data mining method for gene search in a specific process is used to identify the common genomic pathways between periodontitis and type 2 diabetes [69]. ENDEAVOUR software is applied to prioritize all genes of the whole genome in relation to type 2 diabetes [291]. A regularized Bayesian integration system, HEFalMp (Human Experimental/Functional Mapper, http://function.princeton. edu/hefalmp), aims to provide maps of functional activity and interaction networks in over 200 areas of human cellular biology. It allows users to interactively explore functional maps integrating evidence from thousands of genomic experiments, focusing as desired on specific genes, processes, or diseases of interest [155].

Bioinformatics has been widely applied to explore kinase-disease associations. Ingenuity Pathway Analysis (IPA) software (Ingenuity Systems, www.ingenuity.com) was used to construct sub-networks significantly associated with OSA (obstructive sleep apnea) [38]. The results indicate a novel association of Phosphoinositide 3-kinase, the STAT family of proteins and its related pathways with OSA.

IPA, MetaCore (http://www.genego.com/metacore.php), sigPathway algorithm (http://watson.nci.nih.gov/bioc_mirror/packages/2.3/bioc/html/sigPathway.html) were carried out to understand the basis for drug efficacy in the mouse model, by which to map similarities in mTOR pathways in human lupus nephritis [258]. Gene set enrichment analysis (GSEA) version 2.0 [300] identified biological pathways associated with resistance for each chemotherapy agent tested. Based on the rank-ordered gene list provided by GSEA, the top genes up-regulated and down-regulated for docetaxel resistance were analyzed using the Connectivity Map (cmap) to link genes associated with a phenotype with potential therapeutic agents.

The kinase-disease associations can be seen at http://www.cellsignal.com/reference/kinase_disease.html. It provides the information of kinases, including their groups, disease types and molecular basis. By using Hanks classification scheme [128, 129], the human protein kinases can be clustered into groups, families, subfamilies on the basis of the amino acid sequence similarity of their catalytic domains. The reported diseases mainly consist of cancer, diabetes, cardiovascular, behavior, cardiopulmonary, neurodegeneration, vision, cognition, hypertension, inflammation. Table 12.2 presents a summary for kinase-disease associations. The investigation of their associations is useful to create regulatory pathways for drug desgin. For example, AMPK (AMP-activated protein kinase) may have a regulatory role in metabolism [101] and the therapeutic value of activating AMPK in diabetes or metabolic syndrome is described in [64]. It is observed that the associations described in Table 12.2 are crossed. For example, *cancer* and *development* are all related to AGC kinase group, whereas they usually link to different specific kinases, such as Akt1, Akt2, LATS1, LATS2 for cancer, and RSK2 for *development*. In contrast, some diseases may often arise from same kinases, such as p70S6K from AGC for cancer and diabetes. Further, they may have similar or discrepant molecular basses. For example, Abl1 and ACK are all from TK kinase group and are connected to cancer, whereas their molecular bases are translocation and amplification, respectively. In contrast, ACTR2B and ALK1 from TKL kinase group in relation to development and cardiovascular diseases, respectively have the same molecular type, mutation.

Given a known protein kinase, it is not difficult to identify its related diseases in terms of the known relations. If the protein kinase is related to more than one disease, its molecular basis can help us prune unrelated disease. For example, Akt2 are found to link to cancer and diabetes, whereas its molecular basis for cancer and diabetes is overexpression and mutation, respectively. If the protein kinase cannot be found in the database, the sequence and structure similarity can be considered for drug design. Protein kinases have been classified using their sequence and structure, which frequently, though not always, correlates with their biological functions. In [186], it proposes a relevant classification of the protein kinase family based on the structural similarity of its binding sites. The classification can be used to identify protein kinase binding sites that are known experimentally to bind the same drug. Traditional sequence alignment and phylogenetic approaches are used to cluster the prokaryotic kinases. Similarly subfamilies which are specific to an order, sub-order, class,

**Table 12.2** Summary of kinase-disease associations

| Disease types | Kinase group |
|---|---|
| Cancer | AGC, Atypical, CAMK, CK1, CMGC, RGC, TK, TKL, STE, |
| Development | AGC, Atypical, CMGC, RGC, STE, TK, TKL |
| Diabetes | AGC, CMGC, TK |
| Cardiovascular | AGC, CAMK, CMGC, TKL |
| Behavior | CK1, TKL |
| Hypertension | AGC, CAMK, RGC |
| Neurodegeneration | AGC, CAMK, CMGC, CK1 |
| Inflammation | CMGC, STE, TKL |
| Vision | AGC, RGC, TK |
| Epilepsy | CAMK, TK |
| Cognition | AGC, CMGC, STE, TKL |
| Immunity | AGC, TK |
| Reproduction | AGC, TKL |

family and genus have also been identified [309]. Cluster 49 is Chlamydiales specific, and Chlamydia trachomatis belonging to same order causes trachoma which leads to blindness and sexually transmitted disease in human beings. Cavbase [194], a method for describing and comparing protein binding pockets, is applied to the functional classification of the binding pockets of the protein family of protein kinases. A diverse set of kinase cavities is mutually compared and analyzed in terms of recurring functional recognition patterns in the active sites. As a result, the investigation of correlations between protein kinases, diseases, and molecular types assists in correct and accurate drug design for kinase related diseases.

## 12.3   Bioinformatics and Protein Kinase

### 12.3.1   Kinase Data Resources

There has been an increasing growth of diverse protein kinase data. The tremendous data is not only valuable resource for deep understanding of kinase pathways and is a big challenge for further data analysis for drug design. A number of kinase databases have been established for storage, management and other purposes. Table 12.3 presents a collection of data sources of protein kinases.

**KKB** (Kinase Knowledgebase) is Eidogen-Sertanty's database of kinase structure-activity and chemical synthesis data. Eidogen-Sertanty's knowledgebase provides high quality training sets for computational scientists to build predictive QSAR models. This is designed to support medicinal chemists during all project stages of drug discovery, and aims to ensure that the clients receive all the relevant information around their targets and anti-targets.

The availability of structural information makes kinases ideal targets for SBDD (Structure-Based Drug Discovery) techniques. The KKB has been used in drug

**Table 12.3** Resources of Information about Kinases

| Data source | Contents |
|---|---|
| http://bioinf.uta.fi/KinMutBase/ | Information about kinases, gene and mutation in KinMutBase, and alignments of sequences in KinMutBase |
| http://www.kinasource.co.uk/Database/substrates.html | kinase substrate |
| http://kinase.com/ | Kinome, the full complement of protein kinases in any sequenced genome |
| http://kinasedb.ontology.ims.u-tokyo.ac.jp:8081/ | Classification of protein kinases and their functional conservation ortholog tables among species, protein-protein, protein-gene, and protein-compound interaction data, domain information, and structural information. |
| http://www.itb.cnr.it/kinweb/ | A collection of protein kinases encoded in the human genome |
| http://www.proqinase.com/content/view/82 | Protein Kinase Technology Platform for preclinical drug development of protein kinase inhibitors in oncology and other therapeutic areas |
| http://sequoia.ucsf.edu/ksd/ | A comprehensive compilation of aliases for each kinase |
| http://hodgkin.mbu.iisc.ernet.in/king2/cgi-bin/index | A detailed classification based on sequence similarity of eukaryotic protein kinases, assignment of functional domains to the gene products containing the kinase catalytic domain |

discovery projects to investigate a number of different hypotheses. An in-house X-ray structure of a high-throughput screening hit revealed the hinge-interaction binding motif [31]. In structure-based design practices, an analysis of a known drug target can reasonably start with a review of ligands that have been crystallized with the target. The KKB was used to investigate this observation further and to see what other kinases have been crystallized in the DFG-out form with ligands that do not conform to the common DFG-out pharmacophore [32].

**KinBase** explores the functions, evolution and diversity of protein kinases, the key controllers of cell behavior. It focuses on the kinome, and the kinome of an organism represents the set of protein kinases in its genome [146]. The term was first used by Gerard Manning and colleagues in their papers analyzing the 518 human protein kinases [215] and the evolution of protein kinases throughout eukaryotes. KinBase holds information on over 3,000 protein kinase genes found in the genomes of human, and many other sequenced genomes. Users can search the database by different gene names and accessions, or in terms of the sequence based classification. It provides Blast analysis of the human kinome by comparing mouse kinome to human kinome, and carried out kinome analysis of several important organisms.

A study [197] developed kinome-wide proteochemometric models for the prediction of kinase-inhibitor interaction profiles, in which the sequences for the kinase domains were retrieved from KinBase database. It shows the routes to concomitant proteochemometric kinome wide modelling will markedly speed-up the discovery and optimization of protein kinase targeted and multi-targeted drugs.

Base on the data from KinBase, structurally conserved mutational hotspots are found to be probably shared by multiple kinase genes and are often enriched by cancer driver mutations with high oncogenic activity [81]. Structure-based functional annotation and prediction of cancer mutation effects in protein kinases are found to able to facilitate an understanding of the mutation-dependent activation process and inform experimental studies exploring molecular pathology of tumorigenesis.

**Kinweb** [229] includes a collection of protein kinases encoded in the human genome. It provides: a comprehensive analysis of functional domains of each gene product; a prediction of secondary and tertiary structure motifs by using machine learning based programs; a collection of conserved sequence elements identified by comparative analysis of human kinase genes and their murine counterparts, useful to the identification of additional coding sequences. The users can query the database by gene name or query the database by selecting a classification group or a protein domain.

**KSD (Kinase Sequence Database)** is a collection of protein kinase sequences grouped into families by homology of their catalytic domains. The aligned sequences are available in MS Excel format, as well as in HTML. The current version of database features a total of 287 families, which contain 7128 protein kinases from 948 organisms. Protein kinase inhibitors are important targets for designing therapeutic drugs. A comparative sequence/structure analysis finds the amino acid distributions of a large number of protein kinases near the ligand-binding sites [116]. This analysis provides useful guiding principles for designing specific inhibitors targeted towards a particular kinase.

KinAce is a platform technology for the protein-sequence-based development of small peptide-derived kinase inhibitors [157]. The initial step in developing the KinAce platform was the identification and characterization of key well-defined regions within protein kinases involved in substrate binding. The next step in KinAce platform development was the systematic derivation of potential peptide inhibitors based on the sequence of these novel substrate-binding regions. These technologies have already been used to develop potential chemotherapeutic drug candidates and to reveal novel targets for various indications. One such candidate is KRX-123, which has been developed as a treatment for hormone refractory prostate cancer–a highly lethal disease for which therapeutic interventions are limited.

**KPD (Kinase Pathway Database)** is an integrated database involving major completely sequenced eukaryotes. It also provides an automatic pathway graphic image interface. The protein, gene, and compound interactions are automatically extracted from abstracts for all genes and proteins by natural-language processing (NLP). With this database, pathways can be compared among species using data with more than 47,000 protein interactions and protein kinase ortholog tables.

Despite the valuable protein kinase data, their deep analysis are insufficient and their communication are underdeveloped. This prevents us from obtaining a comprehensive understanding of the kinase pathways and their potential usage in drug discovery. Thus, it is critical to apply bioinformatics to deal with protein kinase data for accurate and efficient drug design.

## 12.3.2  Data Analysis for Drug Design

There are many methods or tools used to address the above kinase data, such as features of kinase sequence and structures, kinase classification and identification. This article focuses on extending these databases for the purpose of drug design, and elucidating the procedures or methods to design the drug delivery system based on the data analysis.

**Kinase Pathways.** To fully understand protein kinase networks, it is critical to identify regulators and substrates of kinases, especially for weakly expressed proteins. The kinase pathways mainly include:

- *Kinase docking site.* A hybrid computational search algorithm has been developed, which integrates machine learning and expert knowledge to discover kinase docking sites. This algorithm was used to search the human genome for novel MAP kinase substrates and regulators focused on the JNK family of MAP kinases [306].

  There are many efforts to target MAPK/D-site interactions for therapeutic purposes, using either peptides or more traditional small molecule compounds [18]. Clearly, they will be facilitated by information regarding D-site selectivity. The docking interacting sites facilitate interaction with protein partners, such as substrates, upstream regulators, or adaptor proteins. Disruption of these interactions may be a way to impair selective kinase-mediated signaling pathways, and, thus, peptide-based docking sites may be exploited for selective inhibition and is viewed as potential nontoxic drug compound [171]. A study uses multiple bioinformatics tools to discover candidate MAPK docking site motifs on HIV proteins known to be phosphorylated by MAPKs, and discusses the possibility of targeting docking sites with drugs. ERK1/2 docking with HIV proteins is examined from a drug design perspective using multiple alignments of HIV proteins classified according to subtype [95].

- *Phosphorylation profiles of regulators.* Cluster 3.0 [75] is used to classify the phosphorylation profiles of regulators, which are constructed by quantifying response regulator bands in each profile. Further, the profile is visualized using Java Treeview [268]. It is applied to dissect the basis of phosphotransfer specificity in two-component signaling pathways in [36].

- *Kinase isoform association.* Association rule mining is used to analyze the AMPK regulation data derived from the published experimental results [47]. A number of rules of interest are discovered from mining AMPK data, such as $A = \{moderate\ intensity\ treadmill\} \Rightarrow B = \{high\ expression\ of\ \beta_{2a}\ ,\ high\ expression\ of\ \gamma_{2a}\ \}$. They reveals numerous potential associations between the states of subunit isoforms of AMPK, or between the stimulus factor and the state of isoforms, many of which are useful for drug design. Further, negative rule association [324], represented as the forms of $X \rightarrow \neg Y$, $\neg X \rightarrow Y$ or $\neg X \rightarrow \neg Y$ can be applied for investigating the potential inhibitive regulatory correlation between the subunit isoforms of protein kinases, and the stimulus factors. In addition, advanced bioinformatics and systems biology tools assist in unlocking network properties and modeling kinase pathways. Recent examples are the development of a predictor for breast cancer prognosis based on the modularity of protein interaction networks and the identification of cancer-associated phosphorylation networks through the combined alignment of conserved phosphorylation sites and kinase-substrate networks [192]. An efficient framework based on hidden Markov models (HMMs) is presented for finding homologous pathways in a network of interest [255].

The obtained kinase pathways provide valuable sources for drug design. Kinase cascade presents novel opportunities for the development of new cancer therapies designed to be less toxic than conventional chemotherapeutic drugs. Furthermore, as a signal transduction-based approach to cancer treatment, inhibition of any one of these targets has the potential for translational pharmacodynamic evaluation of target suppression [282]. Deciphering the operation of protein interaction network is important to understand disease processes and therapeutic opportunities [5]. A fuzzy logic approach is applied to model the responses of colon cancer cells in culture to combinations of pro-survival and pro-death cytokines, making it possible to interpret quantitative data in the context of abstract information drawn from the literature. This establishes that fuzzy logic can be used to understand complex kinase pathways with respect to multi-factorial activity-based protein data and prior knowledge. Microarray-Assisted Pathway Analysis identifies mitogen-activated protein kinase signaling as a mediator of resistance to the Green Tea polyphenol epigallocatechin 3-Gallate (EGGG) in Her-2/neu-overexpressing breast cancer cells [122]. Treatment of the resistant cells with the MAPK inhibitor U0216 reduced growth in soft agar and invasive phenotype, whereas the combination of EGCG and U0216 resulted in cells with a cobblestone epithelial phenotype. Thus, activation of the MAPK pathway mediates resistance to EGCG.

**Kinase Gene.** A rational approach is presented for identifying and ranking protein kinases that are likely responsible for observed changes in gene expression [14]. By combining promoter analysis, it can identify and rank candidate protein kinases for knock-down, or other types of functional validations, based on genome-wide changes in gene expression. This describes how protein kinase candidate identification and ranking can be made robust by cross-validation with phosphoproteomics data as well as through a literature-based text-mining approach. Inappropriate activation of AKT signaling is a relatively common occurrence in human tumors, and can be caused by activation of components of, or by loss or decreased activity of inhibitors of this signaling pathway. Causal network modeling is a systematic computational analysis that identifies upstream changes in gene regulation that can serve as explanations for observed changes in gene expression [195].

An evidence might suggest a role for fyn-kinase in modulating GABAA receptor function, possibly via direct interactions between the kinase and receptor. It is observed that deletion of the fyn-Kinase Gene alters sensitivity to GABAergic Drugs by depending $\beta_2/\beta_3$ GABAA Receptor Subunits [29]. One of the recent strategies for gene therapy as a cancer control is the targeted introduction of a drug-sensitivity gene into tumor cells. The gene transfer of herpes simplex virus type I thymidine kinase (HSV-TK) gene is investigated as a drug-sensitivity gene into human lung cancer cell lines. ACV and GCV are nucleoside analogs specifically converted by HSV-TK to a toxic form capable of inhibiting DNA synthesis. These findings suggest that the gene transfer of HSV-TK gene into tumor cells would be one of the models for the use of gene therapy to control lung cancer [133].

Resistance to a particular drug can also occur if there is a deletion or disabling of an enzyme required to activate that drug. For example, for the drug cytosine arabinoside to become cytotoxic, it must first be activated by deoxycytidine kinase in the cancerous cells. Cancers with mutations or deletions in this kinase gene are resistant to the drug [149]. A study identifies the association between the casein kinase 1 epsilon gene region and subjective response to D-Amphetamine [312].

The correlations between expression levels of drug target genes and the activity of the drugs against the NCIs 60 cell line panel were calculated across and within each tumor tissue type, using published drug activity and gene expression data. TCN-Ps mechanism of action and the observed TCN-P:ADK association present catalytic drug activation provides a rational, mechanistic basis for personalizing cancer treatment based on tumorspecific differences in the expression of drug-activating enzymes [286].

**Kinase Inhibition.** While system biology and personalized medicine are becoming increasingly important, there is a urgent need to map the inhibition profile of a compound on a large panel of targets by using both experimental and computational methods. This is especially important for kinase inhibitors, given the high similarity at the binding site level for the 518 kinases in the human genome. A new method is proposed and validated to predict the inhibition map of a compound by comparison of binding pockets [231].

The discovered kinase inhibitors using bioinformatics have potential for treatment of many diseases. However, current inhibitors interact with a broad variety of kinases and interfere with multiple vital cellular processes, which causes toxic effects. Bioinformatics approaches that can predict inhibitor-kinase interactions from the chemical properties of the inhibitors and the kinase macromolecules might aid in design of more selective therapeutic agents, that show better efficacy and lower toxicity. Proteochemometric modelling is applied to correlate the properties of 317 wild-type and mutated kinases and 38 inhibitors to the respective combination's interaction dissociation constant (Kd) [197]. A report of protein kinases as targets for inhibitor design in [219] is presented as follows:

- **Receptor tyrosine kinases.** Dysregulation of growth factor signaling networks has been reported in multiple human cancers. Binding of growth factors to extracellular domains of receptor tyrosine kinases activates the intracellular kinase domain. Based on EGFR (epidermal growth factor receptor) and VEGFR (the vascular endothelial growth factor receptor), different therapeutic agents have been developed for anticancer drug development.
- **Nonreceptor tyrosine kinases.** About one third of tyrosine kinases are classed as nonreceptor tyrosine kinases.
- **Phosphatidylinositol 3-kinase (PI3K).** Resistance to radiation treatment in a number of cancers has been linked to activation of the PI3K-AKT pathway, which suggests that inhibition of PI3K to overcome resistance and to improve the efficacy of radiation treatment is an attractive clinical goal [226].
- **Signal-transducing serine-threonine kinases.** p38 selective inhibition could be a therapeutically useful target route to treatment of a number of inflammatory and autoimmune diseases [250].
- **Cyclin-dependent kinases (CDKs) and other cell cycleCcontrol kinases.** Nature has provided many useful CDK inhibitors that have reached clinical

trials. High-throughput screening of compound libraries has also disocvered many
CDK inhibitors.

The study of kinase inhibitors interaction assists us to find optimized pathways
with less side effect for drug design, whereas structure analysis for inhibitors is
needed to guarantee correct and accurate drug development. Structures information have provided insights into targeting the inactive or active form of the kinase,
for targeting the global constellation of residues at the ATP site or less conserved
additional pockets or single residues, and into targeting noncatalytic
domains [219]. Computer-aided efforts, including molecular dynamics (MD) simulations and anisotropic network model (ANM) normal mode analysis, are used
for generating potential ligand-bound conformers starting from the apo state of
p38 [16]. A structure modeling-based method is developed for sequence and structure analysis, which is helpful in identifying the ligand binding sites and molecular function of the Leishmania specific mitogen-activated protein kinase [273].
SiteAlign algorithm [275] is used to measure the similarity of druggable protein-
ligand binding sites to the ATP-binding site of Pim-1 kinase (PDB entry 1yhs with
bound inhibitor staurosporine) [74].

## 12.4  Kinase Genes for Drug Tragets

Many kinase genes have been identified in the human genomes, and other sequenced
genomes. For example, KinBase holds information on over 3,000 protein kinase
genes. Many databases provide searching tools in terms of a variety of different
gene names and accessions, or according to the sequence based classification. The
challenge to bioinformatics is evolving from that of identifying long lists of genes
to that of determining short lists of the targets most likely to play central roles in
diseases.

A variety of gene identification algorithms have been developed in drug discovery, including the identification of positions, secondary structures and functions.
Nevertheless, the discussion of these algorithms are not the key point in this article.
In contrast, this paper focuses on describing the drug design targeted by the kinase
gene identification.

### 12.4.1  Kinase Gene Identification and Drug Design

A number of algorithms and tools are developed for gene identification. As described in [193], they can include software tools for 1) *Ab initio* gene prediction, 2)
*splicing site* prediction, and 3) *homology-based* prediction. *ab initio* gene prediction
relies on the own information in the DNA sequence, such as promoter, intro or exon,
and use statistical parameter to predict genes. In contract, *homology-based* prediction depends primarily on finding homologous sequences in other genomes and/or in

public databases using BLAST, or Smith-Waterman algorithms. This method compares newly obtained sequence data from experiments with known gene information. It uses sequence alignment to construct gene models and validates the predicted genes through similarity searches including sequence similarity or structure similarity. *Splicing site* prediction is commonly used as complement in the gene prediction tools.

***Ab Initio* Gene Prediction.** Many software tools can be publicly accessed for *ab initio* gene prediction. The representative works include GeneMark (`http://exon.gatech.edu/GeneMark/`), GENSCAN (`http://genes.mit.edu/GENSCAN.html`), GeneBuilder (`http://http://zeus2.itb.cnr.it/~webgene/genebuilder.html/`). GeneMark employed a non-homogeneous Markov model to classify DNA regions into protein-coding, non-coding, and non-coding but complementary to coding. GENSCAN uses a complex probabilistic model of the gene structure that is based on actual biological information about the properties of transcriptional, translational, and splicing signals. GeneBuilder is an integrated computing system for protein-coding gene prediction.

Gene predictions from ab initio or sequence similarity can be used against databases of known effective drug target classes, such as GPCRs, proteases, ion channels, hormone nuclear receptors, kinases, and so on, to uncover novel members of these gene families. Using this approach, it is relatively easy to identify novel genes belonging to high-value, therapeutic target classes. Discovery genomics using databases and informatics tools is not the only strategy to identify genes of interest to the industry. By using human disease populations and identifying gene variants, it is possible to identify disease susceptibility genes, which is known as discovery genetics. Using this approach, novel genes will be disease validated but might not belong to a tractable class of targets, and functional analysis will focus on the disease allele and might require pathway expansion to identify a tractable gene target.

***Splicing Site* Prediction.** NNSplice (`http://www.fruitfly.org/seq_tools/splice.html`). Spliceview (`http://zeus2.itb.cnr.it/~webgene/wwwspliceview.html`), NetGene2 (`http://www.cbs.dtu.dk/services/NetGene2/`) are three typical methods for *splicing site* prediction. NNSplice uses a decision tree method called maximal dependence decomposition (MDD), and enhances it with Markov models that capture additional dependencies among neighboring bases in a region around the splice site. Spliceview is based on prediction of splice signals by classification approach. Neural networks in combination with sequence similarity are trained to recognize splice sites by NetGene2.

***Homology-Based* Prediction.** PipMaker (`http://pipmaker.bx.psu.edu/pipmaker/`) and GeneWise(http://www.ebi.ac.uk/Tools/Wise2/index.html) are tools for *homology-based* prediction. The former compares two long DNA sequences to identify conserved segments in terms of the alignment engine called BlastZ and a scoring matrices. The latter was developed from a combination of hidden Markov models to predict gene structure using similar protein sequence.

Sequence similarity and structure similarity are widely used strategies in gene identification for functional genomic. A variety of approaches have been developed for measuring the similarities, such as BLAST and FASTA for sequence similarity, DALI (distance alignment matrix method used a Monte Carlo simulation) [141] for protein alignment and FOLDALIGN for RNA structural alignment [135]. Recent studies indicate that RNA structures perform many important regulatory, structural, and catalytic roles in the cell. They have been found in most organism and comprise functional domains within ribozymes, self-splicing introns, ribonucleoprotein complexes, viral genomes, and many other biological systems [1]. Association rule mining is applied to identify hidden structure-function patterns within RNA [48, 49].

The identified kinase genes are critical for drug design. The prevalent somatic genetic alterations leading to the inactivation of the tumor suppressor gene PTEN and gain-of-function mutations targeting PIK3CA-the gene encoding the catalytic phosphosinositide-3 kinase subunit p110$\alpha$ [89]. A number of the intracellular components of PIK3 pathway have been targeted as anticancer drug discovery activities leading to the current panoply of clinical trials of inhibitors of PI3K, Akt and HSP90 in man.

Recently, multi-target drugs against selective multiple targets improve therapeutic efficacy, safety and resistance profiles by collective regulations of a primary therapeutic target together with compensatory elements and resistance activities. A comprehensive kinome interaction network based not only on sequence comparisons but also on multiple pharmacology parameters derived from activity profiling data [228]. The framework described for statistical interpretation of these network connections also enables rigorous investigation of chemotype-specific interaction networks, which is critical for multitargeted drug design.

Many diseases, including cancer, diabetes, and inflammation, are related to perturbation of protein kinase-mediated cell signaling pathways.The HER2/Neu gene product is upregulated in the tumor cells of about 30% of breast cancer patients. This finding provided the rationale for the development of Herceptin. In clinical trials, Herceptin alone proved effective in treatment for 15% of patients with HER2-overexpressing metastatic breast cancer and was more effective when used in combination with chemotherapy agents.

Chemogenomics as an approach that structures the early-stage drug discovery process in conjunction with gene (or, more correctly, protein) families. It has been described as the discovery and description of all possible drugs for all possible drug targets. Although SAR-based strategies provide excellent opportunities to relate proteins through their selectivity profiles against test compounds they are not able to offer predictions for proteins outside the training set. In comparison, sequence-based strategies can predict ligand affinity profiles for all members of a protein family. However, because they are not explicitly trained to reproduce SAR-based classifications, they lack the same level of resolution as the SAR-based approaches [132].

## 12.4.2  Challenges in Drug Discovery

The completion of Human Genome project had assembled a genetic blueprint for human being. Genome science has accelerated genetic research and revolutionized the diagnosis, prevention and treatment of various diseases. Genetics has showed its significance in clinical medicine. It collects and studies medical histories and DNA samples from family members. Genetic analysis of these samples assists researchers in finding genes or patterns of genes that are different among affected and unaffected family members and that may be related to the disease. Genetic testing aids in defining clinical indicators of a hereditary predisposition to develop cancers.

In recent years, there have been an explosive growth of disease genes such as oncogenies found due to the high throughput screening. For example, Cancer Gene (https://cabig.nci.nih.gov/inventory/data-resources/cancer-gene-index) Index is a collection of records on 6,955 human genes identified from the literature as having an association with cancer. Diabetes Disease Portal (http://rgd.mcw.edu/) provides gene information for several diseases, such as diabetes, obesity and metabolic diseases. It is observed that genes and diseases might be cross-correlated. Bioinformatics is an efficient way to validate those discovered targets and sort out short lists of the targets most possibly to be critical in disease.

The identification of susceptibility genes for cancers allows testing before symptoms become apparent. If a single gene is responsible, testing during pregnancy or at any other appropriated time of life for the specific cancer may predict a high risk or eliminate concern about that particular cancer. For example, if a person is found to carry an inherited mutation in one of the cancer mutation repair genes, he/she could benefit from annual fixed examination. Thus, any pathological changed would be detected and eliminated before they progress to a potentially invasive cancer.

Microarray allow the gene expression profiles of thousands of genes to be measured and compared with each other in cells and tissues between healthy and diseased states. Those genes that are functionally associated usually share similar expression profiles. To ensure the accuracy, the microarray data is combined with pathways that exist in the context of complex protein-protein interaction networks. It is necessary to use gene ontologies (GO), which describes gene products in terms of their associated biological processes, cellular components and molecular functions in a species-independent manner.

Most of the genetic disorders originate from a mutation in one gene. One of the most difficult issues is to determine how genes contribute to diseases that have a complex pattern of inheritance, such as in the cases of diabetes, asthma and cancer. In other words, no one gene is able to definitely say whether a person has a disease or not. It is possible that several mutations occur before the disease is evident, and many genes may each partially contribute to a person's susceptibility to a disease; genes may also affect a person's reactions to environmental factors. It is a big challenge to unravel these networks of events. It will be undoubtedly assisted by the availability of the sequence of the human genome [147].

## 12.5  Conclusions

Emerging varied diseases have been a big challenge to current health care system. Many evidences indicate protein kinases are involved in a number of diseases. Many diseases have their roots in genes. Thus, the study of abnormalities, disorder or mutation of kinase genes is a promising and efficient way for drug target discovery because they can change the function of genes and have an effect on relevant diseases. The discovery of protein kinase networks including kinase types, diseases, inhibitors and kinome assist us in understanding the root cause of diseases. Bioinformatics combing genetics and genomics technologies has become a critical aspect of drug discovery. Applying bioinformatics into target discovery and data management can not only increase the efficiency and accuracy of drug design and generate personalized drug development. This chapter reviews the techniques for protein kinase networks, including kinase data, kinase inhibitors, kinase gene families, and their properties. Further, the relevant algorithms, tools and the associations between kinome and drug discovery are highlighted.

# Chapter 13
# Conclusion and Future Works

In this book, a brief history and survey of the state of the art in the field of data integration, modeling and pattern identification with respect to pathway mining and presented a number of potential and challenging directions in which it could be extended. The prospects of the application of bioinformatics to pathway analysis have attracted increasing attentions in the past two decades due to the importance of pathway in understanding complex regulatory networks of biology systems. In recent years, these approaches and techniques have been showing their maturity and consolidation. A lot of specialized or general-purpose algorithms and tools have been proposed and used to realistic pathway data analysis, in many cases generating interesting and valuable biology knowledge to biologist that can be further applied to enhance and prompt the relevant study of life science, such as disease diagnosis and drug design. However, it is necessary for us to recognize that some emerging challenges, such as new and complex systems biology and meta-genome and new types of regulatory factors, such as long ncRNA, give rise to new requirements to existing pathway data analysis. Any efforts to discover and construct pathways must taken them into account. These give rise some a series of important issues that need to be investigated for improving the correctness and efficiency of pathway mining.

This chapter summarizes those challenging issues as emerging trends to be confronted with and probable future difficult points to be handled. In Section 13.1, a brief summary to the previous twelve chapters is presented. In Section 13.2, several emerging research fields and challenging issues in pathway analysis are discussed and highlighted.

## 13.1 Conclusion

A collection of bioinformatics applications to pathway analysis are presented in this monograph. It starts from the conventional data mining techniques for pathway analysis and related data resources, and move to recently developed methods by us for coping with pathway data integration and featured pattern identification in specific applications of regulatory network. The key points are:

1. Chapter 1 presents the definition of regulatory pathways, including key regulatory components. A survey of relevant works is provided to explain their limitations and the motivation and importance to apply advanced bioinformatics in emerging challenging issues of pathway analysis.
2. A collection of available data resources for pathway analysis are provided in Chapter 2. The databases are presented by separating them into specific classes. Further, some prevalent bioinformatics applications are discussed.
3. Chapter 3 presented an ontology-based framework for evaluating the inconsistency in biological databases. It provides a metric to compute the inconsistency and determine whether the databases are appropriate for further data mining applications.
4. Chapter 4 proposed a framework based on association rule mining especially used for the analysis of AMP-activated protein kinase regulation. Item constraints are used to control the generation of interesting patterns, which assist biologists in understanding the regulation functions of AMPK.
5. Chapter 5 develops a Bayesian network-based graphical models for exploring protein kinase regulation patterns. Unlike association rule, BN identifies kinase regulation in terms of a dependency correlation of probability. In particular, an intuitive graphical model is derived to indicate the frequent connections.
6. Unlike identification of positive association of protein kinase, Chapter 6 aims to study the inhibitive correlation with respect to AMPK subunit and stimulus factors. This unveils a number of hidden and unknown negative patterns. The combination of positive and negative rules gives rise to some new knowledge.
7. In Chapter 7, a novel framework is proposed to model conserved RNA secondary structures according to a collection of distance constraints. Further, a search schema using marked labels and support function is applied to find the matched candidate model. However, it is observed that only the modeling strategy and general searching space reduction is still hard to distinguish high similar structures. As a result, Chapter 8 develops a *Hausdorff distance*-based metric to measure the similarity between RNA pseudoknots. Unlike traditional *Euclidean distance* and *Manhattan distance*, the position of objects are considered, namely *perfect match*, *partially overlapped* and *non-overlapped*. Chapter 9 proposes a novel method by combing association rule with a conditional probability matrix. The obtained results disclose a number of interesting structure-function and structure-category relationships with respect to RNA pseudoknots.
8. Chapter 10 and Chapter 11 present methods for investigating the interesting patterns with respect to miRNA interaction, conserved and divergent miRNA structure patterns by combing sequence and structure similarity. Different methods are provided to bring about different results in terms of specific purpose. In a sense, these actually yield different options for users to deal with different problems in their own right. This is able to prompt the construction of miRNA-related pathways.

9. Protein kinases play important roles in varied pathways. Their deregulation has been proved to be clinically interesting for drug discovery. Thus, Chapter 12 provides a survey to bioinformatics application in data management and analysis.

Most of the aforementioned methods and techniques in this book are recent work carried out by authors. Some of them are derived from the literature review of important and representative outcomes with regard to pathway analysis. Unlike traditional pathway analysis that focuses on pathway databases and visualization, this monograph mainly explores the featured patterns of protein kinases and ncRNA, including data modeling, data integration and varied relationships or interactions. There are several novel and positive aspects to our work.

- Preliminary evaluation while mining heterogenous biology database. Our proposed approach is effective in not only integrating data from different data sources but also providing an intuitive way to measure the inconsistency between databases. The semantic issues are considered and QC model for knowledge base is applied. Further, this model can be combined with GO to deal with semantic heterogeneity of databases. Without doubt, this is able to guarantee correct and efficient data mining and can be done in a systematic way.
- Protein kinase regulation plays important modulatory roles in various pathways of biology systems. The investigation of relationships between subunit isoforms and between isoforms and stimulus can enhance the understanding of deep regulation mechanisms of protein kinases. The discovery of regulatory patterns of protein kinases by using association rule mining and Bayesian network not only uncovers the positive correlation by frequency but also quantifies the dependency by probability. The proposed *Top-N* and graphical model can be extended or adapted for relevant study in pathway mining.
- Mining negative regulatory patterns. The proposed algorithms and techniques include a constraint-based method to discover Top-N interesting frequent itemsets and negative rule group, and contain an entropy-based approach to unveil the underlying dependency between objects. The inhibitive regulation patterns are derived from interesting negative itemset that is actually infrequent. By analogy with support-confidence framework, mutual information assists in finding items with strong dependence, which ensures the mining efficiency and correctness to some extent.
- Modeling complex and diverse RNA secondary structures. The complexity and variation inherent in RNA structures prevent us from understanding their catalytical roles in genetic operating systems. Our developed method transforms the conserved structure into a set of nested stack, parallel stack and multiloop stack, and model them by using a set of distance interval and specific labels. This reduces the searching space and shows better performance than existing searching schema.
- Hausdorff distance-based metric for measuring RNA structure similarity. To distinguish a set of highly similar structures, an appropriate similarity measure must be provided. The relationships between distance intervals are integrated into the similarity computation. This is able to not only further differentiate between

obtained structures by search, but also aids in allocating the query to a correct function class.

- Discovery of miRNA interaction and conserved and divergent RNA structure patterns and sites. Our proposed joint entropy-based method enables the discovery of RNA interaction within-family and cross-family in terms of identified novel bridge rules. The discovered rules help users obtain a deep insight into the sequence and structure properties of corresponding species and specific RNA sites.

Bioinformatics for pathway data analysis is a challenging and extensive field. Unfortunately, it is impractical and impossible to directly range over or touch all the issues and all the ongoing work in this field. Nonetheless, the book attempts to provide a summary of recent and relevant works with regard to pathway study and presents several hot issues of identifying varied featured regulation patterns for pathway analysis, and applied them to realistic biology data mining, including protein kinase and ncRNA. Further, it proposes some novel ways to apply advanced data mining techniques for improving future pathway analysis.

## 13.2   Future Works

Systems biology is an interdisciplinary field within the life sciences that focuses on the systematic study of complex interactions in biological systems. The study of pathways is an important subfield of systems biology that is concerned with pathway algorithms, ontologies, visualizations, and databases. A pathway comprises one or more processes, each of which begins with input signals, uses various combinations of other input signals, such as cofactors, activators and inhibitors, and ends with output that exhibits functions. The most critical issue to be solved by researchers is the development of efficient algorithms for storage, modeling and analysis of complicated pathway data. It is critical to develop innovative approaches that aim at the sequential and cumulative actions of genetically distinct, but functionally related objects. However, there is a lack of intelligent technological strategies to tackle high-dimensional pathway data and investigate the properties of regulatory factors in pathways. There have been considerable efforts to develop effective methods for integration of biological databases and identification of kinase and gene-mediated pathways. It is essential that these aspects are understood and integrated into new algorithms and tools used in pathway data collection, analysis and interpretation.

**The Importance of Signalling Pathways.** Cells depend on a large number of clearly defined signalling pathways to regulate their activity. These signalling systems not only control development and regulate specific processes in adult cells, such as metabolism, proliferation, information processing in neurons and sensory perception. In general, cell signalling pathways coordinate with each other to regulate many different cellular processes. This intimate relationship between cell signalling and biology leads to valuable insights into the underlying genetic and phenotypic defects responsible for many of the major diseases of numerous species. A large number of diseases are caused by defects in signalling pathways, such as interference by pathogenic organisms and viruses. Most of the serious diseases in humans, such as heart disease and diabetes, appear to arise from subtle phenotypic modifications of pathways. This enables discovery of new ways of correcting many disease states.

MAPK/ERK pathway and cAMP dependent pathway are two major signalling pathways. The former is able to alter the translation of mRNA to proteins and regulates the activities of several transcription factors. By altering the levels and activities of transcription factors, MAPK gives rises to altered transcription of genes that are important for the cell cycle. The latter can activate enzymes and regulate gene expression. Many different cell responses are mediated by cAMP, such as increase in heart rate, and breakdown of glycogen and fat.

Many studies have been performed for characterizating signalling pathways. Nevertheless, the criteria by cells to determine the specific pathways and their regulatory networks are still unclear. It is thus important to explore the mechanisms that different pathways are combined to control a set of cellular processes, especially interaction between involved components, such as gene expression and phosphorylation for mediating enzyme inhibition, regulating protein-protein interaction and protein degradation. A number of pathway databases and repositories have been generated for management of the information of pathways together with their molecular components and reactions. It is critical to apply advanced data mining techniques for extraction of interesting knowledge about signalling pathways.

**The Need for Efficient Data Mining Strategies.** It is observed that the regulatory signals usually function in complex networks, characterized by an abundance of activators or inhibitors. Further, multiple specific inhibitors of all conserved signal pathways have been identified as modulators in organ or tissue development, regulators in metabolism, and cause of diseases. All these findings generate tremendous and diverse pathway data with respect to varied species. The deep analysis of the data have been a big challenge issue to comprehensively understand the complex regulatory networks during evolution.

To meet these requirements, we must develop innovative approaches aimed at the sequential and cumulative actions of genetically distinct, but functionally related objects. However, there is a lack of intelligent technology strategies to tackle the high-dimensional pathway data. Although a number of algorithms and tools have been developed for pathway data analysis, the emerging computation issues in post genome era become more challenging due to the increasing growth of data and components of regulatory networks. These require a systematic way of combining technologies, pathways and genomic data.

This book thus includes the original articles that propose solutions for this exciting new computational biology paradigm. It focuses on practical technologies and applications for pathway data analysis. We have tried to include articles from different research fields, such as plant biology and computer science, and different topics, such as protein- protein interaction and gene expression, which range over key issues of pathways.

The primary relevant fields can be divided into three main topics.

- **protein regulation.** Many approaches have been developed to predict protein-protein interaction(PPI) based on sequence alignment, which makes use of the similarity of two protein pairs through alignment. Nevertheless, the PPI is still far from determining their specific functions and complicated regulatory mechanisms in pathways. Genome-scale interaction networks yield a great deal of valuable resources for studying the functional organization of cells and understanding their regulatory roles and mechanisms. Biological networks can be naturally and conveniently viewed as graphs, in which the nodes represent the participated entities (such as proteins) in a given network and the edges highlight the interactions between them. It may be an effective and feasible ways to apply network alignment for comparing the networks of different organisms by aligning these graphs and identifying their common substructures. This is able to facilitate the discovery of conserved functional modules and eventually assist us explore their functions and the detailed molecular mechanisms that contribute to these functions.
- **Inhibitory regulatory network.** The deregulation pathways have been proved to result in a variety of growth defects and abnormalities and physiological disorders. Many evidences show a tight correlation between pathways and inhibitory genes of diseases. In real regulatory network, the inhibition of genes is usually stronger than activation, and many genes interact with their upstream and downstream genes to construct a regulatory network. Organisms often rely on a family of protein kinases to regulate important biological process, such as memory, anti-hormones and cell growth. These protein kinases are usually activated due to changes in cellular energy level, and the activation have a long-term effect on the levels gene expression and protein synthesis. Thus, the analysis and interpretation of protein kinase inhibition regulation data promote a better understanding of its structure, function and expression characteristics. With the introduction of systems biology, many researches have been done to identify various biological conserved interaction networks, such as protein interaction (PPI) networks, gene regulatory networks. Not only do they effectively find many known biological pathways, and successfully predict a statistically significant new pathways. However many algorithms show limitations while dealing with large or complex sub-structures. The emergence of high-throughput technologies for molecular interactions to promote large-scale systematic study. Since biological functions are realized by a large number of activated and inhibitive regulation network, a comparative analysis of these networks assists us in comprehensively understanding the functional organization of biological systems.
- **gene expression.** With the rapid development of bioinformatics, the complex and varied regulation data makes it difficult to analyze by using traditional clustering methods. The introduction of bi-clustering method into multi-objectives inhibitive regulation pathway analysis might be a very effective way. Different types of genes and proteins may have discrepant expression while the condition is different. In particularly, the same gene or protein may have different expression under different times, different states or different environments. And there may be some degree of contact between their differential expression. How to

improve the existing bi-clustering algorithm to better describe and discover these regulatory networks is an important and challenging research issue.

The pathway analysis have become a ubiquitous research topic in post genome era since they play central roles in many cellular functions. Thus, the study of characterized pathways and their components is not only a big challenge and a good opportunity for researchers. The inherent complexity and diversity of system biology demand for collaboration of scientists from biology, computer science and mathematics. This gives rise to promising and challenging research issues for pathways described in this monograph.

- Protein regulation, including protein-protein interaction network, annotation and analysis of large scale proteome, phosphorylation sites.
- Gene regulatory network, including genes related stress-resistance mechanisms and gene transcriptional regulatory network.
- Gene expression, including sequential, temporal and inhibitive behaviors, and multi-objectives and bi-direction mining in gene expression analysis.

# References

1. Aalberts, D.P., et al.: Asymmetry in RNA pseudoknots: observation and theory. Nucleic Acids Res. 33(7), 2210–2214
2. Aalberts, D.P., Parman, J.M., Goddard, N.L.: Single-strand stacking free energy from DNA beacon kinetics. Biophys. J. 84, 3212–3217 (2003)
3. Adams, P.L., Stahley, M.R., Kosek, A.B., Wang, J., Strobel, S.A.: Crystal structure of a self-splicing group I intron with both exons. Nature 430(6995), 45–50 (2004)
4. Agrawal, R., Imielinshki, T., Swami, A.: Mining Association Rules between Sets of Items in Large Databases. In: Proceeding of ACM-SIGMOD International Conference on Management of Data, pp. 207–216 (1993)
5. Aldridge, B.B., Saez-Rodriguez, J., Muhlich, J.L., Sorger, P.K., Lauffenburger, D.A.: Fuzzy Logic Analysis of Kinase Pathway Crosstalk in TNF/EGF/Insulin-Induced Signaling. PLoS Comput. Biol. 5(4), e1000340 (2009)
6. Altschul, S.T., Gish, W., Miller, W., Myers, E.W., Lipman, D.J.: Basic local alignment search tool. Journal of Molecular Biology 215(3), 403–410 (1990)
7. AmiGO browser, http://www.godatabase.org/dev/.
8. Anderberg, M.R.: Cluster Analysis for Applications. Academic Press, New York (1973)
9. Andrieu, C., Freitas, N.D., Doucet, A., Jordan, M.I.: An introduction to MCMC for machine learning. Machine Learning 50, 5–43
10. Anholt, R.R., Williams, T.I.: The Soluble Proteome of the Drosophila Antenna. Chemical Senses 35(1), 21–30 (2010)
11. Arad, M., Seidman, C.E., Seidman, J.G.: AMP-activated protein kinase in the heart: role during health and disease. Circ. Res. 100(4), 474–488 (2007)
12. Argaman, L., et al.: Novel Small RNA-Encoding Genes in the Ontergenic Regions of Escherischia Coli. Current Biology 11, 941–950 (2001)
13. Ashburner, M., et al.: The Gene Ontology Consortium, Gene Ontology: Tool for the Unification of Biology. Nature Genetics 25(1), 25–29 (2000)
14. Avi, M., John, C.H.: Protein Kinase Target Discovery From Genome-Wide Messenger RNA Expression Profiling. Mt. Sinai. J. Med. 77(4), 345–349 (2010)
15. Baeza-Yates, R.A.: Introduction to data structures and algorithms related to information retrieval. In: Frakes, W.B., Baeza-Yates, R. (eds.) Information Retrieval: Data Structures and Algorithms, pp. 13–27. Prentice-Hall (1992)
16. Bakan, A., Bahar, I.: Computational generation inhibitor-bound conformers of p38 map kinase and comparison with experiments. In: Proceedings of the Pacific Symposium Biocomputing, pp. 181–192 (2011)

17. Baker, P.G., Goble, C.A., Bechhofer, S., Paton, N.W., Stevens, R., Brass, A.: An Ontology for Bioinformatics Applications. Bioinformatics 15(6), 510–520 (1999)
18. Bardwell, A.J., Frankson, E., Bardwell, L.: Selectivity of docking sites in MAPK kinases. J. Biol. Chem. 284(19), 13165–13173 (2009)
19. Barnes, B.R., Zierath, J.R.: Role of AMP-Activated Protein Kinase in the Control of Glucose Homeostasis. Current Molecular Medicine 5(3), 341–348 (2005)
20. Barzilai, N., Huffman, D.M., Muzumdar, R.H., Bartke, A.: The Critical Role of Metabolic Pathways in Aging. Diabetes 61(6), 1315–1322 (2012)
21. Bebek, G., Yang, J.: PathFinder: mining signal transduction pathway segments from protein-protein interaction networks. BMC Bioinformatics 8, 335 (2007)
22. Benjamin, C., et al.: An endogenous small interfering RNA pathway in Drosophila. Nature 453, 798–802 (2008)
23. Benson, D.A., Karsch-Mizrachi, I., Lipman, D.J., Ostell, J., Wheeler, D.L.: GenBank Update. Nucleic Acids Research 32, 23–26 (2004)
24. Bertone, P., et al.: Global Identification of Human Transcribed Sequences with Genome Tiling Arrays. Science 306(5705), 2242–2246 (2004)
25. Betel, D., Koppal, A., Agius, P., Sander, C., Leslie, C.: Comprehensive Modeling of microRNA Targets Predicts Functional Non-Conserved and Non-Canonical Sites. Genome Biology 11(8), R90 (2010)
26. Birk, J.B., Wojtaszewski, J.F.P.: Predominant $\alpha2/\beta2/\gamma3$ AMPK activation during exercise in human skeletal muscle. J. Physiol. 577(3), 1021–1032 (2006)
27. Bjarne, K., Jotun, H.: RNA secondary structure prediction using stochastic context-free grammars and evolutionary history. Bioinformatics 15(6), 446–454 (1999)
28. Blanco, E., Ruiz-Romero, M., Beltran, S., Bosch, M., Punset, A., Serras, F., Corominas, M.: Gene expression following induction of regeneration in Drosophila wing imaginal discs. Expression profile of regenerating wing discs. BMC Dev. Biol. 10, 94 (2010)
29. Boehm, S.L., Peden, L., Harris, R.A., Blednov, Y.A.: Deletion of the fyn-kinase gene alters sensitivity to GABAergic drugs: dependence on beta2/beta3 GABAA receptor subunits. J. Pharmacol. Exp. Ther. 309(3), 1154–1159 (2004)
30. Brennecke, J., Stark, A., Russell, R.B., Cohen, S.M.: Principles of microRNA- target recognition. PLos Biol. 3(3), 404–418 (2005)
31. Brooijmans, N., Chang, Y.W., Mobilio, D., Denny, R.A., Humblet, C.: An enriched structural kinase database to enable kinome-wide structure-based analyses and drug discovery. Protein. Sci. 19(4), 763–774 (2010)
32. Brooijmans, N., et al.: A structural informatics approach to mine kinase knowledge bases. Drug Discovery Today 15(5-6), 203–209 (2010)
33. Bruner, J., Goodnow, J.J., Austin, G.A.: A study of thinking. Wiley, New York (1956)
34. Burdick, D., Calimlim, M., Gehrke, J.: MAFIA: A maximal frequent itemset algorithm for transactional databases. In: Proceedings of ICDE 2001, pp. 443–452 (2001)
35. Cai, X., Hagedorn, C.H., Cullen, B.R.: Human microRNAs are processed from capped, polyadenylated transcripts that can also function as mRNAs. RNA 10(3), 1957–1966 (2004)
36. Capra, E.J., Perchuk, B.S., Lubin, E.A., Ashenberg, O., Skerker, J.M., et al.: Systematic Dissection and Trajectory-Scanning Mutagenesis of the Molecular Interface That Ensures Specificity of Two-Component Signaling Pathways. PLoS Genet. 6(11), e1001220 (2010)
37. Carlson, D., Kim, K.H.: Regulation of Hepatic Acetyl Coenzyme A Carboxylase by Phosphorylation and Dephosphorylation. Journal of Bio. Chem. 248(1), 378–380
38. Castiglioni, E., et al.: Sequence Variations in Mitochondrial Ferritin: Distribution in Healthy Controls and Different Types of Patients. Genet. Test. Mol. Biomarkers 14(6), 793–796 (2010)

39. Cavalieri, D., Castagnini, C., et al.: Eu.Gene Analyzer a tool for integrating gene expression data with pathway databases. Bioinformatics 23(19), 2631–2632 (2007)

40. Cawley, S., et al.: Unbiased mapping of transcription factor binding sites along human chromosomes 21 and 22 points to widespread regulation of noncoding RNAs. Cell 116(4), 499–509 (2004)

41. Chen, J.H., Lee, S.Y., Shapiro, B.: A Computational Procedure for Assessing the Significance of RNA Secondary Structure. Computer Applications in the Biosciences 6, 7–18 (1990)

42. Chen, J.L., Greiger, C.W.: Functional analysis of the pseudoknot structure in human telomerase RNA. Proc. Natl. Acad. Sci. of the USA 102(23), 8080–8085 (2005)

43. Chan, K.P., Fu, A.W.: Efficient time series matching by wavelets. In: Proceeding of ICDE, pp. 126–133 (1999)

44. Chen, M., Han, J., Yu, P.: Data mining: An overview from a database perspective. IEEE Trans. Knowledge and Data Eng. 8(6), 866–881 (1996)

45. Chen, F., Chen, Y.P.: Exploring cross-species-related miRNAs based on sequence and secondary structure. IEEE Trans. Biomed. Eng. 57(7), 1547–1553 (2010)

46. Chen, Q.F., Chen, Y.P.P.:
    http://www.biomedcentral.com/1471-2105/7/394/additional/

47. Chen, Q.F., Chen, Y.P.P.: Mining frequent patterns for AMP-activated protein kinase regulation on skeletal muscle. BMC Bioinformatics 7(394) (2006)

48. Chen, Q.F., Chen, Y.P.P.: Discovery of Structural and Functional Features in RNA Pseudoknots. IEEE Transactions on Knowledge and Data Engineering 21(7), 974–984 (2009)

49. Chen, Q.F., Chen, Y.P.P.: Mining Characteristic Relations Bind to RNA Secondary Structures. IEEE Transactions on Information Technology in Biomedicine 14(1), 10–15 (2010)

50. Chen, Q.F., Chen, Y.P.P.: Modeling conserved structure patterns for functional noncoding RNA. IEEE Trans. Biomed. Eng. 58(1), 1528–1533 (2011)

51. Chen, Q., Chen, Y.P.P., Zhang, C.Q.: Detecting Inconsistency in Biological Molecular Databases using Ontology. Data Mining and Knowledge Discovery 15(2), 275–296 (2007)

52. Chen, Q.F., Li, G., Chen, Y.P.P.: Interval-based distance function for identifying RNA structure candidates. J. Theor. Biol. 269(1), 280–286 (2011)

53. Chen, Q.F.:
    http://bioinformatics.gxu.edu.cn/bio/data/
    LNAI8335/8335-3.zip

54. Chen, Q.F.:
    http://bioinformatics.gxu.edu.cn/bio/data/
    LNAI8335/8335-4.zip

55. Chen, R.O., Felciano, R., Altman, R.B.: RiboWeb: Linking Structural Computations to a Knowledge Base of Published Experimental Data. In: Proceeding of the 5th International Conference on Intelligent Systems for Molecular Biology, pp. 84–87. AAAI Press (1997)

56. Chen, Z.P., McConell, G.K., Michell, B.J., Snow, R.J., Canny, B.J., Kemp, B.E.: AMPK signaling in contracting human skeletal muscle: acetyl-CoA carboxylase and NO synthase phosphorylation. Physiol. Endocrinol. Metab. 279(5), 1202–1206

57. Chen, Y.P.P., Qin, Q.M., Chen, Q.F.: Learning Dependency Model for AMP-Activated Protein Kinase Regulation. In: Zhang, Z., Siekmann, J.H. (eds.) KSEM 2007. LNCS (LNAI), vol. 4798, pp. 221–229. Springer, Heidelberg (2007)

58. Cheng, J.: Transcriptional Maps of 10 Human Chromosomes at 5-Nucleotide Resolution. Science 308(5725), 1149–1154 (2005)
59. Cheung, Y.L., Fu, A.W.C.: Mining Frequent Itemsets without Support Threshold: With and Without Item Constraints. IEEE Transaction on Knowledge and Data Engineering 16(9), 1052–1069
60. Chomsky, N.: Syntactic Structures Mouton. The Hague (1957)
61. Chowbina, S.R., Wu, X.G.: HPD: an online integrated human pathway database enabling systems biology studies. BMC Bioinformatics 10(suppl. 11), S5 (2009)
62. Clark, S.A., Chen, Z.P., Murphy, K.T., Aughey, R.J., McKenna, M.J., Kemp, B.E., Hawley, J.A.: Intensified exercise training does not alter AMPK signaling in human skeletal muscle. Physitol. Endocrinol. Metab. 286(5), 737–743 (2003)
63. Coffey, V.G., Zhong, Z., Shield, A., Canny, B.J., Chibalin, A.V., Zierath, J.R., Hawley, J.A.: Early signaling responses to divergent exercise stimuli in skeletal muscle from well-trained humans. FASEB Journal 20(1), 190–192 (2006)
64. Coghlan, M.P., Smith, D.M.: Introduction to the Kinases in Diabetes Biochemical Society focused meeting: are protein kinases good targets for antidiabetic drugs? Biochemical Society Transactions 33(2), 339–342 (2005)
65. Cohen, P.: Protein kinases–the major drug targets of the twenty-first century? Nat. Rev. Drug. Discov. 1(4), 309–315 (2002)
66. Cong, G., Tan, K.-. L., Tung, K.H., Xu, X.: Mining top-K covering rule groups for gene expression data. In: Proceedings of the 2005 ACM SIGMOD International Conference on Management of Data, pp. 670–681 (2005)
67. Cooper, G.: A simple constraint-based algorithm for efficiently mining observational databases for causal relationships. Data Mining and Knowledge Discovery 1(2), 203–224 (1997)
68. Cooper, G.: Computational complexity of probabilistic inference using Bayesian belief networks. Artificial Intelligence 42, 393–405 (1990)
69. Covani, U., Marconcini, S., Derchi, G., Barone, A., Giacomelli, L.: Relationship between human periodontitis and type 2 diabetes at a genomic level: a data-mining study. J. Periodontology 80(8), 1265–1273 (2009)
70. Dagum, P., Luby, M.: Approximating probabilistic inference in bayesian belief networks is np-hard. Artificial Intelligence 60, 141–153
71. David, W.S., Samuel, E.B.: Pseudoknots: RNA Structures with Diverse Functions. PloS Biology 3(6), 956–959 (2005)
72. Dawson, W.K., Fujiwara, K., Kawai, G.: Prediction of RNA pseudoknots using heuristic modeling with mapping and sequential folding. PLoS ONE 2(9) (2007)
73. Dee, U.S.: Human Physiology: An Integrated Approach, 4/E. Benjamin Cummings (2007)
74. Defranchi, E., Schalon, C., Messa, M., Onofri, F., Benfenati, F., Rognan, D.: Binding of protein kinase inhibitors to synapsin I inferred from pair-wise binding site similarity measurements. PLoS One 5(8), e12214 (2010)
75. de Hoon, M.J., Imoto, S., Nolan, J., Miyano, S.: Open source clustering software. Bioinformatics 20, 1453–1454 (2004)
76. Deiman, B.A.L.M., Kortlever, R.M., Pleij, C.W.: The role of the pseudoknot at the 3' end of turnip yellow virus RNA in minus-strand synthesis by the viral RNA-Dependent RNA polymerse. J. Virol., 5990–5996 (1997)
77. de Oliveira Dal Molin, C.G., Quek, L.E., Palfreyman, R.W., et al.: AraGEM, a genome-scale reconstruction of the primary metabolic network in Arabidopsis. Plant Physiol. 152, 579–589 (2010)

78. Deshmukh, A.S., Long, Y.C., Barbosa, T.C., Karlsson, H.K.R., Glund, Z.W., Gibbs, E.M., Koistinen, H.A., Wallberg-Henriksson, H., Zierath, J.R.: Nitric oxide increases cyclic GMP levels, AMP-activated protein kinase (AMPK)$\alpha$1-specific activity and glucose transport in human skeletal muscle. Diabetologia 53, 1142–1150 (2010)

79. Ding, J., Huang, S., Wu, S., et al.: Gain of miR-151 on chromosome 8q24.3 facilitates tumour cell migration and spreading through downregulating RhoGDIA. Nature Cell Biology 12(20), 390–399 (2010)

80. Dirks, R.M., Pierce, N.A.: A partition function algorithm for nucleic acid secondary structure including pseudoknots. J. Comput. Chem. 24, 1664–1677 (2003)

81. Dixit, A., Yi, L., Gowthaman, R., Torkamani, A., Schork, N.J., Verkhivker, G.M.: Sequence and structure signatures of cancer mutation hotspots in protein kinases. PLoS One 4(10), e7485 (2009)

82. Doddi, S., Marathe, A., Ravi, S.S., Torney, D.C.: Discovery of Association Rules in Medical Data. Med. Inform. Internet. Med. 26(1), 25–33 (2001)

83. Drysdale, R.A., et al.: FlyBase: genes and gene models. Nucleic Acids Research 33(1), 390–395 (2005)

84. Dubes, R.C.: How many clusters are best? - an experiment. Pattern Recogn. 20(6), 645–663 (1987)

85. Dudley, J.T., Pouliot, Y., Chen, R., Morgan, A.A., Butte, A.J.: Translational bioinformatics in the cloud: an affordable alternative. Genome Medicine 2, 51 (2010)

86. Durante, P.E., Mustard, K.J., Park, S.H., Winder, W.W., Hardie, D.G.: Effects of Endurance Training on Activity and Expression of AMP-activated Protein Kinase Isoforms in Rat Muscles. Am. J. Physiol. Endocrinol. Metab. 283(1), 178–186 (2002)

87. Durbin, R., Eddy, S., Krogh, A., Mitchison, G.: Biological sequence analysis: Probabilistic Models of Proteins and Nucleic Acids. Cambridge University Press (1998)

88. Dyck, J.R.B., Gao, G., Widmer, J., Stapleton, D., Fernandez, C.S., Kemp, B.E., Witters, L.A.: Regulation of 5'-AMP-activated Protein Kinase Activity by the Noncatalytic $\beta$ and $\gamma$ Subunits. J. Biol. Chem. 271(30), 17798–17803 (1996)

89. Echeverria, C.G., Sellers, W.R.: Drug discovery approaches targeting the PI3K/Akt pathway in cancer. Oncogene 27, 5511–5526 (2008)

90. Eddy, S.R.: Non-coding RNA genes and the modern RNA world. Nat. Rev. Genet. 2, 919–929 (2001)

91. Edwards, A.C., Zwarts, L., Yamamoto, A., Callaerts, P., Mackay, T.F.C.: Mutations in many genes affect aggressive behavior in Drosophila melanogaster. BMC Biology 7, 29 (2009)

92. Eijnde, B.O., Derave, W., Wojtaszewski, J.F., Richter, E.A., Hespel, P.: AMP kinase expression and activity in human skeletal muscle: effects of immobilization, retraining, and creatine supplementation. J. Appl. Physiol. 98(4), 1228–1233 (2005)

93. EMBL-the European molecular biology laboratory, http://www.ebi.ac.uk/embl/.

94. Etzold, T., Ulyanov, A., Argos, P.: SRS: Information Retrieval System for Molecular Biology Data Banks. Methods Enzymol. 226, 114–128 (1996)

95. Evans, P., Sacan, A., Ungar, L., Tozeren, A.: Sequence alignment reveals possible MAPK docking motifs on HIV proteins. PLoS One 5(1), e8942 (2010)

96. Faloutsos, C., Ranganathan, M., Manolopoulos, Y.: Fast subsequence matching in time-series databases. In: Proceeding of SIGMOD 1994, pp. 419–429 (1994)

97. Feuk, L., Carson, A.R., Schererc, S.W.: Structural variation in the human genome. Nature Reviews Genetics 7, 85–97 (2006)

98. Forsdyke, D.R.: Evolutionary bioinformatics. Springer (2006)

99. Freier, S., Kierzek, R., Jaeger, J., Sugimoto, N., Caruthers, M., Neilson, T., Turner, D.: Improved free-energy parameters for predictions of RNA duplex stability. Proc. Natl. Acad. Sci. 83(24), 9373–9377 (1986)

100. Frosig, C., Jorgensen, S.B., Hardie, D.G., Richter, E.A., Wojtaszewski, J.F.: 5'-AMP-activated protein kinase activity and protein expressed are regulated by endurance training in human skeletal muscle. Physitol. Endocrinol. Metab. 286(3), 411–417

101. Fryer, L.G.D., Carling, D.: AMP-activated protein kinase and the metabolic syndrome. Biochemical Society Transactions 33(2), 362–366 (2005)

102. Fujibuchi, W., Goto, S., Migimatsu, H., Uchiyama, I., Ogiwara, A., Akiyama, Y., Kanehisa, M.: DBGET/LinkDB: an integrated database retrieval system. In: Proceeding of the Pacific Symposium on Biocomputing, pp. 683–694 (1998)

103. Fujii, N., Hayashi, T., Hirshman, M.F., Smith, J.T., Habinowski, S.A., Kaijser, L., Mu, J., Ljungqvist, O., Birnbaum, M.J., Witters, L.A., Thorell, A., Goodyear, L.J.: Exercise Induces Isoform-specific Increase in 5'AMP-activated Protein Kinase Activity in Human Skeletal Muscle. Biochem. Biophys. Res. Commun. 273(3), 1150–1155 (2000)

104. Gardner, P., Daub, J., Tate, J.G., Nawrocki, E.P., Kolbe, D.L., Lindgreen, S., Wilkinson, A.C., Finn, R.D., Griffiths-Jones, S., Eddy, S.R., Bateman, A.: Rfam: updates to the RNA families database. Nucleic Acids Research 37, 136–140 (2009)

105. Gardner, P., Giegerich, R.: A comprehensive comparison of comparative RNA structure prediction approaches. BMC Bioinformatics 5, 140 (2004)

106. Gautheret, D., Lambert, A.: Direct RNA motif definition and identification from multiple sequence alignments using secondary structure profiles. J. Mol. Biol. 313, 1003–1011 (2001)

107. Gehlenborg, N., ODonoghue, S.I., Baliga, N.S., et al.: Visualization of omics data for systems biology. Nat. Methods 68, S56–S68 (2010)

108. Gelman, A., Bois, F., Jiang, J.: Physiological pharmacokinetic analysis using population modeling and informative prior distributions. J. Am. Stat. Assoc. 91, 1400–1412

109. Gene ontology, http://www.geneontology.org/.

110. Giegerich, R., Voss, B., Rehmsmeier, M.: Abstract shapes of RNA. Nucleic Acids Research 32(16), 4843–4851 (2004)

111. Giudici, P., Castelo, R.: Improving Markov Chain Monte Carlo Model Search for Data Mining. Machine Learning 50(1-2), 127–158

112. Gene ontology (2000), http://www.geneontology.org/

113. Gkirtzou, K., Tsamardinos, I., Tsakalides, P., et al.: MatureBayes: A Probabilistic Algorithm for Identifying the Mature mirRNA within Novel Precursors. PLoS One 5(8), 1–14 (2010)

114. Göta, G., Zhu, J.: Efficiently Using Prefix-trees in Mining Frequent Itemsets. In: Proceeding of the First IEEE ICDM Workshop on Frequent Itemset Mining Implementations, pp. 123–132 (2003)

115. Goldberg, J.M., Manning, G., Liu, A., Fey, P., Pilcher, K.E., Xu, Y.J., Smith, J.: The Dictyostelium Kinomel Analysis of the Protein Kinases from a Simple Model Organism. PLoS Genetics 2(3), 291–303 (2006)

116. Gould, C., Wong, C.F.: Designing specific protein kinase inhibitors: insights from computer simulations and comparative sequence/structure analysis. Pharmacology Therapeutics 93(2-3), 169–178 (2002)

117. Grahne, G., Zhu, J.: Efficiently Using Prefix-trees in Mining Frequent Itemsets. In: Proceeding of the First IEEE ICDM Workshop on Frequent Itemset Mining Implementations (FIMI 2003), pp. 257–262 (2003)

118. Grant, M.R., Jones, J.D.: Hormone (dis)harmony moulds plant health and disease. Science 324, 750–752 (2009)

119. Griffiths-Jones, S., Saini, H.K., Dongen, S.V., Enright, A.J.: miRBase: Tools for mi-croRNA Genomics. Nucleic Acids Research 36(1), 154–158 (2008)
120. Grün, D., Wang, Y.L., Langenberger, D., Gunsalus, K.C., Rajewsky, N.: microRNA tar-get predictions across seven Drosophila species and comparison to mammalian targets. PLoS Comput. Biol. 1(1), 51–66 (2005)
121. Guo, Z., Kozlov, S., Lavin, M.F., Person, M.D., Paull, T.T.: ATM activation by oxidative stress. Science 330(6003), 517–521 (2010)
122. Guo, S., Lu, J., Subramanian, A., Sonenshein, G.E.: Microarray-assisted pathway anal-ysis identifies mitogen-activated protein kinase signaling as a mediator of resistance to the green tea polyphenol epigallocatechin 3-gallate in her-2/neu-overexpressing breast cancer cells. Cancer Res. 66(10), 5322–5329 (2006)
123. Haas, L.M., Schwarz, P.M., Kodali, P., Kotlar, E., Rice, J.E., Swope, W.C.: Discov-eryLink: A System for Integrated Access to Life Sciences Data Sources. IBM Systems Journal 40(2) (2001)
124. Han, D.W., Tang, G.L., Zhang, J.: A Novel Method for MicroRNA Secondary Struc-ture Prediction Using a Bottom-Up Algorithm. In: Proc. 47th Ann. Southeast Regional Conf., pp. 1–6 (2009)
125. Han, J.W., Cai, Y., Cercone, N.: Data-driven discovery of quantitative rules in relational databases. IEEE Trans. on Knowledge and Data Engineering 5(1), 29–40 (1993)
126. Han, J.W., et al.: Mining frequent patterns without candidate generation. In: Proceed-ings of the 2000 ACM SIGMOD International Conference on Management of Data, pp. 1–12 (2000)
127. Han, J.W., Kamber, M.: Data Mining: Concepts and Techniques. In: Data Mining: Con-cepts and Techniques, 2nd edn., Morgan Kaufmann Publishers (2006)
128. Hanks, S., Quinn, A., Hunter, T.: The protein kinase family: conserved features and deduced phylogeny of the catalytic domains. Science 241, 42–52 (1988)
129. Hanks, S., Hunter, T.: Protein kinases 6. The eukaryotic protein kinase superfamily: kinase (catalytic) domain structure and classification. FASEB J. 9(8), 576–596 (1995)
130. Hardie, D.G.: AMP-activated protein kinase: the guardian of cardiac energy status. J. Clin. Invest. 114, 465–468 (2004)
131. Hardie, D.G., Scott, J.W., Pan, D.A., Hudson, E.R.: Management of cellular energy by the AMP-activated protein kinase system. FEBS Lett. 546(1), 113–120 (2003)
132. Harris, C.J., Stevens, A.P.: Chemogenomics: structuring the drug discovery process to gene families. Drug Discov. Today 11(19-20), 880–888 (2006)
133. Hasegawa, Y., Emi, N., Shimokata, K., Abe, A., Kawabe, T., Hasegawa, T., Kirioka, T., Saito, H.: Gene transfer of herpes simplex virus type I thymidine kinase gene as a drug sensitivity gene into human lung cancer cell lines using retroviral vectors. Am. J. Respir Cell. Mol. Biol. 8(6), 655–661
134. Hastings, W.K.: Monte Carlo sampling methods using Markov chains and their Appli-cations. Biometrika 57, 97–109
135. Havgaard, J.H., Lyngso, R.B., Stormo, G.D., Gorodkin, J.: Pairwise local structural alignment of RNA sequences with sequence similarity less than 40%. Bioinformat-ics 21(9), 1815–1824 (2005)
136. Heckerman, D.: A tutorial on learning with bayesian networks. Technical Report MSR-TR-95-06, Microsoft Research (1995)
137. Heckerman, D., Geiger, D., Chickering, D.: Learning Bayesian networks: The combi-nation of knowledge and statistical data. Machine Learning 20, 194–243
138. Helfrich-Forster, C., Homberg, U.: Pigment-Dispersing Hormone-Immunoreactive Neurons in the Nervous System of Wild-Type Drosophila melanogaster and of Sev-eral Mutants with Altered Circadian Rhythmicity. J. Comparative Neurology 337(2), 177–190 (1993)

139. Hines, P.J., Zahn, L.M.: Green Pathways. Science 336(6089), 1657 (2012)
140. Hofacker, I.L., Priwitzer, B., Stadler, P.F.: Prediction of Locally Stable RNA Secondary Structures for Genome-Wide Surveys. Bioinformatics 20(2), 186–190 (2004)
141. Holm, L., Sander, C.: Mapping the protein universe. Science 273, 595–603 (1996)
142. Hsu, P.W., et al.: miRNAMap: genomic maps of microRNA genes and their target genes in mammalian genomes. Nucleic Acids Research 34(1), 135–139 (2006)
143. http://bnt.sourceforge.net/.
144. http://www.abgent.com/docs/article_kinases
145. http://www.cellsignal.com/reference/kinase/index.html.
146. http://kinase.com/
147. http://www.ncbi.nlm.nih.gov/books/NBK22183/
148. http://www.sciencemag.org/site/products/drugdiscnew.xhtml.
149. http://unmc.edu/.
150. Huang, D., Chow, T.: Identifying the biologically relevant gene categories based on gene expression and biological data: an example on prostate cancer. Bioinformatics 23(12), 1503–1510 (2007)
151. Hunter, L. (ed.): Artificial intelligence and molecular biology. MIT Press (1993)
152. Hunter, A.: Evaluating the Significance of Inconsistencies. In: Proceedings of the International Joint Conference on AI (IJCAI 2003), pp. 468–473 (2003)
153. Hunter, A.: Measuring Inconsistency in Knowledge via Quasi-Classical Models. In: Proceedings of AAAI 2002, pp. 68–73 (2002)
154. Hurst, D., Taylor, E.B., Cline, T.D., Greenwood, L.J., Compton, C.L., Lamb, J.D., Winder, W.W.: AMP-activated protein kinase kinase activity and phosphorylation of AMP-activated protein kinase in contracting muscle of sedentary and endurance-trained rats. Am. J. Physiol. Endocrinol. Metab. 289(4), 710–715 (2005)
155. Huttenhower, C., Haley, E.M., Hibbs, M.A., Dumeaux, V., Barrett, D.R., Coller, H.A., Troyanskaya, O.: Exploring the human genome with functional maps. Genome Res. 19(6), 1093–1106 (2009)
156. Ideker, T., et al.: Integrated genomic and proteomic analyses of a systematically perturbed metabolic network. Science 292, 929–934 (2001)
157. Wexler, I.D., Niv, M.Y., Reuveni, H.: Sequence-based protein kinase inhibition: applications for drug development. BioTechniques 39(S10), S575–S576 (2005)
158. Ivry, T., Michal, S., Avihoo, A., Sapiro, G., Barash, D.: An image processing approach to computing distances between RNA secondary structures dot plots. Algorithms for Molecular Biology 4(4), 1–19 (2009)
159. Jacob, F., Monod, J.: Genetic Regulatory Mechanisms in the Synthesis of Proteins. J. Molecular Biology 3, 318–356 (1961)
160. Jain, A.K., Dubes, R.C.: Algorithms for Clustering Data. Prentice Hall (1988)
161. Jain, A.K., Murty, M.N., Flynn, P.J.: Data Clustering: A Review. ACM Computing Surveys 31(3), 264–323 (1999)
162. Janssen, S., Reeder, J., Giegerich, R.: Shape based indexing for faster search of RNA family databases. BMC Bioinformatics 9, 131 (2008)
163. Jhoti, H., Leach, A.R.: Structure-based Drug Discovery. Springer (2007)
164. Jia, M., Choi, S.Y., Reiners, D., et al.: MetNetGE: interactive views of biological networks and ontologies. BMC Bioinformatics 11, 469 (2010)
165. Jørgensen, S.B., Jensen, T., Richter, E.A.: Role of AMPK in skeletal muscle gene adaptation in relation to exercise. Appl. Physiol. Nutr. Metab. 32, 904–911 (2007)

166. Jørgensen, S.B., Viollet, B., Andreelli, F., Frosig, C., Birk, J.B., Schjerling, P., Vaulont, S., Richter, E.A., Wojtaszewski, J.F.P.: Knockout of the $\alpha_2$ but not $\alpha_1$ 5′-AMP-activated protein kinase isoform abolishes 5- Aminoimidazole-4-carboxamide-1-$\beta$-4-ribofuranoside but not contraction-induced glucose uptake in skeletal muscle. J. Biol. Chem. 279(2), 1070–1079 (2004)

167. Jones-Rhoades, M.W., Bartel, D.: Computational identification of plant MicroRNAs and their targets, including a stress-induced miRNA. Mol. Cell. 14(6), 787–799 (2004)

168. Jose, M.A., et al.: The Ethylene Signaling Pathway. Science 306, 1513 (2004)

169. Joung, J.G., Zhang, J.F.: Identification of microRNA regulatory modules in Arabidopsis via a probabilistic graphical model. Bioinformatics 25(3), 387–393 (2009)

170. Kaczkowski, B., Torarinsson, E., Reiche, K., Havgaard, J.H., Stadler, P.F., Gorodkin, J.: Structural profiles of human miRNA families from pairwise clustering. Bioinformatics 25(3), 291–294 (2009)

171. Kaidanovich-Beilin, O., Eldar-Finkelman, H.: Peptides targeting protein kinases: strategies and implications. Physiology 21, 411–418 (2006)

172. Kaj, A.E.S., Pentti, T.R., Mauno, V.: KinMutBase, a database of human disease-causing protein kinase mutations. Nucleic Acids Research 28(1), 369–371 (2005)

173. Kampa, D., et al.: Novel RNAs identified from an in-depth analysis of the transcriptome of human chromosomes. Genome Res. 14(3), 331–342 (2004)

174. Kandasamy, K., et al.: PathBuilderɪopen source software for annotating and developing pathway resources. Bioinformatics 25(21), 2860–2862 (2009)

175. Karlin, S., Burge, C.: Trinucleotide repeats and long homopeptides in genes and proteins associated with nervous system disease and development. Proc. Natl. Acad. Sci 93(4), 1560–1565 (1996)

176. Karp, P.D., Riley, M., Saier, M., Paulsen, I.T., Paley, S.M., Pellegrini-Toole, A.: The EcoCyc and MetaCyc Databases. Nucleic Acids Research 30(1), 59–61 (2000)

177. Karp, P.D.: An ontology for biological function based on molecular interactions. Bioinformatics 16(3), 269–285 (2000)

178. Karp, P.D.: A strategy for database interoperation. J. Comput. Biol., 59–61 (1995)

179. Kawahara, Y., Zinshteyn, B., Chendrimada, T.P., Shiekhattar, R., Nishikura, K.: RNA editing of the microRNA-151 precursor blocks cleavage by the Dicer-TRBP complex. EMBO Rep. 8(1), 763–769 (2007)

180. Ke, Y.P., Cheng, J., Ng, W.: An information-theoretic approach to quantitative association rule mining. Knowl. Inf. Syst. 16(2), 213–244 (2008)

181. Kemp, B.E., Mitchelhill, K.I., Stapleton, D., Michell, B.J., Chen, Z.P., Witters, L.: Dealing with energy demand: The AMP-activated protein kinase. Trends Biochem. Sci. 24(1), 22–25

182. Kemp, B.E., Stapleton, D., Campbell, D.J., Chen, Z.P., Murthy, S., Walter, M., Gupta, A., Adams, J.J., Katsis, F., van Denderen, B., Jennings, I.G., Iseli, T., Michell, B.J., Witters, L.A.: AMP-activated protein kinase, super metabolic regulator. Biochem. Soc. Trans. 31, 162–168 (2003)

183. Kevin, B.K., Ann, E.N.: Bayesian Artificial Intelligence. Chapman & Hall /CRC

184. Kdnuggets (2013), http://www.kdnuggets.com/datasets

185. Kim, W.S., Lee, Y.S., Cha, S.H.: Berberine improves lipid dysregulation in obesity by controlling central and peripheral AMPK activity. Am. J. Physiol. Endocrinol. Metab. 296(4), 812–819 (2009)

186. Kinnings, S.L., Jackson, R.M.: Binding site similarity analysis for the functional classification of the protein kinase family. J. Chem. Inf. Model. 49(2), 318–329 (2009)

187. Kitano, H.: A robustness-based approach to systems-oriented drug design. Nature Reviews Drug Discovery 6, 202–210 (2007)

188. Klein, R., Eddy, S.: RSEARCH: finding homologs of single structured RNA sequences. BMC Bioinformatics 4, 44 (2003)

189. Knighton, D.R., Zheng, J.H., Ten Eyck, L.F., Ashford, V.A., Xuong, N.H., Taylor, S.S., Sowadski, J.M.: Crystal structure of the catalytic subunit of cyclic adenosine monophosphate-dependent protein kinase. Science 253(5018), 407–414 (1991)

190. Knut, E., Stuart, J.I., Carsten, J., Rolf, J., Vladimir, K., Georg, K., Rolf, W.: Kinase Data Mining: Dealing with the Information (Over-)Flow. Chem. Bio. Chem. 6(3), 567–570

191. Kohler, J., Philippi, S., Lange, M.: SEMEDA: ontology based semantic integration of biological databases. Bioinformatics 19(18), 2420–2427 (2003)

192. Kolch, W., Pitt, A.: Functional proteomics to dissect tyrosine kinase signalling pathways in cancer. Nat. Rev. Cancer 10(9), 618–629 (2010)

193. Koonin, E.V., Galperin, M.Y.: Sequence-Evolution-Function: Computational Approaches in Comparative Genomics. Kluwer Academic (2003)

194. Kuhn, D., Weskamp, N., Hllermeier, E., Klebe, G.: Functional classification of protein kinase binding sites using Cavbase. Chem. Med. Chem. 2(10), 1432–1447 (2007)

195. Kumar, R., Blakemore, S.J., Ellis, C.E., Petricoin, E.F., Pratt, D., Macoritto, M., Matthews, A.L., Loureiro, J.J., Elliston, K.: Causal reasoning identifies mechanisms of sensitivity for a novel AKT kinase inhibitor, GSK690693. BMC Genomics 11, 419 (2010)

196. Kunin, V., Sorek, R., Hugenholtz, P.: Evolutionary Conservation of Sequence and Secondary Structures in CRISPR Repeats. Genome Biology 8(4), R61 (2007)

197. Lapins, M., Wikberg, J.E.S.: Kinome-wide interaction modelling using alignment-based and alignment-independent approaches for kinase description and linear and non-linear data analysis techniques. BMC Bioinformatics 11, 339 (2010)

198. Lauritzen, S.: Graphical models. Oxford University Press, Oxford (1996)

199. Lee, R.C., Ambros, V.: An Extensive Class of Small RNAs in Caenorhabditis elegans. Science 294, 862–864 (2001)

200. Lee, Y., Kim, M., Han, J., Yeom, K.H., Lee, S., Baek, S.H., Kim, V.N.: MicroRNA Genes are Transcribed by RNA Polymerase II. EMBO J. 23(20), 4051–4060 (2004)

201. Le, S.Y., Chen, J.H., Maizel, J.: Structure and Methods: Human Genome Initiative and DNA Recombination, vol. 1, pp. 127–136. Adenine Press (1990)

202. Lim, L.P., Lau, N.C., Weinstein, E.G., Abdelhakim, A., Yekta, S., Rhoades, M.W., Burge, C.B., Bartel, D.P.: The MicroRNAs of Caenorhabditis elegans. Genes and Developtment 17, 991–1008 (2003)

203. Lin, W.Y., Tseng, M.C.: Automated support specification for efficient mining of interesting association rules. Journal of Information Science 32(3), 238–250 (2006)

204. Liu, B., Hsu, W., Ma, Y.: Mining Association Rules with Multiple Minimum Supports. In: Proceedings of the Fifth ACM SIGKDD International Conference on Knowledge Discovery and Data Mining, pp. 337–441 (1999)

205. Liu, B., Li, J., Tsykin, A., Liu, L., Gaur, A.B., Goodall, G.J.: Exploring complex miRNA-mRNA interactions with Bayesian networks by splitting-averaging strategy. BMC Bioinformatics 10(1), 408–427 (2009)

206. Lin, J.X.: Integration of Weighted Knowledge Bases. Artificial Intelligence 83(2), 363–378 (1996)

207. Lin, W.Y., Tseng, M.C.: Automated support specification for efficient mining of interesting association rules. Journal of Information Science 32(3), 238–250 (2006)

208. Ling, Y., et al.: Mining Frequent Itemsets without Support Threshold: With and Without Item Constraints. IEEE Transaction on Knowledge and Data Engineering 16(9), 1052–1069 (2004)

209. Liu, B., Liu, L., Tsykin, A., Goodall, G.J., Green, J.E., Zhu, M., Kim, C.H., Li, J.: Identifying Functional miRNA-mRNA Regulatory Modules with Correspondence Latent Dirichlet Allocation. Bioinformatics 26(24), 3105–3111 (2010)
210. Luptak, I., Shen, M., He, H., Hirshman, M.F., Musi, N., Goodyear, L.J., Yan, J., Wakimoto, H., Morita, H., Arad, M., Seidman, C.E., Seidman, J.G., Ingwall, J.S., Balschi, J.A., Tian, R.: Aberrant activation of AMP-activated protein kinase remodels metabolic network in favor of cardiac glycogen storage. J. Clin. Invest. 117(5), 1432–1439
211. Lyngso, R.B., Pedersen, C.N.: RNA pseudoknot prediction in energy-based models. J. Comput. Biol. 7(3-4), 409–427 (2000)
212. Lyngso, R.B., Zuker, M., Pedersen, C.N.S.: Fast evaluation of internal loops in RNA secondary structure prediction. Bioinformatics 15(6), 440–445 (1999)
213. Lysenko, A., Hindle, M.M., Taubert, J., et al.: Data integration for plant genomics Cexemplars from the integration of Arabidopsis thaliana databases. Briefings in Bioinformatics 10, 676–693 (2009)
214. Madigan, D., York, J.: Bayesian graphical models for discrete data. International Statistical Review 63, 215–232
215. Manning, G., Whyte, D.B., Martinez, R., Hunter, T., Sudarsanam, S.: The Protein Kinase Complement of the Human Genome. Science 298, 1912–1934 (2002)
216. Mani, R., Onge, R.P., Hartman, J.L.T., Giaever, G., Roth, F.P.: Defining genetic interaction. Proc. Natl. Acad. Sci. USA 105, 3461–3466 (2008)
217. Maji, P.: f-Information Measures for Efficient Selection of Discriminative Genes from Microarray Data. IEEE Transactions on Knowledge and Data Engineering 56(4), 1063–1069 (2009)
218. Markowetz, F., Spang, R.: Inferring cellular networks-a review. BMC Bioinformatics 8(suppl. 6), S5 (2007)
219. Martin, E.M.N., Jane, A.E., Louise, N.J.: Protein Kinase Inhibitors: Insights into Drug Design from Structure. Science 303(5665), 1800–1805 (2004)
220. Ma, S., Hellerstein, J.L.: Mining mutually dependent patterns. In: ICDM, pp. 409–416 (2001)
221. Mathews, D.H., Turner, D.H.: Prediction of RNA secondary structure by free energy minimization. Curr. Opin. Struct. Biol. 16(3), 270–278 (2006)
222. Mattick, J.S.: Non-coding RNAs: the architects of eukaryotic complexity. EMBO Rep. 2, 986–991 (2001)
223. Mattick, J.S.: Challenging the dogma: the hidden layer of non-protein-coding RNAs in complex organisms. Bioessays 25, 930–939 (2003)
224. Mattick, J.S.: RNA regulation: a new genetics. Nat. Rev. Genet. 5(4), 316–323 (2004)
225. McConell, G.K., Lee-Young, R.S., Chen, Z.P., Septo, N.K., Huynh, N.N., Stephens, T.J., Canny, B.J., Kemp, B.E.: Short-term exercise training in humans reduces AMPK signalling during prolonged exercise independent of muscle glycogen. J. Physiol. 568(2), 665–676 (2005)
226. McKenna, W.G., Muschel, R.J.: Genes Chromosomes. Cancer 38, 330 (2003)
227. Melnikova, I., Golden, J.: Targeting protein kinases. Nature Reviews Drug Discovery 3, 993–994 (2004)
228. Metz, J.T., Johnson, E.F., Soni, N.B., Merta, P.J., Kifle, L., Hajduk, P.J.: Navigating the kinome. Nat. Chem. Biol. 7(4), 200–202 (2011)
229. Milanesi, L., et al.: Systematic analysis of human kinase genes: a large number of genes and alternative splicing events result in functional and structural diversity. BMC Bioinformatics 6(suppl. 4), S20 (2005)
230. Milanowska, K., Mikolajczak, K., Lukasik, A., et al.: RNApathwaysDB–a database of RNA maturation and decay pathways. Nucleic Acids Res. 41, D268–D272 (2013)

231. Milletti, F., Vulpetti, A.: Predicting Polypharmacology by Binding Site Similarity: From Kinases to the Protein Universe. J. Chem. Inf. Model. 50, 1418–1431 (2010)

232. Miyazaki, S., Sugawara, H., Gojobori, T., Tateno, Y.: DNA Data Bank of Japan (DDBJ) in XML. Nucleic Acids Res. 31(1), 13–16 (2003)

233. Morgane, L.B., Karim, B., Thierry, S.: Data mining the p53 pathway in the Fugu genome: evidence for strong conservation of the apoptotic pathway. Oncogene 22, 5082–5090 (2003)

234. Murphy, K.P.: Active Learning of Causal Bayes Net Structure, Tech. Rep. UC Berkeley

235. Musi, N., Goodyear, L.J.: AMP-activated protein kinase and muscle glucose uptake. Acta Physiologica 178(4), 337–345 (2003)

236. Musi, N., Fujii, N., Hirshman, M.F., Ekberg, I., Froberg, S., Ljungqvist, O., Thorell, A., Goodyear, L.J.: AMP-activated Protein Kinase (AMPK) Is Activated in Muscle of Subjects with Type 2 Diabetes During Exercise. Diabetes 50(5), 921–927

237. Musi, N., et al.: AMP-activated Protein Kinase (AMPK) Is Activated in Muscle of Subjects with Type 2 Diabetes During Exercise. Diabetes 50(5), 921–927 (2001)

238. Napthine, S., Liphardt, J., Bloys, A., Routledge, S., Brierley, I.: The role of RNA pseidoknot stem 1 length in the promotion of efficient-1 ribosomal frameshifting, J. Mol. Biol. 288, 305–320 (1999)

239. NCBI (The national center for biotechnology information),
     http://www.ncbi.nlm.nih.gov/.

240. Neerincx, P.B., Leunissen, J.A.: Evolution of web services in bioinformatics. Briefings in Bioinformatics 6, 178–188 (2005)

241. Nielsen, J.N., Mustard, K.J., Graham, D.A., Yu, H., MacDonald, C.S., Pilegaard, H., Goodyear, L.J., Hardie, D.G., Richter, E.A., Wojtaszewsji, J.F.: 5′-AMPactivated protein kinase activity and subunit expression in exercise-trained human skeletal muscle. Appl. Physiol. 94(2), 631–641 (2003)

242. Nixon, P.L., Giedroc, D.P.: Energetics of a strongly pH dependent RNA tertiary structure in a frameshifting pseudoknot. J. Mol. Biol. 296, 659–671 (2000)

243. Nybakken, K., Vokes, S.A., Lin, T.Y., McMahon, A.P., Perrimon, N.: A genome-wide RNA interference screen in Drosophila melanogaster cells for new components of the Hh signaling pathway. Nature Genetics 37(12), 1323–1332 (2005)

244. O'Dushlaine, C.T., Edwards, R.J., Park, S.D., Shields, D.C.: Tandem repeat copy-number variation in protein-coding regions of human genes. Genome Biology 69 (2006)

245. Omiecinski, E.R.: Alternative interest measures for mining association rules. IEEE Transactions on Knowledge and Data Engineering 15(1), 57–69 (2003)

246. Oinn, T.M.: Talisman–rapid application development for the grid. Bioinformatics 19(suppl.), 212–214 (2003)

247. Okazaki, Y., et al.: Analysis of the mouse transcriptome based on functional annotation of 60,770 full-length cDNAs. Nature 420(6915), 563–573 (2002)

248. Olson, E.N.: Gene Regulatory Networks in the Evolution and Development of the Heart. Science 313(5795), 1922–1927 (2006)

249. Pang, K.C., Stephen, S., Dinger, M.E., Engström, P.G., Lenhard, B., Mattick, J.S.: RNAdb 2.0-an expanded database of mammalian non-coding RNAs. Nucleic Acids Res. 35, D178–D182 (2007)

250. Pearson, G., et al.: Mitogen-activated protein (MAP) kinase pathways: regulation and physiological functions. Endocr. Rev. 22, 153 (2001)

251. Philippi, S., Kohler, J.: Using XML Technology for the Ontology-based Semantic Integration of Life Science Databases. IEEE Trans. Inf. Technol. Biomed. 8(2), 154–160 (2004)

252. Piatetsky-shapiro, G.: Discovery, analysis, and presentation of strong rules. In: Knowledge discovery in Databases, pp. 229–248. AAAI/MIT (1991)
253. Pleij, C.W., Rietveld, K., Bosch, L.: A new principle of RNA folding based on pseudoknotting. Nucleic Acids Res. 13(5), 1717–1731 (1985)
254. Popov, O., Segal, D.M., Trifonov, E.N.: Linguistic complexity of protein sequences as compared to texts of human languages. Biosystems 38, 65–74 (1996)
255. Qian, X.N., Sze, S.H., Yoon, B.J.: An efficient framework based on hidden Markov models (HMMs) that can be used for finding homologous pathways in a network of interest. Jounral of Computational Biology 16(2), 145–157 (2009)
256. Quinlan, J.R.: C4.5: Programs for Machine Learning. Morgan Kaufmann, San Mateo (1993)
257. Rastogi, T., Beattie, T.L., Olive, J.E., Collins, R.A.: A long-range pseudoknot is required for activity of the Neurospora VS ribozyme. EMBO J. 15(11), 2820–2825 (1996)
258. Reddy, P.S., Legault, H.M., Sypek, J.P., Collins, M.J., Goad, E., Goldman, S.J., Liu, W., Murray, S., Dorner, A.J., O'Toole, M.: Mapping similarities in mTOR pathway perturbations in mouse lupus nephritis models and human lupus nephritis. Arthritis Res. Ther. 10(6), R127 (2008)
259. Rietveld, K., Van Poelgeest, R., Pleij, C.W., Van Boom, J.H., Bosch, L.: The tRNA-like structure at the 3' terminus of turnip yellow mosaic virus RNA. Differences and similarities with canonical tRNA. Nucleic Acids Res. 10, 1929–1946 (1982)
260. Rivas, E., Eddy, S.R.: The language of RNA: a formal grammar that includes pseudoknots. Bioinformatics 16(4), 334–340 (2000)
261. Roepstorff, C., Vistisen, B., Donsmark, M., Nielsen, J.N., Calbo, H., Green, K.A., Hardie, D.G., Wojtaszewski, J.F., Richter, E.A., Kiens, B.: Regulation of hormone sensitive lipase activity and Ser563 and Ser565 phosphorylation in human skeletal muscle during exercise. Physiology 560(2), 551–562 (2004)
262. Rose, B.A., Force, T., Wang, Y.: Mitogen-activated protein kinase signaling in the heart: angels versus demons in a heart-breaking tale. Physiol. Rev. 90(4), 1507–1546 (2010)
263. Rote, G.: Computing the Minimum Hausdorff Distance Between Two Point Sets on a Line Under Translation. Information Processing Letters 38(3), 123–127 (1991)
264. Ruan, J., Stormo, G.D., Zhang, W.X.: An Iterated loop matching approach to the prediction of RNA secondary structures with pseudoknots. Bioinformatics 20(1), 58–66 (2004)
265. Ruppender, N.S., Merkel, A.R., Martin, T.J., Mundy, G.R., Sterling, J.A., Guelcher, S.A.: Matrix Rigidity Induces Osteolytic Gene Expression of Metastatic Breast Cancer Cells. PLoS One 5(11), e15451 (2010)
266. Sachs, K., Perez, O., Pe'er, D., Lauffenburger, D.A., Nolan, G.P.: Causal protein-signaling networks derived from multiparameter single-cell data. Science 308(5721), 523–529 (2005)
267. Sakakibara, Y.: Pair hidden markov models on tree structures. BMC Bioinformatics 19, i232–i240 (2003)
268. Saldanha, A.J.: Java Treeviewextensible visualization of microarray data. Bioinformatics 20, 3246–3248 (2004)
269. Salinthone, S., Yadav, V., Schillace, R.V., Bourdette, D.N., Carr, D.W.: Lipoic acid attenuates inflammation via cAMP and protein kinase A signaling. PLoS One 5(9), e13058 (2010)
270. Sambandan, D., Yamamoto, A., Fanara, J.J., Mackay, T.F.C., Anholt, R.R.H.: Dynamic genetic interactions determine odor-guided behavior in Drosophila melanogaster. Genetics 174(3), 1349–1363 (2006)

271. Sanghamitra, B., Ramkrishna, M.: TargetMiner: microRNA target prediction with systematic identification of tissue-specific negative examples. Bioinformatics 25(20), 2625–2631 (2009)

272. Sanz-Clemente, A., Matta, J.A., Isaac, J.T., Roche, K.W.: Casein kinase 2 regulates the NR2 subunit composition of synaptic NMDA receptors. BMC Bioinformatics 10(suppl. 12), S6 (2010)

273. Saravanan, P., Venkatesan, S.K., Mohan, C.G., Patra, S., Dubey, V.K.: Mitogen-activated protein kinase 4 of Leishmania parasite as a therapeutic target. Eur. J. Med. Chem. 45(12), 5662–5670 (2010)

274. Saraiya, P., North, C., Duca, K.: Visualizing biological pathways: requirements analysis, systems evaluation and research agenda. Inf. Vis. 4, 191–205 (2005)

275. Schalon, C., Surgand, J.S., Kellenberger, E., Rognan, D.: A simple and fuzzy method to align and compare druggable ligand-binding sites. Proteins 71(4), 1755–1778 (2008)

276. Scheffer, U., Okamoto, T., Forrest, J.M.S., Rytik, P.G., Muller, W.E.G., Schroder, H.C.: Interaction of 68-kDa TAR RNA-binding protein and other cellular proteins with prion protein-RNA stem-loop. J. Neurovirol. 1, 391–398 (1995)

277. Schuster, B.: Polymeric Nanoparticles as Imaging Probes for Protein Kinase Activity in Cells. Angewandte Chemie International Edition 46(46), 8744–8746 (2007)

278. Scott, J., et al.: Efficient algorithms for detecting signaling pathways in protein interaction networks. J. Comput. Biol. 13, 133–144 (2006)

279. Searls, D.B.: The language of genes. Nature 420, 211–217 (2002)

280. Searls, D.B.: Using bioinformatics in gene and drug discovery. Drug Discovery Today 5(4), 135–143 (2000)

281. Searl, D.B.: Linguistic approaches to biological sequences. Bioinformatics 13(4), 333–344 (1997)

282. Sebolt-Leopold, J.S.: Development of anticancer drugs targeting the MAP kinase pathway. Oncogene 19(56), 6594–6599 (2000)

283. Sengupta, S., Peterson, T.R., Sabatini, D.M.: Regulation of the mTOR complex 1 pathway by nutrients, growth factors, and stress. Mol. Cell 40(2), 310–322 (2010)

284. Shamoo, Y., Tam, A., Konigsberg, W.H., Williams, K.R.: Translational repression by the bacteriophage T4 gene 32 protein involves specific recognition of an RNA pseudoknot structure. J. Mol. Biol. 232(1), 89–104 (1993)

285. Shao, L., Goronzy, J.J., Weyand, C.M.: DNA-dependent protein kinase catalytic subunit mediates T-cell loss in rheumatoid arthritis. EMBO Mol. Med. 2(10), 415–427 (2010)

286. Shedden, K., Townsend, L.B., Drach, J.C., Rosania, G.R.: A rational approach to personalized anticancer therapy: chemoinformatic analysis reveals mechanistic gene-drug associations. Pharm. Res. 20(6), 843–847 (2003)

287. Costford, S.R., Bajpeyi, S., Pasarica, M., Albarado, D.C., Thomas, S.C., Xie, H., Church, T.S., Jubrias, S.A., Conley, K.E., Smith, S.R.: Skeletal muscle NAMPT is induced by exercise in humans. Am. J. Physiol. Endocrinol. Metab. 298, 117–126 (2010)

288. Shen, L.X., Tinoco, I.: The structure of an RNA pseudoknot that causes efficient frameshifting in mouse mammary tumor virus. J. Mol. Biol. 247(5), 963–978 (1995)

289. Song, G., Zeng, H., Li, J., Xiao, L., He, Y., Tang, Y., Li, Y.: miR-199a regulates the tumor suppressor mitogen-activated protein kinase kinase kinase 11 in gastric cancer. Biol. Pharm. Bull. 33(11), 1822–1827 (2010)

290. Song, J., Wu, L., Chen, Z., Kohanski, R.A., Pick, L.: Axons guided by insulin receptor in Drosophila visual system. Science 300(5618), 502–505 (2003)

291. Sookoian, S., Gianotti, T.F., Schuman, M., Pirola, C.J.: ENDEAVOUR software is applied to prioritize all genes of the whole genome in relation to type 2 diabetes. Genet. Med. 11(5), 338–343 (2009)

292. Srikant, R., Agrawal, R.: Mining Quantitative Association Rules in Large Relational Tables. In: Proceedings of the 1996 ACM SIGMOD International Conference on Management of Data, pp. 1–12 (1996)

293. Staple, D.W., Butcher, S.E.: Pseudoknots: RNA Structures with Diverse Functions. PLoS Biology 3(6), 2 (2005)

294. Starke, K., Born, G., Eichelbaum, M., Ganten, D., Hofmann, F., Kobilka, B., Rosenthal, W., Rubanyi, G., Pinna, L.A., Cohen, P.: Protein Kinase Inhibitors for the Treatment of Disease: The Promise and the Problems. Inhibitors of Protein Kinases and Protein Phosphates 167, 1–7 (2004)

295. Stefan, W., Ivo, L.H., Melanie, L., Alexander, H., Peter, F.S.: Mapping of conserved RNA secondary structures predicts thousands of functional noncoding RNAs in the human genome. Nature Biotechnology 23, 1383–1390 (2005)

296. Steffen, M., et al.: Automated modelling of signal transduction networks. BMC Bioinformatics 3, 34 (2002)

297. Stevens, R., Goble, C., Horrocks, I., Bechhofer, S.: OILing the Way to Machine Understandable Bioinformatics Resources. IEEE Trans. Inf. Technol. Biomed. 6(2), 129–134 (2002)

298. Stilou, S., Bamidis, P.D., Maglaveras, N., Pappas, C.: Mining Association Rules from Clinical Databases: An Intelligent Diagnostic Process in Healthcare. Medinfo 10(2), 1399–1403 (2001)

299. Strobel, S.A.: Biochemical identification of A-minor motifs within RNA tertiary structure by interference analysis. Biochem. Soc. Trans. 30, 1126–1131 (2002)

300. Subramanian, A., Tamayo, P., Mootha, V.K., et al.: Gene set enrichment analysis: a knowledge-based approach for interpreting genome-wide expression profiles. Proc. Natl. Acad. Sci. USA 102, 15545–15550 (2005)

301. Sucaet, Y., Deva, T.: Evolution and applications of plant pathway resources and databases. Briefings in Bioinformatics 12(5), 530–544 (2011)

302. Suderman, M., Hallett, M.: Tools for visually exploring biological networks. Bioinformatics 23, 2651–2659 (2007)

303. Tan, P.N., Michael, S., Kumar, V.: Association Analysis: Basic Concepts and Algorithms. In: Introduction to Data Mining, ch. 6. Addison-Wesley (2005)

304. ten Dam, E.B., Pleij, C.W.A., Bosch, L.: RNA pseudoknots: translational frameshifting and readthrough on viral RNAs. Virus Genes. 4, 121–136 (1990)

305. Thakur, V., Wanchana, S., Xu, M., et al.: Characterization of statistical features for plant microRNA prediction. BMC Genomics 12(1) (2011)

306. Thomas, C.W., David, T.H., Ryan, W.B., Jeffrey, S.R., Robyn, M.K., Elizabeth, A.G., Lan, H., Pierre, B., Lee, B.: Computational Prediction and Experimental Verification of New MAP Kinase Docking Sites and Substrates Including Gli Transcription Factors. PLoS Computational Biology 6(8), 1–21 (2010)

307. Tinoco, I., Borer, P.N., Dengler, B., Levine, M.D., Uhlenbeck, O.C., Crothers, D.M., Gralla, J.: Improved estimation of secondary structure in ribonucleic acids. Nature New Biology 246(150), 40–41 (1973)

308. Torkamani, A., Schork, N.J.: Accurate prediction of deleterious protein kinase polymorphisms. Bioinformatics 23(21), 2918–2925 (2007)

309. Tyagi, N., Anamika, K., Srinivasan, N.: A framework for classification of prokaryotic protein kinases. PLoS One 5(5), e10608 (2010)

310. van Batenburg, F.H., Gultyaev, A.P., Pleij, C.W.: PseudoBase: structural information on RNA pseudoknots. Nucleic. Acids Res. 29(1), 194–195 (2001)

311. van Batenburg, F.H., Gultyaev, A.P., Pleij, C.W., Ng, J., Iliehoek, J.: PseudoBase: a database with RNA pseudoknots. Nucleic Acids Res. 28(1), 201–204 (2000)

312. Veenstra-VanderWeele, J., Qaadir, A., Palmer, A.A., Cook Jr., E.H., de Wit, H.: Association between the casein kinase 1 epsilon gene region and subjective response to D-amphetamine. Neuropsychopharmacology 31(5), 1056–1063 (2006)

313. Verdino, P., Witherden, D.A., Havran, W.L., Wilson, I.A.: The molecular interaction of CAR and JAML recruits the central cell signal transducer PI3K. Science 329(5996), 1210–1214 (2010)

314. Verma, T., Pearl, J.: Equivalence and synthesis of causal models. In: Proceedings of Sixth Conference on Uncertainty in Artificial Intelligence, pp. 220–227

315. Vieth, M., et al.: Kinomics-structural biology and chemogenomics of kinase inhibitors and targets. Biochim. Biophys. Acta 1697(1-2), 243–257 (2004)

316. Wadley, G.D., Lee-Young, R.S., Canny, B.J., Wasuntarawat, C., Chen, Z.P., Hargreaves, M., Kemp, B.E., McConell, G.K.: Effect of exercise intensity and hypoxia on skeletal muscle AMPK signaling and substrate metabolism in humans. Am. J. Physiol. Endocrinol. Metab. 290(4), 694–702 (2005)

317. Wakefield, J.: The Bayesian analysis of population pharmacokinetic models. J. Am. Stat. Assoc. 91, 62–75 (1996)

318. Wang, K., He, Y., Han, J.: Pushing Support Constraints into Association Rules Mining. IEEE Transaction on Knowledge and Data Engineering 15(3), 642–658 (2003)

319. Wang, X., Zhang, J., Li, F., et al.: MicroRNA identification based on sequence and structure alignment. Bioinformatics 21, 3610–3614 (2005)

320. Williams, N.: Bioinformatics: how to get databases talking the same language. Science 275(5298), 301–302 (1997)

321. Wojtaszewski, J.F., Nielsen, P., Hansen, B.F., Richter, E.A., Kiens, B.: Isoform- specific and Exercise Intensity-dependent Activation of $5'$-AMP-activated Protein Kinase in Human Skeletal Muscle. J. Physiol. 528(1), 221–226 (2000)

322. Woltering, J.M., Durston, A.: MiR-10 Represses HoxB1a and HoxB3a in Zebrafish. PLoS ONE 3(1), e1396 (2008)

323. Worby, C.A., Simonson-Leff, N., Clemens, J.C., Huddler, D., Muda, M., Dixon, J.E.: Drosophila Ack targets its substrate, the sorting nexin DSH3PX1, to a protein complex involved in axonal guidance. J. Biol. Chem. 277(11), 9422–9428 (2002)

324. Wu, X.D., Zhang, C.Q., Zhang, S.C.: Efficient mining of both positive and negative association rules. ACM Transactions on Information Systems 22(3), 381–405 (2004)

325. Xiao, F., Zuo, Z., Cai, G., Kang, S., Gao, X., Li, T.: miRecords: an integrated resource for microRNA-target interactions. Nucleic Acids Research 37(1), 105–110 (2008)

326. Xiong, H., Tan, P.N., Kumar, V.: Mining Strong Affinity Association Patterns in Data Sets with Skewed Support Distribution. In: ICDM, pp. 387–394 (2003)

327. Xu, X., Ji, Y., Stormo, G.D.: RNA Sampler: a new sampling based algorithm for common RNA secondary structure prediction and structural alignment. Bioinformatics 23(15), 1883–1891 (2007)

328. Yang, J.Q., Liu, H., Diaz-Meco, M.T., Moscat, J.: NBR1 is a new PB1 signalling adapter in Th2 differentiation and allergic airway inflammation in vivo. EMBO J. 29(19), 3421–3433 (2010)

329. Yang, M., Yang, P.: MIC_FS: A novel model feature selection by mutual information guided by clustering. In: Proceedings of 8th IEEE International Conference on Cognitive Information, pp. 390–398 (2009)

330. Yeh, I., Karp, P.D., Noy, N.F., Altman, R.B.: Knowledge acquisition, consistency checking and concurrency control for Gene Ontology (GO). Bioinformatics 19(2), 241–248 (2003)

331. Yousef, M., Showe, L., Showe, M.: A study of micrornas in silico and in vivo: bioinformatics approaches to microrna discovery and target identification. FEBS J. 276(8), 2150–2156 (2009)

332. Yu, M., Stepto, N.K., Chibalin, A.V., Fryer, L.G., Carling, D., Krook, A., Hawley, J.A., Zierath, J.R.: Metabolic and Mitogenic Signal Transduction in Human Skeletal Muscle after Intense Cycling Exercise. J. Physiol. 546(2), 327–335 (2003)

333. Zahid, M., Phillips, B.E., Albers, S.M., Giannoukakis, N., Watkins, S.C., Robbins, P.D.: Identification of a cardiac specific protein transduction domain by in vivo biopanning using a M13 phage peptide display library in mice. PLoS One 5(8), e12252 (2010)

334. Zaki, M.: Scalable algorithms for association mining. IEEE Transactions on Knowledge and Data Engineering 12(3), 372–390 (2000)

335. Zaki, M., Gouda, K.: Fast vertical mining using diffsets. In: In Proceedings of ACM SIGKDD 2003, pp. 316–325 (2003)

336. Zanin-Zhorov, A., Ding, Y., Kumari, S., Attur, M., Hippen, K.L., Brown, M., Blazar, B.R., Abramson, S.B., Lafaille, J.J., Dustin, M.L.: Protein kinase C-theta mediates negative feedback on regulatory T cell function. Science 328(5976), 372–376 (2010)

337. Zeng, C.Y., Wang, W.Q., Zheng, Y., et al.: Conservation and divergence of microRNAs and their functions in Euphorbiaceous plants. Nucleic Acids Res. 38(3), 981–995 (2010)

338. Zhang, B., Pan, X., Cannon, C.H., et al.: Conservation and divergence of plant microRNA genes. Plant J. 46(2), 243–259 (2006)

339. Zhang, C.Q., Zhang, S.C.: Association Rule Mining. LNCS (LNAI), vol. 2307. Springer, Heidelberg (2002)

340. Zhang, J., Michalski, R.S.: An integration of rule induction and exemplar-based learning for graded concepts. Mach. Learn. 21(3), 235–267 (1995)

341. Zhang, S., Haas, B., Eskin, E., Bafna, V.: Searching genomes for noncoding RNA using FastR. IEEE/ACM Trans. Comput. Biol. Bioinform. 2(4), 366–379 (2005)

342. Zhang, S.C., Chen, F., Jin, Z., Wang, R.L.: Mining class-bridge rules based on rough sets. Expert Systems with Applications 36(3), 6453–6460 (2009)

343. Zhang, S.C., Zhang, C.Q., Yang, Q.: Information Enhancement for Data Mining. IEEE Intelligent Systems 9(2), 12–13 (2004)

344. Zhang, S.C., Yang, Q., Zhang, C.Q.: Data Preparation for Data Mining. Applied Artificial Intelligence 17, 375–382 (2003)

345. Zhang, S.J., Haas, B., Eskin, E., Bafna, V.: Searching Genomes for Noncoding RNA Using FastR. IEEE/ACM Transaction on Computational Biology and Bioinformatics 2(4), 366–379 (2005)

346. Zhang, Z., Yu, J., Li, D., Zhang, Z., Liu, F., Zhou, X., Wang, T., Ling, Y., Su, Z.: PMRD: Plant microRNA Database. Nucleic Acids Research 38(1), 806–813 (2010)

347. Zhao, Y., Thomas, H.D., Batey, M.A., et al.: Preclinical evaluation of a potent novel DNA-dependent protein kinase inhibitor NU7441. Cancer Res. 66(10), 5354–5362 (2006)

348. Zuker, M.: On finding all suboptimal foldings of an RNA molecule. Science 244(4900), 48–52 (1989)

349. Zuker, M., Stiegler, P.: Optimal computer folding of large RNA sequences using thermodynamics and auxiliary information. Nucleic Acids Res. 9(1), 133–148 (1981)

# Index